MARX'S PRACTICAL MATERIALISM
THE HORIZON of POST-SUBJECTIVITY PHILOSOPHY

MARX'S PRACTICAL MATERIALISM
THE HORIZON of
POST-SUBJECTİVİTY PHILOSOPHY

Wang Nanshi, Xie Yongkang
Translated by, Wedo Translation Ltd.

CANUT INTERNATIONAL PUBLISHERS
Berlin, London

Originally published as Contemporary Interpretation of Marx's Materialism Vision of Post-subjectivity in 2006 by China Renmin University Press.
Original Chinese Edition Copyright © 2006 by Wang Nanshi   Xie Yongkang
ISBN: 7-300-05508-7/B-339

Marx's Practical Materialism: The Horizon of Post-subjectivity Philosophy
ISBN: 978-3-942575-05-8
Published by
Canut International Publishers
Yorck Street. 66
10965 Kreuzberg Berlin-Germany
Canut International-London
12a Guernsey Road E11
London 4BJ –England-U.K
URL: http// www.canut.us
E-Mail: canut@aol.com

CONTENTS

TITLES in the BOOK

FOREWORD

When I was invited to form several books on contemporary Marxist philosophy by Chinese authors, it had not seemed so challenging. Pleased to experience, it was hard to select and decide. Besides scholarship endeavor, the trends and focus spheres have largely increased. It is no surprise that the German Springer has responded to that already and leads the periodical article publication on contemporary Chinese philosophy.

Opening up has brought many foreign products into China , as well as once discarded Western Marxism, as generally termed in Chinese academy; re-reading Marx and re- reading texts has been widely accepted, and book translations from foreign Marxism has reached a peak. Thus,an inspiration to study humanism, alienation, subjectivity and practical materialism, epistemology and aesthetics, interchange and social ontology as well as cultural philosophy, existential philosophy, philosophy of daily life, has entered into the scope. I believe, they are quite happy with that experience, but I have a strong feeling that, the Chinese would like to do things in their own way, based on practical wisdom and they have another understanding on theories.

Wang Nanshi and Xie Yongkang , in this book on practical materialism , have succeeded a comprehensive study to reflect the major aspects and theoretical bases of this philosophy. Although, the aim to change the world for the better was so highly desired among Marxists living in both socialist and non-socialist countries, Marxist philosophical theoretical research had not been so successful for some time. This has been fairly evaluated and investigated in this book to open a new scope, looking into the present and future. But authors have fully revealed their theoretical regress. On the one shore was dialectical and historical materialism theory of Marxist philosophy propagated in college text books which was scientist, and naturalist and on the other shore was critical historical materialism of Young Lukacs and Korsch, which put the subject- proletarian practice in the center, to solve the problem of unity between subject and object isomorphic with the unity of nature and history.

The issue put by the former was the existence of general principles applicable to both spheres. The latter had centered the issue on the existence of natural being opposite to social history. Lukacs' gave a negative answer to these two issues. As to history, general principles would be abstract and Lukacs had viewed the nature as a "socio-historical category". Although both schools led their own journey, co-existed and argued with passion, both had failed to grasp the real essence of Marx's philosophical theories on materialism, metaphysics, dialectic and all-sided, integrated human practice. This is only a"thorny" but tiny part of the in-depth scholarly effort offered by Wang Nanshi and Xie Yongkang in this book. The essence of the philosophical revolution achieved by Marx, which makes him an outstanding modern philosopher was his theory and view on practice and theory, historical circumstances and problem/questions brought by capitalism was the background and also the target on which he had established practical materialism. He had challenged capital and the giant geniuses of the theoretical philosophy tradition and re-established practical philosophy trend. Marx had wisely inherited the rational and logical elements in theoretical philosophy to go forward. It could also be named as question oriented philosophical exploration. Readers will surely find a thought provoking debate and vision in the text.

Lastly, I will express my appreciation on the authors' strong empathy with all philosophies, joining with their wisdom. I also thank our tireless translator and all those who have greatly contributed to this great communication in world Marxism.

Daivya Jindal

January 2011 London

ACKNOWLEDGMENTS

A special phenomenon was seen in history time and time again, some theories of a great philosopher and even his whole doctrine show its immanent value and draw people's attention often after a long historical movement behind him. The historical fate of Marx's philosophy is not an exception. Marx's philosophy has emerged in the 19th century. It has adapted to and transcended that specific era. It is impossible that a philosophy only adaptable to the era is synoptic. The historical process in the 20th century and the progress predicament of contemporary philosophy throws the immanent value of some theories of Marx's philosophy into relief and reveal the original spirit and contemporary significance of Marx's philosophy. Contemporary philosophers have spontaneously shifted their attention to Marx's philosophy. Foucault has recently said, it has been impossible for the research of history to transcend ideological horizon defined and described by Marx. Jameson points out that Marx's philosophy is a cognitive mode we use to restore the relation between ourselves and being today. It provides an insurmountable horizon of meaning. Derrida affirms, we are all the successors of Marx and Marxism, we still speak with Marxist codes and we can't leave Marx in the future, either.

Foucault, Jameson and Derrida's comments on Marx's philosophy are sincere and just. In contemporary era, the confrontation of positivism,structuralism, neo-thomism, existentialism, Freudism, de-constructivism and modern neo-confucianism against Marx's philosophy is doomed to be powerless. In my view, this confrontation is like the confrontation of Pompeii against Vesuvio volcanic magma. Marx's philosophy indeed is still the only insurmountable philosophy in contemporary era. It is still the truth and conscience in our times.

We can't agree with the view below: in today's China, following the establishment of market economic system, the research of Marx's philosophy is getting "quieter" and even declining. This view sees a reasonable fact, but it also dissolves this reasonable fact into unreasonable understanding. Compared with the "flourishing scene" of "all-people learning philosophy" before reform and opening up, particularly during "Cultural Revolution", currently it is obvious that philosophy indeed sounds desolate in social life. Many people give a cold shoulder to Marx's philosophy. However, we have to say the flourish of philosophy before reform and opening up was a false flourish.

However, the current "quietness" in the research of Marx's philosophy in fact is people's intensive reflection on Marx's philosophy and is an enthusiastic academic return to Marx's philosophy. Concretely speaking, philosophical community completes this academic return through critical reflection on modern Western philosophy, Chinese traditional philosophy and Marxist philosophy and through reorientation of philosophy. In my opinion, it is exactly the three "critical reflections" and the "reorientation" are those, that drive the research of Marx's philosophy in China to maturity. In other words, the current "quietness" of the research of Marx's philosophy doesn't mean a decline of the research on Marx's philosophy in China. On the contrary, it presupposes the maturity of the research of Marx's philosophy in China.

In fact, the relation between market economy and Marx's philosophy is not as incompatible as ice and charcoal. Without the market economy, there wouldn't be Marx's philosophy. Marx's philosophy was originally generated under the background of the market economy. Following the gradual establishment of the system of socialist market economy, Marx will get closer to us other than farther. It is exactly in the practice of socialist market economy that we, truly understand market economy is the epoch of man's independence on the basis of material's dependency and also the epoch of transition from man's dependency to man's free individuality, truly understand the extreme importance of man's comprehensive development and human orientation, truly understand socialist public ownership and the real meaning of reconstruction of individual ownership. … In a word, Marx's philosophy still has an amazing sense of space.

Meanwhile, in today's China the marketization, modernization and socialist reform are interwoven and progresses in the same space-time. It is unprecedented and will certainly trigger a series of major and profound philosophical issues and certainly provide a broad social space and thinking space for our re-interpretation and re-evaluation of Marx's philosophy.

This book is a part of twelve book series titled as ; "Archives of Contemporary Research on Marxist Philosophy" under the entrustment of Chinese Renmin University Press. I have presided over the compilation of this set including twelve works in the first batch.

They are: Contemporary Interpretation of Marx's Materialism written by Professor Wang Nanshi and Xie Yongkang,Meet Marx Emancipative Philosophy – Contemporary Interpretation of Marx's Philosophical View written by Professor Sun Zhengyu, Meet Marx - Contemporary Interpretation of Historical Materialism written by Professor Yang Geng, Empathize Marx - Contemporary Interpretation of Original Marx's philosophy written by Professor Zhang Yibing, Mythology of Supersensuous World and Its End - Contemporary Interpretation of Marx's Ontology written by Professor Wu Xiaoming, Modernity and Man's Fate - Contemporary Interpretation of Marx Existentialism written by Professor Zhang Shuguang, Between Brainstorming and Real Changes - Contemporary Interpretation of Marxian Practical Theory written by Professor Ouyang Kang et al, Hermeneutics of Power - Contemporary Interpretation of Marx's Interpretive Theory written by Professor Yu Wujin, Existentialist Basis of Dialectic - Contemporary Interpretation of Marx's Dialectic written by Professor He Lai, Reflection and Exploration of Development - Contemporary Interpretation of Marxist Social Development Theory written by Professor Feng Ziyi, Make Resolute Appearance – Contemporary Function of Marxist in the Visual Field of Western Scholars written by Professor Chen Xueming, and Humanistic Critical Theory – Review of Neo-Marxism in East Europe written by Professor Yi Junqing.

In regard to the authors of these works, they are from Peking University, Beijing Normal University, Nankai University, Jilin University, Heilongjiang University, Fudan University in Shangai, Nanjing University and Huazhong University of Science and Technology. Those authors are a special academic group. By and large, they were born in 1950s, have entered the university in 1970s - the "ice thawing" era and later on obtained doctor's degree and have deserved their titles. Basically they all have experienced the wind and rain, natural and man-made disasters in China, while their academic career is linked with the course of reform and opening up, almost synchronously. It is exactly this special experience that enables them to have unique and profound cognition on the society, human life and Marx's philosophy. As a matter of fact, experience is wealth.

Their works involve, ontology, dialectic, existentialism, practical theory and epistemology of Marx's philosophy and etc., and show different theoretical content and theoretical visual angles, like a symphony of different chords. I can't say these works have reached the top, but they are by no means superficial. They are the results of authors' two decades' exploration and deep reflection and are the mind portrait and honest record of their philosophical research. Here the authors try to speak what their predecessors have not dared. This reminds me a famous sentence of Hegel: What is known well is not truth.

I don't think these works have restored the "true colors" of Marx's philosophy and these interpretations fully tally with the "text" of Marx's philosophy because I deeply know the reasonableness of hermeneutics and deeply know these works are restricted by authors' knowledge structure, philosophical attainment and value concept. In terms of time, the farther Marx is from our era, the greater the divergence of the cognition on him will occur, just like the farther a passerby is from us, the more difficult to identify him. Therefore, I don't deny this set of archives may have some defects, prejudices or mistakes. In future academic research, we will keep the pursuit to perfection though we will never reach it. "What undergoes development is imperfect; development ends only with death" (Marx's words). Contemporary Interpretation of Marx's Materialism written by Professor Wang Nanshi and Xie Yongkang, opens a new vision on Marxism studies and investigates Marx's profound post-subjectivity more deeply.

Yang Geng

PART I

THEORETICAL PHILOSOPHY AND PRACTICAL PHILOSOPHY

CHAPTER ONE

Conceptual Study on Theory and Practice

Theory and practice as a clue to the history of philosophy

Our task here is to give a contemporary interpretation on Marx's materialism. No doubt, it is a work concerning "history". Therefore, we need to select a way to conceive the history of philosophy at first. As a matter of fact, some ways have existed. For example, Hegel conceives it as a development process in which clear consciousness is obtained continuously in the "category" of reason and subsequently developing into the form of conception; Windelband believes the history of philosophy should be a development process in which Europeans apply scientific concepts to concretely reflect their viewpoints at the universe and their judgment on human life;[1] Martin Heidegger equates the history of philosophy with the history of metaphysics. In regard to the task of this book, the way we conceive the history of philosophy here must be the one most suitable to Marx's materialism, or the way adopted by Marx's materialism.

---

1 [German] Wilhelm Windelband: A History of Philosophy, Vol.1, p.18 & 22, Beijing, Commercial Press, 1987.

Talking of Marx's understanding on the history of philosophy, we might as well take a look at the following two paragraphs in Theses on *Feuerbach* at first:

> The chief defect of all hitherto existing materialism - that of Feuerbach included - is that the thing, reality, sensuousness, is conceived only in the form of the *object or of contemplation,* but not as *sensuous human activity, practice,* not subjectively. Hence, in contradistinction to materialism, the active side was developed abstractly by idealism -- which, of course, does not know real, sensuous activity as such[1]

The philosophers have only interpreted the world, in various ways; the point is to change it.[2]

In the first paragraph, obviously, Marx regards the realistic grasp on "sensuous human activity" and "practice" as a symbol distinguishing his philosophy from old materialism and idealism; and in the second paragraph, apparently, Marx uses the influence and effect of philosophical activity on the real world to distinguish his new materialism from previous philosophies. It appears that whether practice can be truly grasped and how philosophy acts upon the reality are a same issue, i.e.: the issue of the relation between theory and practice. In fact, it implies Marx's treatment method on previous philosophical theories, that is: to perceive the essence of a philosophical theory from its way to treat or grasp practice, because Marx thinks how to handle the relation between theory and practice is a fundamental issue all philosophies must face. By now, we may preliminarily conclude Marx studies previous philosophies and the history of philosophy from the perspective of the relation between theory and practice.

However, this conclusion does not seem to be a big progress to our understanding on the issue of the history of philosophy, since we know, Marx did not write any formal book about philosophy or the history of philosophy and from his later works, we can not find any advanced dis-

---

1 Marx/Engels Collected Works, Edition 2, Volume 1, P.54, Beijing, People's Publishing House, 1995

2 The same book above, P. 57

sertation on this, either. Once facing the whole history of philosophy, we will find theory and practice, as a clue to the history of philosophy, are still unobvious. Philosophy has an extremely complex history. Even by now, it seems that people have never reached a universal consensus on the definitions of these two concepts. Nevertheless, we should not recklessly rule out this clue, as we find all philosophers in the history were puzzled by the issue of the relation between theory and practice and we have an increasingly strong feeling that this relation does involve the fundamental issues of philosophy. Therefore, we can say although Marx consciously uses the relation between theory and practice as a clue to conceive the history of philosophy, the illustration on this clue is a task not fulfilled by him. I think this task is still not fulfilled by now. Hence, it also becomes the preparatory work we face when we interpret Marx's materialism. But how to understand the theory and practice which can run through the whole history of philosophy as believed by Marx? Obviously, this is a question we must make clear at the first step.

Although we apply the concepts of theory and practice and handle "theoretical" and "practical" issues everyday, we have to admit "theory" and "practice" are still a pair of concepts full of ambiguity, and many arguments in the history of philosophy, the history of Marxist philosophy in particular have aroused from them. Therefore, the intention to draw a clear distinction between these two concepts with a few definitions is certainly unrealistic. It is necessary for us to take a historical approach to this issue.

Aristotle was the first person who made clear differentiation and dissertation on theory and practice. His definitions on these two concepts had inherited Plato, Socrates and the whole Greek philosophy's tradition before him and influenced the subsequent Western philosophy so deeply that we have to refer to his dissertation when we study each change in the meanings of these concepts. In other words, from Aristotle we can find the primary clue to each and every change of the meanings of these two concepts. Even the philosophers in the 20th century, such as: Gadamer and Habermas, had to consciously or unconsciously trace back to Aristotle when they related to the issue of practice.

Triple meanings of theory as "gazing"

In fact, in the beginning Aristotle had not only discussed theory and practice but also talked about another activity mode -- technology. The opposition between theory and practice (generally they are conceived as knowledge and action) and the either/or choice between them afterwards did not exist in Aristotelian philosophy. Therefore, we say Aristotle not only is the first person who profoundly and systematically studied the issue of theory and practice but also opened a broad sphere for it. In the beginning of *Nicomachean Ethics*, Aristotle wrote: "Every art and every inquiry, and similarly every action and pursuit, is thought to aim at some good."[1] Although the terms Aristotle used in the beginning indeed have some difference from those he used later on, the "inquiry", "action" and "art" here can find correspondence to the three modes of life he mainly discussed – theory, practice and technology. We find the later study of the whole Western philosophy on this issue has never gone beyond Aristotle's this framework; and on the contrary, in some later historical periods, they were often limited to some parts of this framework. Therefore, it is necessary for our study here to take Aristotle's ideological framework as a reference.

First of all, let's take a look at theory and the concepts in relation to it (science and reason). The term of "theory" has a religious origin: the theoros (theorist) was the representative sent by Greek cities to public celebrations. Through *theoria* (theory), the theoros presented loyalty to Holy Spirit.[2] How could *theoria* present loyalty? It has to do with the activity mode of *theoria*. The word of *theoria* consists of "God" and "see" and can be conceived as seeing or contemplating God. In ancient religious doctrine, the "one who is seen" is God, while in the sense of later philosophers, it can only be the nature. Of course, this nature was related to God in the very beginning. The research objects of the theories of ancient Greek are mainly invariable things, while "invariable" obviously can be related to nothing but divinity. For this reason, Aristotle

---

1 Ancient Greek] Aristotle: Nicomachean Ethics, p.1, Beijing, China Social Sciences Press, 1999.

2 German Habermas: Technology and Science as "Idology", p.118, Shanghai, Acdemia Prss,1999.

thinks the life of theory (philosophy) is the real activity closest to God and the happiest life.

No doubt, philosophy is a theory. What is more, philosophy endues ancient theory with a novel meaning, for philosophy is generated from the first rational "seeing" of the invariable, i.e.: the exploration to the origin of the world. Aristotle said: "for it is owing to their wonder that men both now begin and at first began to philosophize"; they wondered originally at the obvious difficulties, then advanced little by little and stated difficulties about the greater matters.[1] This statement is to find out the basis and the invariable behind phenomena. The first trier is Thales. We often regard Thales' famous saying – water is the origin of all things – as the symbol of the birth of philosophy. In fact, it only stands for an attempt of theoretical thinking and cannot be considered as the theoretical thinking in a real sense, because Thales lets a variable (water) play a role of invariable. Here theory neither separates the objects it researches from the multiplicate rheologic things nor forms the activity method exclusive to theory. In other words, Thales does not explicitly distinguish contemplation from sense, whereas theoretical "seeing" is not the observation of sensuous objects with eyes but a view of soul. Therefore, neither the theory which considers the origin of all matter is "water" nor the theory which considers the origin of all matter is "fire" is a thorough theory. Only by Heraclitus, the invariable object of true theory had appeared, which is **Logos**. Logos is not a sensuous thing and cannot be grasped by sense. Only theoretical contemplation can approach it. Later on, Parmenides defined the way of truth and the way of opinion: The way of truth is the way of "existence". That is to ideologize existence as existence and maintain existence as timeless and indiscerptible existence other than inexistence.[2] Only in thought, can existence be maintained as existence and as invariable and integral existence. On the contrary, the way of opinion is a way of sense. In sensuous world, just as Heraclitus put it, everything flows. Based on this, only some unreliable opinions can be concluded. Parmenides' theoretical thought was presented in another

---

1 [Ancient Greek] Aristotle: Metaphysics, p.5, Beijing, Commercial Press, 1959.

2 Huang Yusheng: Truth and Freedom, p.4, Nanjing, Jiangsu People's Press, 2002.

way and developed by Plato. In his Republic, through famous allegory of "cave", Plato points out two possible worlds where people live. One is a world of shadows without sunlight, i.e.: the familiar sensuous world. The other is the real and eternal ideal world where sun is visible. The activities of philosophical theories are to deal with the absolute thing in the ideal world and approach this eternal thing. The one which has the same essential state as the eternal thing is wisdom.

Before Plato, theoretical "contemplation" had always been advocated as an activity pursuing wisdom and thus being noble, but theoretical contemplation had never been studied as a kind of life. In fact, as believed by Windelband, philosophy had both the meaning of pure theory and the connotation of "practice" in the beginning. Sophists and Socrates had paved a road for this connotation,[1] or theoretical activity is a rational or scientific mode of life in the very beginning. However, for Plato, this mode of life was yet to be studied systematically. In a sense, people were not conscious of it. Above we have mentioned the first person who studied this activity is Aristotle, the disciple of Plato.

In *Metaphysics*, Aristotle's study on philosophical theory shares a same spirit with the predecessors, i.e.: underlining its aspect of pure theory: philosophy should pursue wisdom, while "wisdom is knowledge about certain principles and causes".[2] Only Aristotle synthesized the invariable things like origin, the highest good and form into his "four causes". In Nicomachean Ethics, Aristotle observes the idiosyncrasy of theoretical contemplation as a mode of life. If theory is observed as a kind of life, essentially it will be to explore how theoretical life becomes a life of virtues. Aristotle classifies virtues into intellectual virtue and moral virtue. The virtue that theoretical life should possess is intellectual virtue – live in line with the intellect of which core is logical thinking. This intellect has its roots in the nature of human, so leading this kind of life is to give full play to human nature. Any consummate play of intellectual virtue can be called wisdom. Same as "virtue", the term "wisdom" was widely

---

1 [German] Windelband: A History of Philosophy, Vol.1, p.9.
2 [Ancient Greek]Aristotle: Metaphysics, p.4.

used in ancient Greek language. All consummate virtues can be called wisdom, so politics and technologies all have their wisdom; but in a narrow sense, wisdom only refers to theoretical wisdom. "The wise man must not only know what follows from the first principles, but must also possess truth about the first principles."[1] In the sense of Aristotle, happiness is virtuous real life. As theoretical contemplation is to see the invariable thing and sacred thing, it is sacred or the part of our soul closest to God. Therefore, theoretical contemplation is the highest happiness. Obviously, in the sense of Aristotle, intellectual virtue takes the first place and theoretical activity is the "first activity".

Pure theory

Here Aristotle discusses theoretical activity as an ethical issue. It is different from Socrates' "virtue is knowledge". The knowledge in the sense of Socrates is the knowledge of ethics, or the knowledge which knows virtues. This knowledge keeps people from making mistakes, whereas ignorance seduces people to make mistakes. In this case, this knowledge cannot come from the observation on eternal and absolute thing and can only come from the cognition on virtues, or as it was stated in Delphic Oracle: "know yourself!" What Aristotle discusses here is the ethical meaning of theory. This theory is still a pure theory and only pure theory is virtuous activity, so Aristotelian ethics has a broader significance, which can be understood only by taking the life in the states of ancient Greece into consideration, because the advent of the state and the birth of philosophy are so closely linked that the origin of rational thought must be seen as bound up with the social and mental structures peculiar to Greek state. Here the concept of practice has been involved and we'll discuss it in detail later. The above explanation is about ancient Greek theory. We may summarize it into a metaphor of "seeing" or "gazing", as said by Griffith, "seeing" is the main image of "thinking" in Greece.[2] Ancient Greek people had particular preference to vision, while acquiring knowl-

---

1 [Ancient Greek] Aristotle: Nicomachean Ethics, p.129.
2 Bao Limin: Life and Logos, p.184, Beijing, Orient Press, 1996.

edge is the "seeing" of soul. In a sense, this "seeing" is the nature of human.[1] As known to all, the most important headstream of Western philosophy is ancient Greek thought, and each step of the development of Western philosophy can be traced back to the initial meaning in this headstream. In consultation with the later Western philosophy, we can interpret the deep meaning of the "theory" in ancient Greece as follows:

(1) Although theory was "the first activity" or the highest activity in ancient Greece and this superiority was maintained in the later philosophy, early-modern philosophy in particular, it is "a kind of" activity mode after all and must be distinguished from other activity modes. The philosophers before Aristotle did not realize this point and took it for granted, while in Aristotelian ethics, this fact is systematically studied. Here the superiority of theory to other activity modes is affirmed, but this affirmation is also the affirmation for the finity of theory. The information we obtain from it is that theory can only "speculatively" grasp the so-called "immobile", but cannot "practically" or "artistically" "know" this world. The knowledge in theory is finite. This is a fact we cannot deny even today.

As known to all, for a time, theory was deemed as the only omnipotent thing in the history. This can be fully proved from early-modern philosophical theory's absorption of instrumental activity mode and its infiltration to ethical sphere. The theory's absorption of instrumental activity mode firstly should be credited to Francis Bacon. Francis Bacon was not satisfied with Aristotle's deductive approach to theory and advocated inductive approach. This means theory should study empirical and multiple things at first in his sense. This idea runs in the opposite direction to ancient Greek theory, for in the eyes of ancient Greek, empirical things should be the objects of making and technical treatment only. Not only that, Francis Bacon also thinks the purpose of knowledge is application, for results and works are seen as if they are the guarantee for philosophers' truth. "Human knowledge and human power meet in one; for where the cause is not known the effect cannot be produced. Nature to

---

1 Aristotle ever said: "All men by nature desire to know" ([Ancient Greek] Aristotle: Metaphysics, p.1)

be commanded must be obeyed; and that which in contemplation is as the cause is in operation as the rule."[1] We know, theory possesses the highest virtue in ancient Greece due to its perfection and self-content-ment, while making is incomplete due to its another end outside activity. Francis Bacon introduces this outward structure of technology into the-ory. The result is to lead to a powerful force of human when it faces the nature. It is Francis Bacon's "new science" which is different from an-cient theory. The "new science" has profoundly influenced the natural sciences since early modern times. It is limited to a visual sphere in which except theories and their application, there are no other activities, or ra-tional activities, for in a sphere where there is no "application" and "no result can be produced", and there will be no guarantee on truth. If the theoretical direction of Francis Bacon starts with experience, then Rene Descartes completes the acceptance of the concept of instrumental activity from an opposite direction, which is the mathematization of theoretical science. Not like Galileo who only cognizes the necessary structure of mathematics in the nature, Rene Descartes' mathematization of sciences intends to endue the nature with the necessary structure of consciousness and make the nature "real" due to the framework of mathematics – geom-etry immanent in subject consciousness. Though Rene Descartes does not underline the direct utility of theory, "application" has its root in the es-sential structure of this theory. Rene Descartes firmly believes that all knowledge must be deduced from some fundamental causes, while these causes must contain forced "generalization" to everything. From then on, the theories of early-modern philosophy were developed towards an in-creasingly abstract and pure direction, but the purer the direction is, the wider the scope of required interpretation will be. The extremalization of this requirement led to Hegelian absolute spirit system.

Here inevitably comes a question: how does ethical sphere which has long been the representative of the spheres outside theory, become reason and science? According to the theoretical directions of Francis Bacon and Rene Descartes, ethical sphere must be "reconstructed". In fact, early-modern ethics as a whole is ethics reconstructed by theory. The typical ones are the "geometric" ethics of Spinoza et al, Hume's empirical

---

1 [British] Francis Bacon: The New Organon, p.8, Beijing, Commercial Press, 1984.

ethics and Kant's formalistic ethics. The difference of these ethics can be reduced to the difference of the principles they follow, i.e.: the difference in theoretical reason. As a matter of fact, the position of ethics had always been an issue in the history of early-modern philosophy. The rise of various kinds of ethics and their retrospect to ancient Greek thoughts, particularly Aristotelian ethical thought in the 20th century, prove the existence and seriousness of this issue.

In fact, ethics is only a "representative" of the spheres outside theory. We know, in the sense of Aristotle, outside theory and ethics, there is also the sphere of technology. In his works, we also consumingly feel the common things of these three spheres. Certainly it is an integral vision. Contemporary philosophers' criticism at early-modern theories in fact is always based on an integral vision similar to this. For example, Martin Heidegger reveals the derivational nature of theory and thinks theory is generated because "what is present-at-hand" becomes not "present-at-hand" and must undergo some "observation". The view of only making "theoretical" observation on things lacks the apprehension on readiness-to-hand. This indicates the "knowing" to theory is exactly the "unknowing" to "readiness-to-hand".[1] Gadamer thinks every theory has its elements of hermeneutic structure, so theory should not be antagonistic to practice and instead should be subordinate to practice. Irrespective of their routes, modern philosophers have universally accepted this notion: theory is only a specific activity, a way and a limited way to "know". This notion comes from an even broader sphere of vision. We may call it "life-world", "practice" and even "being".

(2) In the sense of Aristotle, theoretical contemplation is the pursuit of intellectual virtue (wisdom), while virtue is a character, so theory is to give full play to human's own nature of intellect. In this way, theory finds connection with human nature and Aristotle may say all men by nature desire to know, and we may say only human can engage in theoretical activity, and the engagement of theoretical activity is first of all awareness of human, because the structure of theoretical activity intrinsically embodies human's self-consciousness. Theory is human's "seeing" and the "seeing" implies

---

1 [German] Martin Heidegger: Being and Time, p.82, Beijing, Sanlian Bookstore, 1999.

the seeing and the seen – subject and object. Initially, human has realized that it itself rests with the separation from the nature, while this separation embodied the structure of theory. Therefore, we may say theory concerns human nature and self-consciousness, and thus becomes the headstream of later developed subjectivity in philosophy.

But strictly speaking, the headstream of subjectivity cannot be reckoned as real subjectivity. In fact, in the philosophy of ancient Greece, we cannot find the subjectivity in the sense of early-modern philosophy. The mission of the ancient Greek theory is to "see" the eternal presence behind the ever-changing things and the invariable substance behind phenomena. However, the thought conceived by Greek is not any subjective thing belonging to human but objective reason and Logos, or in other words, the real present. Therefore, in Greek philosophy, "subject" is not human. It only means the basic thing which constitute beings. This thing follows through all changes of the contingent things and constitutes things as things. Therefore, it is subject that is applicable to any being, whether it is table, plant, bird or human.[1] Martin Heidegger also says the concept of subject initially did not have any outstanding relation with human, particularly any relation with ego.[2] Therefore, Ancient Greek had "self-consciousness" in a sense, but absolutely did not have the subjective consciousness in the sense of early-modern philosophy. In fact, the "self-consciousness" of Greek is rather "limited". We often trace the self-consciousness and cognition in Western philosophy back to Socrates' interpretation on Delphic oracle, but this interpretation makes sense. On the one hand, it stands for the pursuit to acquire certainty through cognizing our own soul. On the other hand, the result of this pursuit is negative, i.e.: can only make certain that they cannot make certain on anything. In short, while discovering ego, Socrates had also discovered the finity of ego. Similar thought can be seen in Aristotelian philosophy. Aristotle ever addressed self-thinking and thought of thought, but the "self" here largely does not mean "own" or "self" which

---

1 [German] Gunten Seubold: Heideggers analyse der neuzeitlichen technik, p.44, Beijing, China Social Sciences Press, 1993.
2 [German] Martin Heidegger: Holzwege, p.84, Shanghai, Shanghai Translation Publishing House, 1997.

is the ultimate starting point of intrinsic acts or soul activities, because behind "self", there is still sense, the highest good, real being, justice and other non-intrinsic backgrounds. If we say Aristotle's "self" is law executor, then behind it there is always a legislator.[1] We may say the ego of ancient Greek philosophers is the subject under a certain background. Strictly speaking, it is only "one type of" subject and has an essential difference from the subject which is the ultimate basis for certainty in early-modern philosophy.

The generation of subjectivity in early modern times, in fact is the process in which the concept of the subject in ancient Greece integrates man and ego. The Christianity in the Middle Ages conceived Logos as the God, in this way subject was impersonated in a sense. According to Christianity, it is the God who created the world and God is the eternal presence, while the world is in the God – the Logos. In a sense, we may regard the God in the Middle Ages as the transition from the impersonalized "subject" in ancient times to the personalistic subject in early modern times. Augustine grasps the concept of God through analyzing human spirit. He believes the elements of spiritual life are not only embodied in human spirit but also presented in Trinitarian God spirit.[2] Augustine's thought of seeking certainty in personality was severed from religion by Rene Descartes, hence the subjectivity of early-modern philosophy was generated in a real sense. The significance of Rene Descartes' famous proposition- "ego cogito ergo sum" (I think, therefore I am) is that it for the first time explicitly resorted certainty to ego, thus ego became subject and the "Archimedean Point" that supports the existence of all beings. This is equal to announcing the completion of the transformation from ancient substantial philosophy to early-modern subjective philosophy. Hegel's comment on it is that: hence philosophy has found its own "home".

Nevertheless, the two meanings of Delphic oracle have accompanied early-modern philosophy all the time, and it seems that the finity of subject has been an unsolvable fundamental problem since the very begin-

---

1 Ni Liangkang: Self-knowledge and Reflection, p.24 and30, Beijing, Commercial Press, 2002.
2 The same book as above, p.37~38.

ning. This can be seen in Kantian philosophy at first. Kant clearly knew the finity of subjective reason, thus had limited its validity to phenomenal world. However in this way, the thing-in-itself becomes a perpetual problem indeed. Almost all early-modern philosophers after Kant have consciously regarded eliminating the thing-in-itself as their top task (such as: Johann Fichte, Hegel and Edmund Husserl), but they had all failed; on the contrary, like Kant's "thing-in-itself", both Hegel's "history" and Edmund Husserl's "life-world" indicate, a kind of paradox, the existence of the spheres outside the realm of subject, thus also indicate the "predestination" of the finity of object. Modern philosophy takes the acceptance of this "predestination" as its premise.

(3) The metaphor of theoretical "contemplation" also contains the meaning that "the seeing" must have a visual angle and a theory only has one "visual angle". If a theory cannot "see" the world from multiple angles, it must be abstract. In other words, in terms of its essential structure, theory is abstract, and that theory separates "the seeing" from the world, is the most primordial abstraction although the earliest theorists did not realize it.

The "visual angle" of theory is the foothold of theory. Since the very beginning, theory has attempted to explain the multiplicate world, i.e.: explore the basis behind it. On this basis, all phenomena can be understood. Phenomenal world is multiplicate, while multiplicity cannot be its own basis, so before understanding the world, we must find out the unitary thing among multiplicity, or in other words the common thing in numerous phenomena, and seek the identity of the world. Only based on this identity, can we theoretically apprehend the world. Therefore, the very first issue for philosophy is the issue of one and the many. Through solving this issue, theory finds the origin of the world. As Habermas said:

> This origin, whether it is the Creator above the world, or the essential reason of the nature or more abstractly the being, forms a visual angle. By this token, although the things and events inside the world are rich and colorful, they can still maintain order and uniformity and become a special entity and meanwhile can be understood as the parts of an integral body.[1]

---

1 [German] Habermas: Post-Metaphysical Thinking, p.29, Nanjing, Yilin Press, 2001.

Identical process is also an abstract process. Identical process aims to obtain the form and category of the world. In the inquiry by ancient Greek natural philosophers, on the start and origin of the world, to the Aristotelian categories system, it is the development of this abstract process. Aristotelian categories are also called predicative relations or predicates. These predicates state essentially the things called. In other words, they tell us what on earth these things are.[1] Theorists comprehend the world through philosophical categories. This comprehension is formal comprehension, because category is fundamentally established in form.

In ancient Greek philosophy, the knowledge on the form of theory assumed a special position, but it was not the only knowing. In *Metaphysics* and *Nicomachean Ethics*, Aristotle discusses experience, technology, practice and other forms of knowing, "knowing" is classified by sphere and thus he admits the existence of the spheres outside theory. However, this circumstance was thoroughly changed in early-modern philosophy. If the category of ancient theory is the formal relations of objects, then the category of early-modern theory will be the formal relations of subjects. Above we have discussed early-modern theory's idea as: "forced generalization" of the form of subject to the nature. This form is a category system. The most typical ones in them are Kantian system and Hegelian system. The formality and abstractness of category system reflect the incompleteness of category system. Thing-in-itself has always been a haunted shadow in Kantian system. Hegel brought "history" into his category system by force, but it is exactly "history" that has blasted the first breach in this system. The incompleteness of this formal system is exposed in modern philosophy. Will and history has received the attention of philosophy, whereas the most prominent characteristic of these spheres is the inability to be conceptualized and formalized.

By now, we have interpreted the meaning of theory as "seeing" of the world in three aspects and also indicated from these three aspects the finity of theory in terms of its structure. This finity is relative to the broader sphere outside theory. To understand this sphere, we must relate to practice, because practice has always presented itself as the opposite of theory or thus as the representative of the sphere outside theory.

---

1 [British] W.D. Ross: Aristotle, p.27, Beijing, Commercial Press, 1997.

The concept of practice and its historical evolution

The concept of practice has two meanings today: one is the action of carrying out the results of theoretical thinking, and the other is the actions in moral and ethical sphere. The first meaning had appeared after theory changed direction and was no longer pure "seeing" but a plan was needed for implementing in early modern times; we can say the second meaning has directly originated from Aristotelian tradition, because in Aristotelian ethics, practice was explicitly included into moral and political sphere.

In fact, the word "practice" was used in various senses in ancient Greek language. This can be seen in Aristotle's works. In the widest sense, practice is not exclusively used on human. It can be referred to all movements, such as: motions of celestial bodies and life activities. In Nicomachean Ethics, practice is further defined and distinguished from other two major types of activities (theory and technology). Firstly, animals have no practice and practice exclusively belongs to human. However, not all human activities are practice. In comparison with theoretical science, the objects of practice are variable things and "practical". This has obvious difference from the above statement that the objects of theory are the timeless and invariable things; secondly, not all activities whose objects are variable things, are regarded as practice, because the objects of making are also variable. The difference is that "making has an end other than itself, action cannot; for good action itself is its end".[1] Then what does practice actually mean? Aristotle thinks practice is the correct behavior it itself constitutes an end. Concretely speaking, it is political and ethical activity.

With today's concepts of politics and ethics, we can hardly understand the practice in the sense of Aristotle. The politics and ethics in his sense are the politics and ethics in the Greek state, while state life firstly means a form of life essentially different from current society. Therefore, to really understand the connotation of the concept of practice in the sense of Aristotle, we must study it in combination with the state life in ancient Greece. In Aristotelian philosophy, politics and ethics are integrated, be-

---

1 [Ancient Greek] Aristotle: Nicomachean Ethics, p.127.

cause they all regard the whole state life as the research object. In this sense, we can regard Aristotle's Ethics as a political book, while Politics belongs to ethics in a broad sense. At the first paragraph of *Politics,* Aristotle wrote:

> Every state is a community of some kind, and every community is established with a view to some good; for mankind always acts in order to obtain those which it thinks good. But if all communities aim at some good, the state or political community, which is the highest of all, and which embraces all the rest, aims at good in a greater degree than any other, and for the highest good.[1]

It expresses the same content as the first sentence in Nicomachean Ethics: "every art and every inquiry, and similarly every action and pursuit, is thought to aim at some good". Since all activities in the state aim at some good, we can also say that it is practical, but here we must know the state described by Aristotle is the whole human society or civilized society in a sense. In the concept of Greek, the world outside the state is a world of barbarism, and a barbaric world cannot be considered as a human society. Hence, it is not difficult to understand why Aristotle considered state the highest and broadest community. State is a consortium of free men, so it is free. As freedom itself is its end, state itself is its end.

In this way, it is not difficult for us to discover the two meanings of the concept of practice in Aristotle's works: firstly, it is the practice of the state in its totality. In this sense, all human activities are practice; secondly, it is the practice as ethical activity, i.e.: the practice which is separated from theory and technology as stated in *Nicomachean Ethics*. Aristotle did not explicitly give the above separation, because it seems that the simultaneous use of these two meanings needed no reason. However, from the perspective of today, if we do not make such separation, the overall connotation of practice as human activity will be negligible. That is what had happened. The integral meaning of practice was forgotten for a long time after Aristotle.

---

2 [Ancient Greek] Aristotle: Politics, p.3, Beijing, Commercial Press, 1965.

In fact, in Aristotle's works, Politics in particular, and state practice is higher than individual practice in a sense. This has something to do with the community form of state life. Aristotle said:

> The state [though posterior to individual and family in its occurrence procedure] is by nature clearly prior to the family and to the individual, since the totality is by necessity prior to the part ... because [individual is only a part of the state] isolated individual is not self-sufficing and therefore he is like a part in relation to the totality [people can meet their needs only in this way].[1]

In the sense of Aristotle, human is a political animal, and politics essentially is state life. The essence of human is endowed by the state. He, who is unable to live in the state must be either a god or a barbaric person or beast. Therefore, state is the headspring of individual essence and the background of individual activities. All concrete activities should be observed under this background.

In this way, it is not difficult for us to understand "contemplation is the greatest happiness", and we can also understand the concrete personal practical activities that are different from theoretical contemplation. Individual concrete practice is also the activity taking itself as its end. This activity distinguishes itself from theoretical contemplation because it takes variable and practical things as objects, and also distinguishes itself from technology because, it has no end outside activity. This is the political activity and moral life of concrete individuals. Different from intellectual wisdom in theoretical activity, the wisdom in practical activity is practical wisdom. "Practical wisdom is to be able to deliberate well about what is good and expedient for himself, not in some particular respect, e.g. about what sort of things lead to health or to strength, but about what sort of things lead to the good life in general."[2] Therefore, "practical wisdom, then, must be a reasoned and true state of capacity to act with regard to human goods".[3] No doubt, this is the original meaning of moral life.

---

1 [Ancient Greek] Aristotle: Politics, p.8.
2 [Ancient Greek] Aristotle: Nicomachean Ethics, p.126.
3 The same book as above, p.127.

In the sense of Aristotle, the two meanings in the concept of practice, we have analyzed above are integral, and separating them may even affect the understanding on it. However, in later philosophy, the concept of practice did not maintain this integral state. First of all, it does not mean that the later philosophers consciously separated these two meanings. The fact is that in a fairly long history after Aristotle, the concept of practice was used only in a narrow sense (moral life) even in a technical sense.

The change in the meaning of practice firstly was triggered by the change in lifestyles. After Roman Empire was formed, the lifestyle of ancient Greek state had no longer existed and political and ethical life was integrated with religion. Therefore, the concept of practice in the Middle Ages certainly had the connotation of religion. In the eyes of medieval philosophers, practice firstly means the life of compassion for Jesus Christ. The concrete content (usually some altruistic behaviors) of this life is not very important, for this activity is to practice the compassion of God. Certainly this activity is not as perfect as the direct contemplation on God (theory), but it is necessary. In fact, Christians often had saved no pain to carry out this activity. In the sense of some Christian thinkers – Augustine in particular, practice also means the self-perfecting of the life by Christians. Under the influence of Augustine, most of the later Christian thinkers regarded everyday life as a saintly life, whereas whether it was a private life or public life was not important at all. This was also one of the important bases for Martin Luther's religious reform. Martin Luther was an Augustinian, too. Obviously, the concept of practice in the Middle Ages, no longer had the integral sphere of vision as it had in ancient Greece and was practice in a narrow sense at most, because the position of integrity had been surrendered to empire and God.

The concept of practice in early modern times was developed in this narrow direction. As mentioned above, through the formation of the concepts of Francis Bacon's "new science" and Rene Descartes' "universal mathematics", theory was trying to become something all inclusive. Under such circumstances, practice could exist only in two ways:

(1) Practice is still a moral and ethical sphere, but this sphere must be reconstructed by theory. At the beginning, i.e.: by Rene Descartes, this construction was not successful. Rene Descartes considered all knowledge mathematical knowledge. In this case, moral sphere either has mathematical structure and becomes rational or is irrational (becomes temporary morality). The followers of Rene Descartes chose the former. They have all firmly believed in the "objectivity" and "scientificalness" of the concepts in ethical sphere. For example, John Locke thinks the moral and political concepts may be "as undisputable as the fact that three angles in a triangle are equal to two right angles"; Gottfried Leibniz also thinks moral law and mechanics law are both inherent, so moral science and mathematics are both self evident; Spinoza explicitly said that he would observe human's behaviors and desire as if he observed line, plane and volume.[1] He had created a "geometric ethics" system. Of course, Spinoza's ethics had exceeded the range of morality and ethics described here, or rather is his ontology, but this mathematized effort undoubtedly contains the theorization and scientification of moral and practical sphere.

In the sense of Kant, mathematics and geometry are no longer paradigms of philosophical theories, so practice should be reconstructed in another theoretical mode. Generally, it is believed that Kant's three critiques in fact give another trichotomy. The first critique handles the issue of theory, the second critique handles the issue of practice and the third critique is a means integrating the two parts of philosophy. Therefore, there is only dichotomy: theory and practice. In the sense of Kant, "Now there are but two kinds of concepts, and these yield a corresponding number of distinct principles of the possibility of their objects. The concepts referred by him are those of nature and that of freedom". The former makes cognition's compliance of apriori principles possible. The latter establishes fundamental principles which enlarge the scope activities by will. The development which belongs to the former is natural philosophy and that belongs to the latter is moral philosophy.[2] We can easily understand Kant's concept of theory, but can hardly understand his concept

---

1 [Dutch] Spinoza: The Ethics, p.97, Beijing, Commercial Press, 1991.
1 [German] Kant: Critique of Judgment, Vol.1, p.8, Beijing, Commercial Press, 1964.

of practice. Kant's practice in fact does not involve any concrete human activity, because all empirical things have been included into the spheres of theory and necessity. This practice at most is the totality of the laws of unconditional order. After Kant, particularly by Johann Fichte and Hegel, practice was given a broader meaning, almost referring to all human acts without any discrimination, nevertheless the practice as moral sphere was still its most fundamental meaning.

(2) Another meaning of the concept of practice in early-modern philosophy almost had nothing to do with moral sphere, but it is another manifestation of theoretical structure. Francis Bacon stresses that fruits and works are the guarantees for the philosophers' truth, thus certainly theory contains a link of application and verification. However, old traditional theory is not intended for application, so "practice" undertakes this function. Rene Descartes ever advocated a practical philosophy through which people may become the master of the nature. Kant also clearly differentiated "technical practice" and "moral practice" and regarded technical practice as the "extension of theoretical philosophy".[1] Hegel did not differentiate between these two meanings of practice. In his sense, practice is the objective and purposely activities to the external world and includes productive activities (technology). Of course, Hegel's concept of production is not limited to the "extension" of theory. Its rich connotation was developed by Marx. Nevertheless, the practice as the application link or verification mean for theory is still widely used today. In fact, such practice is almost identical to Aristotle's concept of technology and is the concept of technology in the narrowest sense.

Generally speaking, the concept of practice in early-modern philosophy does not possess an independent position, or in other words, it is constructed by theory. This construction process is intermingled with the elements of technology. Contemporary philosophers have fundamentally changed this circumstance and given more and more attention to practice and richer connotation to it. In fact, Johann Fichte had stressed the superiority of practice, only he did not directly use the concept of "practice", instead he used the concept of "Tathandlung". The so-called

---

2 [German] Kant: Critique of Judgment, Vol.1, p.9.

"Tathandlung" is a pure activity from oneself without any object, so it is the act directly causing fact .[1] This act not only determines ego but also determines non-ego, so it is the "foundation of all theories of knowledge and also the source of selfdom. In the sense of Hegel, all outward activities of the spirit can be called practice. Therefore, we may say the stress of Hegel and Johann Fichte on practice was still a "theoretical" behavior. What we can determine is, that practice is resuming its integral dimension and linking to the essence of man. This concept was decisively developed by Marx, but the practice in the sense of Marx is no longer egocentric or spiritual activity but concrete human activity and just because of this human activity, social life essentially is "practical".

The philosophers in the 20th century have developed the concept of practice. In addition to the enlightenment of Marx, this development mainly stemmed from the elucidation on Aristotle's concept of practice and Edmund Husserl's concept of life-world. In fact, Edmund Husserl's philosophy pays main attention to the research of theoretical reason. His work was done under the guidance of the powerful theoretical concepts since Rene Descartes. However, later on Edmund Husserl had deeply realized the "crisis of European science". During his effort to get rid of the "crisis of European science", Edmund Husserl introduced the concept of "life-world". Although the introduction of this concept was out of the need of theoretical method for Edmund Husserl, its "theoretical" significance was much weaker than its influence on practical concept. We can say the philosophies of Martin Heidegger, Habermas and so on are the extensions of "life-world".[2] In addition, a distinct feature of the concept of practice in the philosophy in the 20th century is to resume Aristotle's differentiation between practice and technology. For example, Habermas introduced the concept of communicative behavior to draw a distinction from labour or instrumental behavior, while he thinks communicative activity is the power to constitute life-world; Gadamer thinks that following the overall dominance of technology over life, practice and practical wisdom are losing ground, while his hermeneutics is an effort to restore practice and practical wisdom. Therefore, hermeneutics is

---

1   Li Wentang: The Light of Truth, p.46~47, Nanjing, Jiangsu People's Press, 2002.
2   Ni Liangkang: Phenomenology and Its Effect, p.118 & 138, Beijing, Sanlian Bookstore, 1994.

not merely a method or technology, and as a philosophy, it is practical philosophy. Gadamer's interpretation on practice has directly originated from Aristotelian tradition and in a sense is a representative for the revival of Aristotle's concept of practice.

Above, we have all referred to technology when we have discussed theory and practice: Aristotle particularly discusses technology which is separated from theory and practice, while many early-modern philosophers regarded technology as a kind of practice. With the contemporary era, technology became a "hotspot" of theory due to many realistic problems. Nevertheless we have to admit our understanding on technology is not deep. As Martin Heidegger has put it, when we pursue technology, usually we will have two answers. "One says: Technology is a means to an end. The other says: Technology is a human activity. The two definitions of technology belong together. For to posit ends and procure and utilize the means to them is a human activity".[1] Saying technology is an instrumental behavior in fact is to say technology itself does not contain an end, or in other words to say the end that governs technology is beyond technology, so technology is incomplete or fragmentary. Generally, it is believed that the basis of this notion can be initially found in Aristotelian ethics. Aristotle thinks both theoretical activity and practical activity take themselves as end, or their ends lie in activity, but "making has an end other than itself", and the "origin of making is in the maker and not in the thing made".[2] From the above, people often get such a conclusion: technology has nothing to do with human essence and social essence, just like the slaves in ancient Greece who are only speaking "instruments", so cannot be reckoned as human. From this conclusion, two attitudes towards technology are naturally generated: worshipping the power of technology and applying it without restriction; and denounce its influence on the spheres (theory and practice) concerning human "essence".

The first thing we want to call into question is whether Aristotle's concept of technology is merely equal to instrument? In fact, the technology discussed by Aristotle is the character reflected by making or productive

---

1 Selected Works of Martin Heidegger, Vol.2, p.925, Shanghai, Shanghai Sanlian Bookstore, 1996
2 [Ancient Greek] Aristotle: Nicomachean Ethics, p.126~127.

activity – the character of rational creation. Firstly, this activity is an activity inside state and a part of the integral practice of state. Furthermore, same as theory and practice, it also "aims at some good", so we cannot say it has no concern on human essence. Secondly, it is not true that technology has no common point with theory and practice. On the contrary, Aristotle thinks technology is also a kind of "knowing" of integral practice. Martin Heidegger thinks technology is also a way of unconcealment. Initially technology and cognition were interwoven, while Aristotle's differentiation between these two in his Ethics is also based on their different roles and ways of unconcealment.[1] In fact, Aristotle had also discusses the "knowing" of technology in Metaphysics. He thinks knowledge and understanding belong to technology rather than to experience, men of experience know that the thing is so, but they do not know why, while the others know the 'why' and the cause. Therefore, technology had contained the insight to cause and basis.[2] If we do not look at Aristotle only, we will discover technology almost covers all human acts in the conception of ancient Greek and even their language and politics are both technology.[3]

In early-modern philosophy, technology no longer had the meaning of "knowing" and has been disintegrated into an instrument and become an implementation link of theory. As technology is considered a non-essential sphere, it could not obtain an independent position in early-modern philosophy, and the philosophers in early modern times have seldom made deep observation on technology. However, in real life it is quite the contrary and technology is intensively influencing human's social life. This sharp contrast can find reason from the early-modern concept of technology. Nowadays, due to the numerous issues aroused by it, technology has become a "focus" of attention in contemporary philosophy, but this attention is often just a kind of "emotional" denouncement, or ascribing these issues to people's "misuse" of the instrument with neutral value. This essentially is still based on the "instrumental"

---

1 Selected Works of Martin Heidegger, Vol.2, p.931.
2 [Ancient Greek] Aristotle: Metaphysics, p.2~3.
3 [French] Bernard-Stiegler: Technics and Time, 1: The Fault of Epimetheus, after p.236, Nanjing, Yilin Press, 1999.

understanding on technology. Only, few philosophers have thought over the essence of technology and subsequently went deep into the essence of human life, Marx and Martin Heidegger for instance. Obviously, the research on technology is an unfulfilled task. We will further discuss it in the second chapter.

Above, we have roughly observed the significance of the concepts of theory, practice and technology in the history of philosophy under the framework of Aristotle. Although the position of theory varies with times, its most fundamental meaning maintains unchanged all the time. In comparison, it is much more difficult to comprehend the meaning of the concept of practice. However, we can easily obtain the differentiation between the practice in a broad sense as totality and background, and on the other hand human's specific activity modes (theory, practice in a narrow sense, technology and so on). Only after we make such a differentiation, can we study the relation between theory and practice, otherwise this study will become invalid. In this case, the above mentioned clue of philosophical history must be the relation between theoretical activity and practice only in a broad sense, for if we take the concept of practice in a narrow sense, this relation can be converted into the relation between knowledge theory and ethics, thus we will be unable to understand the numerous major revolutions in the history of philosophy. Obviously, on this issue, Marx also explores the practice in its broad sense. Only in this sense, can the whole social life be considered practical and can Marx criticize the previous theories as "abstract" theories. Of course,

Marx's concept of practice also has the facet including its narrow sense, i.e.: productive activity. We will expound this point in detail in the second chapter.

CHAPTER TWO

Differentiation and Evolution of Theoretical Philosophy and Practical Philosophy

Introduction

As mentioned above, theory and practice are angles from which we understand the history of philosophy. After we observe the meaning and historical evolution of these two concepts, it is necessary for us to think about the reasonableness of this angle. Hegel thinks the development of philosophy and the unfolding of truth or logos are the same process, so the way to study the history of philosophy, which is the closest to its nature, is to regard it as the history of logos and spirit. Others can only be regarded as "extrinsic history" of philosophy.[1] We cannot agree with Hegel's interpretation on the nature of philosophy, but his view that the study on the history of philosophy must have a clue that hits its nature is unquestionably right. We think philosophy is a kind of theoretical activity

---

1 [German] Hegel: Lectures on the History of Philosophy, Vol.1, Introduction, Beijing, Commercial Press, 1959

in essence, so we must look for the clue to the history of philosophy from theory, and the things relevant with theory. Since philosophy is a kind of theoretical activity, the critical content which differentiates various kinds of philosophies should be the ways of their activities or the theoretical standpoints they take. What theoretical standpoint a philosophy takes is fundamentally determined by how it handles its relation with life practice, or in a broad sense the relation between theory and practice. In this way, it is not difficult to understand why Marx chooses the relation between theory and practice as a clue to study the history of philosophy.

Relation between theory and practice as a clue to study the history of philosophy have two meanings at least: on the one hand, theory and practice are two philosophical concepts, so they can be studied as an issue inside the realm of philosophy or as a theoretical issue; on the other hand, the theory here, is usually philosophy per se, or in other words, philosophy usually regards itself as the most representative theory. In this sense, practice is not only a content considered by theory but also a sphere opposite to philosophical theory -- a sphere the subject of theoretical activity must face. These two meanings are connected, for theory must operate according to its "notion". That is to say, a philosophy will inevitably adopt a theoretical standpoint corresponding to its concepts of theory and practice. For this reason, we normally do not differentiate these two meanings in our discussion.

However, here the issues to which theory refers are investigated and seemingly the contradiction similar to "Antinomy of Russell" is generated. If we use the method by which Russell solves this "antinomy", the self-involved discussion of philosophy will never become possible. In fact, the theory we discuss here is not the theory of formal logic. It is more like Martin Heidegger-style "inquiry". Martin Heidegger thinks "Dasein" assumes a priority position in the issue of being and regards it as the entrance to being in Being and Time. One of the reasons is Dasein is a being who can question about its being. The study on theory and practice in a sense is philosophy's "questioning" about its essence. Apparently, theory and practice have the particularity and priority to the studies of philosophy and the history of philosophy, because the issue of theory and practice is an issue philosophy refers to and also an issue closest to philosophy. This issue as a clue and angle for our studies of philosophy and the history of philosophy has essential difference from other angles for our studies of the history of philosophy. Usually we use a "notion" as the standard to judge a philosophy or a philosopher, for example: materialism and idealism, nominalism and realism, and empiricism and rationalism. We should say all these ways have their reasons and are necessary. However, they only hit partial content of philosophy and do not study the issue from the nature of philosophy. The issue of the relation between theory and practice is both an indispensable content of the study of philosophy and philosophy's interpretation on its own activities. Therefore, the study of the history of philosophy from this angle not only shows universality in the involved range, but also has undoubted priority in the comprehension of the essence of philosophy.

The issue of the relation between theory and practice essentially is the issue of how philosophy carries out its activities. The view on this issue decides the modality of theoretical existence of a philosophy, and also decides its attitude towards life practice. In view of the history of Chinese and Western philosophy, we can easily find philosophical theory has two activity directions in terms of its attitude towards life practice. One believes theoretical thinking is a part of life practice, and theory cannot fundamentally surpass life or find a foothold outside life practice, so theoretical reason should be subordinate to practical reason; the other thinks theory can surpass life, it can find its own "Archimedean point" outside life, and theoretical reason is superior to practical reason. Here we call the philosophy in the first direction as practical philosophy, and the philosophy in the second direction as theoretical philosophy.

It must be noted that our differentiation between practical philosophy and theoretical philosophy here is not from the perspective of theoretical object or theoretical subject, but from the perspective of the way of theoretical activity or the way of thinking. In fact, classifying philosophy into theoretical philosophy and practical philosophy according to the objects involved has long been emplyed in the history of Western philosophy. For example, Kant's practical philosophy refers to the philosophy involving the sphere of narrow-sense practice (such as: morals, ethics and politics), while theoretical philosophy on the opposite refers to the part involving ontology, metaphysics and epistemology. Although we often underline the difference between these two types of philosophy as theoretical methods used, it is rather a difference which derives from the spheres they involve. Obviously, this classification cannot cover all spheres of philosophy, so today we think there are still other spheres apart from theory and practice. Different from this differentiation, our discussion here proceeds from the way of theoretical activities, thus it involves all spheres of philosophy. With such an approach, the study on the sphere of "practice" may be a kind of theoretical philosophy, for example: Kant's "critique of practical reason"; while ontology or epistemology may also be studied as practical philosophy, for example: the ontology of Marx, Martin Heidegger and so on.

In view of the history of Chinese and Western philosophy from the perspective established above, we can see without difficulty that the mainstream tradition of Western philosophy in the past, i.e.: the tradition from Plato and Aristotle in ancient Greece to Rene Descartes, Kant and Hegel is theoretical philosophy, since Aristotelian ethics which had been neglected for a long time, its revival in contemporary era as well as the shift of philosophical direction fulfilled by Marx, Martin Heidegger and other philosophers can be deemed as the tradition of Western practical philosophy. In comparison, the mainstream of Chinese philosophy is practical philosophy, and we can say the tradition of theoretical philosophy in a real sense does not exist in China. For a long time, people have usually simply conceived Western philosophy as the tradition of theoretical philosophy, but haven't had clear knowledge about the tradition of Chinese practical philosophy, so it is not difficult to understand why the "dialogue" between Chinese philosophy and Western philosophy always ends up with failure. Nevertheless, the shift in Western philosophy from theoretical philosophy to practical philosophy in current days seemingly has created more opportunities for such dialogue.

Ancient Greece, the common headstream of theoretical philosophy and practical philosophy

Before we apply the classification of theoretical philosophy and practical philosophy to ancient philosophy, we need to make clear that ancient philosophy as a whole is "unconscious" philosophy, in other words, ancient philosophy does not have the subjectivity similar to that of early-modern philosophy, and subsequently does not have a strong consciousness on the opposition between subject and object. Therefore, in ancient times, theoretical philosophy only meant the basis of the world, the spontaneous worship and pursuit to the ultimate and the "negligence" to life practice (of course it is only limited to theory per se. It does not mean early philosophers did not value life. In fact, they were active interveners even "sages" in the that society); while we can understand practical philosophy as the revelation of the natural link between theory and life practice. The spontaneity of ancient philosophy often makes a philosopher's attitude ambiguous, but the later theoretical philosophy and practical philosophy with a clearer stance exactly grew out of this state.

The "powerful theories" of Western philosophy, particularly in early modern times, has originated from the tradition of ancient Greece – we can roughly call it the tradition of metaphysics. The starting point of this metaphysics tradition is also the starting point of Western theoretical philosophy. According to the saying of Aristotle, philosophy originated from the wonder about the world, the curiosity about "why" or in other words; the inquiry about the causes of the world. This inquiry implies the differentiation in two aspects: the first is the differentiation between the world and the asker, i.e.: between the "seeing" and the "seen". In fact, this differentiation is hidden in the structure of theory, and ancient people did not have a strong consciousness on it; the second is the differentiation between empirical world and ontological world, or one and the many. "Inquiry" implies the thing before us is different from its cause. The cognition on the latter is the real mission of philosophy. We should say that in the vision of ancient Greek philosophers, the second differentiation is the most important, while the first became outstanding only in early-modern philosophy.

In the sense of ancient Greek, both the cause and the result from the cause (the world before us) are the nature. In the early philosophy of ancient Greece, we can hardly find any attention to "life practice". Of course, from some historical records, we may know the life of the most ancient philosophers and the wisdom and sapience they demonstrated in reality (for example: Thales as one of the "Seven Sages" of ancient Greece). However, their philosophies only involve the issue of the nature and it seems to be one issue only – the issue of one and the many. This tendency has deeply influenced the later Greek philosophy and even the whole Western philosophy. As Windelband put it, the result of the objective thinking over the nature is that Greek science contributed all youthful joy and energetic knowledge to the issue of the nature at first. During this work, in order to understand the external world, basic concepts or thinking modes were formed.[1] From today's point of view, the particular attention to the issue of the nature firstly implies the negligence of other spheres, and moreover, the initial purpose of this attention is to find an eternal supporting point to interpret the whole world. In the beginning, the issue aimed only to find the basic matter of the world, for example: Thales claimed the basic matter of the world was water, while Anaximenes declared it was gas. The reason for regarding a particular matter as the basic matter of the world is that it is changeable and the changeability makes it adaptable to multiplicate experiences. However, explaining experience with empirical matter contains a contradiction. To solve this contradiction, we must find a non-empirical thing, or exclude the empirical content of things. Only such super-empirical things can govern all experiences. This is the origin of the world. Anaximander's "infinity", Heraclitus' "Logos", Parmenides' "being", Pythagoras' "number" and Leucippus and Democritus' "atom" are all the results of the exploration on the origin of the world. Plato had differentiated ideal world and real world. The latter is the Teilhabe-part- (germ.) of the former. Philosophy regains the logos of the world through memory. Therefore, philosophy's love for wisdom is the love for logos. However, Plato's method is not satisfying. Logos is not abstracted from real world but imposed on the world, so it cannot properly explain the real world. Aris-

---

1 [German] Windelband: A History of Philosophy, Vol.1, p.40.

totle, criticizes Plato's logos not only because it cannot explain the real world but also doubles real things. In the sense of Aristotle, the interpretation on the world must get help from a category system corresponding to world structure. The base of this system is "particular substance" in reality. The highest type is "pure form", i.e.: the God.[1] It is commonly thought that Aristotle is the culminant figure of ancient Greek philosophy, because he had established a complete metaphysical system. Meanwhile we also see his great contribution to practical philosophy. People usually consider him the initiator of Western practical philosophy.

It is believed that with the rise of Sophists, the theories of Greek philosophy took a turn from nature to human and social life. Windelband called the period from this turn to the days of Socrates as an "era of anthropology" or "era of practice" in Greek philosophy, while some critics also simply call the philosophy in this era as "practical philosophy". Indeed, the issues of ethics and politics were mainly discussed in this era, but does it mean the philosophy is the practical philosophy we discuss here? It is doubtful. **Firstly,** here we do not regard research sphere as the basis for the classification of philosophy into theoretical philosophy and practical philosophy. **Secondly,** philosophers in this era studied ethical issue often by the way of natural philosophy, and these studies had failed to grasp the totality of social life and only involved some concrete issues. For example, the issue of law was put forth as such: The essence of everything in the world does not change. It always exists regardless of changes in things. And this essence was called nature. Now, we want to ask whether there is also a law which is determined by the eternal nature and is superior to all changes and differences. Hence Greek ethics had started with a question similar to the first question of physics. The issue of one and the many, was reflected here as the contrast between nature and custom.[2] The way of "learning" in early physics had even deeply influenced Socrates' ethics. "Virtue is knowledge", this was Socrates' objective ethical standard. Of course, the knowledge referred here is not only the exact knowledge about external things but rather about the knowledge and in-

---

1 Deng Xiaomang: Fate of Western Metaphysics, Social Sciences in China, 2002(6).
2 [German] Windelband: A History of Philosophy, Vol.1, p.104.

sight of the good. The proposition of Socrates may have the meaning in two aspects. Firstly, knowledge is enough to make people do the good; secondly, only the life of knowledge or insight is virtuous life. Today, it seems that the former has a logical problem, and the knowledge about the good is at most the necessary condition for doing the good other than a sufficient condition; the latter is close to Aristotle's saying: "contemplation is the highest happiness", but the knowledge in the sense of Socrates is not identical to Aristotle's theoretical contemplation. In any case, Socrates had faced the difference and contradiction between the two spheres of which previous philosophers were not aware – the difference and contradiction between science and ethics.

If we say the vision of early natural philosophers was limited to the inquiry of the nature, i.e.: the scope of theory, one of the sophists' great achievements was, to broaden the vision of philosophy and introduce the sphere of narrow-sense practice into philosophy; moreover in the days of Socrates, the relation between those two spheres (science and ethics) had become an issue. Socrates solved this issue by giving stress on the priority of ethics and enabling science to meet ethical need, even regarding ethics as the first philosophy as mentioned by some critics. Apparently, sophists did not develop the practical philosophy as described above by us, but have created conditions for the generation of practical philosophy, because, to solve the issue of the relation between the two spheres, people must be based on a broader vision and must be aware of life practice as a totality.

We see the vision of this integral life practice, first in Aristotelian philosophy. Above we have stated the direction of ancient Greek theoretical philosophy was established by Aristotle and he had formed a metaphysical system; here we will see the direction of ancient Greek practical philosophy was first formed in Aristotelian philosophy. This seems to be a contradiction. It is unbelievable that two thoroughly different philosophical directions can be found in the same philosophical system, and both later theoretical philosophers and practical philosophers have regarded Aristotelian philosophy as an important resource. We must find the reason for it in the "unconsciousness" of ancient philosophy. Due to such unconsciousness, the "Archimedean point" of ancient theoretical philosophy can only be found in external world. That is the highest entity. In this way, theoretical philosophy may not involve "human" activity; in contrast, practical philosophy is based on the sphere of human activities, i.e." based on state life. We find both the highest entity and the state have the meaning of ultimacy, their co-existence needs an appropriate medium, and in Aristotelian philosophy, this medium is God. In theoretical philosophy, god is the highest entity; while in practical philosophy, God can be practice and life, and theoretical life is a life closest to God. Here in fact, is a role change for God that covers the conflict between the two philosophical directions, because God can be the ultimate supporting point of theory and inherent in theoretical philosophy, and in the meantime, the life of God as a perfect life beyond the state was acceptable to Greek. In this way, the theory of theoretical philosophy can be an absolute theory, while human's theoretical life in reality (this is the study object of practical philosophy) is to long for this "absolute" life, so God and the absolute theory supported by God are also beyond the state and practical philosophy. This mutually extrinsic type of state seemed natural for ancient Greek.

When observing Aristotle's concept of practice, we have seen the special meaning of the state in the eyes of Greek. In fact, if we do not consider this special meaning, we will be unable to understand Aristotle's practical philosophy, because state as the life-world of ancient Greek has an ultimate meaning. At the very beginning of Politics, Aristotle stresses the state as the highest and broadest which community should aim at good in a greater degree than any other and at the highest good. State is a community where people live together, and also the offerer of the meaning to all concrete human activities, i.e.: the giver of human essence. Aristotelian ethics is to study the form of state and all kinds of activities in the state. In this sense, we may also say that ethics is Aristotle's "first philosophy", but this should be differentiated from the ethics which analyzes concrete moral activities. Under the background of state, we can easily grasp the finity of theoretical activities, although its position in Aristotelian ethics is still very high. Theory takes eternal thing as object and thus is closest to the life of God, but human's theoretical activities are not the life of God, and God is beyond the state life. In this way, we may understand theory as the lifestyle of the human in reality, in parallel with the lifestyle of practice and that of technology. We may say that these three lifestyles have covered all life of human in Aristotelian theory, but these three kinds of activities are hierarchical: according to the saying in his book, theoretical activity is closest to the life of God and is the highest happiness due to the eternity of its object and its inward end; practical activity takes variable and practicable things as objects and assumes the second place; technical activity is the lowest activity due to its outward end and non-possession of leisure. This hierarchy has something to do with the tradition of strong ancient Greek theoretical philosophy.

In comparison, the tradition of Chinese ancient philosophy is principally practical philosophy. Strictly speaking, in ancient China, no theory like metaphysics and a pure category system in ancient Greece was created. Therefore, in the eyes of traditional Western people, Chinese philosophy cannot be regarded as "science". From Hegel, we can deeply feel the heterogeneity between Chinese philosophy and the tradition of Western theoretical philosophy. Hegel said:

> China stays in abstraction; when they go on to what is concrete, which is the extrinsic connection of sensuous objects; it has no order (logic and necessity) and no fundamental intuition. The concrete at a further step is moral.

> The further concrete developed from the beginning is moral, art of governing state, history and so on. However, such concrete is no philosophy.[1]

The so-called philosophy in the sense of Hegel is undoubtedly theoretical philosophy, but his assertion that Chinese ancient ideology is "no philosophy" exactly proves that Chinese philosophy belongs to another type of wisdom and philosophy.

---

1 [German] Hegel: Lectures on the History of Philosophy, Vol.1, p.132.

Early-modern age theoretical philosophy and its problems

From the above observation, we find ancient philosophy, ancient Greek philosophy in particular, has contained both theoretical philosophy and practical philosophy. These two different directions, but with the development of history, this "dual" state gradually became impossible. Since its generation, Chinese philosophy has not experienced fundamental changes and practical philosophy has taken absolute advantage all the time; while Western philosophy gradually developed into a pure theoretical philosophy following a continuous expansion in subjectivity.

If we say the "Archimedean point" of ancient theoretical philosophy was God – the highest entity, then early-modern philosophy regards the subject as the ultimate supporting point of its theory. Therefore, some critics consider subjectivity the essential stipulation of early-modern philosophy [German] Kane: *Life-world as A Basic Issue of Objective Science and an Issue of Universal Truth and Being.*[1] It is extremely accurate. Above we have stated that the essential structure of theory has an intrinsic association with subject-object differentiation and subjectivity. This association indicates the development of theoretical philosophy will certainly result in a kind of powerful subjectivity, while this powerful subjectivity will become the support and guarantee of an even stricter theoretical philosophy -- subjective metaphysics. The most distinct difference between early-modern theoretical philosophy and ancient theoretical philosophy is former's "consciousness" and latter's "unconsciousness". Although every theory contains the separation between subject and object, thus containing "consciousness" in a sense, ancient philosophy did not realize this. In ancient philosophy, concepts such as: spirit and soul were discussed as "things", while the concept of "ego" did not exist. In comparison, in early-modern philosophy, human has transcended itself from the existence order of nature and in a sense has become the only one who stick it out and the foundation of the relation of all beings. Through pure "confrontation" with subject, all beings obtain their positions and

---

1 Ni Liangkang: Phenomenology and Its Effect, p.123.

become objects, thus losing their independence and being-for-itself. In this way, human obtains a superior position before other beings; by now, it no longer regards itself as a being of beings but a subject opposite to its object.[1]

However, the consciousness of subject not only means human has achieved "a superior position" but more importantly it means that "human establishes the law for nature". Although "human establishes the law for nature" is only a statement by Kant, it can be applied to the whole early-modern philosophy, because subjectivity can find a real "Archimedean point" only when nature finds its basis in subject. Rene Descartes used the method of universal doubt to determine "Cogito" as the only undoubted thing. In as much, subject becomes the supporting point of the being of other beings. Rene Descartes thinks that the most fundamental attribute of a thing is extension and the thing without an extension does not exist. Extension as a geometric form is the "endowment" of subject. In this way, Rene Descartes had summarized the being of things as the being of subject or "I". And Hegel had highly praised Rene Descartes:

> "It is not until Descartes is arrived at that we have really entered upon a philosophy which is, properly speaking, independent, which knows that it comes forth from reason as independent, and that self-consciousness is an essential moment in the truth. Here, we may say, we are at home, and like the mariner after a long voyage in a tempestuous sea, we may now hail the sight of land".[2]

> Kant had recognized the knowledge of pure mathematics and pure geometry as comprehensive judgment. In fact, it contains the recognition to Rene Descartes – apriori validity of extension to nature; however Kant also thinks Rene Descartes' extension is only a sensuous and intuitive form (space), so it is not enough to govern the nature, or guarantee the objectivity of an empirical judgment, because beyond empirical things, generally speaking, beyond things which give sensuous intuition, some special concepts must be added. These concepts are completely apriori and stem from pure reason, each perception must be procured under these concepts at first. After that,

---

1 [German] Gunten Seubold: Heideggers analysis on contemporary technic, p.44.
2 [German] Hegel: Lectures on the History of Philosophy, Vol.4, p.59, Beijing, Commercial Press, 1978.

it can become experience with the help of these concepts.[1] Hence, Kant had introduced the concept of pure reason. Only the things procured under this kind of concept have necessity and universal validity, i.e.: the "objectivity" in the sense of Kant. Kant for the first time had ascribed objectivity to subjectivity, while this should belong to nature in ancient philosophy and in the early-modern philosophy before it. The meaning of nature in the sense of Kant is fundamentally changed, too. He said : "the formal [aspect] of nature in this narrower sense is therefore the conformity to law of all the objects of experience, and so far as it is known a priori, their necessary conformity."[2]

We may say Kant had established the authority of subject, but this authority is limited, and thing-in-itself is always a "problem" in Kantian philosophy. Kant was indeed very conscious of this problem and limited the valid range of subject. From today's point of view, it is a wise approach at least, but from theoretical philosophy's point of view, it means the ultimate supporting point of his theoretical system was not firm enough. Therefore, most German classical philosophers after Kant were dedicated to removing this "thing-in-itself". Johann Fichte's approach is pure unification of subjectivity and objectivity into ego, and hence the issue of object and subject is traced back to their common basis – ego. This ego knows it itself is in action, so it knows the subject of the action; it also knows the result of the action, so it knows the object of the action.[3] Johann Fichte's basic method to solve the problem of thing-in-itself is to put the issue of pure subject and pure object under a more primordial subject and make it a product of Tathandlung (ger. something like practice), thus converting it into a secondary issue. Hegel had criticized Kant: if conceptual knowledge is unable to grasp thing-in-itself, and reality is totally outside concept ... it will immediately indicate that: the reason which cannot establish consistence between itself -- thing-in-itself and its object, the thing-in-itself inconsistent with the concept of reason, the concept inconsistent with reality, and the reality inconsistent with concept are all unreal concepts.[4] In the sense of Hegel, Kant's concept of

1 [German] Kant: Prolegomena to Any Future Metaphysics, p.63, Beijing, Commercial Press, 1978.
2 The same book as above, p.60~61.
3 Ni Liangkang: Self-knowledge and Reflection, p.225.
4 [German] Hegel: The Logic, Vol.1, p.259, Beijing, Commercial Press, 1966

thing-in-itself is ridiculous, for it claims it can correctly cognize phenomena but cannot cognize thing-in-itself, just like a person, who says he has correct insight, but he adds he can have insight into no real things but the unreal.[1] Hegel's truth is all inclusive, i.e.: the last part of his logic – absolute idea. Inside his absolute idea, it is impossible to contain Kant's thing-in-itself. If you must insist, it can only be an abstract and one-sided link.

> If we say Hegel removes Kant's thing-in-itself with absolute spirit – with his historical-dialectic subjectivity, then Edmund Husserl had realized this task through transcendental subjectivity. Edmund Husserl said: "Kant tries to find, from subjectivity or the mutual relation between subjectivity and objectivity, the final regulations of the meaning of subjectivity which are cognized by cognition. At this point, we are consistent with Kant......"[2] However, Kant is not thorough. He still leaves thing-in-itself. In this way, the yield to transcendentality under the excuse of "thing-in-itself" has ruined the purity of subjectivity . "Subjectivism can be sublated only by the most universal and consistent subjectivism (transcendental subjectivism). In this form, subjectivism is at the same time objectivism, insofar as it defends the rights of every objectivity that is to be demonstrated by harmonious experience".[3] The function of this transcendental subjectivity was similar to Hegel's absolute spirit, since transcendental subjectivity also means absolute subjectivity, and the meaning and being of all constructed things are on the basis of transcendental subjectivity.[4] Transcendental subjectivity ultimately may surpass the transcendental essence of each self and thus be conceived as transcendental inter-subjectivity. It can be considered as the constructive foundation of a same objective world.[5]

Our above studies indicate that early-modern philosophy has always expressed in different ways a kind of subjectivity which surpasses life-world ; which is used as the ultimate supporting point of its theory.

---

1 The same book as above, p.27.

2 Ni Liangkang: Explanation on the Concepts of Edmund Husserl's Phenomenology, p.458, Beijing, Sanlian Bookstore, 1999.

3 [German] Edmund Husserl: Phenomenology and the Crisis of Philosophy, p.30, Beijing, International Culture Publishing Co., Ltd., 1988.

4 [German] Edmund Husserl: Phenomenological Method, p.187, Shanghai, Shanghai Translation Publishing House, 1994.

5 Ni Liangkang: Explanation on the Concepts of Edmund Husserl's Phenomenology, p.446.

However, until the systems of Hegel and Edmund Husserl, we cannot see the realization of such subjectivity, on the contrary, often the immanent contradictions of these systems had aroused more concern. Is this subjectivity not thorough enough, or does this theoretical direction contain a fundamental problem? In view of the subsequent development of philosophy, the reason is the latter without doubt, for the starting point of contemporary philosophy is the disclosure of this contradiction.

When we analyzed the metaphor of "seeing" of theory, we have indicated that the essential structure of each theory contains a kind of separation between subject and object, and meanwhile it is also a kind of consciousness of human. If it is thought that theory can be independent of life practice and find an "Archimedean point" outside it, inevitably the structure of theory will be regarded as an ultimate structure. However, the "binary" structure of theory will certainly conflict with the "unitary" goal it pursues. This is the logical paradox of theoretical philosophy, or the unsoundness of the premise of theoretical philosophy. In other words, theoretical philosophy regards binary opposition (extremalization of the structure of theory) as its ultimate framework. In this case, whether truth is determined to be in object or subject, it is unable to effectively connect the other party. Hence we can understand without difficulty, how object "faithfully" and "objectively" reaches the observer was always a fundamental issue in ancient theoretical philosophy. On thee other side what puzzles early-modern theoretical philosophy is how subject can effectively govern its object. History tells us that the decomposition of these issues is the solution of them.

The inherent problems of ancient theoretical philosophy were revealed by the earliest skepticism. Ancient skepticism had mainly interrogated the reliability of the channel between object and subject, i.e.: the reliability of the feeling. Protagoras has a famous saying: "man is the measure of all things".[1] It means that every thing is what it presents itself to a man. Therefore, true or not, it depends on man. Gorgias went one step

---

1 [British] D.W. Hamlyn: A Brief History of Western Epistemology, p.1, Beijing, China Renmin University Press, 1987.

further. He claimed: "Nothing exists; even if something exists, nothing can be known about it; and even if something can be known about it, knowledge about it cannot be communicated to others".[1] The skeptical object of early-modern philosophers usually is not the communication channel between subject and object but the "capacity" of subject, because in the concept of early-modern philosophy, object is the construction of subject. Therefore, Rene Descartes cannot be reckoned as a skeptic; while for Hume's skepticism, we may consider it as an examination on the capacity of subject. Nevertheless, if the power of subjectivity is infinitely expanded, the only result will be the thorough abandonment of the stance of theoretical philosophy. Theoretical philosophy does not eliminate suspicion in the end. The root cause here, is the "dubiety" in the foundation of theoretical philosophy. Above we have indicated this dubiety originates from the contradiction between the "unitary" goal of theoretical philosophy and the "binary" structure of theory. This contradiction not only reflects the finity of theory but also reveals the fundamental problem of theoretical philosophy.

The problem of theoretical philosophy is not only seen in its immanent contradiction but also manifested by the contradiction between theoretical sphere and life practice – the non-theoretical sphere. In Aristotelian philosophy, we have seen that non-theoretical sphere has two meanings. One is practice as human's concrete activities and technology. The other is the state practice as totality. Since the very beginning, early-modern theoretical philosophy had tried to include these spheres into the theoretical system of subjectivity, but this process was always accompanied with some unsolvable problems, and all these problems imply the existence of the spheres outside theory.

In the philosophy of Rene Descartes, this problem is seen as an issue of the legality of ethical sphere and ethics. Rene Descartes tried to use geometric form to define the existence of the world. He had first suffered setback in ethical sphere, because obviously we cannot use geometric form to define morals and also cannot use mathematical knowledge to demonstrate human behaviors. Thus, we may easily understand why

---

1 Philosophy of Ancient Greece and Rome, p.133, Beijing, Sanlian Bookstore, 1957.

Rene Descartes resorted to extreme irrationalism in the sphere of ethics and politics. However, this irrationalism is incompatible with the system of his theoretical philosophy. The geometric ethics after Rene Descartes had always tried to solve this problem based on Rene Descartes' theoretical principle. Kant's method to solve this problem was to regard ethical and moral sphere as the result of the practical capacity of transcendental subject. Due to the subjective construction of subject's practical capacity, moral law must be expressed as order, the behaviors tallying with them must be expressed as responsibilities, and reason uses "should" to express this necessity. In the sense of Kant, this necessity and the necessity in natural sphere have equal effect. Hence Kant uses theoretical way to construct moral and ethical sphere, thus this sphere can be called "reasonable". Unfortunately, Kant's theoretical reason had met with an unsolvable problem – the thing-in-itself. Above we have mentioned that Kant had limited subjectivity to phenomenal world and avoided "illegal" involvement of thing-in-itself. Do not step beyond the boundary of experience and do not try to judge any thing which is beyond the boundary of experience and is thing-in-itself.[1] Thing-in-itself is an unremovable nick of Kant's theoretical system and is also a sign of imperfection in his theoretical system. Kant had realized the finity of human's theoretical reason, and always limited the unity of subject and object to the phenomenal world, and avoided discussing thing-in-itself, so critics think what Kant advocates is a finite subjectivity. This was an unharmonious "note" in early-modern philosophy. The criticism of later German classical philosophy at Kant and the new interpretation of modern philosophers on Kant often concentrate on this point.

However, classical philosophers had encountered their own problem while trying to solve the problem of Kant. From Johann Fichte on, subjectivity has no longer been a transcendental form, and historicity and timeliness were gradually introduced as media to synthesize thing-in-itself.[2] In the sense of Hegel, historicity has become the only way for rea-

---

1 [German] Kant: Prolegomena to Any Future Metaphysics, p.148.
2 Johann Fichte's concept that "I" exist in the present moment must contain a dimension of time (refer to Li Wentang: The Light of Truth, p.58); Schelling's System of Transcendental Idealism contains the preliminary principle of world historical structure , he articulated (refer to [German] Habermas: Post-Metaphysical Thinking, p.146)

son to unify the whole world. It seems that historicity had enabled Hegel to establish a powerful theoretical system, but in fact, historicity and timeliness had hit a fatal blow at both Hegelian philosophy and the entire theoretical philosophy. Same as Hegelian theoretical system, to determine an "Archimedean point", theoretical philosophy must establish a closed system with this as the end point, whereas the infinity of history just implies the finity of this system and the existence of the spheres outside theory. But in this way, the "Archimedean point" of philosophical theory will become invalid. Engels thinks this is a contradiction between Hegel's conservative system and revolutionary method.[1] Here, what Engels really wants to express is that Hegel would certainly introduce historicity to realize the unity between subject and object, while this introduction also implies the existence of the spheres outside the duality of subject and object and the failure of this unity. Martin Heidegger had said that: "we might have a try to establish the connection between spirit and time and this would disclose the etymological kinship between them".[2] Below we will see it was based on this "kinship" that Martin Heidegger developed his ontology. Certainly, it is beyond the framework of theoretical philosophy. We can easily discover that the influence of historicity on Hegelian philosophy is similar to the influence of thing-in-itself in Kantian philosophy. It was impossible for Kant to deny the existence of thing-in-itself, otherwise the content of experience will lose headspring, but admitting the existence of thing-in-itself is equal to admitting the finity of theoretical reason; historicity is necessary for Hegelian philosophy, but it announces the failure of the construction while it is used as Hegelian theoretical construction. It was undoubtedly a paradox.

Similar paradox can be seen in the philosophy of Edmund Husserl. Above we have mentioned Edmund Husserl solves Kant's problem of thing-in-itself by means of transcendental subjectivity or transcendental ego, but "I myself, as transcendental ego, 'constitute' the world, and at the same time, as soul, I am a human ego in the world".[3] Edmund

---

1 Marx & Engels Selected Works, Edition 2, Vol.4, 214~223, Beijing, People's Publishing House, 1995.

2 [German] Martin Heidegger: Being and Time, p.491.

3 [German] Edmund Husserl: Crisis of European Sciences and Transcendental Phenomenology (English version), p.202, Evanston, 1970.

Husserl thinks that thorough subjectivism he can solve this paradox. However, "Edmund Husserl's paradox is not really solved and under this paradox, a greater paradox is implied", because ; to realize transcendental ego, it must be restored through phenomenon, and moreover, to enable the restoration, it must break through natural attitude and has the consciousness of transcendental ego. Therefore, "the paradox: the premise of restoration is the awakening of transcendental ego, while the premise of the awakening of transcendental ego is restoration".[1] In addition, in his late years, Edmund Husserl introduced "life-world" as a channel to transcendental phenomenology, but life-world also implies it is beyond objective – scientific world, and implies the failure of the ultimate identity of theoretical reason. In the sense of Martin Heidegger and Habermas, life-world which is outside theoretical world is a more primordial sphere, or in other words, the sphere of theory stems from life-world.

Practical philosophy as the trend of modern philosophy

We may say Edmund Husserl's philosophy of transcendental phenomenology is the acme of subjective philosophy, so it is also the acme of the development of theoretical philosophy. From substantial philosophy to subjective philosophy, theoretical philosophy has walked through a fruitful road, but as described above, problems were not solved. Apparently, for the tradition of theoretical philosophy, what troubles it is not the numerous trivial problems but the fundamental problem. This problem rests with the "contemplation" standpoint at human life brought by its fundamental metaphor of "seeing" or "gazing". The highest realm pursued by this "contemplation" is to eliminate all the pure consciousness existing in reality, even set aside the existence of its own body. Under such a "out of body" circumstance, to solve the problem concerning the relation between a thinking subject and the real world will be as impossible as fishing in the air. This impossibility means that to solve the problems of theoretical philosophy, we must break through the tradition of theoretical philosophy and embark on a way different from it.

---

2 Chen Lisheng: Ego and the World, p.122~123, Guangzhou, Guangdong People's
   Publishing House, 1999.

This approach different from early-modern theoretical philosophy can only be modern practical philosophy. The concept of modern practical philosophy, we use, on the one hand implies the reversion and transcendence to the standpoint of early-modern theoretical philosophy, and on the other hand, indicates that after the stage of early-modern subjective philosophy, it has inherent difference from ancient practical philosophy. Above, we have explained the paradoxical nature of the fundamental logic of early-modern philosophy. In the mature stage of theoretical philosophy, i.e.: Hegel, Edmund Husserl and so on, this paradoxical nature was sufficiently exposed. All modern philosophies in the 20th century have proceeded from critique of it. Therefore, we may also say modern practical philosophy was born from early-modern philosophy. This can be fully proved by the relation between Marx's philosophy and Hegel's philosophy and the relation between Martin Heidegger's philosophy and Edmund Husserl's philosophy. In the same time, ancient practical philosophy is another important source of modern practical philosophy. The interpretation on classical philosophers, Aristotle in particular, is often an important content of the theoretical activities of modern philosophers. Modern practical philosophy has inherited a kind of consciousness and subjectivity from early-modern philosophy. This is a point distinguishing it from ancient practical philosophy. In Aristotelian philosophy, we can see the phenomenon of the co-existence of theoretical philosophy and practical philosophy, because of the "unconsciousness" of ancient philosophy. This phenomenon would never happen in modern philosophy, because modern philosophy is intolerable to an "Archimedean point" by any theory. In addition, from Aristotle's practical philosophy, we can also find that the channel between theory and life practice was not noticed, either. Aristotle, just regards theoretical activity as a natural part and the highest part of state life; however theoretical activity is not aware of the fontal relation between it itself and state life, so it is impossible to regard returning to life-world as its end, and it only takes "divinity" as its special definition. Therefore, we can say ancient practical philosophy is the natural expression of the fontal relation between theory and life practice. The conscious awareness of this relation had not occurred till modern practical philosophy.

The process in which the standpoint of practical philosophy was born from early-modern philosophy in fact is the process in which the life practice in a broader sense was noticed. Its starting point is Marx's practice and theory. However, neither the supporters nor opponents of Marx have clearly realized this point. We will discuss it in detail in next section. Only by the 20th century, modern practical philosophy became a worldwide trend. Usually we call it as the rise of the discourse of life-world.

We know life-world is a concept first put forth by Edmund Husserl. Although Edmund Husserl also thinks the natural life-world is priori to objective scientific world, the foundation-laying role of this concept has never been thoroughly affirmed, because the life-world in the sense of Edmund Husserl is subordinate to subjectivity, and is the sum of the visual spheres constructed by subject. This subject is a separate subject in the beginning and later it is extended into inter-subject. The formation process of life-world is the construction process of life-world from a subject to object and inter-subject even to the whole nature and society.[1] Martin Heidegger reverses this view. He thinks men -at first -live in a common world in a selfless state. Only when they pull away from this communality, will they meet as other persons or even other things. When a human being breaks away from this communality, nature and other persons will become its objects, while theory is generated from this objective relation.[2] Ludwig Wittgenstein does not consciously put himself in the tradition of Edmund Husserl, but he explicitly expresses the concept of life-world. Later on Ludwig Wittgenstein gave up the binary mode of "logical atomism", and converted philosophical research into daily "language games" and "forms of life". The rules of these games and the forms of life are what we must accept, i.e.: the things given. For humans, they possess quasi transcendental nature. Habermas has directly inherited Edmund Husserl's concept of life-world, but he has also made an important reform on it. Habermas thinks the bias of Edmund Husserl's concept of life-world rests with its subjectivity and subject's priority to it. He underlines the background of life-world and its foundation-laying role for concrete activities. He thinks the background of

---

1 Ni Liangkang: Phenomenology and Its Effect, p.354.
2 [German] Martin Heidegger: Being and Time, p.81~82.

life-world has multiple features, such as: definiteness, totality and integrity.[1] It is to underline the unsurpassability of life practice for theoretical subject.

We can easily discover that today's philosophies, regardless of approach, all try to open a vision of modern practical philosophy, and modern practical philosophy has become a general trend in philosophical development.

---

1 [German] Habermas: Post-Metaphysical Thinking, p.79~80.

CHAPTER THREE

Marx's Philosophy As a Modern Practical Philosophy

Modern practical philosophy: reasonable orientation of Marx's philosophy

Since the mainstream tradition of Western philosophy is theoretical philosophy and this tradition has realized logical completion in early-modern subjective philosophy, one question we must face is whether Marxist philosophy belongs to theoretical philosophy or practical philosophy? In fact, our analysis above has dropped a hint on the answer of this question: Marx's philosophy belongs to the way of practical philosophy, or in the other words, Marx is the founder of Western modern practical philosophy.

Here undoubtedly, the issue of the orientation of Marx's philosophy will be reviewed. The author believes that this issue has not aroused people's attention for a long time. Even in Western academic community, people usually only stress the importance of Marx and regard him as a resource of theoretical innovation, but the position of Marx's philosophy is often ambiguous. For example, Martin Heidegger thinks that like Nietzsche, Marx had completed the "reversal" of Western metaphysical standpoint, but he also thinks Marx could not break away from this tradition. In China, this issue has not been seriously thought over for a long time, and the evident position of Marx's philosophy in our mind is an ambiguous position in fact: Marxism is neither Chinese philosophy nor Western philosophy (Western bourgeois philosophy); neither ancient philosophy nor real modern philosophy or contemporary philosophy. Proving Marxist philosophy suits our era is only to prove it suits any era. Therefore, generally it is believed that the philosophy before Marx is discarded by Marx, while the philosophy (modern Western philosophy) after Marx has no necessity for existence due to the perfectness of Marx's philosophy. It seems that Marx's philosophy is hung in the air and does not belong to history. In 1980s, the academic community in China seemed to be aware of this issue. They gave up the second thought,--the previous dogmatic interpretation on Marx's philosophy-- and proved that it was a modern philosophy and adaptable to our era. However, this proof only says the issue of the relation between thought and being is a basic issue for all philosophies, and Marx had introduced the concept of practice when solving this issue, thus obtaining an answer superior to all of the previous philosophies. In this case, it seems that the only uniqueness of Marx's philosophy is to provide a better answer to the so-called basic philosophical issue, while it bears no fundamental difference from previous philosophies. This result on the contrary indicates that Marx's philosophy only belongs to modern philosophy. This orientation of Marx's philosophy is the biased understanding on the essence of Marx's philosophy, while this can boil down to the biased understanding on the history of philosophy and even philosophy per se. Below we will indicate the issue of the relation between abstract thought and being is only a core issue and basic issue of early-modern philosophy. If we observe the history of philosophy and Marxist philosophy from this perspective, misunderstanding will be certainly induced. As described above, regarding the relation between theory and practice as a way to understand the history of philosophy is the closest to the essence of philosophy. No doubt, understanding Marx's philosophy in this way is the most appropriate. As a matter of fact, it was a method used by Marx himself.

The most direct evidence proving Marx's philosophy is practical philosophy is certainly lay in the expressions made by Marx himself. The most famous is Article 11 of Theses on Feuerbach. In this article, Marx summarizes his new philosophical thought: "The philosophers have only interpreted the world, in various ways; the point is to change it." Of course, changing the world is not only "doing" without theory as misunderstood by some people. Instead, it is to change the understanding on the relation between theory and practice and changing the contemplative attitude towards the world. It is not to regard theory as "out of body" mediation outside the world but to regard it as theoretical practice connecting life practice and which constitutes a part of life. The termination or negation of philosophy mentioned by Marx (and Engels) on many occasions should also be deemed as the negation of traditional theoretical philosophy. When they had talked of the termination of philosophy, they did not explicitly refer to theoretical philosophy, but had considered its mainstream position in Western philosophy, the philosophy they wanted to negate can only be the philosophy belonging to theoretical philosophy, other than practical philosophy. This can be clearly seen from their relevant dissertations. As early as in Introduction to a Contribution to the Critique of Hegel's Philosophy of Right, Marx had criticized German philosophers "philosophy up to the present itself belongs to this world and is its completion".[1] In *The German Ideology*, they had further criticized these philosophers "it has not occurred to any one of these philosophers to inquire into the connection of German philosophy with German reality, the relation of their criticism to their own material surroundings."[2] Therefore, they think "When reality is depicted, philosophy as an independent branch of knowledge loses its medium of existence.",[3] but "at the best its place can only be taken by a summing-up of the most general results, abstractions which arise from the obser-

---

1 Marx & Engels Selected Works, Edition 2, Vol.1, p.8.

2 The same book as above, p.66.

3 The same book as above, p.73.

vation of the historical development of men".[1] "Viewed apart from real history, these abstractions have in themselves no value whatsoever."[2] Apparently, such thing which cannot be apart from real history and is the general results of it can be nothing but a kind of practical philosophy.

Of course, the most important is not the expression of a few paragraphs of words but that in this philosophical logic, Marx's philosophical theses can be best explained. We should proceed from the relation between theory and practice. Above we have indicated that no matter what understanding is on theory and practice, since Kant separated theoretical reason and practical reason into phenomenal world and noumenal world, the issue of the relation between theory and practice has always been the central issue in German philosophy from Kant to Hegel. As the reason or self-consciousness were the bases on which these philosophical systems were established; and they were a kind of absolutely independent and self-existent abstract thing, and the solution of this classical idealism could only be to absorb practical sphere into this absolute abstract thing. The result was nothing but the sufficient exposure of the essential paradox in theoretical philosophy. Early-modern materialism does not in the least exceed the vision of classical idealism but just substitutes the absolute subjectivity of idealism with absolute objectivity, but the abstractness degree of this objectivity is not inferior to the former. Therefore, the old materialism is also a kind of theoretical philosophy, and its solution to the relation between theory and practice was unsuccessful, too. The standpoint of Marx's practical philosophy is generated amidst the critique of old philosophy.

In *Theses on Feuerbach*, the central point of Marx's critique of Feuerbach and all old materialism is to criticize their ignorance of practice's foundation-laying role in theory. In fact, in the sense of Marx, the old materialism does not break away from the logic of old metaphysics -- theoretical philosophy, still regards theoretical activity as real human activity,[3] and can be called as a kind of "contemplative materialism". There-

---

1 The same book as above, p.73~74.
2 The same book as above, p.74.
3 Marx & Engels Selected Works, Edition 2, Vol.1, p.54.

fore, the greatest problem of such materialism is that it thinks human is the product of circumstances and education. This doctrine forgets that "circumstances are changed by men and that it is essential to educate the educator himself. This doctrine must, therefore, divide society into two parts, one of which is superior to society."[1] That is to say:

> When theorists see their tasks in this way, they do not realize that they have made strict differentiation between how they understand themselves and how they understand the people who are their research objects. They use their own theory to explain the activity experience of these people and understand them as the products thoroughly decided by environment and education. Their biological and social heritage independent of and priori to their own will of reason make them only the inherited products. In contrast, here theorists see themselves as proxies of reason and they are capable and determined to reflect their ambition in natural world and social world. They look at other people with a deterministic vision and look at themselves with the principle of rational will.[2]

Then how to solve this difficult problem? Marx had pointed out: "The coincidence of the changing of circumstances and of human activity or self-changing can be conceived and rationally understood only as revolutionary practice."[3] This sentence is familiar to every researcher of Marxist philosophy, but its meaning is not simple. We may say it contains the most critical secrete to understand the change in Marx's philosophy – based on it, Marx solves the above mentioned antinomy between determinism and rational voluntarism. But how do we understand this solution? If we still think theoretical reason is independent and theoretical activity may be independent of life practice, then the above antinomy will not be solved in the least. Only when we consider theoretical reason is subordinate to practical reason, and theoretical activity is a part of life practice, can the above antinomy be solved. When we deal with the relation between theory and practice in this way, it means we have taken the side of practical philosophy.

---

1 The same book as above, p.55.
2 [American] McIntyre: The Theses on Feuerbach: A Road. not Taken, Social Sciences Abroad, 1995(6).
3 Marx & Engels Selected Works, Edition 2, Vol.1, p.55.

Obviously, Marx criticizes old philosophy by basing himself on real life practice. This critique was further developed in The German Ideology. Since "all social life is essentially practical. All mysteries which lead theory to mysticism find their rational solution in human practice and in the comprehension of this practice",[1] then the critique of mysterious theory should be the foundation and premise on which its reality is disclosed, other than use phrases to oppose phrases. In the sense of Marx, all of the then critiques aimed at Hegel were based on Hegelian system. "This dependence on Hegel is the reason why no one of these modern critics has even attempted a comprehensive criticism of the Hegelian system, however much each professes to have advanced beyond Hegel".[2] Therefore, these critics only grasp some aspects of Hegelian philosophy and from them they create various kinds of other abstract theories. Consequently, this criticism becomes a criticism of an abstraction at another abstraction. They are merely combating "the phrases of this world" and in no way combating "the real existing world".[3] Obviously, Hegel's critique essentially is the criticism of a theoretical philosophy by another theoretical philosophy, while Marx thinks only the critique standing outside theoretical philosophy, i.e.: based on real life practice can be valid. The standpoint based on life practice is the standpoint of practical philosophy. Therefore, it is wrong to say Marx's theory for critique does not have a starting point. "It starts out from the real premises and does not abandon them for a moment. Its premises are men, not in any fantastic isolation and rigidity, but in their actual, empirically perceptible process of development under definite conditions".[4] The "men" in the sense of Marx in fact are the collection of real relation and are real life practice. Hence, theory is not "falling from the heaven" as claimed by classical idealism but "rising from the earth to the heaven".

---

1 The same book as above, p.56.
2 The same book as above, p.64.
3 Marx & Engels Selected Works, Edition 2, Vol.1, p.66.
4 The same book as above, p.73.

Basic significance of Marx's practical philosophy

In this way, Marx completes the "reversal" of the standpoint in theoretical philosophy. The basic significance of this "reversal" is to indicate theory is inherent in practice and subordinate to practice other than beyond practice. However, if we stop here, we will be still unable to fully understand all the connotation of Marx's practical philosophy. In fact, Marx only simply "announced" the standpoint of "practice" in his theoretical activity and did not give systematic and theoretical definition, since it wasn't Marx's primary task in that time. Today, we can find much "evidence" to prove Marx's philosophy belongs to practical philosophy, i.e.: find his way dealing with the relation between theory and practice is apparently different from the standpoint of theoretical philosophy. However, the definitions on this "new" relation is still simple and sometimes even extrinsic. Of course, this does not in the least affect the revolutionary significance of Marx's philosophy, but it becomes a task of later generations to give a theoretical definition on this "new" relation between theory and practice. Unfortunately, our prolonged theoretical studies seldom entered the visual sphere of Marxist philosophy and no real awareness on this task was achieved, either.

In fact, the asymmetry between theory and practice developed by Marx's philosophy just reveals the "distance" between theory and practice, and obviously, this "distance" also belongs to the content of the "new" relation between theory and practice in Marx's practical philosophy. In other words, the asymmetry between Marx's theoretical activity and our theoretical grasp on this activity reflects the "distance" between theory and practice in a general sense. More importantly, it is the existence of this distance between theory and practice that makes the reversal of the standpoint of theoretical philosophy possible. It can be seen that how to understand this "distance" in fact has involved the issue of how to understand the "new" relation between theory and practice, because once the fact that theory is subordinate to life practice is recognized, their differentiation will become critical.

Since our task is to "theoretically" understand this "new" relation, we should not only announce theory's subordination to life practice. Instead we should do some logical reasoning of this subordination. Above we have mentioned that Aristotle classified three different activity modes based on the purpose and object of activity. This includes a classification method of theory. Now we must describe the relation between theory and practice based on the inherent properties of theory and practice. Of course, due to different understanding on many concepts, this relation will inevitably be different from that of Aristotle. As the practice in Marx's philosophy has two meanings, the relation between theory and practice, here must involve the relation between theory and the life practice as the totality and background, and the relation between theory and the productive practice as a concrete mode of activity.

Then, what enables us to distinguish theory from life practice, or what causes the "distance" between theory and life practice? Our answer is the abstractness and unicity(singleness) of theoretical activity. According to our above analysis, theory is the abstract activity of subject. Just because of this abstractness, it obtains relative independence and stands out from the totality of life practice. The opposite to the abstractness of theory is the concreteness of life practice. Our description on the relation between theory and practice starts with the difference between the abstractness and concreteness. In fact, the issue of the relation between abstract and concrete has been studied in Marx's *Introduction to the Contribution to Political Economy as* "the method of political economy". Marx differentiated the two roads for research on political economy. The first is to "start with the real and concrete elements, with the actual preconditions",[1] and in the end "meaningful images are attenuated to abstract definitions";[2] "the second leads from abstract definitions by way of reasoning to the reproduction of the concrete situation".[3] In the sense of Marx, "this latter was obviously the correct scientific method",[4] while the first is wrong, because theory certainly is a process from abstract to

---

1 Marx & Engels Selected Works, Edition 2, Vol.2, p17, Beijing, People's Publishing House, 1995.
2 The same book as above, p.18.
3 Marx & Engels Selected Works, Edition 2, Vol.2, p.18, Beijing, People's Publishing House, 1995.
4 The same book as above, p.18.

concrete, and concrete cannot be the logical starting point of theory and can only be its result. Then what is the concrete concept? Marx said: "The concrete concept is concrete because it is a synthesis of many definitions, thus representing the unity of diverse aspects."[1] From the dissertation of Marx, we can see that there are two kinds of concrete. One starts with political economy, i.e.: the real premise before abstraction of theory. The other is the result of theoretical activity, i.e.: the concrete as thought and which is the totality of the methods with many definitions and relations. Here Marx mainly explores the issue of theoretical method, so naturally he has mainly considered the latter concrete. Nevertheless, his differentiation of the two kinds of concrete is extremely important for our understanding on the relation between theory and practice, because it contains all contents of abstract and concrete.

According to Marx's description, the two ends of theoretical activity are both concrete. Although the first concrete cannot be regarded as the "starting point" of theory, it is the premise of theory or the starting point in reality, while the latter concrete as the result of theoretical activity is the concrete grasping and the reproduction of the reality. The latter can be easily comprehended, but Marx does not spread his dissertation on the former and only defines it with words like "real premise", "perception" and "image". Apparently, "perception" and "image" are concepts from old epistemological philosophy. If we still understand these terms Marx used, in the sense of such old epistemology, we will misunderstand Marx, because if we understand them in this way, inevitably we will equate the differentiation between concrete and abstract with the differentiation between perceptual knowledge and rational knowledge, i.e.: the differentiation between the higher stage and lower stage of cognition. This differentiation can be traced back to Kant's differentiation between sense and intellect, Plato's differentiation between ideal world and sensuous world, and even Parmenides' differentiation between truth and opinion. If we use this framework for interpretation, the method of Marx's political economy will be not a great method. In fact, the issue Marx explores is not this issue at all. Marx regards the first concrete as a

---

1 The same book as above, p.18.

sphere outside theory other than a stage of theoretical activity, so this is no longer a simple epistemological issue and it involves the relation between theory and life practice. As concrete cannot be exhausted by simple definitions, while theory is based on this simplicity in essence, it will not be difficult to understand why Marx chooses such words like "chaos", "image" and "perception". The "non-theory" nature can be reflected only in this way. Obviously, this sphere is nothing but real life practice. By its concreteness, life practice distinguishes itself from theory. In terms of the concept, category and logic of theory, life practice is infinite and thus shows it infinite complexity in comparison with the logical simplicity of theory. In this sense, theory is always finite.

Although theory must start with abstractness and cannot thoroughly get rid of this starting point, theory is not contented by abstractness from the very beginning. In fact, theory also aims for a kind of concreteness. This is the second concrete as mentioned by Marx, i.e.: the concrete of thinking. Since the interior of theory also contains a kind of concreteness, can we equate or partially equate it with the first concrete? Absolutely not. Marx said: "the concrete totality regarded as a conceptual mental totality, as a mental fact, is indeed a product of thinking, of comprehension; but it is by no means a product of the idea which evolves spontaneously and who think proceeds outside and above perception and imagination, but is the result of the assimilation and transformation of perceptions and images into concepts."[1] The latter concrete is inherent in theory and the "theoretical" manifestation of the first concrete. Marx strictly differentiates these two concretes and regards this differentiation the key to his philosophy, and particularly as a key step to draw a clear distinction with Hegelian philosophy. Marx thinks the result that Hegel erases this differentiation is "the result of thinking, which causes its own synthesis, its own deepening, and its own movement; whereas the method of advancing from the abstract to the concrete is simply the way in which thinking assimilates the concrete and reproduces it as a concrete mental category".[2] As the concrete of thinking is inherent in the concrete of theory, this concrete is finite in the end. In fact, the approach of Hegel

---

1   Marx & Engels Selected Works, Edition 2, Vol.2, p.19.
2   The same book as above, p.18~19.

is simply the extremalization of theoretical philosophy, while Marx's criticism is applicable to the whole theoretical philosophy. Only when theory and life practice are qualitatively separated, will the finity of theory and its subordination to life practice be able to be implemented, and thus can the standpoint of practical philosophy be really established by a "theoretical" mean.

By now we have only articulated the relation between theory and the life practice in a broad sense. Only on this premise, can the relation between theory and productive practice be comprehended. Like theoretical activity, productive activity is also a conscious activity of subject, so it must act upon the world from a specific angle. Therefore, productive activity is also an abstract activity. This point is connective with theoretical activity. Below we will review that production and theory are both concrete human activities and share structural similarity or isomorphism. The difference is that the abstractness of theory is manifested through the abstractness and unicity(singleness) of concept, while the abstractness of productive activity is manifested through a physical object – production tool. As production tool can only be a physical object, its abstractness is extremely finite, and it is impossible that its relation with this world is a real unitary relation, whereas concept can achieve this and we can even say the generation of concept is aimed at overcoming the unicity(singleness) of physical object. In this sense, theory can be regarded as a kind of symbolized and utopian production. In this way, it will not be difficult to understand why Marx says, theory is the process of "assimilation and transformation of perceptions and images into concepts". Then, the relation between theory and production will certainly contain two aspects. One is their structural similarity and the other is their difference in abstractness degree. Although production is also an abstract activity, this abstractness cannot "divorce" itself from concrete life practice, just like a certain degree of concreteness may exist within the range of theory. However, this concrete of thinking cannot go beyond the range of theory, and thus can only be finite concretization. If theory wants to reach the concreteness of life practice, it must realize that through the decomposition of theory per se. We will discuss the aspects of the relation between theory and practice below.

The issue of the relation between theory and practice further involves the comprehension on activity subject. Above we have stated the relation between theory's essential structure and subjectivity as well as the difficulties of absolute subjectivity in early-modern philosophy. The question at present is how Marx understands subject and subjectivity, or how should we understand subject based on real life practice. We know the subject in ancient philosophy is believed to be unconscious and has no subjectivity, while the subjectivity in early-modern philosophy can be considered as an absolute subjectivity. At first, it is certain that the subject in the sense of Marx is by no means the unconscious subject like in ancient philosophy or the frequently criticized absolute subject in early-modern philosophy, and can only be a conscious and finite subject.

Talking of finite subject, we have to relate it to Kant. Although Kant inherited and developed Rene Descartes' path of subjective philosophy, seemingly he had realized the finity of subject and theoretical reason. Kant thought that real scientific knowledge must be apriori and synthetic. What makes apriori and synthetic proposition possible is the cognitive ability of subject – the ability to govern multiplicate sensuous materials. Therefore, we may say the knowledge in the sense of Kant is no longer the faithful reflection of subject on object, let alone the construction of subject and the "product" of subject. The uplift of subjectivity is obvious. However, we have discovered that Kant had never separately discussed subjectivity in departure of the sphere of experience, to say nothing of giving an ultimate ontological position to subject. He had always set foothold in the sphere of experience, while experience is "both subject and object" and no experience can be formed without transcendental subject or absolute object (thing-in-itself). Therefore, Kant's subjectivity is finite subjectivity which is limited to experience. The limit of this subjectivity is thing-in-itself. Above we have made clear that as a theoretical philosophy, this finity was the failure of Kantian philosophy, but from today's point of view, this finity provides revelation and reference for us to understand the concept of subjectivity in modern philosophy. Here we might as well make comparison between Marx and Kant. The finity in Kant's subjectivity refers to the incomprehensibility of thing-in-itself, while the opposite to Marx's finite subject is the background of life practice, or in other words the concept of practice as life-world; the limit of subjectivity in the sense of Kant is Anderssein (germ.) which is completely outside subject, while the limit of subjectivity in the sense of Marx is the world where man lives. We cannot say it is outside subject and should say subject is inside it. Here, the issue of the unity between man and nature as faced by Kant is no longer an issue, for "man establishes a relationship with the world through his very existence, and this relationship is already there before he ever starts contemplating it, before he turns it into an object of investigation, and before he practically or intellectually affirms or negates it".[1] The finity of subject means it cannot go beyond the background of life-world and must have a lifestyle. Individuals are like what they manifest themselves,[2] but it is impossible for people to manifest themselves arbitrarily, and human beings must be an nsemble of social relations. Further speaking, if man cannot go beyond life-world, it will mean he can neither take the whole life-world as his object nor theoretically perceive the totality of life-world. Although subject is constructing life-world all the time and inherently "knows" this background, it cannot exist alone outside life-world, to say nothing of absorbing the whole world into it. If the finity of Kant's subject implies the failure of his theoretical construction, then Marx's finite subjectivity will indicate his standpoint of practical philosophy.

Then, what does Marx's finite subject concretely refer to? Undoubtedly, it is the "real individuals" who are historical activity subjects as he repeatedly stresses in The German Ideology. These real individuals engage in activities and carry out material production, and thus act with certain material and under the limits, premises and conditions not freely controlled by them.[3] Such activity subjects are certainly the individuals who are concrete in a specific social relation, or as Gould said, "what Marx proposed is individual ontology in relation.[4] In comparison, the old philosophy criticized by Marx conceived the subject of activity as either "absolute spirit", "self-consciousness" and "the One" or "man". Apparently,

---

1 [Czech] Karel Kosik: Dialectic of the Concrete, p.166, Beijing, Social Sciences
  Academic Press, 1989.
2 Marx & Engels Selected Works, Edition 2, Vol.1, p.67~68.
3 Marx & Engels Selected Works, Edition 2, Vol.1, p.72.
4 [American] Carol Gould: Marx's Social Ontology (English version), p.30, MIT Press, 1980.

conceiving subject as an abstract being which could be independent of life practice is the absolute requirement of the starting point proposed by theoretical philosophy. Once subject is conceived as an abstract being which can be independent of life practice, the above antinomy between determinism and voluntarism in the relation between theory and practice will become unsolvable. Apparently, regarding subject as "real individual" is the intrinsic necessary requirement of practical philosophy, for only when subject is defined in this way, can the antinomy in the relation between theory and practice be reasonably solved.

The assertion that Marx's philosophy belongs to the tradition of practical philosophy may also be proved from the misunderstanding of the people in later generations on his philosophy. After Marx, two main trends has dominated the interpretation on his philosophy: one is the mechanical determinism starting from Plekhanov and fixed by Stalin. The other was rational voluntarism starting from Lukacs and developed in Western Marxism movement. The first interpretation is obviously an interpretation of substantial philosophy, while the latter undoubtedly is an interpretation of subjective philosophy. The former underlines the objective necessity of a historical process. The latter gives prominence to the role of historical subject. Both interpretations have contradictions which cannot be sublated. Just as Alasdair Mac Intyre put it, in later debate, each side has great diagnosis of the counterpart's errors: One side is very clear that if man is the product of circumstances and education, then it will be impenetrable to transcend the limit of that circumstances and education through revolutionary force. The other side also clearly advocates that if revolutionary force is what Lukacs suggests in his History and Class Consciousness, then the subjectivity of social and historical course will become rather unclear.[1] Obviously, the fundamental reason which brings the interpretations of two sides into trouble and back to the antinomy between determinism and rational voluntarism as seriously interrogated by Marx in Theses on Feuerbach is that the two depart away from the logic of Marx's practical philosophy, and go back to the tradi-

---

1 [American] McIntyre: The Theses on Feuerbach: A Road not Taken, Social Sciences Abroad, 1995(6).

tion of theoretical philosophy. The difference is that one goes farther and back to the tradition of ancient substantial philosophy, while the other goes back to the tradition of early-modern subjective philosophy during the struggle of opposing the counterpart's substantial philosophy (of course we may also say "move ahead to" in this sense).

Marx conceives the subject as a "real individual". This certainly provides the most ideal visual angle for the description of the existent state of subject and meanwhile also solves another fundamental problem in theoretical philosophy – the issue of the relation between subjects. This in fact also concerns the issue of the legality of ethical sphere as mentioned above. Although the separation between subject and object has taken place in the structure of theory, subjectivity was not awakened in ancient philosophy, so even if people realized the difference of individuals as the observers and conceived practice as the planning of polis affairs, the issue of the relation between subjects was yet to become an issue, whereas ethics attached more importance to the relation between human and "the good", i.e.: the issue of virtue. Similar circumstances have also appeared in Chinese ancient philosophy. Although Chinese philosophy, particularly Confucianism, sets its foothold in the sphere of social ethics, it pays main attention to the relation between man and moral ontology, for example: the relation between "doctrine" and "virtue". Although the way to heaven is often reduced to human affairs, human affairs do not have the meaning of subjectivity. In early-modern philosophy, subjectivity becomes the "Archimedean point" of theory and is used as the supporting point of theory, but it can only be unitary, so the relation between subjects will become groundless and the existence of other people becomes an issue of theoretical philosophy. Therefore, the ethics of early-modern philosophy is also abstract, and only one subject can exist. This will inevitably lead to solipsism.

Edmund Husserl had apparently realized this issue and put forth the issue of "inter-subjectivity". Putting forth the issue of "inter-subjectivity" firstly does not mean he will demonstrate the identity of objectivity to all subjects but implies the intention that transcendental phenomenology extends itself from "single subject" to "multiple subject", and from "solipsist self-taught" to "inter-subjectivity phenomenology".[1] We should say that the work by Edmund Husserl had created the possibility of surpassing theoretical philosophy, but in the end he fell back to the standpoint of theoretical philosophy, "Otherness" in the end was traced back to transcendental subjectivity, and transcendental solipsism is an Archimedean point Edmund Husserl had set for the analysis of transcendental inter-subjectivity.[2] If subject is understood as "real individuals", this cycle of Edmund Husserl will be solved. Firstly, this finite subject is neither the only supporting point of a theoretical system nor the final basis of world unity, so the existence of "otherness" can be tolerated. Secondly, the "otherness" is not totally isolated substance existing in an atomic state, they share a common living background and certain identity, and among individuals, it is likely to have Rawls' "overlapping consensus" on the issue of ontology. Hence we may describe such subjectivity as a real individual which cannot be fully summed up into otherness. The affirmation on this feature enables the superiority of the relation between a man and others to the relation between a man and other beings as required by Levinas to be satisfied. Consequently, the reduction and disregard of theoretical philosophy to otherness from the vantage of ego can be avoided. In other words, it provides an ontological foundation for the first philosophy of ethics so that it does not have to put ethics and ontology in an antagonistic state. In this way, ethics as a sphere of the relation between subjects gets rid of its awkward position in early-modern philosophy.

---

1 Ni Liangkang: Phenomenology and Its Effect, p.140.
2 The same book as above, p.144~145.

PART II

MATERIALISM AND MODERN MATERIALISM

MATERIALISM AND MODERN MATERIALISM

In the first chapter, we have oriented Marx's philosophy as a modern practical philosophy. Through the debates on the contemporary significance of Marx's philosophy in recent years, this orientation has gradually become a common understanding in the academic community. At present, we may say that the studies on Marx's philosophy has walked out of the subjective paradigm of early-modern theoretical philosophy. However, the understanding on it is still incomplete or unclear. We often underline the rupture of Marx's philosophy from early-modern philosophy as well as its superposition with the schools of modern philosophy and interpret its contemporary significance among them, but another fundamental character of Marx's philosophy – materialism has been neglected all the time. As a result, our understanding on Marx's materialism still has not stepped out of the textbook system. In this case, the incompatibility between the two discourses becomes inevitable: on the one hand, we underline the modernity of Marx's philosophy, while on the other hand we often have to debate on Marx's materialism in an early-modern age approach or even ancient times. Therefore, re-interpreting Marx's materialism has become the most critical and urgent step to comprehensively and concretely understand Marx's philosophy.

CHAPTER ONE

General Connotation and History of Materialism

Although Marx claims his philosophy as materialism, and we are used to mark the whole Marxist philosophy as dialectic materialism and historical materialism, few people have probed into the meaning and history of the concept of "materialism". As a general approach, we have first regarded the issue of the relation between thought and being as a basic issue of philosophy, and then based on different answers to this issue, classified the philosophies in the history into two blocks: materialism and idealism. Thus the entire history of philosophy is written into a history of the struggle between materialism and idealism. Undeniably, although "materialism" is a term appearing only till early modern times (the 18th century), materialism had indeed run through the whole history of philosophy. According to Friederick Albert Lange, materialism has existed since the emergence of philosophy. Materialism is as old as philosophy.[1] But, evaluating the history of philosophy in this way in fact simplifies this issue. In different historical periods, materialism had different connotations due to the difference of philosophical themes.

1 [German] Friederick Albert Lange: A History of Materialism, Vol.1, p.1 & 231, Beijing, Zhonghua Book Company, 1936.

Talking about the understanding on Marx's materialism without knowing the historical evolution of this tradition would be by no means proper.

Misunderstandings on materialism

It seems impossible to give an accurate definition of materialism in the very beginning. It also has no good for our discussion. As this concept has been used arbitrarily for quite some time, particularly even frequently used in a non-philosophical sense, it is necessary for us to distinguish its real meaning from non-philosophical and philosophical misuse of it before we discuss this concept.

Some people conceive materialism as an attitude and mode of life, of course the attitude and mode of life which is opposite to "idealism". In Ludvig Feuerbach and the End of Classical German Philosophy, Engels said: "by the word materialism, the philistine understands gluttony, drunkenness, lust of the eye, lust of the flesh, arrogance, cupidity, avarice, covetousness, profit-hunting, and stock-exchange swindling -in short, all the filthy vices in which he himself indulges in private. By the word idealism he understands the belief in virtue, universal philanthropy, and in a general way a 'better world'".[1] This without doubt was the result of the vulgarization of the concept of materialism.

Besides, some people also link materialism with political stance and think materialism represents a progressive and revolutionary political stance, whereas idealism represents conservation and counter-reaction. We cannot say the antagonism between philosophical schools has nothing to do with politics, but equating philosophical schools with the schools in political struggle not only has no good for philosophical studies but also will create serious results in real life. In fact, above we have mentioned the generation of philosophy and the philosophical activity have a sense of politics. For example, Jean Pierre Vernant had said: "The advent of the polis, the birth of philosophy – the two sequences of phenomena are

---

1 Marx & Engels Selected Works, Edition 2, Vol.4, p.232.

so closely linked that the origin of rational thought must be seen as bound up with the social and mental structures peculiar to the Greek city."[1] Polis had made the political life in an initial sense possible, while philosophy should be a part of such political life from the very beginning. Philosophers' advocacy on a rational and proper life and even their pure research on nature can be deemed as a political event in a sense, for philosophy per se is an attitude towards the mode of polis life and the tradition of this mode. In an even broader sense, a philosophy may try to transcend real life (of course the way of this transcendence is always abstract), but a philosopher is unable to live in a sphere that transcends reality. He certainly lives in the spheres outside philosophy, where other human beings live. Particularly, he is unable to live outside the real political and economic spheres. In this way, philosophy may form various links with real politics through philosophers.

However, saying philosophy and politics are linked does not mean philosophical schools and political schools must be linked together. In fact, this view is a misunderstanding on both philosophy and politics, a simplified misunderstanding at least. In ancient Greek polis, philosophy represented a reflective and rational life in contradistinction to traditional religion and was a kind of activity with "political" nature; while since early modern times, following the infiltration of technical structure to philosophical theory, people gradually considered philosophy a "neutral" thing, and a means to realize goals. Since it is a neutral thing, it may serve different goals and certainly may serve different political schools. Therefore, strict antagonism between materialism and idealism not only is improper to evaluate ancient philosophy but also does not make sense in early-modern philosophy. In view of historical facts, the view that fixes the connection between philosophical stance and political stance is hopelessly flawed. For example, to address people's misbelief that human progress should be attributable to idealism, Engels had said: "it has absolutely nothing to do with the antagonism between materialism and idealism. The French materialists no less than the deists Voltaire and Rousseau had raised this conviction to an almost

---

1 [French] Jean Pierre Vernant: Origins of Greek Thought, p.117, Beijing, Sanlian Bookstore, 1996.

fanatical degree, and often enough made the greatest personal sacrifices for it".[1] Obviously, the political conviction of human progress has no necessary connection with idealism or materialism. Equating materialism and idealism in philosophy with the revolution and counter-reaction in politics has even less support of facts. Without question, many revolutionary movements in history chose a kind of materialism as their theoretical weapon, but there were almost as many reverse examples as them. For example, Engels had ever stated that in the period of British revolution, materialism was reactionary force's "aristocratic, esoteric doctrine", while the religion as theological idealism (Protestantism) became a banner of revolutionary bourgeois in the struggle against Stuart Dynasty.[2] Engels had explained: "materialism is hateful to the middle-class both for its religious heresy and for its anti-bourgeois political connections."[3] The ones who contradicted British aristocrats in the Restoration period were extreme religious fantast; in order to do what is opposite to them – reactionaries, the aristocrats had to choose materialism.[4] Obviously, this relation between philosophical schools and political schools in the period of British revolution best explains the non-inherent inevitability of this connection.

The above two misunderstandings on materialism is due to non-philosophical factor. The more serious understanding on this concept is sheerly a matter of philosophy. We should say the differentiation and antagonism between materialism and idealism was unconscious in ancient philosophy. The materialism we generally call should be a concept of early-modern philosophy. In other words, although materialism existed in ancient times, to study on it as an object is only a matter in modern times. Both idealism-the opposer of materialism and the self-claimed materialists misunderstood the concept of materialism out of consideration of their own theoretical standpoint. When discussing this issue, Horkheimer wrote:

1 Marx & Engels Selected Works, Edition 2, Vol.4, p.232.
2 Marx & Engels Selected Works, Edition 2, Vol.3, p.709~710, Beijing, People's Publishing House, 1995.
3 Marx & Engels Selected Works, Edition 2, Vol.3, p.709.
4 [Russian] Plekhanov: The Development of the Monist View of History, p.165, Beijing, Sanlian Bookstore, 1961.

Materialism is thus reduced to the simple claim that only matter and its movements are real. Whether the attacking philosopher be himself an idealist or a realist, he quickly rejects the materialist thesis. Materialism is understood either as trying to explain everything spiritual, and especially consciousness and reason, as pure illusion (in contradiction to the most instinctive thrust of reason itself) or as trying to derive the spiritual from material process with the aid of artificial hypotheses and questionable appeals to future scientific discovery. Given such an understanding of materialism, it is obviously easy to provide a refutation "to which there is no answer," according to Friedrich Albert Lange, the historian of materialism.[1]

If materialism was understood as such a simple logic, materialism would collapse at the first blow of its component, because if matter was considered the only real thing, the generation of spiritual phenomena which are heterogeneous with it would become an unsolvable problem. The facts tell the same. Since modern times, the popular way idealists treat materialism is to "reduce" it into some simple and ridiculous propositions and then refute them in the same simple way. Therefore, the conclusion is usually the same: the reason why materialism is obviously unacceptable is its superficiality and inadequacy at the level of basic principle.[2] However, if it were the case, the logic of idealism would not be better than that of materialism and materialism might use the same logic to attack idealism: if spirit were considered the only real thing, then how is matter generated and how does this spirit reach the sphere of matter? Kantian thing-in-itself has exposed this logical difficulty of the idealism in early modern times. If Hegel's solution to the issue of thing-in-itself is acceptable, then general materialists' explanation on spirit will become irrefutable for the same reason. Horkheimer thinks the reason why the views on materialism often go astray is that these views put their primary interest in those metaphysical issues and thus regard materialism as a kind of metaphysics; he thinks "contemporary materialism is not principally characterized by the formal traits opposite to idealist metaphysics. It is characterized rather by its content: the economic theory of society.[3]

---

1 [German] Horkheimer: Critical Theory, p.12, Chongqing, Chongqing Publishing House, 1989.
2 [German] Isaac Ehrlich: Self-exhibited Modern German Philosophy, Vol.2, p.20, Leipzig, 1921, Excerpt from [German] Horkheimer: Critical Theory, p.14~15.
3 [German] Horkheimer: Critical Theory, p.43

The "contemporary" materialism stressed by Horkheimer here in fact is Marxist materialism, while he has not made a deep research on the materialism in ancient and early modern times. However, the materialism as a kind of metaphysics did exist in the past. We would rather understand idealist misunderstanding as wrongly regarding a special kind of materialism as all kinds of materialism and considering all kinds of materialism are the same. Therefore, the attack by idealism is inapplicable to Marx's materialism, but we cannot say it is inapplicable to all kinds of materialism. As a matter of fact, many materialists do also possess such an understanding, including many so-called "Marxists".

Due to lack of profound understanding on Marx's modern materialism, our interpretation on Marx's philosophy has often been a kind of metaphysical materialism for a long time. The metaphysical materialism mentioned here is not the mechanical materialism criticized in textbook system and which is opposite to dialectic materialism. Instead, it stresses, same as the idealists, these materialists have a metaphysical attempt: this attempt makes philosophers entangled in the "riddle" of being, in the "totality" of the world, in "life" and in "themselves", or in some describable objects, so it expects a positive conclusion can be deduced for behavior.[1] Metaphysics expects the ultimate interpretation on this world, which may support the past, present and future. In fact, the dialectic materialism advocated by textbooks is exactly an answer to this metaphysical issue.

Materialism as a theoretical visual angle

Accurately speaking, the reason for many misunderstandings on materialism (here referring to philosophical misunderstandings) should be the theoretical framework of early-modern metaphysics, i.e.: the binary opposition between mind and matter or the opposition between man and world, or in other words, limiting problems in the problem domain of early-modern philosophy, regarding the materialism of early-modern

---

1   [German] Horkheimer: Critical Theory, p.22.

philosophy as the essence of all materialism and disregarding the difference in times. We know subjectivity is an essential definition of early-modern philosophy, while in the same time when the subject in the early-modern sense was generated, the object as its object was generated, too. According to Martin Heidegger's research, the word "subject" did not have the implication of man in ancient Greece and was monopolized by "man" only from early-modern philosophy on. Once the concept of subject in the early-modern sense was formed, "object" as its object was generated accordingly to fill the denotation gap of all things outside subject, while the "opposition between subject and object" – this major issue of philosophy thus was formed.[1] Although the opposition between subject and object was generated due to the emergence of the concept of subject and the essence of the whole early-modern philosophy must be defined with subjectivity, it is not necessary for philosophy as a theory to select subject as its ultimate supporting point under such macro framework, because this framework logically allows two possibilities. One is subject and the other is object. Usually, we call the one choosing the former idealism, and that choosing the latter materialism. Due to the particularity of early-modern philosophy, the differentiation and opposition between materialism and idealism were usually manifested in form of epistemology.

We trace the opposition between materialism and idealism in early modern times back to the differentiation and opposition between subject and object, but is this differentiation applicable to ancient philosophy and modern philosophy? We have been accustomed to use the concept of materialism without discrimination. Now it appears not correct indeed, because subjectivity was unconscious in ancient philosophy, whereas for modern philosophy, this opposition needs to be sublated – the sublation here is not thorough elimination, but to avoid accepting it as an ultimate framework. Therefore, we can posit that defining materialism and idealism with mind and matter is only applicable to early-modern philosophy, while materialism has other special meanings in ancient philosophy and modern philosophy.

---

1 Guan Ziyin: Kant and Phenomenological Tradition, Chinese Phenomenology and Philosophic Review, Issue 4, p.152, Shanghai, Shanghai Translation Publishing House, 2001.

Here it must be stressed that we haven't found materialism in the ancient practical philosophy represented by Aristotle, or in other words, ancient practical philosophy does not need to use the differentiation between materialism and idealism as a way to discuss issues. In the first chapter, we have indicated ancient practical philosophy is a spontaneous practical philosophy, and its spontaneity implies the spontaneous overflow of the kinship between man and world. By contrast, modern practical philosophy was evolved from theoretical philosophy after subjectivity was developed in early modern times. The differentiationbetween materialism and idealism have represented different visual angles from the very beginning. Therefore, for the materialism in ancient philosophy, our discussion should be limited to the scope of theoretical philosophy. The facts also indicate ancient materialists are all theoretical philosophers.

The theme of ancient theoretical philosophy is to explore the origin of the world, i.e.: to think over the unified, eternal and invariable being behind phenomena. From today's point of view, this exploration may adopt two angles at least. One is the elements constituting things or the ulee (material) of things. The other is the composition way of these elements, i.e.: the forms of things. Of course, we may say things should be integrated in these two aspects, but if we are only limited to the scope of theory, this statement will become questionable, because exploring the origin of all things is to find the "one" behind complex and numerous phenomena, while paralleling the two will inevitably result in incompleteness of theory. In fact, Aristotelian system faces such a problem. From the etymons of materialism and idealism, we may discover without difficulty the differentiation between materialism and idealism exactly represents the differentiation of these two theoretical visual angles in ancient philosophy. The "matter" in materialism was ulee or matter essentially in ancient Greek people. Since materialism is matter + ism, it should indicate the special status of matter in this doctrine. In Aristotelian philosophy, ulee is the first cause of the "four causes", but this matter is not the "object" opposite to subject. It is the "understratum" and "substrate" constituting things and the undertaker of changes. In the sense of Aristotle, from the earliest philosophers till Leucippus and

Democritus, they all regarded the "material cause" of things as the origin of everything.[1] We usually call these philosophers ancient materialists. Idealism opposite to materialism obviously came from Plato's idea. Idea in the sense of Plato does not have the subjective sense as conceived by ordinary people but lays stress on expressing the form of things. Plato thinks particular things are variable and must experience the process from birth to death, while only their form is not changed and is the undertaker of these changes. Aristotle thinks Plato's idea is a doctrine which regards formal cause as the origin of the world.[2] Pythagoras' "number theory" and Socrates' "definition" are two examples.[3] We usually call this tradition ancient idealism. Here naturally comes a question: does Aristotle belong to idealism or materialism? We used to define Aristotle as a philosopher without a firm stance. Below we will indicate that Aristotle had attempted to integrate these two stances, i.e.: integrate two theoretical angles of view.

Anyway, we find another meaning of materialism from ancient philosophy. This meaning is different from the materialism in early modern times, because the two eras have different philosophical themes. As philosophical theme is different, the selection of different theoretical visual angle will have different implication. Nevertheless, since we call both of them materialism, they must have something common. It is the visual angle of "matter". We may define this visual angle as a method to solve problems from a perceptible and spatial[4] being. This method is the ulee constituting things and particular being in ancient philosophy, and is

---

1 [Ancient Greek] Aristotle: Metaphysics, p.7~12.
2 In Plato' works, idea and eidos are interchangeable and have no marked difference (refer to [Ancient Greek] Aristotle: Metaphysics, p.17; [Ancient Greek] Plato: Parmenides, p.39~41, Beijing, Commercial Press, 1982). Aristotle differentiated them in order to criticize Plato's idealism. In fact, Aristotle's form and ulee can find a pair of corresponding concepts in Plato's philosophy: idea and dektikos, but their relation is changed a lot. Form and dektikos are only a superficial relation, while ulee is the undertaker of things, and becomes a part of ousia after form is accepted. (Chen Kang: About Greek Philosophy, p.421~430, Beijing, Commercial Press, 1987)
3 [Ancient Greek] Aristotle: Metaphysics, p.12~36.
4 Generally speaking, spatiality is the precondition of perceptibility, i.e.: only the things occupying space are perceptible and substantial. Just for this reason, Descartes considers extension as the only attribute of matter.

the perceptible object in early-modern philosophy. Therefore, when ide-alism interrogates materialists with the question of "where does spirit come from", this question refers to early-modern materialism only.

Here naturally comes a question: is this concept of materialism applicable to modern materialism, particularly Marx's materialism. Just like we an-alyze the materialism in ancient and early modern times, firstly we should make clear the theme of modern philosophy. As indicated above, modern philosophy was generated through overcoming early-modern subjectivity philosophy and the framework of subject–object separation. In fact, this framework has been embodied in the essential framework of theory, so this sublation essentially is to sublate the philosophical paradigm which regards theoretical structure as an ultimate structure, i.e.: to sublate the-oretical philosophy. For this reason, we call modern philosophy modern practical philosophy. The difference of modern practical philosophy from ancient practical philosophy is its consciousness. This consciousness de-cides it is different from the spontaneous overflow of the relation between man and life-world like in ancient practical philosophy and must re-enter the life-world with unified subject and object by means of theory. By which way to transcend theory's framework of subject-object separa-tion and enter life-world is exactly the theme of the theoretical activities in modern practical philosophy. We find different schools of modern philosophy chose the "entrance" to life-world from different special an-gles. For example, Martin Heidegger chose the emotional activity of "Da-sein", Habermas and Ludwig Wittgenstein chose communicative activity and everyday linguistic activity. We should say these special activities cannot stand for the whole of life-world, but undoubtedly they assume a priority position in their respective theories, because these are the visual angles they adopt. We can easily find this kind of special visual angle from Marx's theory. It is the material activity of human society, or pro-ductive activity. Comparing with other aspects of life-world, human's productive activity is the real and sensuous aspect of this world. Marx regards this aspect as a channel through which his theory enters life-world. In this sense, we say Marx's philosophy is materialism and modern materialism. It seems that it is also reasonable for Horkheimer to think modern materialism should be a "social and economic theory".

It should be noted that as a visual angle of theory, the meaning of materialism in ancient philosophy and early-modern philosophy is different from that in modern philosophy. We know the materialism in ancient and early modern times is a theoretical philosophy, so "materialism" as a visual angle of theory must be an absolute visual angle; but modern materialism is a practical philosophy, so its visual angle of theory can only be a finite visual angle. The visual angle of theoretical philosophy is a supporting point to constitute and grasp the world, while the visual angle of practical philosophy is a way to enter life-world. The former is conceived as eternal and absolute, while the latter must be transcended and abandoned.

In a general sense, materialism and idealism are different visual angles chosen by philosophical theories. Their meanings vary with the themes of philosophy in different eras. Therefore, when we discuss materialism, we should differentiate their different existing forms. It is not correct to think they are integral. It is also extremely harmful for our discussion on the meaning of modern materialism in current days. In fact, our longstanding misunderstanding on Marx is the result that we study Marx from an angle of early-modern or ancient philosophy and disregard the epoch-making significance of Marx's philosophy. However, here we only obtain the era division of materialism from the perspective of concept. It still has some distance from the real history. In fact, materialism had developed into a tradition long before and has its own logic. Of course, we can reveal this logic only through studying the history of materialism.

Ancient age materialism

Materialism of early natural philosophers

Although materialism represents a theoretical visual angle opposite to idealism, idealism is not the only one opposite to materialism. In fact, the opposite of materialism was mainly religious view of world in the beginning other than idealism in philosophy. At that time, materialism was the representative of philosophical thinking. At the beginning of his History of Materialism, Friedrich Albert Lange wrote:

> Materialism is as old as philosophy, but it is not the oldest. The view of nature of the physics which supported the development of cultural history in the initial period could never get rid of the contradiction of dualism and the illusion of personification. It wanted to avoid such contradiction, interpret the world in a unified way and transcend the common sensory mistakes. The initial attempt imported philosophical sphere. Since the numerous initial attempts, materialism has maintained its position.[1]

This paragraph at least contains the information in the following aspects: materialism and philosophy were generated in the same time; materialism had appeared as a challenger of primitive religious view of world; the primitive religious view of world is not philosophy and is neither materialism nor idealism, for it does not explain the world with a single principle and does not "interpret the world in a unified way". This circumstance is extremely consistent with the history of ancient Greece. Ancient Greek philosophers' attempt of interpreting the world in a unified way is a kind of theoretical activity in essence, and both the result of such activity (a rational view of the world) and the activity per se have imposed threat to the old belief in the polis, so we may say philosophy was generated in the conflict with primitive worship, while what see is ; initially was mainly the conflict between materialism and primitive religion. Therefore, we were used to call all theistic concepts idealism. Apparently, it is not accurate, because if we say a thought is materialism or idealism, first of all it must be a philosophical theory.

The generation of theory symbolizes the awakening of subjectivity in a sense, because as indicated above, the structure of theory has contained the separation between subject and object in a sense. However, regardless ideology or real life, this subjectivity was rather limited in ancient people, and in real life, the range of human's reform of the world was rather narrow and man and the external world (as an abstract entity) were still in a same primitive state, much inferior to the development and conquest of early-modern people over the nature; in terms of concept, ancient

---

1 [German] Friedrich Albert Lange: A History of Materialism, Vol.1, p.1.

people did not have self-consciousness in a strict sense, even discussed the concepts like mind and soul as "things", and were not conscious of the opposition between subject and object. In this state, theory only explored nature -- an entity, and in this theory, nature is equal to the whole of the world.

The exploration on nature logically has two different angles at least. They are the angle of ulee and the angle of form as mentioned above. However, what we see first is the former. That is to say, most of the early Greek philosophers are materialists. Aristotle thinks:

> Of the first philosophers, then, most thought the principles which were of the nature of matter were the only principles of all things. That of which all things that are consist, the first from which they come to be, the last into which they are resolved (the substance remaining, but changing in its modifications), this they say is the element and this the principle of things.[1]

From the perspective of Aristotle's "doctrine of four causes", "taking elements as principle" is to be dedicated to exploring the ulee aspect of nature. In the sense of Friedrich Albert Lange, it is reasonable to explore the nature from the perspective of ulee aspect at first:

> In Greece, people must liberate their line of sight from magical fog, and lead the research on the world to the intelligent and calm theoretical sphere from the dazzling fable world of religious and poetic concepts. However, the success of the first step must have materialism as its medium, because external things are closer to natural consciousness than "ego".[2]

Although Friedrich Albert Lange saw the special position of materialism at the beginning of the generation of philosophy, his understanding here is still problematic. As described above, "ego" as a concept of philosophy was officially generated only by Rene Descartes in early modern times. In ancient philosophy, the one in contradistinction to the "matter" in materialism was not the concept of "ego" but "form". Apparently, Friedrich Albert Lange here also discusses ancient materialism in an early-modern way. We would rather ascribe the reason for the first emergence of materialism to the then development level of human thinking, because

---

1 [Ancient Greek] Aristotle: Metaphysics, p.7.
2 [German] Friedrich Albert Lange: A History of Materialism, Vol.1, p.7.

to think the form of a thing needs higher abstract ability than to think ulee. Of course, it does not mean materialism was the product of low-level human thinking, thus a shallow theory. The abstractness level of Democritus' atomism is enough to explain this issue.

Based on the above understanding on ancient materialism, we may call the universally accepted first philosopher Thales a materialist. His famous saying "water is the origin of all things" is not only a proposition of phi-losophy but also a proposition of philosophical materialism because it is an attempt to make "unified explanation" on the world through a kind of perceptible being. Most of the natural philosophers after him put forth similar propositions. For example: Anaximenes and Diogenes think air is priori to water and is the origin of all matter; Heraclitus thinks it is fire; Empedocles thinks things are composed of four basic elements: earth, air, fire and water.[1] It is worth noting that these natural philoso-phers all used some natural things – the natural things most familiar to people in everyday life to interpret the world; the reason for using them to interpret the world is very intuitive, for example: The reason why Thales thinks water is the origin of all matter is that all seeds grow due to moisture, while water is the source of moisture. In fact, people had checked what "ulee" can explain more natural things.

Although we reduce these thoughts of natural philosophers into the effort to interpret the world from the aspect of ulee, the prime matter here still has certain difference from Aristotle's concept of ulee. On the one hand, it is because of the intuition of basic elements; on the other hand, natural philosophers think prime matter not only explains the constitution of things but also undertakes the function of explaining the movements and changes of things. Originally, the task of natural philosophers is to interpret this multiplicate and ever-changing world, but if the world is finally reduced to a prime matter, the basis for changes of things must be found from such matter. The common approach of natural philoso-phers is to endue vitality to prime matter and think the matter is a living thing and full of vitality, just like a special organism. Therefore, these doctrines were usually called "animatism" later on. We know Aristotle's

---

1 Ancient Greek] Aristotle: Metaphysics, p.8

ulee is an abstract concept and does not possess the function of explaining the changes of movements. These prime matters still have some distance from pure matter or ulee, but in terms of other visual angles of the initial philosophical exploration, this will not prevent us from calling these natural philosophers as materialists.

Mature ancient materialism

As a matter of fact, the most typical materialism after these natural philosophers in ancient Greece is Leucippus and Democritus' atomism. The basic argumentation of atomism is to regard void and the atoms moving in void as real being and the essence of the world. The most distinctive difference of atomism from the thought of previous natural philosophers is that atom is not a natural matter but a product abstracted by philosophers; atoms are separated or combined by pure physical method, thus resulting in the movements and changes of things and they themselves do not possess vitality. On the contrary, things like soul are constituted by thin, scare and tiny (atom of fire for instance). We used to include atomism into materialism because atomism simplifies everything into the quantitative relations among atoms, atomic sequence and atomic motions, while all these are spatial, perceptible and intuitive; moreover, the interpretation of atomism also particularly contains soul and mental activities. When talking of atomism, Windelband said:

> This principle[1] is applied in whole experience based on the strictness of an integral system, so atomism regards spiritual life and all of the elements and values in connection with spiritual life as phenomena, while the truly existing atomic motion and atomic form that constitute such phenomena will certainly be explained with this theory. Therefore, the matter with form and motion is considered the sole real thing and the entire mental life or spiritual life as derivative and superficial reality. Here, Democritus' system first is manifested with a conscious and open materialist character.[2]

---

1 The principle in which the world is interpreted with the quantitative relations between atoms – quoter's note.

2 [German] Windelband: A History of Philosophy, Vol.1, p.154.

Democritus indeed reduces mental activity into the mechanical form of atoms, but here we should never think his materialist characteristic is to reduce spiritual things opposite to matter into atoms. Above we have indicated that it is a typical understanding of early-modern philosophy, and its use is also within early-modern philosophy. It is alleged that Windelband used the standard of early-modern philosophy to evaluate Democritus. However, if we conceive in this way, inevitably we will consider the view that is opposite to this standpoint and interprets the world with mental and spiritual things as idealism, but this has nothing to do with the ancient Greek idealism as we often relate to, particularly the understanding on Plato, the most typical idealist in ancient Greek. In fact, we may also find such a viewpoint from Windelband's works:

> In order to avoid endless misunderstandings, we must make clear that Plato's concept of non-material has no common point with the concept of spirit or soul, whereas the thinking mode of modern people may easily lead to such supposition. ... spirit or soul is integrated with non-material and the world is divided into spirit and matter. All these are non-Platonic. The non-material world indoctrinated by Plato is not a spiritual world yet.[1]

If we define ancient materialism and idealism as the opposition between spirit and matter, obviously we will be unable to explain the relation between Democritus' system and Platonic system, for with such an approach the two seem to have more similarities than differences. Both Democritus' atom and Plato's idea are principles interpreting the world – the entity. The differentiation of the two is only the differentiation between different theoretical visual angles inside substantial philosophy. In essence, the opposition between subject and object, and between matter and spirit belongs to the model of early-modern epistemological philosophy, while the issue of epistemology is only a subordinate part of ancient philosophy and its role was only the reflection of ontology and an opposite which stimulates the development of ontology.

In fact, the opposition between ontology and epistemology has been reflected in the opposition of Democritus and Plato against the sensationalism of sophist school. We say Democritus uses the perceptible and

---

1 [German] Windelband: A History of Philosophy, Vol.1, p.162.

intuitive aspect of things as the principle for interpreting the world, but this absolutely does not mean Democritus' trust in sensation, because this principle is the abstraction of the perceptible aspect of things other than the perceptible natural things. In fact, Democritus and Plato both believe sensation is just a product of natural process, can only be the cognition of a thing and emerges and perishes with this thing, so sensation only generates opinion and can only indicate what a thing is like to an individual and cannot indicate any true or real thing.[1] The opposite of it is sensationalism represented by Protagoras. Protagoras thinks everybody cognizes a thing not according to the original look of the thing but according to the sensation it presents to him, so it is impossible to really know a thing. For this reason, Protagoras said: "man is the measure of all things".[2] In a sense, Democritus' atomism and Plato's theory of idea are in allusion to sensationalism as well as the skepticism resulting from it. The way they solve problems is to only give an appropriate position to sensation and make it relevant with the ever-changing, relative and temporary things and not affect people's deliberation over the invariable and absolutely eternal things. In fact, this approach evades problems, but for substantial philosophy, this evasion seems logical. Here a contradiction of materialism is embodied: since Democritus' materialism observes the world from the perceptible aspect of things, it should logically come to a conclusion of attaching importance to sensory perception and deeming it as the only source of knowledge; on the other hand, sensation is the "content" of knowledge and its role to knowledge is like the role of matter or ulee to external nature. Simply speaking, sensation is the "ulee" of knowledge. If materialism follows through its principle, it should recognize the significance of sense for knowledge. However, the fact is the contrary. This creates the contradiction between the ontology and epistemology in ancient materialism. The root cause of this contradiction lies in substantial philosophy.

As described above, epistemology is only a part of ancient philosophy, so the above contradiction did not become outstanding. Aristotle is the

---

1 [German] Windelband: A History of Philosophy, Vol.1, p.145.
2 Selected Readings of the Original Works of Western Philosophy, Vol.1, p.54, Beijing, Commercial Press, 1983.

culminant figure of ancient Greek philosophy. His system is the most typical ontological system. In the words of Windelband, Aristotle used the concepts of relation and development to further solve the fundamental issues of Greek philosophy – how to think over the issue of unified and eternal being behind the kaleidoscopic phenomena.[1] We still do not have a clear answer to the issue of whether Aristotelian philosophy is materialism or idealism and only say it "sways" between these two standpoints, for Aristotle as the student of Plato had both inherited and criticized the theory of idea. This state of "ambiguous" standpoint essentially is the negation of the previous either/or concept. If we conceive materialism and idealism as theoretical visual angles, this "ambiguity" of standpoint will be understandable, for the attempt from multiple visual angles is always possible. In fact, a culminant figure of the philosophy in an era will always consider different visual angles of his predecessors.[2]

The significance of Aristotelian system to ancient materialism is that it defines materialist visual angle as one of the "four causes" and also as a part of solution to the "fundamental issue" of ancient Greek philosophy. Aristotle reduced previous materialist thought into the exploration to the "ulee (material) cause" of all matter, while "ulee cause" assumes a unique position in the "four causes" and cannot be reduced. In this way, Aristotle gave a corresponding position to ancient materialism. However, we cannot therefore equate the matter in ancient materialism with Aristotle's ulee. For materialists, matter is the unitary visual angle from which everything is interpreted. For Aristotle, any unitary visual angle is limited and must be supplemented by other visual angles. Therefore, Aristotle's "ulee" is the result of the critique and further abstraction of "matter": In the sense of materialists, the form of a thing can be restored to quantitative combination of matter, whereas in the sense of Aristotle, ulee and form are two different causes; matter in ancient materialism is not only the only true being but also the only real being, but Aristotle's ulee is only in a potential state, ulee (or the substrate of ulee) is a possibility, a possibility of becoming a real thing among the completed things by re-

---

1 [German] Windelband: A History of Philosophy, Vol.1, p.189.
2 Below we will indicate this attempt with non-unitary visual angle has essential relation with dialectic

lying on form". In ulee, essence is endowed with possibility only. Ulee exists in reality only with the help of form.[1] Therefore, Aristotle's concept of ulee is the result of abstracted materialist visual angle. On the other hand, Aristotle's inheritance of Platonic theory of idea is very obvious. The opposition between the materialism represented by Democritus and the idealism represented by Plato is manifested as the opposition between ulee and form in Aristotelian metaphysical system, but apparently Aristotle lays particular stress on form, because the other "two causes" are often reduced into form. In addition, ulee essentially is only a part of his conceptual system. Hegel had also praised that Aristotle "comprehends the essence of spirit and nature in particular aspects in a simple way – conceptual form.[2] It seems not groundless that Friedrich Albert Lange has named Aristotle as one of the "reactionaries" of materialism. In fact, the materialism after him (the Stoics and the Epicureans) have all explicitly opposed against Plato and Aristotle, only they completely took the stance of Leucippus and Democritus' atomism and did not go beyond their scope. While in terms of the development course of materialism, it had no much significance.

Materialism in early modern age

Initial form of early-modern age materialism

We know the starting point of early-modern philosophy was a real self-conscious standpoint.[3] It appeared along with people's self-reflection on being, so the principle of early-modern philosophy was not simple thinking but the opposition between thinking and nature.[4] As early-modern philosophy has realized the opposition between self-consciousness and entity, it was impossible for it to directly study the issue of ontology as a dogmatic attitude as before; instead, before it studied the issue of on-

---

1 [German] Windelband: A History of Philosophy, Vol.1, p.190.
2 [German] Hegel: Lectures on the History of Philosophy, Vol.2, p.282, Beijing, Commercial Press, 1960.
3 [German] Hegel: Lectures on the History of Philosophy, Vol.4, p.7.
4 [German] Hegel: Lectures on the History of Philosophy, Vol.4, 7.

tology, it should solve the issue of the opposition between thought and being, and prove the identity between thought and being and prove the objective validity of our knowledge. Therefore, in early-modern philosophy, epistemology had gained an unprecedentedly important position and become the foundation and the focus of whole philosophy, while all other issues must be re-perceived on this basis. We know not only Rene Descartes had proved the existence of "ego" from "cogito" and thus proved the existence of God and the world, and not only Berkeley defined existence with the perceived, but also materialists like Holbach had defined the existence of matter from the relation between our thought and external being. Thus it indicates the conversion of philosophical theme: the "simple thinking" of ancient philosophy corresponds to an ontological philosophy, while the prominence of "the opposition between thinking and nature" will certainly lead to a subjective philosophy or epistemological philosophy; the theme of the former is the exploration on the origin of the world, while the latter had always dedicated for the unification of subject and object.

Therefore, by what way to realize the unification of subject and object becomes an issue of early-modern philosophical theory which it must face at first. Above we have indicated early-modern philosophy may seek the unification between subject and object at least from two angles: subject and object. If the former is chosen as a way to solve problems, there might appear two circumstances. One is "to seek truth from the independence of thinking" as advocated by Hegel;[1] the other is to define being and truth from the perspective of sensation, but assertively refuse the objectivity of the perceived "object". If object is chosen as an angle to solve problems, it means accepting the objectivity of external things as objects as well as their priority to subject, and underlining that sensory experience is the only effective channel to communicate subject and object. Generally, we call the notion of choosing subject as a way to solve problems as idealism, while call the notion of choosing object as a way to solve problems materialism. Apparently, the differentiation here can be reduced to the differentiation between subject and object. We may

---

1 The same book as above, p.8.

also see that early-modern materialism is inevitably a kind of special empiricism, though empiricism is not necessarily materialism.

Same as ancient materialism, early-modern materialism also vehemently criticizes Platonic system and Aristotelian system, but the meaning of their criticism is different. The object criticized by ancient materialism is the ontological visual angle opposite to it, while the criticism of early-modern materialism contains the criticism on ontology. Interestingly, the then spokesman of Plato and Aristotle was Catholic theology, so it seems that early-modern materialism again plays a role similar to ancient materialism, and fights against traditional belief on behalf of scientific spirit. In fact this struggle may be traced back to the argument between nominalism and realism inside scholasticism. According to Hegel's definition, the ones who believe universal is outside thinking subject, is different from particular things and is an existing entity and think only idea is the essence of a thing are called realists, and on the contrary, nominalists and formalists affirm that universal is only the product of the generalization of image and subject as well as mind and soul; when people form concepts, these universals are only names, forms, subjective things constructed by soul and the images created by us – therefore only particular things are concrete.[1] Here a major symbol of particular things is sensory perceptibility, thus the research on concrete things will have only one route – sensory experience. Therefore, generally nominalists are empiricists, too. These empiricists are also the pioneers of early-modern materialism. As most of these nominalists were British, Marx and Engels said, nominalism is one of the main components of British materialist theory, and generally speaking it is the earliest manifestation of materialism;[2] "materialism is the natural-born son of Great Britain".[3] From today's point of view, the major consequences from the argument between nominalism and realism include the generation of empiricism as described above and the changes of universal(s) and general view. The universal(s) in ancient philosophy are substantial, and Plato's idea, Aris-

1 [German] Hegel: Lectures on the History of Philosophy, Vol.3, p.307, Beijing, Commercial Press, 1959.
2 Collected Works of Karl Marx and Frederick Engels, Chinese version 1, Vol.2, p.163, Beijing,
3 Marx & Engels Selected Works, Edition 2, Vol.3, p.698.

totle's categories and even the God in the medieval period are all irrelevant with subject. After the above argument, the definition on universal was changed: universal is oneness, but it is not abstract and is the oneness which is presented and the thought to contain everything.[1] This in fact has contained the basic standpoint of early-modern idealism, so Hegel thinks it is extremely important and significant for early-modern culture. The argument between nominalism and realism has contained many factors of early-modern philosophy. In these potential factors, we even can see the internal differentiation of early-modern philosophy.

Contradictory relation between early-modern materialism and idealism

Nominalists were the pioneers of early-modern materialism. The totality of the particular and concrete things defined by nominalists is the nature in the sense of materialists. The concept of matter in early-modern materialism is closely related to the concept of nature. The concept most frequently studied by materialism in the beginning was not the concept of matter but the concept of nature. It should be stressed that the nature in early modern times is different from the nature seen by ancient philosophers, but it was the nature as the object of subject. Nature is not only the object studied by human but also the object of "practice". These two aspects were unified in the sense of Francis Bacon from the very beginning. Above we have indicated that a logical result of nominalism is empiricism. Francis Bacon had obviously accepted the view of nominalism and created a new empirical method for the research of the nature to supersede the Aristotelian pure theoretical deduction. Francis Bacon thinks although Aristotle does give experience a position, this position is too insignificant to mention; conceptual deduction can only be limited to the range of existent knowledge, while experience is the only source of new knowledge. In addition, ancient philosophers' research on nature is a pure non-utility activity, whereas Francis Bacon thinks the ultimate single mission of all human knowledge is to conquer the world with

---

1 [German] Hegel: Lectures on the History of Philosophy, Vol.3, p.312.

human's cognition on the world; power is knowledge; to conquer the nature, man must obey it (research on nature).[1] Francis Bacon thinks "application" is not only the value manifestation of experience research but also the guarantee for the truth of this research. It is not difficult to understand that experiential knowledge is verifiable and must be verified. In the first chapter, we have stated that Francis Bacon in fact endues the structure of ancient technology to theory. We may say Francis Bacon's this notion has extreme significance to the development of natural science and technology since early modern times. Windelband has ever criticized that Francis Bacon had become the enemy of pure theoretical knowledge and contemplative cognition due to his excessive stress on technology: in the hands of Francis Bacon, philosophy faces such a risk: degraded from the dominance for religious purpose to the dominance for the interest of craftsmanship.[2] In comparison, Windelband rather favors the theoretical way of Galileo and Rene Descartes. But just as indicated by us, these two theoretical ways are nothing but two expressions of the subject-object divided structure of early-modern philosophy. According to Martin Heidegger, the essence of contemporary technology has its root in whole metaphysics. Rene Descartes is the real founder of early-modern metaphysics. His theory contains the structure of technology.

Usually we regard Francis Bacon and Rene Descartes as the founders of early-modern materialism and idealism, respectively, so always stress the opposition between the two. But the fact is that: Rene Descartes was remarkably influenced by Francis Bacon and the influence was positive;[3] while the later materialists' standpoints on nature and matter were also remarkably influenced by Rene Descartes. Without clearing the relation between the two, we will be unable to fully understand the essence of early-modern materialism. The most obvious common point between Francis Bacon and Rene Descartes is the attitude towards ancient philosophy. They had both started their philosophy with the suspicion and

---

1 [British] Francis Bacon: The New Organon, p.102~104.
2 [German] Windelband: A History of Philosophy, Vol.2, p.531, Beijing, Commercial Press, 1993.
3 Ni Liangkang: Self-knowledge and Reflection, p.12.

rebellion against ancient philosophy, Aristotelian philosophy in particular, just like Friedrich Albert Lange said:

> Only in this way, can Francis Bacon get the discovery of truth from external
> experience. Only in this way, can Rene Descartes who suspects everything
> except self-consciousness get the discovery of truth from self-consciousness
> through deductive reasoning.[1]

This indicates that the two both consciously stand on the side of early-
modern philosophy, while their difference is only the approach in their
theories. What corresponds to Francis Bacon's empiricism should be a
mechanical view of nature, but Francis Bacon fiercely criticizes ancient
teleological view of nature and gives little positive statement on it. Interestingly, later materialists' mechanical view of nature mostly came
from Rene Descartes. Though Rene Descartes often uses the concept of
god, the use is often in a strategic sense. In regard to the exploration to
nature, although Rene Descartes regards god as the ultimate end and
cause, beyond this point he thinks natural objects all develop and move
in line with mechanical principle, and one object is the cause of the motion of another object. In this way, the nature becomes an infinite set of
objects and motions, and the "essential" differentiation between form
and ulee and between celestial bodies and earth in ancient philosophy
no longer exists. At this point (the world of matter must follow mechanical law), Rene Descartes is consistent with later materialists, such as: La
Mettire and Holbach. However, nature is only a half of Rene Descartes'
view of world and which is the unimportant half. In the sense of Rene
Descartes, every known thing is either the being of space (extension) or
the being of consciousness (thinking) and without doubt the two are
heterogeneous. We usually consider Rene Descartes a dualist (although
he also arranged the perfect God above the two), but for a theory, no
dualism is possible in the end. In fact, Rene Descartes thinks the certainty
of the being (nature) outside subject is ultimately determined by subject
(thinking). This view is unacceptable for all materialists.

By now, we can easily see both early-modern materialism and idealism
had given mechanical explanation on nature in the beginning. Differ-

---

1 [German] Friedrich Albert Lange: A History of Materialism, Vol.1, p.235.

ently, the former follows this principle throughout the whole world, while the latter aims to leave some space for spirit. The later idealists could not accept Rene Descartes' mechanical view of nature, but we may say they were all successors of his "theory of spirit"; while the most distinctive sign of materialism is to interpret spirit with the rule of nature. Francis Bacon only admits that man possesses "perceptual" soul, and like ancient materialists, he regards this soul as a fine ulee; non-material entity with thinking is unimaginable for him. La Mettire directly claims "man is a machine". Holbach had said that like generating various kinds of entities without feeling and thinking, the nature generates plants, animals and men – these organic entities with sensation and thinking.[1]

When materialists had tried to apply the rule of nature to the world, the use of the concept of matter became conscious and the term as "materialism" was formally generated. Although materialism thinks matter is the component of nature, the concept of matter was generated from the concept of nature, the concept of matter in modern materialism essentially is the generalization and abstraction of the concept of nature. We know the "matter" in ancient materialism is the ulee aspect which constituted entities, early-modern materialists also often use such concepts as ulee and atom, but they are absolutely not identical to the "matter" in early-modern philosophy, because the concept of matter in early-modern philosophy must be in a relation opposite to subjective consciousness, or in other words, --only the one which is defined in this opposite relation,-- can be the concept of matter in early-modern philosophy. Here it seems that materialists have faced a contradiction: on the one hand, matter must be defined in the relation with consciousness. And this relation indicating consciousness, by no means, can be reduced to matter; on the other hand, materialist principle requires spirit must be explained with the principle of matter, otherwise it could only be idealism or dualism. It seems to be a contradiction between materialists and the spirit of the era they live in. Nevertheless, materialists still put forth their own concept of matter and gave the concept of spirit accordingly:

---

1 [French] Holbach: The System of Nature, Vol.2, p.149, Beijing, Commercial Press, 1964.

> Matter is all that affects our senses in any manner whatever; the various prop-
> erties we attribute to matter, by which we discriminate its diversity, are
> founded on the different impressions we receive on the changes they produce
> in us.[1]

> Nature provides all kinds of objects for us; these objects form some relations
> with us and some relations among them are formed, too; the cognition on
> these relations constitutes the so-called spirit.[2]

The way to introduce these concepts is empirical. Matter is all that affects
our senses and spirit is our cognition on these matters. For a materialist,
cognition without experience is unimaginable. Here the ambiguity is
"we". In essence, these concepts do not form any explicit antagonistic
relation between matter and spirit, because spirit is defined by means of
matter; however this concept itself reflects the antagonistic relation between matter and "we", although "we" usually does not form the explored object. With Francis Bacon, the force of "we" had become
extremely powerful and it was even comparable with the spirit in idealism; in addition, most early-modern materialists were natural scientists,
i.e.: the people who actively promoted historical development process
since early modern times. It appears that the spirit of materialism and
the spirit of early-modern philosophy do not conflict with each other in
essence. If we find a contradiction inside materialism, this contradiction
usually has its root in the essence of early-modern philosophy, and idealism has it, too. Here what we want to analyze is how materialism's
"subjective" spirit is presented.

The opposite preset by materialists for the material world is, "we",
whereas the definition on "we" brings the trouble for this theory. In fact,
since Harvey had discovered blood circulation of human body, mechanistic view of nature has contained the mechanical interpretation on
human. However, if "we" as human is completely reduced to matter and
its mechanical motion, the opposition between "we" and nature will no

---

1 Selected Readings of the Original Works of Western Philosophy, Vol.2, p.216, Beijing,
   Commercial Press, 1983.

2 [French] Helvetius: Spirit of Laws, Ge Li: French Philosophy in the 18th Century,
   p.555~556, Beijing, Social Sciences Academic Press, 1991

longer exist. If the impression of objects on us has no difference from the mechanical actions between objects, then how can "our" "obedience" to nature and "commanding" of nature (Francis Bacon) be possible? Obviously, early-modern materialists must preset a being that is different from the essence of nature and matter. However, if in this way, it will become impossible to follow through the principle of materialism. In this sense, early-modern materialism is not a thorough materialism. Then, will Rene Descartes' approach of dividing the world into two kinds of entities solve problems? In fact, as Friedrich Albert Lange put it, the thorough philosophy of Rene Descartes should be idealism. Later on, Kantian thing-in-itself most clearly reveals that idealism faces similar problems. This indicates the contradiction early-modern materialism faces is the inherent contradiction of early-modern philosophy, and to thoroughly sublate this contradiction, the paradigm of early-modern theoretical philosophy needed to be abandoned.

CHAPTER TWO

Practice and Marx's Modern Materialism

The ancient materialism and early-modern materialism as analyzed above both have insurmountable contradictions, because they are both in the domain of theoretical philosophy and thus have the limitations of theoretical philosophy. Consciously or unconsciously, theoretical philosophy sets the world as the observed object according to theoretical structure, while man is the observer. The result is that theorists are often put outside the world. Nevertheless, men by no means can get rid of their life-world. We may say ancient materialism basically did not involve the issue of subject, but once facing the issue of epistemology, which is relevant with it, its inherent contradiction was thoroughly exposed; the early-modern materialism also regards the opposition between subject and object in theoretical structure as its preset premise, so it was unable to explain the existence of spirit, which is certainly heterogeneous with matter. To fundamentally solve these fundamental contradictions, the standpoint of theoretical philosophy needed to be surmounted. That is to take the stance of modern practical philosophy, or move towards modern materialism leaving back the perspective of traditional development. Marx's materialism was exactly a modern materialism.

Marx's practice concept and materialism

Misinterpretation of Marx's materialism as a "theoretical philosophy"

The one relevant together with the above misunderstanding on materialism is our longstanding misunderstanding on Marx's materialism. As "materialism" is a concept emerging till early modern times, people are prone to mistake the materialism in early modern times as the essence of all types of materialism; our interpretation on Marx's materialism used to follow an approach of early-modern philosophy. Consequently, the original meaning of Marx's materialism has been concealed for a long time. Even today, after it has become a common understanding that Marx's philosophy is a practical philosophy, the understanding on Marx's materialism is still not changed accordingly. On the one hand, the discourse of life-world springs up in the research of Marx's philosophy. On the other hand, the understanding of materialism in Soviet textbooks is accepted almost without any amendment. As a result, different discourses run in parallel.

The "materialism" in textbook system was directly from Lenin's dissertations in *Materialism and Empiriocriticism*. In regard to materialism and matter – the basic concept of materialism, Lenin wrote:

> All knowledge comes from experience, from sensation, from perception. That is true. But the question arises, does objective reality "belong to perception," i.e., is it the source of perception? If you answer yes, you are a materialist. If you answer no, you are inconsistent and will inevitably arrive at subjectivism, or agnosticism, irrespective of whether you deny the know-ability of the thing-in-itself, or the objectivity of time, space and causality (with Kant), or whether you do not even permit the thought of a thing-in-itself (with Hume).[1]

> Matter is a philosophical category denoting the objective reality which is given to mall by his sensations, and which is copied, photographed and reflected by our sensations, while existing independently of them.[2]

---

1 Lenin Selected Works, Edition 3, Vol.2, p.87, Beijing, People's Publishing House, 1995.
2 The same book as above, p.89.

Lenin's definition on materialism, in fact the definition on Marxist materialism mainly includes two points: one is to admit the objectivity of matter; the other is to admit knowledge is the reflection of matter, of which the only effective way is sensation. It is almost identical to our above summary on the essence of the materialism in early modern times. Here the definition of matter is same as Holbach's definition of matter. Moreover, during the reasoning, Lenin cited typical early-modern materialists' dissertation other than Marx's, for example: Feuerbach's "my sensation is subjective, but its foundation (or Grund, germ.) is objective", as well as Frank's vocabulary entry in Philosophy Dictionary, "Objective sensationalism is nothing but materialism, for matter or bodies are, in the opinion of the materialists, the only objects that can affect our senses (atteindre nos sens)".[1] Here Lenin is not aware of the significance of Marx's philosophical revolution and does not conceive object as practice. Instead he accepts early-modern philosophy's framework : opposition between subject and object. Karl Korsch thinks Lenin's materialism not only deletes Marx and Engels' materialist reversal to Hegelian dialectic but also drags all arguments between materialism and idealism back to the German idealism spanning from Kant to Hegel. It has exceeded historical stage. In the sense of Karl Korsch, Hegel's conceptual dialectic movement has sublated the opposition between spirit and matter in early-modern philosophy, while it is on this basis that Marx reforms Hegel's conceptual movement with historical and realistic movements, thus generating his materialism. "Lenin went back to the absolute opposition between 'thought' and 'being' and between 'spirit' and 'matter'", thus back to the philosophical level of the seventeenth and eighteenth centuries that had been surpassed by Hegel.[2] Although we do not agree with Karl Korsch's statement that Hegel had sublated early-modern philosophy's framework as opposition between subject and object (in fact, Hegelian philosophy also takes this as its end, and his system is embodies many factors which sublate this framework), we have to say Lenin's criticism at materialism is rather accurate.

---

1 The same book as above, p.90.

2 [German] Karl Korsch: Marxism and Philosophy, p.81~82, Chongqing, Chongqing Publishing House, 1989.

Lenin thinks that apart from the above "philosophical materialism", Marx's philosophy also has another part – a historical materialism or materialist view of history. Historical materialism is the application of philosophical materialism in social sphere. Since the principle of materialism is to interpret spirit with matter, then its application in social sphere will inevitably be to interpret social consciousness with being of social matter. Above we have indicated the finity of materialism as a philosophy, its application is more problematic in social sphere. In fact, it is illegal to differentiate Marx's philosophy in this way. We know that in terms of the foothold of Marx's philosophy, human's social activity is unified with nature, so historical materialism is Marx's philosophy, and the relation between universal principle and special application does not exist. Below we will indicate Marx's materialism is historical materialism.

Lenin's misunderstanding on Marx's materialism is to understand Marx from an approach of early-modern philosophy in fact, thus interpreting Marx's philosophy into a system of theoretical philosophy. Therefore, in order to dispel this misunderstanding, we must articulate the significance of Marx's surpassing and overcoming early-modern theoretical philosophy as well as the meaning of materialism on this basis, at first. Here we will continue to proceed from practice – the basic and core concept of Marx's philosophy.

Practice as the background of all theories

Marx's materialism is a practical philosophy, while practice as its core and basic concept undoubtedly can reflect the basic particularity of this philosophy. British scholar Jorge Larrain also believes the concept of practice is the central category of historical materialism; it constitutes the incorporation and unification between human and nature, society and matter, subject and structure, and consciousness and reality,[1] and also thinks Marx had not realized the essence of his own theory, so it is

---

1 [British] Jorge Larrain: A Reconstruction of Historical Materialism, p.111, Beijing, China Social Sciences Press, 1991.

necessary to reconstruct historical materialism with the concept of practice. Jorge Larrain indeed saw the drawbacks of the previously popular interpretation on Marx's philosophy as a theoretical philosophy, but he did not realize Marx's philosophy was a practical philosophy, so what we need to do is not to "reconstruct" Marx's materialism but restore its original meaning as practical philosophy.

Above we have mentioned materialism, this tradition, has its development clue. Marx had given in-depth studies and criticism of the materialism from ancient atomism to Feuerbach. He also claimed himself a materialist. It goes without saying, Marx belongs to this tradition. Ancient materialism and early-modern materialism had both met with insurmountable difficulties. These difficulties can be traced back to the theoretical philosophy they belong to. Apparently, Marx's materialism as a practical philosophy also has transcended this tradition. So, if we do not want to misunderstand Marx's philosophy in a way mentioned above, first of all we should distinguish Marx's materialism from all kinds of previous theoretical philosophy.

Under the framework of theoretical philosophy, theoretical activity must have an abstract foothold. Ancient materialists chose the ulee aspect of entity, while early-modern materialists chose the abstract object which is opposite to subject. Marx's philosophy is a practical philosophy. The foothold of its theoretical activity must be human's life practice. While, how to understand this foothold? For a time, we have conceived practice as the highest category and "Archimedean point" of the theoretical system of Marx's philosophy and seemingly all dissertations of Marx's philosophy was deduced from it. In this case, in essence, practice is conceived as an abstract concept of theoretical philosophy and as an initial link of theoretical system. If so, it will be difficult to understand Marx's opposition to the abstract concepts of old philosophy. Marx said: "Since the real existence of man and nature has become evident in practice, through sense experience, because man has thus become evident for man as the being of nature, and nature for man as the being of man, the question about an alien being, about a being above nature and man – a question which implies the admission of the unreality of nature and of man – has become impossible in practice."[1] The "being above nature and man" essentially is the conceptual thing constructed by theoretical philosophy, while theoretical philosophy regards it as a foothold and starting point. "Matter" in ancient materialism and early-modern materialism is also such abstract concept. For ancient materialists, "matter" no doubt is alien and even does not have the process of human life; although early-modern materialists regarded "matter" world as the object of recognition and development, but they had still considered this objective relationship a premise, thus the mutual definition of matter and consciousness takes their mutual alienation as a premise. Therefore, this matter after all is not controlled by human and is abstract. Marx's concept of practice firstly means the negation and transcendence of these abstract concepts. Consequently, it is not like old materialism, which conceives object, reality and perception only in an objective or intuitive form, but conceives them as sensuous human activity and practice. For subject, object, spirit and matter, these abstract concepts, their abstractness can be dissolved and they can be concretely conceived only in human's life practice process.

Therefore, regarding actual life practice as the foothold of Marx's philosophy is not regarding practice as a concept of the starting point for the construction of a theory. On the contrary, it means the abstract concepts necessary for previous theories are intactly unified into practice, thus theoretical activity also becomes a kind of practical activity. On this basis, the immanent contradictions of ancient materialism and early-modern materialism (the contradictions rooted in the theoretical philosophy they belong to) can be fundamentally solved. In the process of life practice, human and world, spirit and matter, and subject and object are unified, hence the ultimate structure of theoretical philosophy is sublated. Of course, this sublation is not to completely eliminate all oppositions of these aspects – in fact it is also impossible – but to indicate these oppositions are not ultimate and insurmountable; these oppositions are exactly the basis for the establishment of unification. The visual angle

---

1 Collected Works of Karl Marx and Frederick Engels, Chinese version 1, Vol.42, p.131.

a theory chooses on this basis is impossibly an "Archimedean point", but is a relative "view point" through which we "see" the world. The existence of this "view point" does not repulse the legal existence of other "view points". On the contrary, only when other "view points" exist, may the dialogue and mutual supplement of the "view points" become possible, thus obtaining the concrete understanding on life practice.[1] In this way, the contradiction between practice and theory in the theoretical philosophy is fundamentally solved. In fact, except Marx's concept of practice, modern philosophers have raised similar concepts, for example: Martin Heidegger's "being-in-the-world", Ludwig Wittgenstein's "form of life" as well as the re-interpretation of Habermas on Edmund Husserl's "life-world" all can be deemed as transcendence of the basic structure of early-modern theoretical philosophy.

The contradiction of previous materialism and even all theoretical philosophies is, in the final analysis, abstract concepts concealing the real state of human life, while the introduction of Marx's concept of practice firstly means "unconcealment" and description on the real state of human life. This is the first meaning or primary meaning of Marx's concept of practice. In fact, the discovery of this "truth" of human life is the basic precondition for the generation of modern practical philosophy and reflects the common vision of all modern philosophers.

If we say ancient practical philosophy is the natural disclosure of the unified state between man and world, then modern practical philosophy is to consciously sublate early-modern philosophy's world pattern of subject – object separation, and re-discover this unified state. In ancient Greece, polis is the totality of a unified life-world, and the people who lived in polis seemingly were accepted in apriori. In the concept of ancient Chinese, the exploration to the abstract things that transcend life-world was often naturally believed to be an "illusioned" conduct. At present, after early-modern theoretical philosophy, people need to re-open the vision of man-world unification with the help of a method. No doubt, this method firstly is the method of "smashing" the old theoretical philosophy. In the third thesis of Theses on Feuerbach, Marx wrote:

---

1   Below we will indicate this is the most fundamental meaning of dialectic.

The materialist doctrine concerning the changing of circumstances and up-bringing forgets that circumstances are changed by men and that it is essential to educate the educator himself. This doctrine must, therefore, divide society into two parts, one of which is superior to society.

The coincidence of the changing of circumstances and of human activity or self-changing can be conceived and rationally understood only as revolutionary practice.[1]

For the issue of the relation between man and circumstances, old materialists think man is the product of circumstances and upbringing, while idealists adopt an opposite view and think circumstances are ultimately created and changed by men. Here, the opposition between the two visual angles of theoretical philosophy is typically manifested. Marx as a materialist did not simply accept the past materialist views. He has criticized the common foundation of old materialism and idealism. He has unified the two parts separated by theoretical philosophy into the "revolutionary practice", and therefore we may say all social life is practical in essence. In The German Ideology, this thought is expressed as "circumstances make men just as much as men make circumstances".[2] In this way, we may conceive the state of human life disclosed by Marx's concept of practice at least from two aspects. In one aspect, practice is a kind of activity, accurately speaking, it is the totality of all human activities. Marx has stressed repeatedly the starting point of his theory is "the men engaging in real activities". The men in the activities no doubt have initiative and create the world in their activities. Here Marx obviously absorbs the "active" aspect "abstractly" developed by old idealism. Marx also has stressed that the men as the starting point and premise of his theory are not in any fantastic isolation and rigidity, but in their actual, empirically perceptible process of development under definite given conditions. Hence, Marx drew a demarcation line with the abstract spirit of old idealism. In the other aspect, we should also conceive practice as the whole human life-world constituted by these activities. Human activities are always the activities under certain social conditions and historical situations. Although we say this world is a world formed by men and belong to men, for concrete individual, this world is an apriopri premise

---

1 Marx & Engels Selected Works, Edition 2, Vol.1, p.55.
2 Marx & Engels Selected Works, Edition 2, Vol.1, p.92

which must be accepted at first. Marx said: "This sum of productive forces, capital funds and social forms of intercourse, which every individual and generation finds in existence as something given, is the real basis of what the philosophers have conceived as 'substance' and 'essence of man', and what they have deified and attacked; a real basis which is not in the least disturbed, in its effect and influence on the development of men, by the fact that these philosophers revolt against it as 'self-consciousness' and the 'Unique.'"[1]   Here, it seems that Marx again stands on the side of old materialism, but in fact, no previous materialist would admit men change the world. In this way, Marx dialectically depicts the true relationship between the concrete subject and the world.

Martin Heidegger's analysis on "being-in-the-world" and Habermas' explanation on "life-world" are similar to Marx's concept of practice. Although we cannot ascertain whether Martin Heidegger and Marx have any ideological inheritance relationship,[2] what we may ascertain is that Martin Heidegger deeply has deliberated Marx's philosophy, and in his Letter on Humanism, he gives a high comment on Marx's "alienation" thought. In fact, as they are "cotemporaneous" thinkers, we do not have to prove the similarity of their thoughts through their "direct relationship". What we want to indicate is that Martin Heidegger's analysis of "being-in-the-world" and Marx's theory of practice share common vision. Same as Marx, Martin Heidegger discusses the world in a way different from Rene Descartes' approach which firstly defines spirit and nature (matter) as two heterogeneous things. Heidegger proceeds from the inseparable relation between man and world in activities (labouring), or from the world closest to Dasein, i.e.: "seeks the world-hood of the environment (environmentality) by going through an ontological interpretation of those entities within-the-environment which we encounter as closest to us.[3] Not like the definition given by Rene Descartes, the environmentality is an entity of spatiality. In the sense of Rene Descartes,

---

1 The same book as above, p.92~93.

2 In fact, some critics comment as : Lukacs tend to recognize this relationship and think Martin Heidegger's analysis on "being-in-the-world" and "verfallen" state has a direction relation with Marx. [Refer to The Concept of Alienation in the Works of Martin Heidegger and Georg Lukacs, published in Philosophical Translations Journal, 1994(3)]

3 [German] Martin Heidegger: Being and Time, p.78.

"substance as such – that is to say, its substantiality – is in and for itself inaccessible from the outset. 'Being' itself does not 'affect' us, and therefore cannot be perceived".[1] This essentially is equal to announcing the result of not solving the issue of the unity between man and world (nature) and giving up the exploration to the substantiality of substance. Its result is the incommunicability between Kantian subject and thing-in-itself. Martin Heidegger thinks: "We must show how the aroundness of the environment, the specific spatiality of entities encountered in the environment, is founded upon the worldhood of the world, while contrawise the world on its part, is not present-at-hand in space."[2]

Analyzing spatiality and the world-hood of the world from the things present-at-hand in space is not only a revolution transcending Rene Descartes and Kant's philosophy and also a thorough criticism of the old materialism. Above we have discussed early-modern materialist view of nature and concept of matter. We know the "matter" in early-modern materialism essentially is also an abstract spatial being and an "alien" of spirit. For modern philosophy, the only method to eliminate the gulf between matter and spirit is to find the deeper foundation of this gulf. Marx's approach is to conceive things, reality and perception as human's sensuous activities and as practice, while Martin Heidegger traces these oppositions back to human's most primitive activities, i.e.: Readiness-to-hand of being. In the sense of Martin Heidegger, "zuhandenes"(present-at-hand) has a familiar and unnoticed nature. People will check things only they become "not present-at-hand" from readiness-to-hand, and "only on the occasion of trying to disclose zuhandens, location per se will come to our eyes in a noticeable way and in an incomplete way of labouring activity.[3] The activity of "seeing" essentially is a theoretical activity. If this activity and its structure are regarded as premises of ultimacy, the result will absolutely be theoretical philosophy. Therefore, Martin Heidegger here presents the practical essence of theory in another way, thus opening the vision of practical philosophy.

---

1 French] Rene Descartes: Principles of Philosophy, Chapter 1, excerpt from [German] Martin Heidegger: Being and Time, p.110.
2 [German] Martin Heidegger: Being and Time, p.118~119.
3 German] Martin Heidegger: Being and Time, p.121.

If we say the common ontological vision between Martin Heidegger and Marx is because of their "cotemporaneous" relationship, then Habermas' analysis on life-world consciously inherits the tradition of Marxism and phenomenology. "Life-world" is a concept first used by Edmund Husserl, but in Edmund Husserl's theoretical philosophical system, it is only a channel to transcendental phenomenology and in the end is only a link for the construction of theory. Martin Heidegger's Being and Time obviously is the exploration to "life-world", but Habermas thinks Martin Heidegger's exploration is invalid, because Heidegger's Dasein alone cannot solve the issue of the interrelation in social life. Habermas believes the concept of "life-world" should be introduced as a complementary concept of communicative acts.[1] Habermas thinks the background of life-world should have the following characteristics: the first characteristic is absolute specificity. It endows the knowledge our common life, common experience, common language and common action rely on with a paradoxical characteristic; the second characteristic is its generalized power. Life-world is a kind of totality and has a center and many uncertain limits. These limits are penetrable but insurmountable, because they are shrinkable; the third characteristic is the holism of background knowledge and links with absoluteness and generalization.[2] The most outstanding characteristic of Habermas' life-world is its background. This background is composed of communicative activities. Here we can easily find a dialectic structure extremely similar to Marx's theory of practice. Marx's concept of practice may also refer to some concrete activities, and the totality of these activities constitutes the background of life. In fact, Habermas' stress on communicative and interactive conducts is largely attributable to Marx, not only because Marx has used concepts of "communicative activity" and "communicative way" in The German Ideology, but also because the stress on human's sociality has always been the uniqueness of Marx's philosophy compared with other modern philosophies. Therefore, Habermas has some misunderstanding on Marx's concept of practice. As we have indicated above, the vision opened by his communicative theory is connected to Marx's theory of practice.[3]

---

1 [German] Habermas: Post-Metaphysical Thinking, p.75.
2 [German] Habermas: Post-Metaphysical Thinking, p.75.
3 Below we will indicate the difference between them. It will involve the nature of "matter" in Marxist materialism.

The introduction of Marx's theory of practice firstly implies the sublation and transcendence to the structure of subject-object opposition in theoretical philosophy. This sublation and transcendence are realized through discovering the true state of human life, i.e.: the state of non-separation between subject and object. Reviewing our study on the concept of practice in Introduction, we may easily find that only the practice of the Greek state as totality in Aristotelian philosophy has similar meaning. Alasdair Mac Intyre thinks if we unfold the ideas in Theses on Feuerbach, it will be inevitable to adopt Aristotle's way of expression for articulation.[1] It is also reasonable.

However, we should not believe this is the only content of Marx's concept of practice. In fact, on most occasions, Marx and Engels did not use the concept of practice in this sense. Nevertheless, this can be regarded as the basic and principal meaning of the concept of practice, and many misunderstandings on Marx have resulted from the negligence of this point.

Practice as production - art, and materialism

The first meaning of Marx's concept of practice – the analysis of practice in a broad sense does not involve the materialist nature of Marx's philosophy or does not indicate what "matter" means in Marx's philosophy, but without doubt this analysis is necessary and even is the premise for correct understanding on Marx's materialism.

If we say the practice in a broad sense is the life-world without separation of subject and object as well as the totality of all kinds of human activities, then what must be handled immediately will be the relation of all kinds of human activities. This involves the actual meaning of the "matter" in Marx's materialism. We have mentioned above that the "matter" in Marx's materialism refers to the material activities of human or the material aspect of social life. This kind of activities assumes a priority po-

---

1 [American] McIntyre: The Theses on Feuerbach: A Road. not Taken, Social Sciences Abroad, 1995(6

sition in the vision of Marx's philosophy. However it is extremely diffi-cult to articulate the concrete meaning of this kind of activities and the historical origin of their generation, the relation of human activities has been a complicated issue since ancient Greece. We have to go back to Aristotle. He is the first person who had consciously and systematically studied this issue.

Jorge Larrain said that Marx had mixed Praxis and Poiesis – two activity forms which were differentiated as early as in ancient Greece. Larrain also thinks Marx's practice is not only Poiesis (making or production) but also contains a kind of emancipative practice.[1] No doubt, Jorge Lar-rain has seen the conceptual difference between Marx and ancient Greek, particularly Aristotle's practical philosophy. His stress on the "emanci-pative" significance of Marx's practice also effectively responds to Haber-mas and other people's technology-utility understanding on Marx's concept of practice, but if we stop at this point, it seems only to carve these two meanings and not to obtain a real understanding on human activity - "matter". In fact, without holistic study of theory, practice, production, art and other activity types, it will be impossible to realize this real understanding.

We know that in Aristotelian philosophy, human activities are classified into theory (Theoria), practice (Praxis) and making (Poiesis). The objects of theory are things that are of necessity in the unqualified sense, i.e.: are eternal; while making and practice both take variable things as objects.[2] In terms of the nature of activity, theory and practice are both activities with their own as ends, while making has an end outside activity. In this sense, theory and practice are one type of activity, while making is an-other. The activities including theory have an inner end, so they are free activities, while making has an end outside activity, so it is not a free ac-tivity. Here whether end is inherent – whether it is a free activity is the fundamental standard for the differentiation between making and prac-tice or theory on the other hand.

---

1 [British] Jorge Larrain: A Reconstruction of Historical Materialism, p.112~114.
2 [Ancient Greek] Aristotle: Nicomachean Ethics, p.117~118.

It is noteworthy that the artistic activity we talk of today is not an independent activity in the sense of Aristotle, and belongs to making. Making includes both the productive or technical activity we refer today and the artistic activity in some subjects. Here another key concept must be involved. It is skill or technology (Tekhnee). Ancient Greek had differentiated natural (phusis) growth (genesis) and the generation of the created things, i.e.: making. Natural things grow and emerge naturally, while artificial products need a "power" of creation – the Tekhnee. Therefore, Martin Heidegger said the motive (arkhee) is Tekhnee. Martin Heidegger thinks Tekhnee is neither technology in manufacturing sense nor art, but a cognitive concept, indicating the proficiency at the foundation of any making and manufacturing; a proficiency at where a kind of manufacture (such as: the manufacture of beds) must come, end and complete.[1] Martin Heidegger conceives Tekhnee as a way to know. This approach is not groundless. In the sense of Plato, Tekhnee and episteemee (science) are both the "knowing" opposite to experience; in Aristotle's Metaphysics, technology is oriented as the knowledge and wisdom lower than philosophy and higher than experience,[2] and in Nicomachean Ethics, it is called a quality made for real reason.[3] No doubt, Martin Heidegger has revealed the deeper essence of Tekhnee, but just on the basis of this essence, Tekhnee has the "content" of some concrete activities. By the meaning of Tekhnee, making activities are classified into different "sub-types", for example: in Metaphysics, Aristotle defines two types of "technical inventions": one enriches living necessity and the other increases human entertainment.[4] Of course, these two types of making activities do not stand out independently in Aristotelian philosophy, but this differentiation has played a very important role in the later philosophy. The polysemia of Tekhnee decides the complexity of the concept of making. This complexity provides space for later philosophers' articulation on the issue of practice. Therefore, although the concept of making does not have a very high position in Aristotelian practical

---

1 German] Martin Heidegger: Wegmarken, p.290, Beijing, Commercial Press, 2000.
2 [Ancient Greek] Aristotle: Metaphysics, p.2~3.
3 [Ancient Greek] Aristotle: Nicomachean Ethics, p.126.
4 [Ancient Greek] Aristotle: Metaphysics, p.3.

philosophy, it has generated great influence on the generation of future philosophy. In fact, to analyze Marx's concept of practice (of course, here we refer to the concept of practice in a narrow sense), we must proceed from this concept, because the production repulsed by Aristotle constitutes the basic content of practice in Marx's philosophy, while interpersonal behavior or moral and ethical behavior only a subordinate; theoretical activity loses the sacred position endowed by Aristotle and is based on practice and even can be considered as a special form of practice; the position of Aristotle's practice (Praxis) is substituted by artistic activity standing out from making activity. Marx always regards art as a paradigm of free activity. While, how is the change from Aristotle to Marx was realized? Does this change mean that Marx's concept of practice should be given a technology – utility understanding?

When Aristotle differentiates practice from theory and production, the practice in his sense is interpersonal behavior in fact, while interpersonal behavior or moral and ethical behavior is exactly the theme of ethics and politics.[1] Aristotle excludes productive activity from practice. The theoretical reason is that the end of production is outside itself. As pointed out by many critics, this has a close relation with the fact that the productive activities in Greek society were mostly undertaken by slaves. Just because of this reason, Aristotle's concept of making includes the artistic activities in some categories. In the eyes of Greek, sculptors have no difference from carpenters, for these two kinds of production both need physical labour, which was always looked down upon by Greek.[2] Besides, the mimesis view of art which was dominated among Greek had also contributed to the depreciation of art. Since art is only the imitation of the prototype, and even was thought as imitation of imitation by Plato, thus being a thing far from truth, then artistic activity should be a lower activity. We know under the then social and cultural background, Aristotle's exclusion of making --including production and art-- from free activities was very reasonable. Is Aristotle's differentiation a thorough

---

1 Zhang Rulun: History and Practice, p.102, Shanghai, Shanghai People's Publishing House, 1995.

2 [Polish] Tatarkiewicz: History of Concepts of Western Aesthetics, p.111, Beijing, Academy Press, 1990.

differentiation which implies there is an impassable demarcation line between different types of activities, particularly between free activity and unfree activity? The fact is not so. As indicated above, all activities are embodied with "wisdom" and "knowledge" in a sense. It should also be stressed that Aristotle made this differentiation under a great premise which is the state as totality can be apprehended only when it is a concrete type of state "practice". Since they are in the same indiscerptible integral body, they must have some inherent links. Though Greek were unconscious of such links, we think that without the premise of survival provided by making – non-free activity, theory and practice – free activity would be unimaginable. In fact, Aristotle had realized the necessity of slave labour for the existence of state.

The trichotomous paradigm of Aristotelian practical philosophy has become the basic framework and reference structure for the exploration to this issue, but following the development of history, complicated changes have taken place for raising its significance.[1] Here we center on the concept of practice and try to grasp the "traces" of these changes to fully understand Marx's concept of practice. It is commonly believed that after Aristotle, there are largely two paradigms of understanding on practice. One is ethic – conduct paradigm and the other is technology – utility paradigm. The former is the inheritance from Aristotle, i.e.: conceiving practice as an ethical and political sphere. Although the definition on the concrete content of practice and its relations with other activities differ among people, this understanding maintains consistence with Aristotle at least in form. In fact, most philosophers in the history of Western philosophy did not deny moral and politics as a practical sphere. Although medieval Christian thinkers had changed their attitude towards productive labour and the phenomenon of including labour into practice appeared (Saint Thomas Aquinas for example), ethical and political life as practice is unimpeachable. Such understanding is also applicable in Rene Descartes, but due to his background of theoretical philosophy, the significance of Rene Descartes' practical sphere has changed remark-

---

1   Readers may refer to the studies on the historical evolution of the concepts of theory and practice described in "Chapter 1" of this book.

ably comparing with Aristotle's. Aristotle thinks theory and practice are two types of activities, while Rene Descartes' moral practice must accept the inspection and reconstruction of scientific theory. Rene Descartes thinks ethics is the last wisdom and inaccessible to individual moral behaviors, so there must be a "temporary moral" which supports this behavior and needs to be proved scientifically. We may say this thought of Rene Descartes has directly influenced the "geometric ethics" of Spinoza and et al and indirectly influenced Kant's "critique of practical reason". Although Kant had differentiated between "technical practice" and "moral practice", the former follows the principle of nature, so it is only "the extension of theoretical philosophy" and obviously is not the object of practical philosophy, while the study object of his practical philosophy is the "moral practice" which follows the principle of freedom.[1] However, same as Rene Descartes, Kant's practical sphere is also constructed in a "theoretical" way. Like Kant, the classical philosophers after Kant, such as: Johann Fichte and Hegel, all gave prominence to the position of practical reason as a moral principle in the theory-practice issue. "The differentiation between theoretical reason and practical reason in use, i.e.: the differentiation between cognition and moral was developed by Hegel into a major form of spiritual dialectic."[2] Not only early-modern philosophers have conceived practice in a paradigm of ethical conduct. In fact, the "practical" philosophy advocated by some modern philosophers, such as: Gadamer, Hannah Arendt and Habermas all can be reduced to this paradigm. Gadamer and Hannah Arendt both have tried to revive Aristotle's tradition of practical philosophy. The key is to underline the differentiation between practice and making which had been explicitly stated by Aristotle as well as the fundamental significance of interpersonal behavior sphere on this basis. Hannah Arendt classifies human activities into three basic types: labour, work and action. Labour involves the relation between man and nature. Work involves the relation between man and artificial world. Action involves the relation between man and man, i.e.: political activity. Both labour and work are restricted, while action

---

1 [German] Kant: Critique of Judgment, Vol.1, p.9, Beijing, Commercial Press, 1964.
2 Zhang Rulun: History and Practice, p.258.

is the only activity which does not need any medium and refers to the condition of people other than the group formed by men in the world. All human conditions are related to politics, while group is an important condition for all political life and is not only a sufficient condition but also a necessary condition.[1] The action here is the practice in the sense of Aristotle. Habermas has also claimed his starting point as the fundamental difference between labour and interaction,[2] while interactive activity is interpersonal activity, and it was obviously influenced by Aristotle's concept of practice.

The reason why Aristotelian practice was given so much stress and realized revival unquestionably has to do with instrumental activity's infiltration and invasion to other activity spheres. After Weber, most modern philosophers have realized that many crises in current society stems from technocracy, while the instrumental activity producing this technocracy usually is identical to Aristotelian making activity. In this way, it is not difficult to understand why the differentiation between the two types of activities defined by Aristotle (free and unfree) was stressed and on the stage again – the purpose is to resume the priority of practice to instrumental activity. But here Aristotelian concept of making is quite simplified, but for people like Hannah Arendt, it seems not so important, because the direct motive of this new revival is the domination of the technology-utility understanding on practice since early modern times.

Technology – utility paradigm was founded by Francis Bacon. As mentioned above, medieval Christian ideology changed Europeans' attitude towards labour (a kind of making activity) to some extent. In addition, the significance of technical activity in human life was increasing, and the technical activity thoroughly separated from practical activity in the theory of Aristotle gradually became an element of the concept of practice. Francis Bacon defined "application" as an indispensable element of theory. This not only led to a major change of theory but also formed another way to understand practical activity: "practice" is the conquest

---

1 [American] Hannah Arendt: The Human Condition, p.1, Shanghai, Shanghai People's Publishing House, 1999.
2 [German] Habermas: Technology and Science as "Ideology", p.48~49.

of nature, and the means of the conquest is technology for scientific application. No doubt, Francis Bacon's this thought excludes Aristotle's "depreciation" on technology to some extent and recognizes its important position in human life. In fact, even in ethics – conduct paradigm, this activity also has its position. For example, Kant gave example for a type of "technical" practice. Differently, in the ethics – conduct paradigm, technology is only the extension of theory and is excluded from practice. In comparison, in technology – utility paradigm, technical activity is practice. Apparently, this practice is "labour" as classified by Hannah Arendt – the activity of handling the relation between man and nature. Habermas' instrumental activity is also carries this sense. In fact, the technology – utility paradigm conceives the concepts like theory, practice and technology in a rather simple way, but it is therefore more acceptable to people, particularly to natural scientists. The later positivist concept of "practice" obviously also belongs to this paradigm, for positivism only cares for man's "technically practical" activity and does not care for "morally practical" activity. Although they also talk on the issue of moral behavior, they think all human activities are defined in a "technically practical" way guided by natural sciences.[1]

The current question is: what understanding paradigm does Marx's practice belong to? As Marx recognizes the priority of productive labour and economic activity among many types of human activities, both Marx's opponents and also some "Marxists" usually include it into technology – utility paradigm. The philosophers with ethics–conduct interpretation refute "making", so their misunderstanding and critic on Marx is understandable. Hannah Arendt calls Marx's philosophy "labour philosophy". The labour here refers to the labour which only involves the relation between man and nature and is restricted, thus cannot constitute human "condition". Habermas also believes Marx does not give real explanation on the link between interaction and labour, and only includes interaction into labour under the general title of social practice, i.e.: and thus includes communicative activity into instrumental activity.[2] Instru-

---

1   Yu Wujin: A Concealed "Kantian Issue", Journal of Fudan University (Social Sciences), 2003(1).
2   [German] Habermas: Technology and Science as "Ideology", p.33.

mental activity is the activity done as per technical rules. Such understanding on Marx's concept of practice given by Hannah Arendt, Habermas and so on is out of the criticism on Marx, while the interpretative
system for Marx's philosophy represented by Soviet textbooks "consciously" had also adopted the technology – instrument understanding.
This understanding roughly includes two aspects. One is the practice in
the sense of epistemology, i.e.: the verification link for correct recognition; the other is the practice in the sense of instrument, i.e.: regarding
practice as a means to conquest and rule the world. In fact, the latter was
formed by Francis Bacon. Francis Bacon was also a "materialist", so this
acceptance is generally considered reasonable. However, just as we have
indicated above, both ethics – conduct paradigm and technology – utility
paradigm have indeed simplified Aristotelian making activity and Marx's
concept of practice. Aristotelian making activity is not equal to instrumental activity, and even the technology it contains cannot be understood as the instrumental activity in a modern sense. In fact, instrumental
activity as an affiliate link of theory is a special product of early-modern
theoretical philosophy, because only when this activity possesses a nature
of value "neutrality" like science, it can obtain the all-pervasive penetra-
bility, i.e.: the "perspective" of theory is realized in action. No doubt,
this is the profound cause for technocracy in current times, and also the
object criticized by the people including Hannah Arendt. The understanding on Marx's concept of practice as instrumental activity is same
as employing the thinking mode of early-modern theoretical philosophy
on Marx.

No doubt, Marx's concept of practice (even the concept of the practice
in a narrow sense) has a very rich connotation. Although the framework
of Aristotelian practical philosophy provides a referential framework for
later exploration to the issue of practice, Marx as a model of modern
practical philosophy put forth a set of ideas different from Aristotle's.
Therefore, absolutely it is improper to evaluate Marx with Aristotelian
framework, to say nothing of analogizing Marx with the simplified understanding on Aristotle. If we take Aristotelian framework as a reference,
we may easily find Marx's concept of practice has the following charac-

teristics: (1) Material production activity is considered a form of a priority activity constituting man and man's life essence, while artistic activity is considered as the model of human free activity; (2) Theoretical activity and political ethics has certain unity with productive practice and is even isomorphic.

The first characteristic of Marx's concept of practice

No doubt, the sufficient affirmation on the priority of productive activity is a symbolic characteristic by which Marx distinguishes himself from other modern practical philosophers, and is also the basic connotation in Marx's materialism. If we say Aristotle's stress on moral and political practice is understandable in view of his times and social life background, then after a long history and social evolution, it is also reasonable that Marx has regarded productive activity as "the first activity".

In the sense of Aristotle, the essence of man is given by the state – this community, while belonging to the state has a sense of politics. Therefore, man is both a political animal and a free animal. Theoretical activity is also free activity – the free activity which greatly exceeds human "conditions". In comparison, making activity is a non-free activity, so it is impossible to constitute human "conditions" and it is excluded from the essential range of human life. However, after ancient Greece, people no longer lived in state, and consequently the meanings of man, social essence and freedom were changed, too. A marked change was that making activity (including productive and artistic activities) had entered into the sphere of human essence and human freedom.

Following the introduction and wide influence of Christianity, people gradually changed Greek people's despicable attitude towards productive labour. At monasteries, as everybody must do physical labour, the old-style classical antagonism between slave labour and free leisure had no longer existed.[1] Moreover, labour sometimes became a way of paying "redemption". This had laid groundwork for the further advocacy of the

---

1 [British] Christopher Dawson: Religion and the Rise of Western Culture, p.45, Chengdu, Sichuan People's Publishing House, 1989.

creative significance of labour in early modern times. Hegel attaches great importance to productive labour. He calls the tool-using productive activity "die List der Vernunet".[1] In Phenomenology of Spirit, Hegel considers labour as "edification of things" and negation of things. The mediation process of this negation or action of edification meanwhile is the particularity and pure being-for-itself of consciousness. This consciousness now alienates itself during labour and enters a persistent state. Therefore, this consciousness in labour uses independent being as its own intuition.[2] Hence, labour is no longer a thing irrelevant with human essence. Hegel regards it as an important link through which subject constitutes its essence - although for Hegel the human essence equals self-consciousness.[3] On the other hand, since the Renaissance, a symbolist view of art had grown.[4] By the 19th century, imitation hypothesis was superseded by symbolism, and as art depicts pure form or imaginative concept, it is higher than nature rather than nature is higher than art.[5] Not only that, in German movement of classical philosophy, artistic or aesthetic activity played an even more important role. Kant and Schiller both regard aesthetics or art as a medium solving the conflict between freedom and necessity. One step further, Schelling intuitively regards art as the absolute and highest way to realize subject-object unity. Even Hegel who debases art also thinks real creation is the activity of artistic imagination[6] and aesthetics has an emancipating nature.[7]

In early-modern philosophy, the essence of man lies in its subjectivity, while freedom means that through its own active activity, subject conquests and gets rid of nature. Initially, Marx was undoubtedly influenced by this concept. If we say the philosophers in early modern times think labour and artistic activities are separated, then in Marx's early works – particularly in the Economic and Philosophical Manuscripts of 1844, these two activities regain unity, into productive labour. Productive

---

1 [German] Hegel: The Logic of Hegel, p.394, Beijing, Commercial Press, 1980.
2 [German] Hegel: Phenomenology of Spirit, Vol.1, p.130, Beijing, Commercial Press, 1979
3 Collected Works of Karl Marx and Frederick Engels, Chinese version 1, Vol.42, p.165.
4 Lu Yang: Medieval and Renaissance Aesthetics, p.377, Shanghai, Shanghai Literature & Art Publishing House, 1999.
5 [British] Bernard Bosanquet: A History of Aesthetic, p.367, Beijing, Commercial Press, 1985
6 [German] Hegel: Aesthetics, Vol.1, p.50, Beijing, Commercial Press, 1979.
7 The same book as above, p.147.

labour here not only separates human from animals and constitutes the essence of human but also is an artistic activity in a sense:

> The practical creation of an objective world, the fashioning of inorganic nature, is proof that man is a conscious species-being – i.e., a being which treats the species as its own essential being or itself as a species-being. It is true that animals also produce..., but they produce only their own immediate needs or those of their young; they produce only when immediate physical need compels them to do so, while man produces even when he is free from physical need and truly produces only in freedom from such need; they produce only themselves, while man reproduces the whole of nature; their products belong immediately to their physical bodies, while man freely confronts his own product. Animals produce only according to the standards and needs of the species to which they belong, while man is capable of producing according to the standards of every species and of applying to each object its inherent standard; hence, man also produces in accordance with the laws of beauty.[1]

The influence of early-modern philosophy on Marx is obvious. We may even say Marx here uses "Hegelian" language (for example, view intuitively himself in the world he creates). Notably, Marx directly uses "practice" to address the activity that man reforms object, and thinks this activity is free, conscious, comprehensive and beautiful, thus is also the activity that constitutes human essence. This is unimaginable in the framework of Aristotelian practical philosophy, because Aristotle thinks the free activity symbolizing human essence can only be theoretical, ethical and political activity; while the productive labour Marx stresses here and its artistic content are exactly the unfree and incomplete activity "repulsed" by Aristotle. In terms of the inherent relation between productive activity and artistic activity, it is not an exaggeration to say that there is an inheritance relationship between Marx and Aristotle. But, obviously Marx's understanding on practice here does not belong to the ethics – conduct paradigm represented by Aristotle and cannot be simply reduced to technology – utility paradigm. In fact, Marx has introduced a brand new paradigm to understand practice. At present we are still unable to make fully clear of all connotation of this new paradigm, but we are certain it is closely related to productive activity and artistic activity.

---

1   Collected Works of Karl Marx and Frederick Engels, Chinese version 1, Vol.42, p.96~97.

But, Marx's view on the essence of productive labour and the relation between productive activity and artistic activity experienced a process of change. In the Economic and Philosophical Manuscripts of 1844, productive activity and artistic activity are identical, whereas in The German Ideology, under the influence of French materialism, Marx partially revises this romantic version. He has seen coerciveness in labour and thinks production is the activity people must complete every day and every moment in order to live.[1] However Marx does not therefore deny the significance that productive labour constitutes the essence of human and society. This labour is not a fully free and comprehensive activity, but this limited activity constitutes the essence of human and society. Marx said:

> The way in which men produce their means of subsistence depends first of all on the nature of the actual means of subsistence they find in existence and have to reproduce. This mode of production must not be considered simply as being the production of the physical existence of the individuals. Rather it is a definite form of activity of these individuals, a definite form of expressing their life, a definite mode of life on their part. As individuals express their life, so they are. What they are, therefore, coincides with their production, both with what they produce and with how they produce. The nature of individuals thus depends on the material conditions determining their production.[2]

Marx stresses "labour creates man". And,when productive labour is mentioned, it is always linked with human and human's mode of life. "By producing their means of subsistence men are indirectly producing their actual material life."[3] Therefore, productive labour is not merely an "instrument", and a means by which reason realizes its purpose. The labour of human must borrow a hand from instrument, but during labour, instrument constitutes a part of human's mode of production and mode of life, thus this instrument and instrumental activity is correlated with the essence of man. Just as Karel Kosik put it, labour is a course that permeates into the whole existence of man and constitutes the traits of man. In labour process, things that affect the essence and existence of man occur, and the two questions: "what is labour?" and "who is man?" have inherent links."[4] We may say this view is a major revolution on the con-

---

1 Marx & Engels Selected Works, Edition 2, Vol.1, p.79.
2 The same book as above, p.67~68.
3 The same book as above, p.67.
4 [Czech] Karel Kosik: Dialectic of the Concrete, p.149.

cepts of technology, instrument and labour since Aristotle. Of course, we have to admit the relation between Marx and Aristotle is extremely complex, and production and technology are also recognized by Aristotle as a kind of unique activity. In the very beginning Aristotle cognized technology as an incomplete thing, a thing with an end outside itself. Therefore, artistic and productive activities have always been discussed in "purpose–method" categorical framework. No doubt, today's criticism of "instrumental reason" is also based on this framework. Marx's dissertation on productive labour definitely negates this concept. French scholar Bernard Stiegler recognized Marx's contribution in this aspect and expressed the same thought in another way: "The appearance of the human is the appearance of the technical. ... Lroi-Gourhan specifies this as the appearance of language. The movement inherent in this process of exteriorization is paradoxical because of, ... the tool, that is, tekhne, that invents the human, not the human who invents the technical. Or again: the human invents himself in the technical by inventing the tool – by becoming exteriorized technologically. But here the human is the interior: there is no exteriorization that does not point to a movement from interior to exterior. Nevertheless, the interior is invented in this movement; it can therefore not precede it."[1] Bernard Stiegler thinks tool exposes the deformity and finity of human, while the essence of human and human life exactly originates from it. For Marx, this finity more implies the reality and concreteness of human's social life. Previous exploration was based on human's apriori consummate essence, while the affirmation on the finity of human activity indicates human essence is "constituted" by various kinds of finite activities.

Marx regards "non-free" and finite activity as the essential activity of human life. This not only implies a revolutionary change of the understanding on the concept of "essence" but also means a relative separation between productive activity and artistic activity. This is the difference between the realm of necessity and the realm of freedom. In his 1857-1858 Economic Manuscripts, Marx conditionally (with the conditions of "sociality" and "scientificalness") affirms that productive labour can become a way to realize individual ego, but in another manuscript in his

---

1 [French] Bernard Stiegler: Technics and Time, 1: The Fault of Epimetheus, p.167.

Capital, Marx changes his view and thinks the sphere of material production still remains in the "realm of necessity",[1] while the "realm of true freedom"in which human energy is comprehensively and freely developed "begins only where labour which is determined by necessity and mundane considerations ceases; thus in the very nature of things it lies beyond the sphere of actual material production".[2] This development of human energy which is an end in itself, the realm of true freedom, which, however, can blossom forth only with this realm of necessity as its basis. The shortening of the working-day is its basic prerequisite. This seems to indicate Marx in his late years went back to Aristotle's view on production. Marx had always regarded productive activity as the essential activity of human life and art as a model of free activity. At this point, Marx is fundamentally different from Aristotle. We see if we define free activity admitted by both Marx and Aristotle as the standard judging whether an activity belongs to practice (in a narrow sense), then in the older age of Marx, only artistic activity belongs to practice. On the other hand if we define the activity constituting the essentiality of human and their life as the standard of the practice in a narrow sense, then Marx' concept of practice is always productive activity. Here we may naturally define the practice understanding paradigm proposed by Marx as a production – art paradigm.

The second characteristic of Marx's concept of practice

We have indicated that Marx regards productive activity as "the first activity". Next we will talk on the relation of productive activity with theoretical activity and political and ethical activity. Aristotle realized free activity is based on non-free activity, and dis-engagement from production is a precondition of political activity and theoretical activity, but this relation can not be seen in his practical philosophy. Although Aristotle had mentioned the significance of slaves' labour to Athens citizens' free life, the relations of various kinds of activities was not emphasized, while that was stressed all the time were the difference and hierarchy be-

---

1 Collected Works of Karl Marx and Frederick Engels, Chinese version 1, vol.25, p.927, Beijing, People's Publishing House, 1974.
2 The same book as above, p.926.

tween these activities. An impression this gave later generations is that the three major activities put forth by Aristotle seem irrelevant with each other. The common points of Aristotelian activities were seldom mentioned. In fact, in terms of freedom, it seems that the demarcation line between making activity and political and theoretical activity as defined by Aristotle is impassable, but from another perspective, every activity has its wisdom and all these wisdoms are embodied with a kind of "knowing". For this reason, Aristotle may define technology as a kind of "knowing" in Metaphysics, and stress in his Nicomachean Ethics that "phroneesis" is "practical wisdom" and the moral knowledge necessary for the handling of interpersonal relations.[1] It looks as if there is a kind of unity among the activities differentiated by Aristotle, but after all it was not the emphasis of Aristotelian practical philosophy.

After Aristotle, the development of the relations of these activities shows a general trend of mutual fusion and influence. However, a major premise - "separation" cannot be ignored. We say the unity of all kinds of activities is a profound and essential unity (as conceived by Martin Heidegger) and this unity in the final analysis is not an issue of theoretical category. Due to the standpoint of theoretical philosophy, the philosophers in early modern times are unconscious of this unity. Therefore, the mutual influence and fusion of the activities in the sense of early-modern philosophers was a unity without profound evidence. This unity is usually reflected as the forced entry or absorption of a "strong" activity to another activity. Francis Bacon's integration between technology and theory, and Rene Descartes and Kant's construction of moral sphere in a theoretical way do not mean the inherent unity among different spheres is demonstrated. On the contrary, it was impossible that early-modern philosophers did in-depth research on the profound essence of these activities. Therefore, the theories of early-modern philosophers either have cracks which cannot be made up (such as: Rene Descartes' ethics) or dialectically unify all activities into a powerful "theoretical subject" as Hegel did. This unification is illegal in the sense of some modern practical philosophers. To tackle this illegal unification, it is considered an

---

1 [Ancient Greek] Aristotle: Nicomachean Ethics, p.127.

urgent task to resume the status of Aristotelian "practical" activity. Gadamer, Hannah Arendt and Habermas use this as the growth point of their theories.

Obviously, Marx's solution to this issue is neither a "forced unification" as adopted by early-modern philosophers nor a contemporary revival of Aristotelian differentiation. Then, based on the Marx's production – art paradigm on practice, in what way should the issue of the relations of various kinds of activities be solved? People usually think Marx regards productive activity as the "first activity" and it means other kinds of activities are reduced or unified into this activity, and think this is the essence of Marx's materialism. When enunciating Marx's social theory, Anthony Giddens, thinks that in the process of "reversing Hegel", Marx points out that ; state relies on civil society, does not surpass civil society and reflects the class structure of the civil society.[1] "Marx's above view sacrifices Hegelian insight to a bourgeois society, because Hegel thinks "civil society" is a bourgeois society and in fact is established by a (modern) state; or more correctly speaking, it is jointly generated during the mutual interweaving between the two.[2] This is because Marx has not established any satisfying theory of rights, and this shortcoming originates from some major limitations of his historical analysis framework.[3] Here we particularly mention Anthony Giddens, because he most clearly pointed out that Marx sacrifices Hegelian insight that state and civil society are mutually interwoven and mutually constituted, or in other words, Marx's limitation is that his social theory is a kind of economic reduction or reductionism. This "view of sacrifice" or "economic reductionism" is of course the viewpoint of Marx's critics. The followers of Marx call this view as a materialist reversal to the reversed Hegelistic idealism. Here people may admit the independence of political superstructure to economic foundation, but this admittance is strictly limited to

---

1 [British] Anthony Giddens: Nation – State and Violence, p.23, Beijing, Sanlian Bookstore, 1998.
2 [British] Anthony Giddens: Nation – State and Violence, p.25, Beijing, Sanlian Bookstore, 1998.
3 A.Giddens, A Modern Critique of Historical Materialism Vol.1 Power, Property and the State.The Macmillan Press Ltd 1981, p .3.

"relative" condition which in the final analysis decides the effect of economic foundation. Apparently, regardless of his critics and followers, their criticism and approval are both established on the precondition of assuming Marx denies the mutual interweaving and mutual construction. Although the misunderstanding on Marx is only seen in the layer of social theory, in fact it stems from the intensive misunderstanding on Marx, i.e.: conceives Marx's philosophy as a theoretical philosophy with a single visual angle and thinks Marx reduces all other activities into productive activity.

We may refute this misunderstanding from two aspects at least. One is from the standpoint of Marx's practical philosophy and the other is from Marx's dissertation on the relations between human activities. If we rethink on the first meaning of the concept of practice, we may easily see that this critic is undoubtedly self-contradictory. We say the foothold of Marx's philosophy is practice, but it does not mean Marx regards the material activity (practice) of human as the ultimate supporting point of his theory, nor does he ultimately reduces all human activities into material activity. Otherwise the first meaning of his concept of practice will become groundless, because in a broad sense, practice means the totality of human activities and the life-world constituted by these activities. If all activities were reduced to material activities, then material activities would be the whole life-world, and Marx's view of "social life essentially is practical" would have no difference from the view that social life essentially is productive activity and economic activity. Obviously, no one who has carefully thought over Marx's philosophy will accept it.

In fact, the premise for Marx's discussion of the unity of all kinds of activities is that these activities cannot be reduced. Without this premise, the discussion of these activities would become unnecessary. In reference to Aristotelian "triachotomy", these relations mainly include the relation between production and theory and the relation between production and political and communicative activity. Above we have indicated that through reversing the standpoint of theoretical philosophy, Marx concludes that theory is only a form of human activity and a specific "practice" under the background of the practice in a broad sense, in other words, theory is always inside life-world. Similar to Aristotelian theory, there theory was an activity in the state, but the object of Aristotelian theoretical activity and its truth guarantee the transcendence of state, while in the sense of Marx, this transcendence is illegal and theory must be within life-world, or in other words, it must be "produced". In this way, Marx's theoretical activity is influenced by productive activity – the primary activity which constitutes life-world, and the relation developing under this influence can be easily understood. When Marx opposes theoretical philosophy and those economic doctrines established on the basis of theoretical philosophy, he always stresses that the relation between man and world is firstly a practical relation, i.e.: a relation based on activity" other than a "theoretical relation".[1] "We can see it is only in a social context that subjectivism and objectivism, spiritualism and materialism, activity and passivity cease to be antinomies, and thus cease to exist as such antinomies. The resolution of a theoretical contradictions is possible only through practical means, only through the practical energy of man. Therefore, their resolution is not by any means, only a problem of knowledge, but is a real problem of life which philosophy was unable to solve precisely because it saw there a purely theoretical problem."[2] *In The Poverty of Philosophy,* Marx criticizes Proudhon, "holding this upside down, sees in actual relations nothing but the incarnation of the principles, of these categories,"[3] "which were slumbering in the bosom of the "impersonal reason of humanity",[4] while in fact, "Economic categories are only the theoretical expressions, the abstractions of the social relations of production".[5] "These categories, are as little eternal as the relations they express. They are historical and transitory products."[6] Productive activity (its core is instrumental activity) and theoretical activity are both objective activities, so it is understandable that there is a

---

1 Collected Works of Karl Marx and Frederick Engels, Chinese version 1, Vol.19, p.405, Beijing, People's Publishing House, 1963.
2 Collected Works of Karl Marx and Frederick Engels, Chinese version 1, Vol.42, p.127.
3 Marx & Engels Selected Works, Edition 2, Vol.1, p.141.
4 Marx & Engels Selected Works, Edition 2, Vol.1, p.141.
5 Marx & Engels Selected Works, Edition 2, Vol.1, p.141.
6 The same book as above, p.142.

kind of isomorphism between them. Marx thinks theory is the abstraction of productive sphere or a kind of symbolic and abstract practice (in narrow sense). Emile Durkheim expresses similar concept from another angle. Through studies on a few kinds of "primitive classifications", Emile Durkheim thinks "it is possible to classify other things than concepts, and otherwise than in accordance with the laws of pure understanding".[1] Logical connection is expressed in form of family connection or in the form of economic relation and political affiliation."[2] It seems that there is indeed a kind of isomorphism between theory and productive practice. This isomorphism stems from the life-world to which they both belong as well as productive practice's dominant role in constituting life-world. But, does the stress on the unity between the two in this sense erase the independence of theoretical activity? Apparently, the answer is negative. Marx says the category of a theory is the abstraction of production sphere. This sentence reveals the essential difference between the two: production sphere is realistic and real, while theory is abstract. This can also be applied to Marx's materialism. Below we will indicate it was not an accident that historical materialism was generated in the days of Marx, because only by then productive activity as "the first activity" became the reality for the first time, while together with it materialism had alo become a "real" theory for the first time.

In the sense of Marx, there exists a unity between productive activity and political and communicative activity. This is greatly different from Aristotelian theory. Aristotle thinks practice and making only bear resemblance (changeable) in the form of object, while their natures are completely different. It seems that making activity is irrelevant with political and moral value, while political activity is only "planning" and does not make "creation", because in the state where people live and the principle of political life – virtue- seems ready made and unchanged. In contrast, Marx thinks political activity "produces" political system and influences man's communication way, but political activity is also influ-

---

1 [French] Emile Durkheim and Marcel Mauss: Primitive Classification, p.92, Shanghai, Shanghai People's Publishing House, 2000.
2 The same book as above, p.91.

enced by productive activity. Habermas thinks Marx thus reduces the sphere of social and political communication into productive activity, and consequently does not consider the "social premise" and "pre-economic fact similar to historical development mechanism" of production". Habermas thinks productive labour shall be established on the basis of the interactive connection which uses signs as media.[1] Habermas stresses the social premise of production, but he fails to perceive that this social premise is also constituted by specific activities and productive activity plays a dominant role. Moreover, all communications are individual communications under certain conditions other than pure individual communications. Therefore, Marx regards communism as the production of communication form, and this production essentially possesses economic nature.[2] However, the stress on the influence of production in social communication sphere does not mean Marx reduces this sphere into productive activity and instrumental activity. In fact, if this "reduction" was possible, the social revolution advocated by Marx would become meaningless, because instrumental activity only follows objective laws, thus communism would emerge naturally by only following the same law. This is the economism of the Second International and is also the logical result of Stalinist textbooks, nevertheless it is obviously inappropriate to think this is a Marxist doctrine.

If we regard the first meaning of the concept of practice as the premise of thinking, we may easily obtain such a conclusion that material activity is only a theoretical visual angle of Marx's philosophy and a finite visual angle. Undeniably, the focus of Marx's theoretical activity is productive activity and economic activity (particularly in the later ages of Marx), but we cannot therefore deny the existence of other spheres. In fact, the ontological vision opened by Marx's theory of practice has provided a space for the existence of other "non-material" activities. We define material activity as "a kind of" activity. This definition firstly indicates material activity is finite; as it is a visual angle of theory, and it is abstract. In contrast, the practice in a broad sense is the totality of human activity

1 [German] Habermas: Erkenntnis und Interesse, p.64, Shanghai, Academia Press, 1999.
2 Marx & Engels Selected Works, Edition 2, Vol.1, p.122.

and human life-world, so it is consummate; as a background of theoretical activity which does not separate object and subject, and it is concrete. No doubt, Marx's philosophy is a theory. As indicated above, theory must choose a specific visual angle. The visual angle chosen by Marx's philosophy is human's material activity. Different from theoretical philosophy, this angle was not the ultimate visual angle. Theoretical philosophy sets a theory which can surpass life and find its "Archimedean point" beyond life, so the visual angle it chooses becomes a principle to explain the whole world; while under the premise of practical philosophy, theoretical thinking is a part of life practice and theory cannot fundamentally surpass life practice, so the theoretical visual angle of practical philosophy is finite. Since its visual angle is finite, then the existence of other theoretical visual angles will become legal. Below we will indicate that materialism more obviously possesses a kind of special reality, comparing with idealism in modern society, which is the unity with real life structure.

By now, we may affirm that the "matter" in Marx's materialism is not any previous theoretical visual angle in the sense of theoretical philosophy, but a finite visual angle of practical philosophy. Comparing with previous theoretical philosophy, it is a dialectic theory. Of course, it involves the understanding on the general meaning of dialectic. Below we will discuss this issue further. Here we may outline modern materialism as a dialectic characteristic of the theory of practical philosophy at first. In fact, Marx's modern materialism as the critique and transcendence of the materialism and idealism in early modern times possesses a nature of dialectic. Because human's material practice activity concept has reviewed the ideas proposed by the two opposite visual angles in early-modern philosophy, and compared with the former- early-modern philosophy- the theoretical visual angle chosen by Marx is more inclusive. Below we will indicate dialectic is a process from the abstractness of theory to the concreteness of practice. Without question, the visual angle of Marx's materialism is more concrete than that of early-modern materialism and idealism, but the dialectic nature of modern materialism does not contain this meaning only. Obviously, if we also regard this more inclusive visual angle as an absolute visual angle, it would not be more progressive than early-modern philosophy. In fact, the more important reason why modern materialism surpasses early-modern philosophy is that it is aware of the finity of theoretical visual angle and also aware of the complexity of practical sphere. The awareness of its own finity is equal to awareness of the reasonable significance for the existence of other theories and visual angles and also provides a possibility for a dialogue at a higher level. And awareness on the finity of theory also provides possibility for transcendence of theory. At this point, Marx's philosophy has an essential difference from previous theoretical philosophy. The latter sticks to an abstract visual angle, so it is not dialectic, while the former is aware of the finity of every visual angle, so it provides possibility for further dialogue and "multi-angle" grasp and it is dialectic.

If we conceive Marx's materialism as such a dialectic theory, the above misunderstanding on economic determinism (for example: Anthony Giddens) no doubt will be forcibly refuted, and Marx's materialist theory will show a state of "plural determinism" similar to Althusser's structuralist contradiction. Of course, we cannot simply reduce it to "plural determinism", and should see its evidence of practical philosophy. In any case, when this point is reached and people give stress on the decisive role of economy, it will no longer mean that economy is considered the only essence and other spheres as its manifestation, but mean the dominant role of economic factor and meanwhile the unique role of other spheres can not be eliminated or ignored. How should we understand Marx's priority or primary role he gave to economic sphere? In fact, dialectic interactionism is only a common issue of theoretical method, while the particular emphasis on economic sphere involves Marx's understanding on the characteristics of modern social life. The division of economic foundation and superstructure only means the observation of human's social life from dual visual angles – objective and subjective, and does not mean that the two are separated in social life in any era. In fact, the separation between economic life and political life is only a characteristic of modern social life. Marx's analysis is based on such concrete historical situation. It is also where the reality of Marx's materialism lies. Below we will indicate it is also where its superiority to previous materialism lies.

The materialism in reality and the materialism as a method

We determine Marx's materialism as a specific visual angle from which we observe and enter human's real life practice, but is this visual angle superior to other visual angles? Our answer is certainly positive, because it is more suitable to the condition of modern social life, i.e.: the fact that economic sphere assumes the most important position in social life. However, if we admit that this essence of materialism is relevant with era, its application scope will become an issue we must study in depth. A question related to this is: why is Marx's materialism only a product of modern society and why could it not be generated in ancient times, or in other words, with respect to the differentiation between Marx's modern materialism and previous materialism, in addition to the differentiation between theoretical philosophy and practical philosophy, how should we make a further differentiation?

In fact, in the history of Marx's philosophy, debate on the scope of historical materialism had occured. The essence of this issue is: is Marx's historical materialism applicable to the societies before capitalism? Orthodox view was represented by the textbooks of the former Soviet Union. This view thinks Marx's theory of materialism includes two departments: dialectic materialism and historical materialism. Historical materialism is a theory on the process of social history and thinks the ultimate cause and motive for the development of social history are social and economic development and the changes of production mode and exchange mode. In other words, historical materialism is the application of the general principles of dialectic materialism in the sphere of social history. Another view represented by Georg Lukacs thinks that the essential truth of historical materialism and the truth of classical (bourgeois) economics are the same type: they are the truth in a specific social system and production system. As a truth, only as such truth, can they act unconditionally.[1] Therefore, the historical materialism in its classical form (it is a pity that it has been vulgarized nakedly into general con-

---

1 [Hungarian] Georg Lukacs: History and Class Consciousness, p.311, Beijing, Commercial Press, 1992.

sciousness) means the self-cognition of capitalist society, not only in the sense of the just summarized ideological meaning, and historical materialism first of all is a theory of bourgeois society and its economic structure.[1] In the sense of Georg Lukacs, historical materialism is Marx's philosophy, it is not accidental that this philosophy was generated in the middle of the 19th century, and the social system of capitalism had become the typical foundation for the application of historical materialism. If we apply historical materialism to a pre-capitalist society, we will perceive a fundamental and important methodological difficulty which is never seen in the critique of capitalism.[2]

The view in the textbooks no doubt is seeking a "fundamental" law which is applicable to any historical era and has same certainty as the principles in natural sphere, and it seems that the concept of materialism is independent of concrete historical events, while on the other side the latter can be deduced from the former. In fact, this is a typical approach of theoretical philosophy. We can find typical examples of this approach from Hegel. Since the theory of practical philosophy is the theory under the background of concrete life practice, it cannot ignore the changes in the structure of this life practice. Lukacs stresses the structural difference between modern society and pre-modern society. Certainly, his stress is reasonable. However, we cannot say Marx's historical materialism can study capitalist society only and is unable to give dissertation on pre-modern social forms, or his studies on other social forms are not historical materialism. Obviously it is nonsense. We might as well take a look at Marx's dissertation on relevant issues:

> Production in general is an abstraction, but a sensible abstraction in so far as it actually emphasizes and defines the common aspects and thus avoids repetition. Yet this general concept, or the common aspect which has been brought to light by comparison, is itself a multifarious compound comprising divergent categories.[3]

To recapitulate: there are categories which are common to all stages of production and are established by reasoning as general categories; the so-called

---

1 The same book as above, p.312.
2 The same book as above, p.316.
3 Marx & Engels Selected Works, Edition 2, Vol.2, p.3

general conditions of all and any production, however, they are nothing but abstract conceptions which do not define any of the actual historical stages of production.[1]

Apparently, Marx admits its materialism has general concepts, but says these concepts are abstract. Although this abstraction is reasonable in a sense, we cannot understand any real historical stage just relying on these abstract concepts. No doubt, it does not mean that Marx does not involve other social forms before capitalism. We know that in fact Marx had even made intensive studies on pre-historical society. The critical issue is how Marx had approached to the societies before capitalism. We know, practical philosophy as a theory must set its foothold at a real life-world, while the life-world where Marx's materialism has its root is the established capitalist society. Therefore, that historical materialism can only start with capitalist period as its deep theoretical ground. Does the start with capitalist society mean the distinctive characteristics of capitalist society are promoted to all forms of human societies? Of course not. Marx often stressed the difference between capitalist society and pre-capitalist society. This difference is fundamental to theory. Marx ever said: In every social form in which land ownership assumes a dominant position, natural bond has dominated. In a social form in which capital assumes a dominant position, the factors created by society and history are dominated.[2] Lukacs also underlined this differentiation of Marx and concluded that there would be an important methodological difficulty if historical materialism was applied to a pre-capitalist era.[3] Anthony Giddens, also pointed out, in a non-capitalist society, the equalization of national wealth forms the axle center of social totality and social changes; on the contrary, in a capitalist society, wealth distribution has a very special significance. Based on this point, he had concluded: as currently historical materialism underlines the importance of wealth distribution, it might be spurned as a theory

---

1 Marx & Engels Selected Works, Edition 2, Vol.2, p.6.
2 Collected Works of Karl Marx and Frederick Engels, Chinese version 1, Vol.12, p.758, Beijing, People's Publishing House, 1962.
3 [Hungarian] Georg Lukacs: History and Class Consciousness, p.316.

of the whole history.[1] Jorge Larrain had criticized the views of people
including Lukacs. He thinks the grounds of argument cited by Lukacs
to support his limitation of historical materialism are exactly the grounds
of argument supporting the general theory of historical materialism;
whereas the reasoning of Anthony Giddens cannot get the conclusion
of "authoritative means is the main foundation in pre-capitalist society",
and thinks that if the land possession does not define a specific social relation, there would not be the ruling power over the people.[2] Jorge Larrain reaches a more orthodox conclusion.

We think the only reasonable solution to the problems here is to derive
from the differentiation of the types of social life; and the differentiation
of theories which are applied to these different types of social life. According to Marx's statements described above, we can see the general
concepts he applies to pre-capitalist societies are abstract, while the concrete can only be the understanding on current society - capitalist society.
However, we cannot therefore conclude that Marx's materialism is inapplicable to pre-capitalist societies, because this abstraction is "reasonable". Obviously, Lukacs and Anthony Giddens could not see this point.
This also does not mean we should obtain a conclusion similar to that
of Jorge Larrain, because after all he "applies" capitalist social structure
in pre-capitalist society. The key is how we understand this "abstraction"
is "reasonable". Firstly, we should affirm it is not a relation between "general and particular" in essence, because otherwise we will end up with
the conclusion similar to that of Jorge Larrain. Obviously, this abstraction is the abstraction of "thinking" and the abstraction of theory. Another way to differentiate abstraction and theory is concretion or reality.
No doubt, the understanding of historical materialism on capitalist society is realistic and concrete, while it can only adopt a reasonable and
abstract way to understand pre-capitalist societies. It seems that this abstraction is only a theoretical method, of course also a general method.

---

1 A. Giddens, A Modern Critique of Historical Materialism Vol.1 Power, Property and the
   State. The Macmillan Press Ltd 1981, p.4; [British] Jorge Larrain: A Reconstruction of
   Historical Materialism, p.124.
2 [British] Jorge Larrain: A Reconstruction of Historical Materialism, p.124~125.

In this way, it is not difficult for us to obtain the two layers of Marx's materialism or the two forms of theory – the materialism as a general method and realistic materialism.

In this way, the issue of the application scope of Marx's materialism is reasonably solved: firstly, this materialism is the understanding on the life-world of the modern society at which it sets its foothold, so it is realistic and concrete; but this does not exclude the existence of abstract materialism or the materialism as a general theoretical method. In fact, this materialism as a theoretical method is rather important to both the understanding on Marx and the understanding on the essence of pre-Marx materialism. Above we have only introduced the concrete forms and limitations of ancient materialism and early-modern materialism, while as the essence of them, we only defined them as a theoretical philosophy. Here we must review the relation between these theoretical philosophies and life practice as well as the difference between their abstractness and the abstractness of Marx's materialism as a theoretical method.

If we say that the reality and concreteness of Marx's materialism are because, it is a practical philosophy, or in other words, sets its foothold at real life practice, then the visual angle chosen by its theory must be in real life. The superiority of Marx's materialism to the philosophy in the same era lies in the fact that the material activity it chooses assumes a priority position in capitalist society. In the sense of Marx, it is inevitable to have this kind of dependency relationship among people in any era, but this relationship may have a rather different form in different era. The development from traditional society to a modern society depends on the transformation of the form of this dependency relationships.

> Everybody conquests social power in form of material. If you snatch social power from material, you must endow people with the power to rule the people. The dependency relationship of human (completely spontaneous in the very beginning) is the earliest social form under which human's production capacity was developed only in a narrow range and isolated places.

> Human independency based on material dependency is the second form under which a system with universal social material exchange, comprehensive relations, multi-aspect demands and all-round capacity is formed.[1]

Human's dependency relationship implies economic life is still in the swaddle of social life, political life in particular, and is not independent, to say nothing of a decisive role. Material's dependency relationship implies the universal exchange of activities and commodities have become the existence condition of every individual person. In this universal exchange, their mutual connection is manifested as a heterogeneous and irrelevant thing and an object. In exchange value, the social relation of human is converted into the social relation of material; the capacity of human is converted into the capacity of material.[2] Under such condition, the exchange relations in economy, or civil society possesses a kind of independency from political life. Now economic life not only meets people's need for material subsistence but also produces social order with the help of "universal exchange becoming the production condition of every individual person", i.e.: partially transcending the function of previous political life. Under such a historical condition, the primary and decisive role of economic life in shaping social life becomes inevitable. Although political life and other types of social life still play an extremely important role in shaping the entire social life and particularly economic life, they have to take a back seat and serve economic life to a large extent. Therefore, the visual angle selected by Marx's materialism is also concrete and realistic. However, if this visual angle and the differentiation relevant to it are applied to a pre-modern society, this reality and concreteness will not exist. For this, Marx's approach is a kind of reasonable abstraction and a methodological differentiation from pre-modern society. We should say the two aspects of historical materialism are merged into one by Marx, but as a realistic and concrete theory, we see its essential character as its non-methodology aspect.

The materialism before Marx was outside life-world in terms of the foothold and visual angle of its theory, so undoubtedly it was abstract

---

1 Collected Works of Karl Marx and Frederick Engels, Chinese version 1, Vol. 46
  (1st part), p.104, Beijing, People's Publishing House, 1979.
2 The same book as above, p.103~104.

and purely a method. In ancient times, the true state of human and world integration was naturally revealed in practical philosophy, while ancient theoretical philosophy, including ancient materialism was unable to conceive that. The "matter" in ancient materialism is only one of the internal differentiations in an abstract entity, though these materialists usually recognized it as this entity per se. In Aristotelian system, we may obviously see this point. Therefore, the abstractness in ancient materialism shows its meaning in two aspects. One is the abstractness in the sense of ontology, and the other is the abstractness of the "matter" which is its theoretical visual angle. Apparently, the former is more fundamental. We may understand the latter as a theoretical method (in fact, it is consistent with the aspect of Marx's materialism as a method), while the former facilitates this method with ultimate significance, thus only being a method in the end. The condition of early-modern philosophy is similar to that of ancient philosophy. Its "object" as a theoretical visual angle or nature firstly appears as the opposite of subject, while this opposition is the concealment of the real life in which subject and object are not separated. Therefore, early-modern materialism initially was a method, too and was an ultimate and metaphysical method.

CHAPTER THREE

Modern Materialism As Historical Materialism

Above we have illustrated the generation and basic significance of modern materialism. Next question will be: in what form will the theory under this significance present itself? i.e.: after the ultimate framework of the opposition between subject and object is negated and transcended, when facing a new relation with practice, how will theory adjust itself to show itself in a reasonable form? On this issue, relevant arguments have occurred in the history of Marxist philosophy. The most famous one is the argument on historical materialism and dialectic materialism. We know that in the traditional textbook system, Marx's materialism is divided into two blocks: dialectic materialism and historical materialism, but in fact, these two blocks are comprehended not to have a parallel relation but to have the relation between general theory and the application of particular sphere. In the sense of Marx, this differentiation does not exist and contradicts with the standpoint of modern practical philosophy. In fact, this differentiation model has long been challenged by Western Marxists. The arguments arising from this challenge provide multi-aspect revelation for our studies on this issue today.

Debates between two kinds of materialism

As known to all, the classification model which has been popular for a long time in the textbooks of Marxist philosophy is directly rooted from Stalin's booklet Dialectic Materialism and Historical Materialism. In this booklet, Stalin clearly defines the meaning of this classification: historical materialism is to popularize the principles of dialectic materialism to research social life and apply the principles of dialectic materialism to the phenomena of social life and the research of the society and social history.[1] Dialectic materialism is the integration between the previous old materialism and dialectic, so it possesses the universality advocated by old materialism, while historical materialism becomes a sphere of philosophy, a sphere of philosophy which must maintain a consistence with a universal principle.

In fact, Stalin's booklet does not have much new stuff and at most it only clearly and systematically illustrates the views of Plekhanov and Lenin. The direct ground of these views is Engels' dissertations. However, Marx has never used terms -- dialectic materialism and historical materialism-- these two terms, to symbolize his philosophy, and Marx only claims that his materialism is practical materialism. In The German Ideology, Marx and Engels had criticized and fixed Feuerbach, same as other theorists, who only wish to establish a correct understanding on the existing facts, while the mission of a true communist should be to overthrow all this kind of existing things.[2] For **practical materialists**, i.e.: communists, it is all about revolutionizing the existing world and realistically opposing and changing the current things[3] The "practical materialism" here is no doubt the "new" materialism in contrast with the old materialism as mentioned in the Theses on Feuerbach. We can say this is the original meaning of Marx's materialism. Although Marx himself did not give definite and systematic definition on its content, at least we can see clearly that this materialism is "practical", and its mission is not only to interpret the world but also to change the world. Below we will

1 Selected Works of J.V. Stalin, Vol.2, p.424, Beijing, People's Publishing House, 1979.
2 Marx & Engels Selected Works, Edition 2, Vol.1, p.96~97.
3 The same book as above, p.75.

indicate the interpretation of historical materialism and even the whole Marx's philosophy is be based on this basic point.

However, the orthodox interpretation represented in the textbook system is not principally based on this but on some direct dissertations made by Engels in his late age. Engels has never used the concept of dialectic materialism, either, but he had tried to define historical materialism. This definition from him has provided a possibility for the later classification model in textbook system. In the "English-version of Introduction to "The Development of Socialism from Utopian to Science", Engels uses the term "historical materialism" to express the notion about historical process.[1] This notion believes that the ultimate cause and great motive of all important historical events are the economic development of a society, are the changes in production mode and exchange mode, are the classification of the society into different classes and are the struggle of these classes.[2] Apparently, Engels here regards historical materialism as a historical theory or a historical viewpoint. This is consistent with the idea described in his Anti-Duhring:

> The materialist view of history proceeds from the following principles: production and the product exchange resulting from production are the foundation of all social systems; in each historically emerging society, product distribution as well as accompanied social classification into classes are decided by what is produced, how to produce and how to exchange products.[3]

In fact, Engels here regards historical materialism as a kind of theory of social history or view of history, but this cannot directly effect the differentiation as "two kinds of materialism" as indicated in the textbooks, because in that passage the history was not further defined. However, in his dissertation on dialectic, we may see the differentiation between the two spheres: as history and nature, "because the law of dialectic is abstracted from nature and the history from human society. The law of dialectic is nothing but the most general law of these two stages of historical development and thinking per se.[4] Engels thinks dialectic covers three

---

1 Marx & Engels Selected Works, Edition 2, Vol.3, p.704.
2 The same book as above, p.704~705.
3 The same book as above, p.617.
4 Marx & Engels Selected Works, Edition 2, Vol.4, p.310

spheres: nature, society and thinking. The above mentioned historical materialism obviously belongs to the sphere of social history. Engels has not used the concept of "dialectic materialism", but without doubt, he thinks there exists the most universal dialectic law which is applicable to the three major spheres. We know Marx thinks Hegelian dialectic is mysterious and inverted, and it must be reversed so as to discover the reasonable core inside the mysterious shell. In general, this reversed form is called **materialist dialectic.** Supposing dialectic represents a universal law as conceived by Engels, the differentiation between ordinary philosophy and sphere philosophy will be embodied here.

The later theorists like Lenin and Plekhanov have based themselves on this differentiation. Since Marx's dialectic is the reversal of Hegelian dialectic, it should be "materialist dialectic" opposite to "idealist dialectic", for them while materialist dialectic and dialectic materialism were the same. Plekhanov thinks "Marx's philosophy can be correctly explained" only in this way, and it can distinguish itself from both the idealism of Hegelian philosophy and old materialism. When mentioning Marx's doctrine, Lenin stresses Marx's critique on Hegel and Feuerbach, but it seems that this critique is just integration between Feuerbach's materialism and Hegel's dialectic, thus obtaining a "philosophical materialism".[1] Obviously, the superiority of this philosophical materialism by Marx rests with its sublation of the "non-dialectic" defect of old materialism. Therefore, the Marx's philosophical materialism as evaluated by Lenin and the dialectic materialism generally accepted later was believed to have the same content. Lenin also thinks:

> the inconsistency, incompleteness, and one-sidedness of the old materialism convinced Marx of the necessity of "bringing the science of society... into harmony with the materialist foundation, and of reconstructing it thereupon". Since materialism in general explains consciousness as the outcome of being, and not conversely, then materialism as applied to the social life of mankind has to explain social consciousness as the outcome of social being.[2]

---

1 In fact, the concept of "dialectic materialism" was first used by Plekhanov in a strict philosophical sense. (Refer to [British] Jorge Larrain: A Reconstruction of Historical Materialism, p.42)

2 Lenin Selected Works, Edition 3, Vol.2, p.423.

This was the definition of historical materialism or materialist view of history. In the sense of Lenin, the discovery of materialist view of history had mobilized the complete role of materialism and the application of materialism to social phenomena. Thus,with this definition, the differentiation between two kinds of materialism illustrated by Stalinist textbooks has been formed without question.

Although we have to say we can find some evidence of this differentiation from the works of Marx and Engels, but after all, it is only a kind of interpretation on Marx's materialism. Today, we see it is not compatible with Marx's practical philosophy, so fundamentally speaking, it does not hold water. However, this interpretation was fixed through textbooks and was advocated as mainstream Marxist philosophy after Stalin. Nevertheless, the framework of this interpretation was challenged by Western Marxists in the very beginning and has been under frequent attack for a long time. The earliest challenger was Lukacs.[1] When illustrating Marx's philosophy, Lukacs does not observe this differentiation. For example, in his book History and Class Consciousness, Lukacs equates Marx's philosophy, historical materialism and Marxist dialectic. Above we have reviewed Lukacs' dissertation on historical materialism. By conceiving Marx's philosophy in this sense, no doubt Lukacs opposes orthodox interpretation framework.

Lukacs reveals the fundamental antinomy of classical philosophy and thinks this antinomy is deeply rooted in the materialization of capitalist society.

> Therefore, classical philosophy is in such a self-contradictory situation in the history of development: its aim is to ideologically sublate bourgeois society and contemplatively resuscitate the people who are in this society and ruined by it, but the consequence is only fully ideological re-emergence and transcendental deduction of bourgeois society. Only this deductive way, i.e.: dialectic method transcends bourgeois society.[2]

---

1 The primary and direct object Lukacs challenged is the Second International's scientist and naturalist interpretation on Marx's philsophy, but in terms of the differentiation between social history and the fields beyond it, the view of Bernstein and Kautsky is basically same as Lenin's. Therefore, we may regard the thought of Lukacs as a challenge to textbooks. In fact, the attack of later Western Marxists has adopted a standpoint similar to Lukacs'.

2 [Hungarian] Lukacs: History and Class Consciousness, p.227.

Lukacs thinks that if the methodological transcendence to capitalist society is not satisfied, it will be necessary to find a realistic transcendence,
while the realistic transcendence of capitalist society and classical philosophy can based on history. Only history is the realistic route to sublate
the materialization of bourgeois society and the antinomy of classical
philosophy. In the sense of Lukacs, history is a past thing, is no longer
an elusory process happening on human and things, can be explained
only with the intervention of transcendental force, or in other words, it
can become meaningful only when it is connected to the value which is
transcendental to history. History on the one hand is mainly the product
of human activity (of course it was spontaneous till now) and on the
other hand is a string of processes.[1] The form of human activity and
human relations (with the nature and other people) are thoroughly
changed along with this string of processes . The history as conceived by
Lukacs is a process of unity between subject and object. In terms of the
separation between subject and object in early-modern philosophy, its
functions are similar to Spinoza's nature and Hegel's absolute spirit. Differently, Lukacs thinks the former was an abstract and methodological
unity, while history is realistic unity. This reality rests with the awakening
of proletarian class consciousness, because the previous thoughts and
philosophies could not perceive this unity and only proletariat can truly
realize it while they consciously make history during their struggle. In
the sense of Lukacs, historical materialism was established on the basis
of self-consciousness of this unity. Proletariat should obtain the sharpest
weapon from definite cognition to reality. This weapon is historical materialism. Historical materialism is not a mere scientific method to understand past events. It should become a part of the struggle. From the
perspective of this struggle, theory and practice are consistent. Cognition
without transition may lead to action.[2]

It is obvious that the most critical concept of Lukacs here is history. The
differentiation between the two kinds of materialism in the textbook system in fact is the differentiation between "general" philosophy and

---

1 [Hungarian] Lukacs: History and Class Consciousness, p.275.
2 Refer to the above book, p.306~307.

sphere philosophy, i.e.: thus the existence of the spheres beyond history and the general principles that transcend all spheres is defined. From Lukacs' critique on classical philosophy, we can easily discover his very reason for the introduction of the concept of history is to sublate the division of philosophical vision. For the moment we will not discuss whether the classification in the textbook system is equal to the division of early-modern philosophy, but we can conclude Lukacs' concept of history is a total process and any process outside this process will be considered unrealistic. Here the incompatibility between Lukacs' view and the textbook system is mainly seen in two aspects. One is the issue of the existence of general principles. The other is the issue of the existence of natural sphere opposite to social history. We should say Lukacs' historical materialism gives a negative answer to these two issues. In relation to history, all general principles are abstract. Lukacs thinks that nature is a "social category". Lukacs' ideas has set a basic direction for later Western Marxism. His fundamental divergence from orthodox interpretation system has become the focus of many later arguments. Among these arguments, the most typical one is the argument over natural dialectic and dialectic materialism.

Lukacs' above ideas were criticized by the theorists of the Second International and Soviet theorist Bukharin. Bukharin was one of the key figures contributing to the formation of the textbook system. His argument with Lukacs is an evidence enough to tell us the conflict between these two interpretations on Marx's philosophy. After the orthodox interpretation was written into textbooks, it was fixed as classic and hence there was no revision to it in the following decades. On the contrary, Western Marxists have inherited the rough direction of Lukacs' theory. Although the people in later generations can see the elements from Hegel in History and Class Consciousness as well as the alleged interpretation on Marx from an approach of Hegel, we may say the negation of the two kinds of materialism in textbooks, has become the common understanding by most Western Marxists.

No doubt, we should analyze this argument from a standpoint of practice at first because of the fact that Marx has not used the concept of dialectic materialism or historical materialism and secondly because of the self-claimed "practical materialists". Moreover a more fundamental reason is that Marx's philosophy is a practical philosophy, and the concrete form it should have should be grasped from its fundamental standpoint.

In fact, we may summarize the divergence of the above argument into two points. One is whether there is a dialectic materialism and the other is how to understand historical materialism. Lukacs' attack on natural dialectic is equal to denial of the existence of the general materialist dialectic which transcends all spheres. The reason for his opposition to natural dialectic is that if we admit dialectic can be a law in the nature or a structure of things, then subject will be unable to be combined into this dialectic process, thus we will be facing the issues left over by classical philosophy, i.e.: the issue of mind-matter opposition and the issue of thing-in-itself will become unsolvable. This is equal to announcing dialectic materialism and early-modern philosophy have no difference at all. Here we have to say that at this point Lukacs' criticism is rather accurate. As mentioned above, the interpretation in textbooks does not reflect the essence of Marx's materialism as a modern practical philosophy, and on the contrary it conceives Marx's philosophy as an early-modern or even ancient theoretical philosophy. In modern practical philosophy, all theories and their visual angles shall be inside life practice, whereas the textbook system insists that the most general principle universally applicable to every sphere is a theoretical visual angle that transcends life practice in essence. Japanese scholar Hiromatsu Wataru, has evaluated this interpretation as a "dramatic distortion" of historical materialism.[1] He thinks historical materialism is not only a part of Marxist theoretical system but also the composition of Marxist view of the world.[2] No doubt, Hiromatsu Wataru holds a standpoint similar to Lukacs' on this issue.

Is the historical materialism adhered to by Lukacs problematic or can Lukacs draw a clear demarcation line from the classical philosophy criticized by him? It is still a question calling for observation. In the early

---

1 [Japanese] Hiromatsu Wataru: The Composition of Reification Theory, p.3, Nanjing, Nanjing University Press, 2002.
2 "The same book as above, p.5.

thoughts of Lukacs, what closely related to history is the concept of practice. In order to oppose the scientism and economic fatalism of the Second International and oppose the mechanical materialism put forth by the people including Bukharin, Lukacs re-introduced the concept of practice and elevated it to a central position in Marxist philosophy to highlight the initiative of Marx's philosophy. However, we still must differentiate Lukacs' concept of practice from the concept of practice we have illustrated above. Though Lukacs' practical theory also aims to realize the unification between subject and object, this unification is realized in subject. In the sense of Lukacs, practice is proletarian struggle activity and relies on proletarian class consciousness, which is a collective consciousness similar to Hegel's absolute spirit. Lukacs thinks only in this real practice, can proletariat become the subject and object of history at the same time. Here we have to mention Marx's Theses on Feuerbach again. In the first article of the "Theses", Marx had criticized the old materialists by not grasping things and objects subjectively, and criticized idealists by developing " this active side" - though abstractly. Naturally, the idealism here refers to German classical idealism at first. Obviously, although Lukacs vehemently criticized classical philosophy, his way to solve problems had not departed from the direction of classical philosophy. In fact, Lukacs was obviously influenced by Johann Fichte and Hegel. We know all classical philosophers after Kant have strived to eliminate thing-in-itself – the issue of the unity between subject and object. All these ways to solve problems had endep up with the introduction of the concept of a powerful subject. To some extent, Lukacs' proletarian class consciousness may also be considered as such a way to solve the problem of thing-in-itself and as a substitute of Hegel's "absolute spirit", because this class consciousness is still abstract. Although Lukacs reiterated the reality and concreteness of history, what makes history is a kind of abstract consciousness, so this reality and concreteness cater for this consciousness and we have no difficulty finding similar circumstance from Hegel. No wonder that Alasdair MacIntyre thinks the view of young Lukacs is "rational voluntarism";[1] people universally believe that

---

1 [American] McIntyre: The Theses on Feuerbach: A Road. not Taken, Social Sciences Abroad, 1995(6).

Lukacs' History and Class Consciousness is the "resurgence" of Hegelian philosophy.[1] This certainly indicates Lukacs' historical materialism has not reached the vision opened by Marx's materialism, so it is still a theoretical philosophy.

The above indicates none of the two kinds of materialism(s) both in textbooks and young Lukacs' "sole" historical materialism could break through the framework of theoretical philosophy in the end, so none of them could enunciate the concrete form of Marx's materialism. However, these two tit-for-tat standpoints provide reference for our research on the concrete form of Marx's materialism: only the research that is consciously based on the standpoint of practical philosophy is valid.

The real meaning of "historical" materialism

History as the history of concrete men

As mentioned above, because Marx claims his materialism as "practical materialism", and moreover Marx's philosophy has a nature of practical philosophy, our study here must set a foothold at Marx's theory of practice. From the above argument, we can see without difficulty that the problem with dialectic materialism essentially is how to understand historical materialism. Abstract dialectic materialism is incompatible with Marx's concept of practice, but in the sense of Marx, practice and history are always intrinsically related. Therefore, we may preliminarily determine historical materialism unquestionably can be used to name Marx's philosophy. The key is how to understand this historical materialism. Of course, this concerns the understanding on the concept of Marx's practice. As a matter of fact, no parties in the argument deny historical materialism is Marx's original creation. Only they differ in its position and connotation. No doubt, the key to solving this issue is how to understand Marx's concept of history, or how to understand the concept of history on the basis of Marx's theory of practice. Below we need to explain the

---

1 Zhang Xiping: Reconstruction of Historical Philosophy, Chapter 7, Beijing, Sanlian Bookstore, 1997.

issues in two aspects at least. One is the scope of history, which decides the application scope of historical materialism; the other is whether a brand-new thinking mode is represented which will enable us to see a comprehensive differentiation between Marx's materialism and previous philosophy.

If we say the "matter" in Marx's materialism is the "matter" in real human life, then the connotation of "history" in historical materialism must be closely related to this life practice. In fact, in Marx's philosophy, the concept of history is absolutely no less important than the concept of practice. Marx ever said:

> We know only a single science, the science of history. One can look at history from two sides and divide it into the history of nature and the history of men. The two sides are, however, inseparable; the history of nature and the history of men are dependent on each other so long as men exist. The history of nature, called natural science, does not concern us here; but we will have to examine the history of men, since almost the whole ideology amounts either to a distorted conception of this history or to a complete abstraction from it. [1]

The history mentioned here obviously has broader connotation than our ordinary understanding. If we deem the science of history as a single science, this history must be able to cover the whole scope of human life practice. In other words, history and practice should be concepts with considerable extension. In addition, Marx and Engels say history can be looked at from two sides: the "history of nature" and the "history of men", but it is noteworthy that they neither separate these two spheres nor define them as a "reflective" relation, and instead, they underline they are closely related and mutually restrict each other. Seemingly, looking at history by dividing it into two sides is a "theoretical method", while the "mutual restriction" of the two spheres indicates an ontological unity. Therefore, both the research of the history of nature and the research of the history of men must be aware of a unified history and integral practice. Obviously, the "history" concept of historical materialism is exactly such integral and unified history.

---

1 Marx & Engels Selected Works, Edition 2, Vol.1, p.66, editor's note.

In fact, the history of men was included into the visual sphere of philosophy a long time ago, but just as Marx put it, this history is either "distorted" or "completely abstracted". As early as Vico, the differentiation between the history of nature and the history of men was generated. Vico thinks the latter is created by men, while the former not, and men only can cognize the history created by themselves. In German classical idealism, history is conceived as a general medium of soul.[1] Just as reflected by Lukacs later on, history is conceived as the history of subject, while this subject has always been an abstract subject. But as Habermas said:

> History absorbs the cultivation process of nature and spirit. It must follow the logical form of self-interpretation of spirit; through sublimation, history becomes the opposite of history. To summarize, when a history contains lost past, pre-defined future and criticized present, this history has no longer been a history.[2]

Once the history of classical philosophy is deemed as an all-inclusive totality, it will become an abstract thing same as the "subject" of history.

An outstanding common point between Marx's historical concept and the historical concept of classical idealism is that they both possess a kind of integrity and unity. In the sense of Hegel, history is a comprehensive process in which spirit integrates external world, while in the sense of Marx, this process essentially is a process of human's real activities and a process of labour.

> The nature which develops in human history -the genesis of human society- is man's real nature; hence nature as it develops through industry, even though in an estranged form, is true anthropological nature.[3]

> History does not end by being resolved into "self-consciousness as spirit of the spirit," but that in it at each stage there is found a material result: a sum of productive forces, an historically created relation of individuals to nature and to one another, which is handed down to each generation from its predecessor; a mass of productive forces, capital funds and conditions, which, on

---

1 [German] Habermas: Post-Metaphysical Thinking, p.146.
2 [German] Habermas: Post-Metaphysical Thinking, p.152~153.
3 Collected Works of Karl Marx and Frederick Engels, Chinese version 1, Vol.42, p.128.

the one hand, is indeed modified by the new generation, but also on the other hand prescribes for it its conditions of life and gives it a definite development, a special character.[1]

Through history, Marx transcends the model of separation between subject and object, but this does not mean the subject of history will be naturally absorbed into itself, but instead the inseparable relation between man and the external world in real life practice is discovered. In this way, the so-called independent nature is only an abstract product and a product of theoretical method. Therefore, nature is still the category of social history. Talking nature in departure from human history is unquestionably an abstract approach of theoretical philosophy. At this point, the world of men is a life-world relating to social history and things beyond this sphere are negative to man, so impossibly it is a sphere at which philosophy sets its foothold. Just as Marx put it, "only in a social context that subjectivism and objectivism, spiritualism and materialism, activity and passivity cease to be antinomies, and thus cease to exist as such antinomies."[2]

Superficially, history plays a role of medium in the sense of both Marx and Hegel, but Marx's concept of history avoids the abstractness of Hegel, because what makes history is not "spirit" but real human practical activities. Owing to the abstractness of the subject of history, all the past attempts to profoundly illustrate the nature of history possess a character of mystification. It is the same case from Vico to Hegelian classical historical determinism. Seemingly the profound insight has an indissoluble bond with mystification.[3] Therefore, history is usually incomprehensible to concrete individuals and is manifested as a power of transcendence. As a result, history acquires ultimate interpretation in such concepts as "invisible hand", "cunning of reason" and "natural intention". It seems that this interpretation avoids the division between subject and nature, but it leads to another division – the division of this abstract subject and the history made by it in the real world. In the sense

---

1 Marx & Engels Selected Works, Edition 2, Vol.1,
2 Collected Works of Karl Marx and Frederick Engels, Chinese version 1, Vol.42, p.127.
3 [Czech] Karel Kosik: Dialectic of the Concrete, p.176.

of Marx's materialism, the subject of history is real individual. "Men must be in a position to live in order to be able to 'make history'. But life involves before everything else eating and drinking, a habitation, clothing and many other things. The first historical act is thus the production of the means to satisfy these needs, the production of material life itself."[1] Only such history is true, real and concrete history. Same as Hegel, Marx's history is also a totality. The difference is: in the sense of Hegel, totality is subject and the authority of totality must be guaranteed by an absolute subject; whereas in the sense of Marx, the totality of history originates from the unity of society and nature in real life and moreover, it is finite subjects, i.e.: real men who constitute this totality. Just as Karel Kosik said: "The first basic premise of history is that it is created by man, but its second, equally basic premise is the necessity for continuity of this creation. History is only possible at all because man does not always start over again from the beginning and instead follows up the road and results of past generations."[2] In this sense, the totality of history and the totality of practice are a same thing. In a word, Hegelian history needs an absolute subject to match it, so it is abstract; whereas in the sense of Marx, history includes a kind of finite subjectivity, so this history is concrete.

History as a thinking mode to sublate metaphysics

But, how does Marx realize this unity and avoid the abstractness of the view of history in the early modern times? It appears that the significance of Marx's concept of history is not only its totality and integrity and also represents a unique thinking mode due to which Marx's philosophy obtains for the first time the concretion of modern philosophy. Therefore, the introduction of history into philosophy not only means the discovery of a new sphere and but also means a method and principle able to bring about a qualitative change in philosophy. We know that history had entered into the sphere of philosophy in the early modern times, but by

1 Marx & Engels Selected Works, Edition 2, Vol.1, p.79.
2 Czech] Karel Kosik: Dialectic of the Concrete, p.182.

Marx, history is no longer a "distorted" history but becomes a real history. In other words, only in Marx's theory, history is carried through as a real principle. Therefore, the "history" in Marx's historical materialism means a paradigm different from previous philosophy. As described above, this paradigm is modern practical philosophy.

In fact, history is even repulsive to the earliest philosophical spirit. We know the fundamental issue of ancient Greek philosophy is to contemplate the unified, eternal and invariable being behind the ever-changing phenomena, thus all rheological things were universally deemed unreal. "In the most basic sense, the history called by us stands for "change", "disappearance" and "one-time", in short, the irreversibility of time. This no doubt is opposite to the "eternity" as pursued by ancient Greek philosophy. Therefore, although ancient Greece had a developed history, we can hardly find out the concept of history in Greek philosophy.[1] From Parmenides' differentiation between the way of truth and the way of opinion, then further to Plato's metaphor of cave, and to Aristotle's substance theory and pattern theory, we cannot see history. Although Heraclitus noticed the rheology of the world, same as Parmenides, he had only regarded rheology as a necessary step to the invariable - Logos. Greek philosophers and historians were convinced that whatever is to happen will be of the same pattern and taking a character as past and present events.[2] From today's point of view, this "time pattern of ancient Greek has inherent relation with their substantial philosophy, because the introduction of the dimension of time has no difference from the fundamental destruction of the ultimate visual angle of their theoretical philosophy.

Different from ancient Greek philosophy, the fundamental principle of Christian thought – another headstream of Western thought is "histor-

---

1 Greek usually narrated historical events in a "timeless" way. For example, "the temporal scheme of Herodotos' narrative is not a meaningful course of universal history aiming towards a future goal, but, like all Greek conception of time, is periodic, moving within a cycle. In this view of Herodotos, history shows a repetitive pattern, regulated by a cosmic law of compensation mainly through nemesis which time and again restores the equilibrium of the historico-natural forces." (Refer to [German] Karl Lowith: World History and Salvation History, p.11, Beijing, Sanlian Bookstore, 2002).

2 [German] Karl Lowith: World History and Salvation History, p.10.

ical". We may say that for the first time Christianity had brought human's new attitude at time and events into European world of thought. Christianity is based on historical time. The history of men had started with the initial fall. This fall means the parting from the Garden of Eden and this parting means the parting from the God-like timeless life (this timeless life is exactly the attention focus of ancient Greek practical philosophy. As expressed by Aristotle in his Nicomachean Ethics, "philosophers' life is the closest to divine life, and this life is relevant with eternity). Once departing from timeless static world, men will inevitably live in time or in other words live in a way of time or history. The ideas of Christianity almost all are expressed in the model of time. We may also say Christianity was generated from a strong time consciousness. We can really feel this point from the miserable history of Hebrews as recorded in Bible. The influence of this time consciousness on Western people's world of thought is beyond estimation. Even from Marx – an anti-theist, seemingly people can also find things relevant with this. As a result, some critics mention Marx's historical materialism and Christian view of history in the same breath and think historical materialism is the history of redemption in the language of national economics".[1] Certainly, this view contains some insight to Marx's historical materialism, but the real history in Marx's philosophy has essential difference from the natural disclosure of historical consciousness in the thought of Christianity.

Similar concept was expressed in another way in Chinese ancient history. In the sense of ancient Chinese, history and men are inseparable. Although Chinese ancient genesis does not have the strong sense of time and history as the thought of Christianity does, we can see the strong sense of history from the formation process of the thought of the people in Zhou Dynasty, which had influenced the whole Chinese ancient thought. It can be regarded as the headstream of Chinese historical concept. From ancient literature, we can discover the people in Zhou Dynasty had a history as twisted and miserable as the history of Hebrew. They experienced history amidst the rise and fall of the nation, and this strong historical experience was expressed with "Providence". Generally

---

1 [German] Karl Lowith: World History and Salvation History.

we conceive "Providence" as a personified force, just like the God in Christianity is conceived as a personified god. We do not repulse this understanding, but we must stress that it is not the essence of "Providence" or god and what supports this understanding is the sheer experience of time and fugacity. This experience resulted in the way of existence of these two nations. In the words of Xu Fuguan, it is the existence in "misery". Zhou Yi is a product of "misery", while "misery" originated from the experience of history.

If we say that in the ancient times history and historical consciousness only existed in religion or the beliefs similar to religion, then in the early modern times, this history experienced a process of entering philosophy. In fact, in the thought of Augustine who has a dual identity – religious theologist and philosopher, we have seen the start of this process, but wholly speaking, the fundamental concepts of early-modern philosophy are still static. In the thoughts of Herder, Kant and other early-modern philosophers, history is always a sphere other than a principle, so history is a history of reason; it is reason that owns history or history should be constituted by reason other than history constitutes the fundamental content of reason. This condition was changed to some extent by Hegel. History becomes a principle in Hegelian dialectic. We can see "history" in The Philosophy of History, Lectures on the History of Philosophy, Phenomenology of Spirit and The Logic. On the other hand, Hegel does not depart from the subjective thought of early-modern philosophy, so his principle of history is not thorough. Although Hegel admits to some extent that reason is "historical", history is "reasonable" after all. Hegel's ultimate intention is to regard history as a comprehensive means only and limit it in the system of reason. No doubt, Hegelian philosophy has indicated the development direction of the principle of history. Martin Heidegger said Hegel's "formal dialectical 'construction' of the connection between spirit and time can be ventured at all, manifests that these are primordially akin. Hegel's 'construction' was promoted by his arduous struggle to conceive the 'concretion' of the spirit".[1] Therefore, just as Engels said, Hegelian philosophy was a mixture of conservative system

---

1 [German] Martin Heidegger: Being and Time, p.491.

and revolutionary method,[1] which is also the reason why an overwhelming majority of modern philosophers vehemently criticize Hegelian philosophy, but they cannot cross this philosophy.

The first modern philosopher who directly criticized Hegel is Marx. Here we care most on the relation between Marx's concept of history or time and the thinking mode of practical philosophy. As long as we distinguish the different meanings of history in Hegelian philosophy and Marx's philosophy, the problem will be solved, because as described above, though Hegel considers history a principle of his philosophy, he cannot get rid of the framework of theoretical philosophy; history is also a fundamental principle of Marx's dialectic and by this principle Marx had intensively criticized Hegel. Therefore, the "secrete" and "birth place" of the thinking mode of practical philosophy lies in Marx's "reversal" of Hegelian philosophy. Obviously this "reversal" is not the simple substitution of the concept of matter by Hegel's concept of spirit. This reversal means spurning the abstraction of Hegelian philosophy, going towards concretion and leading Hegelian dialectic from "heaven" to "secular world". Here we see this "reversal" process as a process which was comprehensively carried through historical principle. Hegelian history in the end is only the history of spirit and the history of reason, since Hegel thinks only absolute spirit can prevent historical principle from becoming a relativism, which the philosophers had tried so much to avoid since ancient Greece. Will the thoroughness of historical principle inevitably lead to relativism? From the perspective of Marx's practical philosophy, it is only a special problem facing theoretical philosophy, because theoretical philosophy will certainly require an eternal visual angle. Marx carries through historical principle. In fact, this historical principle requires that theory should always set its foothold on concrete historical circumstances, i.e.: concrete life-world. Although concrete life-world is constituted by man's practice activities, as asserted by Marx, "circumstances make men just as much as men make circumstances", so we may say life-world is not an eternal entity, but in terms of theoretical activity, it is

---

1 Marx & Engels Selected Works, Edition 2, Vol.4, p.214~223.

unquestionably "objective". In this way, we can easily see the close connection between thorough historical principle and the thinking mode of Marx's practical philosophy, because as we have described above, life-world is the first meaning in Marx's concept of practice.

Marx said the previous "history must, therefore, always be written according to an extraneous standard; the real production of life seems to be primeval history, while the truly historical appears to be separated from ordinary life, something extra-super-terrestrial."[1] Regarding history as the history of real life -- in essence—is, to introduce a finite visual angle into the studies of philosophy. Marx refuses all extra-super-terrestrial things. In essence, he refuses all absolute visual angles of theoretical philosophy, then historicity, timeliness and finity must be deemed as things relevant with man and the essence of the world where man lives. The modern philosophers after Marx, such as: Martin Heidegger and Gadamer all place history or time on the most fundamental position of their philosophies. In Being and Time, Martin Heidegger establishes the priority position of Dasein in conceiving the being, while in essence, Dasein has the nature of history or time. No doubt, Gadamer's hermeneutics has developed Heidegger's view on this point.

---

1 Marx & Engels Selected Works, Edition 2, Vol.4, p.93

DIALECTIC AS PRACTICAL WISDOM

DIALECTIC AS PRACTICAL WISDOM

Introduction

Above we have denied the existence of materialist dialectic as a universal abstract law. Then how should we conceive grasp Marx's dialectic? Though Marx has never written any special work on dialectic, we don't doubt that Marx has inherited and reformed Hegelian dialectic and is a great dialectician. In the postscript of *Capital Volume* I Edition 2, Marx claims himself a student of Hegel – a great thinker- and admits that he has applied and even "showed off" Hegelian dialectic in his "Capital". In the sense of Marx, dialectic is mystified by Hegel and "inverted" and must be reversed in order to reveal the reasonable core inside its mysterious shell. This is the dialectic in a reasonable form.[1] However, here we must point out that for a long time, our understanding on Marx's dialectic and even dialectic per se has been confusing and had contained defects and contradictions. In general the concept, dialectic is regarded as a pure and objective naturalist system. It may be said: it tallies with some views of ancient or early-modern materialism,[2] but it is obviously improper to apply this idea on it to the whole dialectic tradition. Apply-

---

1 Marx & Engels Selected Works, Edition 2, Vol.2, p.112.
2 According to this interpretation, French metaphysical materialism which has always been considered "non-dialectic" would also become "dialectic materialism".

ing such a concept to Marx's philosophy will create sharp contradictions in many aspects, and the most fundamental -we should underline -- is the incompatibility between the "objective" laws of dialectic and Marx's theory of practice. The result is either obliterating the thought of Marx's practical philosophy or disintegrating Marx's philosophy into several mutually heterogeneous parts. Therefore, it is an urgent task to enunciate Marx's practical dialectic and even to re-evaluate the concept of dialectic.

CHAPTER ONE

The Concept and the History of Dialectic

First of all we indeed need to enunciate the essential meaning of the concept of dialectic and the tradition of dialectic. We may say dialectic is as old as philosophy, but following the development of the history of philosophy and the changes of the objective of human cognition, the meaning of the concept of dialectic has become vague and ambiguous. Marx's dialectic is mostly misunderstood or cannot be grasped since there is a lack of knowledge on dialectic and its tradition. Here it is necessary for us to identify the concept of dialectic and take a brief look at its history. Only in this way, it will be possible for us to interpret Marx's dialectic thought on the basis of practical philosophy view.

Essence of Dialectic

"Empirical" misinterpretations on dialectic

Same as "materialism", dialectic is also a concept common but quite complex for most people. As Chen Kang said, dialectic "as a philosophical term didn't have a common meaning and was given different meanings when it was employed by different philosophers throughout the history of philosophy".[1] We can generally observe many people employing the concept of dialectic ad arbitrium. Likewise, people may praise and derogate it ad arbitrium, too. Perhaps, among all philosophical terms, none more frequently receives alternative glory and on the other side faces humiliation as "dialectic" does. Dialectic has gained a respect as a way of thinking or a way to accelerate the birth of truth in a time, but due to the discovery of paradox and the prevalence of sophistry, dialectic gradually became a pronoun of confusion or absurdity of thought. People living in our times and cultural atmosphere can hardly imagine or answer why people used the concept of dialectic to describe the absurdity and confusion of a thought, but on the contrary such a thing was praised and applied in the long history. It was even applied in Kantian philosophy. When Kant called the "antinomy" of reason resulting from the misuse of intellectuality beyond the possible experiential scope as "dialectic" or "logic of illusion", he had used this term in a derogatory sense.[2] However, since Hegel, the fate of dialectic had encountered a dramatic turn. In Hegelian philosophy, and particularly in the succeeding Marxist philosophical tradition, dialectic was given a completely positive meaning. It would be a great honor if a philosopher, home or abroad, in the ancient or today, known as a dialectician. In order to recognize the contribution of some accomplished scientists, they might be eulogized to "unconsciously apply dialectic" or "have a tendency of spontaneous dialectic thought" even if they in fact don't know what dialectic is or they explicitly disapprove it. The word "dialectic" has acquired so powerful magic in language that nearly every thought, would like to elevate itself with the help of "dialectic". These facts perhaps indeed imply that dialectic faces a risk of falling back to the opposite. Some people's sophistic conduct under the disguise of dialectic is even present a more alarming blow at dialectic. Considering that dialectic has been quite abused and has partly lost from its reputation, we first suggest to elaborate the real connotation of the term and "distinguish" its essence from many thoroughly different usages from the standpoint of Marx's modern practical philosophy.

---

1 Chen Kang: Discussion on Greek Philosophy, p.193.
2 [German] Kant: Critique of Pure Reason, p.242, Beijing, Commercial Press, 1960.

Among the above various kinds of misuse of dialectic, we observe generally two major forms: one is to integrate the external form of dialectic with daily experience, thus obtaining a "universal" but quite meaningless statements on things; the other is to apply it on the basis of formal logic, thus suggesting that dialectic is a logical contradiction. The former use assembles everything under the name of dialectic, while the latter deems dialectic useless. Although these two result are in remarkably different attitudes towards dialectic, they are quite similar in essence: i.e.: attempting to apply or "verify" it in the experiential sphere. It seems that the misunderstanding on dialectic also has a "dialectic" nature. Here the example of Karl Popper is enough to explain this issue. In his *Conjectures and Refutations*, Popper wrote:

> The vagueness of dialectic is another of its dangers. It makes it only too easy to force a dialectic interpretation an all sorts of developments and even a quite different thing. We find, for instance, a dialectic interpretation which identifies a seed of corn with a thesis, the plant which develops from this seed with the antithesis, and all the seeds which develop from this plant with the synthesis. That such an application expands the already too vague meaning of the dialectic triad in a way which dangerously increases its vagueness is obvious; it leads to a point where by describing development as dialectic we convey no more than by saying that it is a development in stages – which is not saying very much. But to interpret this development by saying that germination of the plant is the negation of the seed because the seed ceases to exist when the plant begins to grow, and that the production of a lot of new seeds by the plant is the negation of the negation – a new start at a higher level – is obviously a mere playing with words. (Is this the reason why Engels said of this example that any child can understand it?)[1]

No doubt, Popper opposes the vulgar understanding on dialectic, but his criticism on dialectic is on the premise of accepting this understanding. Karl Popper's default premise is that "science" should be applied to experiential sphere and should be able to be falsified by experience. The inevitable result is that "dialectic" can be "verified" by anything, but can't be "falsified", so dialectic is a vague and rather elastic theory. No doubt, it is very effective to use Popper's above theory to refute the generalized

---

1 [British] Karl Popper: Conjectures and Refutations, 460, Shanghai, Shanghai Translation Publishing House, 1986.

and vulgarized "dialectic", but this refutation didn't spur Popper to explore the original meaning of the concept of dialectic. We may say he has negated dialectic almost in haste. Obviously, Popper was directly inspired by Kant. In the sense of Kant, dialectic is used in a negatory sense. He calls dialectic an unavoidable contradiction generated when intellectuality attempts to apply "thing-in-self" outside its valid scope, i.e.: "logic of illusion" or "logic of falsehood". The feature of this contradiction is that "the thesis, as well as the antithesis, can be shown by equally clear, evident, and irresistible proofs", and "all these proofs are correct", "reason therefore is divided with itself, a state at which the skeptic thinker rejoices, but which must make the critical philosopher pause and feel ill at ease".[1] Therefore, Kant thinks dialectic should be avoided by philosophers. The way to avoid it is critique, i.e.: to strictly limit intellectuality within the scope of experience. However, Popper and Kant show essential difference over this issue: the former tries to accept and inspect dialectic as a theory of empirical science, while the Kant clearly points out that dialectic doesn't belong to empirical sphere; the former denies the existence of metaphysics outside empirical sphere, while the latter gives a positive conclusion on it, "that the human mind will ever give up metaphysical researches is as little to be expected as that we should prefer to give up breathing altogether, to avoid inhaling impure air".[2] In fact, Hegel thinks Kant's contribution to dialectic is tremendous, because Kant's "antinomy" reveals the finity of the concept of intellectuality. It appears that Popper only unilaterally absorbed Kant's view on this issue and that he considers dialectic an empirical theory which goes against the tradition of dialectic. In fact, dialectic has the nature of metaphysics since the very beginning, while at the level of daily experience, it is impossible to generate the issue of dialectic and dialectic is not used, either.

---

1 [German] Kant: Prolegomena to Any Future Metaphysics, p.122~123.
2 The same book as above, p.163.

Inquire the essence of the most typical dialecticians in history

Then, how to understand the dialectic which has a sense of metaphysics? Firstly we must take a look at the views of important "dialecticians" in the history. If the result of Popper's intentional confusion of the valid scope of dialectic and empirical science is simple negation only, then Kant at least left some space for positive dialectic. Just as Gadamer said:

> Kant's successors, Johann Fichte, Schelling and Friedrich Schleiermacher (and Hegel) accepted in their own philosophies Kant's testimony that reason will inevitably lead to self-contradiction, but contrary to Kant, they gave a positive comment on it. From this self-contradiction, they saw the special power of reason, which may transcend the ideological limit unable to surpass the level of intellectuality. They were aware of the classical nature of dialectic.[1]

This indicates the common point of early-modern dialecticians about the concept of dialectic is evaluated as the transcendence to intellectuality, i.e.: the transcendence of finite empirical sphere. This concept was summarized by Hegel: dialectic is inherently transcendence, and due to the process of this inherent transcendence, the original feature of one-sidedness and finity of intellectuality, i.e.: the self negation of the concept of intellectuality was revealed. All finite things discard themselves.[2] Without doubt, all dialecticians in early modern times brought dialectic into the sphere of "reason". In the sense of Hegel, it is an internal deduction from a pure logical definition to another. Here we should avoid a possible misunderstanding – dialectic is the transcendence to finite empirical sphere, i.e.: a formal system similar to geometry. In fact, it is exactly what the dialectic in early modern times had particularly opposed. Kant thinks both mathematics and geometry are sciences studying "perceptual" world and have objective reality only when sensory object is involved;[3] Hegel thinks the difference of dialectic from geometric models and the pure instrumental deduction of formal logic is the key to conceive the real meaning of Hegelian logic. Dialectic by no means is an empty form (it

---

1 [German] Gadamer: Gadamer on Hegel, p.1, Beijing, Guangming Daily Press, 1992.

2 [German] Hegel: The Logic of Hegel, p.176.

3 [German] Kant: Prolegomena to Any Future Metaphysics, p.47.

is the key to Popper's misunderstanding, because he understood dialectic as an empty "ternary form") and it itself is "content". Hegel conceives dialectic as a science studying pure idea. The idea here is not "formal" thinking of course but the specific stipulations of thinking and the totality developed from laws. The laws and stipulations are endowed by thinking itself and are absolutely not any existent external thing.[1] Therefore, strictly speaking, Hegelian dialectic is not a science which can separate itself from its object. We would rather say it is the laws and stipulations of pure idea and the display of the necessary process of idea movement.

Obviously, the key of the stipulations of dialecticians in early modern times, particularly Hegel on dialectic is pure thinking or pure idea. This sphere corresponds to sensibility and intellectuality and is the direct negation of intellectual sphere. This negation is to transcend the finity of intellectual sphere and reach infinity, or seek the bridge between finity and infinity. Now the question is: is it the essence of dialectic or the original meaning of the concept of dialectic, or the whole meaning of the concept of dialectic? If we do not look at early-modern age philosophy only, we will see without difficulty that not only this dialectic is unacceptable for modern philosophy but also it is improper to apply it to ancient philosophy. Although Hegel claims his dialectic demonstrates a complete and logical necessity, from today's point of view this necessity is not all unconditional. In fact, the guarantee of this absolute necessity, also the premise of his entire logic, is "self-consciousness", while this is exactly the theme of Phenomenology of Spirit. As Martin Heidegger put it, Hegelian dialectic is the generation process of the subjectivity of absolute subject and also the process of the necessary conducts of absolute subject.[2] Above we have indicated this self-consciousness and subjectivity are the products of early-modern philosophy, so we may affirm that although Hegel also emphasizes that his logic is derived from ancient dialectic, obviously this dialectic concept of "subjectivity" cannot be directly applied to ancient dialecticians. Nevertheless, the inheritance re-

---

1 [German] Hegel: The Logic of Hegel, p.63.
2 [German] Martin Heidegger: Wegmarken, (Marks of the Road) p.506.

lationship between Hegelian dialectic and ancient Greek dialectic is undeniable, then what are their common points? This without doubt is another critical issue for our understanding on the essence of dialectic.

Hegel said: dialectic is not new in philosophy. In ancient times, Plato was called the inventor of dialectic, because dialectic first appeared in Platonic philosophy in form of free science – objective form. In this sense, the above sentence is correct.[1] In Lectures on the History of Philosophy, Hegel also calls Zeno a founder of dialectic: "He (Zeno) is the master of the Eleatic school in whom its pure thought arrives at the movement of the Notion in itself and becomes the pure soul of science, - he is the founder of dialectic."[2] The two should not be contradictory, because Hegel separately stressed the movement of pure Notion generated in Zeno and the objective form of this movement obtained in Plato. However, here we must pay constant attention to Hegel's starting point, i.e. the fundamental starting point of early-modern philosophy – subjective spirit. The objectivity of Platonic dialectic in the sense of Hegel is absolutely not the objectivity commonly conceived by us. We would rather say it is the objectivity in the sense of Kant, i.e.: universal validity. In the sense of early-modern age idealism, this universal thing is the product of thinking - thought. Since the product of thinking activity is universal, thought may be called a universal substance. From the perspective that thinking is regarded as a subject –able to think, the shortened form of the subject able to think is me.[3] Apparently, the subjectivity of this pure thought is inapplicable to Zeno. Hegel had said Platonic dialectic exposed the finity of "intellectual stipulation". This saying is inaccurate, because intellectuality is a typical concept of early-modern age philosophy. In fact, concepts in Plato and Zeno are "being-in-itself"; in comparison, if these concepts are added with subjective elements, certainly they will be considered subjective and uncertain. In this way, we discover the two different "metaphysical" natures of dialectic. One is the subjectivity of early-modern philosophy and the other is substantialism in ancient philosophy. Of course,- dialectic- no matter what nature category it has, it is always far from perceptual experience.

---

1 German] Hegel: The Logic of Hegel, p.178.
2 [German] Hegel: Lectures on the History of Philosophy, Vol.1, p.272.
3 [German] Hegel: The Logic of Hegel, p.68.

By now we discover an important divergence between early-modern dialecticians and ancient dialecticians. The revelation of this divergence aims to indicate that it is improper for us to adopt a historical concept of dialectic no matter what it is. However, after we make clear this divergence, we may get to know their common points and get closer to the essence of dialectic. We can find without difficulty that the most obvious common point between ancient dialectic and early-modern age dialectic is the transcendence and run-through of various kinds of finite stipulations. The finite stipulations are transferred and enter their opposites. In the end, they are no longer isolated and still and become flowing. The revelation on this movement is essentially the enunciation of a kind of absolute essence. In Plato, dialectic rests with the mutual relations between idea and idea, while the unified totality of the ideas linked by these relations is the ultimate essence of the world. Hegel thinks that in Plato, he did not find the full consciousness on this nature of dialectic, but he did find out such dialectic.[1] In comparison, Hegelian dialectic is fully conscious. The ultimate essence revealed by Hegelian dialectic is absolute idea, i.e.: a comprehensive truth which includes the stipulations of all previous finite concepts.

Both Platonic dialectic and Hegelian dialectic regard a "rich" unity as their ultimate goal. Here we find another motion. It is not the motion of some concepts but the motion of "cognition" from abstract to concrete. If we put aside the difference between the subjectivity and substantialism of early-modern and ancient dialecticians, this motion will become even more obvious. Interestingly, the development of dialectic experienced a similar process in these two eras, i.e.: from finite stipulations and the contradictions generated by them (this contradiction is typically manifested as a paradox) to the sublation of this contradiction and the transcendence to the finite stipulations. In this development process, the relation between Zeno and Plato is similar to that between Kant and Hegel. It appears that the investigation on the essence of dialectic should not be limited to Plato, Hegel and other most typical dialecticians, because obviously dialectic emerged to address some "issues"

---

1 [German] Hegel: Lectures on the History of Philosophy, Vol.2, p.200.

and to our discussion here, these "issues" are particularly crucial. We may say the mature state of the accepted dialectic has been embodied in these "issues" (finite stipulations and their paradoxes). Plato's criticism at Eleatics and Hegel's emphasis on Kant have disclosed the "kinship" between dialectic and specific paradoxes.

In view of form, Zeno and Kant's famous paradoxes both belong to the paradoxes involving infinity or comprehensiveness.[1] In the beginning, the purpose of Zeno's paradoxes is to defend the doctrine of Parmenides, so these paradoxes are ultimately manifested as the self-contradiction of the viewpoints that proposes "all" is "many", thus arriving at Parmenides' proposition that "all is one". We may say, initially dialectic was used as a technique to attack opponents, so this dialectic was negative. But the positive significance of Zeno's paradox is that it reveals the possibility for the communication between finite stipulations and is realized from one direction, i.e.: "many" may lead to "one". If we say Zeno's dialectic is unilateral only, then we see the reverse motion -- from "one" to "many" also becomes possible in Plato's Parmenides. Therefore, Hegel said Eleatic proposition essentially was the same as that of sophism. Here "one" and "many" are two finite stipulations which concern the fundamental issue of ancient philosophy. However, no matter where the foothold is set, this issue was still unable to be solved.[2] Similar condition is seen in Kant: Kant had listed four groups of antinomies. In fact, he listed four groups of mutually opposite finite stipulations. The two parties in opposition can both be "effectively" proved, while the effectiveness of the proving of one party means the ineffectiveness of the other party. Kant's conclusion is negative, too. He thinks this dialectic is the "false image" created by illegal use of intellectuality, so it should be avoided. However, in Hegel, it obtains a kind of positive significance and these stipulations are unified.

---

1 Distinguish from "semantical" paradox (such as: liar paradox) and self-reference paradox. But due to the subjectivity nature of Kantian philosophy, his "antinomy" also has a feature of self-reference paradox.

2 However, as indicated above, every theoretical philosophy must have an ultimate foothold, so neither Zeno nor Plato had followed this 'dialectic" principle.

For the moment we do not discuss whether Plato and Hegel's unification here is the real solution to the problem. The critical issue here is how to understand these finite stipulations at first. In Plato, they are understood as uncaused ideas, while Hegel conceives them as the result of pure thinking. Today, obviously we cannot accept such understandings, because these understandings proceed from the standpoints of respective theoretical philosophies. If we do not only look at theoretical philosophy when we think over this issue, we will see without difficulty that the finite stipulations stand for specific theoretical visual angles – of course the different theoretical visual angles for the solution of ontological issues. The forms of these visual angles are can be matched with the philosophical paradigms in their times: In ancient times, Eleatics and Sophism represented the two extremes of ontology; while the antinomy revealed by Kant aims to indicate the "world" as a whole is not experienced by us, so it is not the effective range stipulated by intellectuality and Kant warns that the attempt of choosing these finite stipulations to solve metaphysical issues is doomed to failure. The theoretical visual angles represented by various kinds of finite stipulations have already existed. The task of dialectic is to transcend them and bring them into a richer and more comprehensive and thus infinite system. The consequence of this transcendence is typically reflected in Platonic philosophy and Hegelian philosophy.

Is this transcendence the solution to the issue or does this transcendence result in real richness and concretion? In fact, our above analysis has contained the answer. Owing to the finity and abstractness of theory, it is impossible for a theoretical philosophy to realize real concretion and richness. Although Platonic dialectic and Hegelian dialectic both have sublated the contradiction of previous abstract stipulations to some extent, this sublation is realized by another abstract stipulation. Although idea (universal) or absolute spirit may include the multiple visual angles of previous theories, it itself is a single theoretical visual angle. The abstractness and finity of this single visual angle cannot be sublated by Platonic dialectic and Hegelian dialectic. It seems that the situation is: dialectic aims to sublate finite stipulations and thus achieve infinity and concretion, but this infinity is still an abstract stipulation, so it is also a finite stipulation -the situation similar to Zeno and Kant's reappears. By now it seems that we only obtain a negative conclusion- dialectic ultimately will be applied to itself and the consequence is self negation. Nevertheless, just like Zeno and Kant' s paradoxes imply the opening of a possibility for the generation of a kind of dialectic, the contradiction here by no means only indicates the "non-dialecticality" of the most typical dialecticians in the history. It also provides a possibility for our understanding on the essence of dialectic and thus acquiring a higher form of dialectic.

As Hegel put it, Platonic dialectic is not self-conscious, so he did not analyze why the finite stipulations are finite; Hegel's answer to this question is obviously influenced by Kant, i.e.: define it as an intellectual concept. The finity and abstraction of intellectuality are relative to reason. Now we know even Hegel's reason is finite, too, because theory is finite fundamentally. Since the root cause for our affirmation of these finities is the finite theoretical visual angle, then the transcendence and sublation of these finities will certainly be the transcendence and sublation of theory per se. Hence our standpoint of practical philosophy becomes evident, because the result of transcending the finity of theory is practice. Above we have indicated all theoretical activities regarded practice as background, and their abstractness and finity are relative to the concretion and "infinity" of practice. By now the concept of dialectic we have discussed has exceeded the meaning given by Plato and Hegel, or in other words, we have "dialectically" reviewed previous dialectic. In Plato and Hegel, dialectic is manifested as a motion from abstract and finite concept to more concrete and a richer concept. Now we see this motion in fact is only a part of another motion in a broader sense, i.e.: a part of the motion from the abstractness of theory to the concreteness of practice. Therefore, we say practice is the essence and truth of theory, and theory in the end will go to practice to realize the unity of theory and practice. Through analyzing the most typical dialecticians in history, no doubt we have touched the essence of dialectic. Logically speaking, it is an inevitable result of applying previous dialecticians' principles to themselves.

In the real history of philosophy, it is reflected as the result produced after Hegelian theoretical dialectic was transcended. Marx and the modern dialecticians after him all use dialectic in this sense. Here in this book we call it practical dialectic.

Dialectic as a process from abstraction to concretion

Understanding dialectic as a process from the abstractness of theory to the concreteness of practice can be considered as a kind of negation to traditional dialectic, particularly the "affirmative" nature of Hegelian dialectic, because the ultimate goal of dialectic within the scope of theory is to obtain a fixed viewpoint and try to solve problems for good and all. As indicated above, practice absolutely cannot be regarded as a "theoretical" conclusion. In both Hegel and Plato, dialectic serves for an ultimate theoretical conclusion. Hegel thinks that in the sense of Plato, a real thing is a kind of unity, for example: the unity of 'one' and 'many', and 'being' and 'nonbeing'.[1] Hegel regards this as a "model", too. He also thinks that, idea is the truth of thing-in-itself and thing-for-itself [2] and idea includes all relations with intellectuality.[3] If practice is considered as the direction of dialectic motion, then the ultimate result of dialectic will not only be transcendence of finite stipulations or finite categories and more importantly, it will be transcendence of theory. In this way, for theory, dialectic seems purely negative.

This involves the understanding on "negation", this oldest feature of dialectic. In Zeno and Kant's famous paradoxes, dialectic shows its unique negative feature. This negativity can be either a means to attack opponents or a method to break theoretical bigotry. The prominence of this negativity may often cover the "affirmative" result of dialectic. Aristotle conceives dialectic in a completely negatory sense. He thinks "philosophy differs from dialectic in the nature of the faculty", "dialectic is merely

---

1 [German] Hegel: Lectures on the History of Philosophy, Vol.2, p. 207.
2 [German] Hegel: The Logic of Hegel, p.397.
3 The same book as above, p. 400.

critical where philosophy claims to know".[1] The separation between dialectic and "knowledge" has reappeared in Kant, but interestingly, not only Kant was considered by later generations to have made imperishable contribution to dialectic (such as: by Hegel) but also Aristotle was "admitted posthumously as a "dialectician" (such as: by Gadamer). This not only indicates that their thoughts bear the feature of dialectic but also explains that the positivity of dialectic always plays its effect – though often in a "negatory" way. The two aspects are consciously unified by Hegel. In the Hegelian dialectic system, negation is considered the source of all movements, thus it is inseparable from subjectivity and even it is identical to subjectivity. In Phenomenology of Spirit, Hegel had pointed out: "The key of all issues is: Everything turns on grasping and expressing the True, not only as substance, but equally as subject. This substance is, as subject, pure, simple negativity, and is for this very reason the bifurcation of the simple; it is the doubling which sets up opposition, and then again the negation of this indifferent diversity and of its antithesis."[2] It can be seen that, in Hegel, subjectivity and negativity have equal significance. The identity between negativity and subjectivity, on the one hand, finds a "basis" for the negativity of dialectic, thus making it get rid of the pure "destruction" as commonly understood; on the other hand, it also finds an end point of theory for negativity, which is the absolute spirit as the negation of negation.

Adorno has criticized it: To equate the negation of negation with positivity is the quintessence of identification […] in Hegel, what thus wins out in the inmost core of dialectic is the anti-dialectical principle.[3] Generally speaking, negation implies difference, while positivity implies unity. However, in Hegel, once dialectic is linked with subjectivity, inevitably it will regard the unity of subject as its end point and as a "means" to achieve this ultimate positivity. As Adorno put it: as the negatory power of the movement of every single concept and its whole

---

1 [Ancient Greek] Aristotle: Metaphysics, p.62.

2 Deng Xiaomang: Tension of Speculation, p.179, Changsha, Hunan Education Publishing House, 1992.

3 [German] Adorno: Negative Dialectic, p.156, Chongqing, Chongqing Publishing House, 1993

process.[1] Adorno has grasped the negatory factors of dialectic and put forth a "negative dialectic" which is the perpetually consistent consciousness on non-identity and does not take a stance in advance.[2] Adorno's negatory stress on dialectic essentially is the negation of any fixed theoretical standpoint, but if we are not limited to the scope of theory, we will discover without difficulty this negative dialectic is not totally negative, and it may have a positive result, which is the opening of the visual sphere of practice. Indeed, only practice cannot be systemized by the logic of any theory and is the real "heterogeneous experience". Therefore, we may say that "negative dialectic" is a part of practical dialectic.[3] This is consistent with Marx's spirit of criticizing and reversing Hegelian dialectic.

Gadamer's "hermeneutic" dialectic expresses the same idea in a different way. Through illustration of the dialecticians in the history – classical dialecticians in particular, Gadamer tries to discover the most primitive particularity of dialectic. He thinks dialogue is the most essential characteristic of dialectic. During dialogue, questions enjoy priority over all cognitions and conversations which reveal the significance of things, and a conversation which should reveal a thing needs to open this thing through question.[4] Under such an understanding, dialectic essentially possesses a kind of negatory significance: it does not cater for a question per se, but seeks a standpoint that affirms and negates the question, i.e.: its stance is not to gradually approach the question and explain it through a fixed view but to develop various explanations on this question in various directions and in contradiction. It meets things during such explanation. The aim of dialectic is not to form a fixed theoretical view but to achieve more fundamental cognition over the question.[5] In this way, Gadamer achieved a concept of dialectic that is completely different from

---

1　[German] Adorno: Negative Dialectic, p.5.
2　he same book as above, p.3.
3　Zhang Yibing has also has expressed similar view, but he lays main stress on the correspondence between thought and labor process and "negative dialectic originates from revolutionary practical dialectic"(Zhang Yibing: Modeless Dialectic Imagination, p.101, Beijing, Sanlian Bookstore, 2001).
4　German] Gadamer: Truth and Method, Vol.1, p.446, Shanghai, Shanghai Translation Publishing House, 1999.
5　Zhang Rulun: History and Practice, p.329.

the tradition – particularly early-modern philosophy. His concept coincides with Marxist practical dialectic. The necessity of dialogue originates from the finity of the stance and visual angle of dialogists, while the aim of the dialogue is not to stick to another similar stance; if a dialogue does not stop at an abstract theoretical stance, certainly what it opens is a practical sphere. At this point, it is not difficult to understand why Gadamer deems his hermeneutics as a practical philosophy.

In addition, if we say theory is a kind of human activity, this process is essentially also the return of theory to practice. The driving force of this return is the difference and tension between the abstractness of theory and the concreteness of practice. We say the practice as a whole is a concrete totality, but this concreteness is formed by various kinds of abstract activities. Above we have indicated that the structure of theory has embodied the differentiation and separation between subject and object (this is also the condition for the generation of subjectivity), while this separation results in the uni-directivity of theoretical "perspective" and the unicity(singleness) of its "visual angle". Therefore, finity and abstractness are the "pre-destinations" of theoretical activity. In fact, it is not only the "pre-destination of theoretical activity. Human's objective activity universally possesses this finity. The premise of human's objective activity firstly is to differentiate itself from circumstances, while this differentiation means that man has to face the world by setting foothold at a specific angle and act upon the world according to its own "standards" to some extent. The role of these "standards" is to simplify the world and thus make it easily comprehended – this means an abstracting capacity and also the abstraction of human capacity. In this way, the isomorphism among various kinds of human's specific activities will become easily understandable.[1] However, it is exactly these numerous abstract activities that constitute the concreteness of practice. Therefore, we say practice itself is "dialectic", and the "prototype" of dialectic practice as often called by us also bears this meaning.

---

1 In fact, the tools in productive activities, the vocabulary in linguistic activities and the concepts in thinking activities all can be considered abstract factors of human activities. Men always act upon the world through these activities, otherwise human activities will become unimaginable. For details, please refer to Section 2 of this chapter.

However, the dialectic we refer to here is only a theoretical activity. That is to say, we conceive dialectic as a process in which theory as a kind of abstract activity keeps overcoming itself and goes towards practice. Obviously, such a concept of dialectic has a great difference from the understanding of the dialecticians in ancient and early modern times and the understanding of "Marxism". Above we have indicated the concept of dialectic is only a specific stage or aspect of the process in which theory sublates its abstractness and finity, so this difference does not mean there is no common point among different understandings, but for the convenience of the subsequent discussion, here we must highlight the formal difference between our concept of dialectic and the previous concept of dialectic.

Firstly, it is the extension of this concept. Usually people have two tendencies: one is to regard the affirmation of any "movement" or "contradiction" as dialectic, thus generalizing this concept. The other is to emphasize the "purity" of dialectic and think only the one in pure thinking sphere is dialectic, thus only the philosophies of the people like Plato and Hegel become real dialectics. If we conceive dialectic as the process in which theory moves towards practice, then anything that involves the "boundary" of theoretical visual angle can be called dialectic. That is to say, dialectic has existed before the universally accepted "founder" of dialectic – Plato, Zeno or Aristotle. Disclosing the "boundary" of theory took place simultaneously with contradiction and dialogue, so we may say all philosophies possess the nature of dialectic, and the metaphysical nature of philosophy and the metaphysical nature of dialectic are connected. The process in which theory moves towards practical dialectic can be reflected in two different ways. One is to bring contradiction into a theory and realize "dialogue" in a theoretical system; the other is that contradiction is reflected between different theoretical systems, and dialogue happens between theories. The former as dialectic generally will not have much doubt, because the dialecticians which we usually call have adopted this way; while the latter is a dialectic process without extensive awareness. In this way we can obtain a concept of dialectic in a broader sense, which includes the concept of dialectic in previous theoretical philosophy and meanwhile avoid it being vulgarized into common sense known to all.

Secondly, it is the goal of dialectic. In the past we have either conceived dialectic as a set of complex "viewpoints" or conceived it as a process in which contradictions are synthesized in order to reach a "viewpoint", but if dialectic is conceived as a process in which theory moves towards practice, this ultimate viewpoint will become impossible, because practice by no means is a "viewpoint". Therefore, ultimately dialectic will not reach a "theoretical" goal. We would rather say that dialectic is the transcendence of the theoretical sphere. It is not difficult to imagine that the realization of its goal for dialectic is the sublation of the abstractness of theory and also is the self-decomposition of theory. Therefore, we may say, dialectic itself is not a "view of world" but a process in which various world views sublate and transcend themselves; and the goal of dialectic and the place where dialectic is completed is practice.

Various kinds of abstract dialectics

Emergence of dialectic and the earliest dialectic

Dialectic essentially aims the concreteness of practice, but not all dialecticians are conscious of it. In fact, all the dialecticians before Marx were unconscious of it, their dialectics are the dialectics within the scope of theory and their aim is to achieve an ultimate theoretical view. Therefore, this kind of dialectic is not thorough and complete. It is an abstract dialectic. Its abstractness stems from the abstractness of theory. Dialectic itself can be considered a negatory factor of theoretical activity, so abstract dialectic is the immature and unfinished state of dialectic. Corresponding to the two theoretical philosophies we discuss above, we classify abstract dialectic into two categories, namely: ancient dialectic and early-modern dialectic.

Without doubt, the discussion of ancient dialectic must first involve the question: what is the earliest dialectic? The answer varies with the definition of dialectic. Hegel regards dialectic as the knowledge studying pure thought and the transcendence to intellectuality, so naturally he thinks Zeno is the founder of dialectic. This dialectic was "objectified" by Heraclitus and appeared for the first time in the "form of free science" in Plato.[1] Based on Hegel's assertion that dialectic is knowledge studying pure thought, some critics think the founder of dialectic is Parmenides, because Parmenides is the first person who realized "pure" thought.[2] Generally speaking, Marxists used not to accept Hegel's definition on dialectic. Instead, they studied the history of dialectic according to classic Marxists' definition on dialectic. Engels thinks dialectic is a science about the universal law of the movement and development of nature, human society and thinking, and ancient Greek philosophers are all born spontaneous dialecticians.[3] Lenin thinks dialectic is the doctrine of the identity of opposites – how they can be and how they become identical, transforming one into another – why the mind of man must not take these opposites for dead, blocked, but for living, conditioned, mobile, transforming one into the other.[4] If dialectic is a doctrine exploring the general law of the world, then the founder of dialectic should be neither Zeno nor Parmenides, and we should trace back to the beginning of philosophy - Thales.

No doubt, the previous Marxist exploration has opposed Hegel's narrow concept of dialectic, extended the concept of dialectic and is positive. But here comes a problem – the unity between this concept of dialectic and ancient Greek's understanding on dialectic. The word "dialectic" (dielektikee) initially was not a philosophical term in ancient Greece. It had joined the family of philosophy even later than logos. According to Diogenes Laertios' record, the first person who was called a dialectician is Zeno. Aristotle also thinks so.[5] Later Socrates and Plato both used dialectic in the sense of Zeno. The dialectic in the sense of Zeno obviously

---

1 [German] Hegel: The Logic of Hegel, p.178; [German] Hegel: Lectures on the History of Philosophy, Vol.1, p.272~371.

2 Xie Xialing: Parmenides: Founder of Dialectic, published in Research of Philosophy, 1987(1)

3 Marx & Engels Selected Works, Edition 2, Vol.3, p.358.

4 Lenin Collected Works, Chinese Edition 2, Vol.19, p.2, Beijing, People's Publishing House, 1989.

5 [Russian] М.А.Дынника et al: History of Ancient Dialectic, p.24, Beijing, People's Publishing House, 1986.

is not the dialectic which probes into the law of the world. The solution to this issue in History of Ancient Dialectic compiled by the Philosophy Institute of Soviet Academy of Sciences is representative. In the book, dialectic is divided into two forms:

> (1) Positive dialectic, i.e.: the demonstration and research on some dialectic regularities in natural, social or thinking sphere;

> (2) Negative dialectic, i.e.: negating the truth of the things which reveal their own internal contradictoriness.[1]

The author of this book thinks that positive dialectic was spontaneously generated by the natural philosophers of Melisian school, but it took the clearest form till Heraclitus; whereas negative dialectic took its clearest form in Eleatic school. This handling is essentially to equate positive dialectic with philosophy, and meanwhile conceives negative dialectic as a method to explore philosophical issues. Initially, these two forms are separated. Only because the art of debating, revealing and proving truth is becoming an ability which can conceive things from object's inherent opposite stipulations, reduce these stipulations into a unity and see the unity of opposites. Thus as the author writes: it becomes a dialectic method by which people cognize nature, society and thought,[2] and these two forms were integrated. However if it is so, the two forms of dialectic will essentially become the relation between a doctrine and the method adopted by this doctrine. What is more, no evidence shows that this method must be adopted. Therefore, although the Soviet author has claimed that since the era of Socrates, philosophers often developed dialectic from these two meanings. Undeniably, the concept of dialectic is extended by him, i.e.: Engels and Lenin's concept of dialectic the author had cited as a basis cannot incorporate the traditional concept of dialectic, at least it cannot indicate any immanent and necessary relation between these two types of dialectic. Thus we may say, there is always something between the dialectic as understood by us today and the dialectic in the tradition of Western philosophy, ancient Greek philosophy

---

1 The same book as above, p.24.
2 The same book as above, p.24.

in particular, and it is certainly improper to use such a concept of dialectic to discuss the history of dialectic.

Obviously, the failure of the above idea essentially stems from the mutually heterogeneous state between the exploration of the world and the negativity of dialectic, and stems from author's failure to indicate the necessary relation between the negativity of dialectic and this exploration. Even if the two can be combined sometimes, this combination is extrinsic. This no doubt has to do with the predefined concept of dialectic. Both Lenin and Engels define dialectic as exploration of laws, while the basis of this exploration is the objective state of these laws. This approach in fact defines dialectic as a "viewpoint", which can be directly "seen". In this way, even if it is admitted that the law of dialectic has some contradictory elements, they are limited to the positivity of direct "seeing", whereas the negative meaning of this "seeing" is completely ignored. Under the premise of such a concept, the mutually extrinsic state between the two types of dialectic will be easily understood, and it seems that tracing the origin of dialectic back to Melisian school will also become an "illegal" extension.

The key to transcend the failure of this idea is to reveal the contradictoriness and negativity of the "seeing" and indicate it is related to the essence of negative dialectic due to this contradictoriness. Apparently, we have to return to the concept of dialectic we have defined above. Above we have indicated dialectic is essentially a process in which theory transcends its finity and abstractness and moves toward the concreteness of practice. This finity is the "predestination" inherent in the essence of theoretical activity. Due to this "predestination", contradiction will be inevitably generated among different theoretical visual angles. This is the essence of all dialectic contradictions. In this way, negativity is included into the concept of dialectic in an even broader sense. It will become reasonable to study the dialectic before Eleatic school by setting foothold at this concept of dialectic, because although early natural philosophers were unconscious of dialectic contradictions and it was impossible for them to reflect these contradictions in their theories as Zeno did, the contradictions have been embodied in the finity of their theories. We may even say their theoretical activities were unconsciously driven by these contradictions. Since the very beginning, philosophy has touched the "boundary" of theoretical activities. We have indicated above that it can be called dialectic as long as it touches the "boundary" of theoretical activities.

When man attempted for the first time to look at the whole world from a specific angle and give a unified interpretation on the world, he created a new mode of theoretical activity. The object of this theoretical activity is not a specific thing but the whole world. From today's point of view, man is inside this world, so what he can see cannot be the whole world. However, it seems that it is not a problem for ancient people, because man was not conceived as a subject, but they were puzzled by another question: under what principle can the world be interpreted in a unified way? In the sense of ancient Greek, this question can be expressed as the issue of the unified essence behind the complicated phenomena and also the issue of the contradiction between "one" and "many". Strictly speaking, this contradiction initially is not the contradiction between different theoretical visual angles as we usually refer to, because "many" does not form a theoretical visual angle here; we would rather say this contradiction is the contradiction between theory and pre-theory state or common sense phase. Even from this initial contradiction, we may clearly see the finity of theory. This finity was initially manifested as the fact that early natural philosophers could not find out the "archee" of all things – the world.

From Thales' famous proposition "water is the origin of all things", we see the earliest manifestation of the contradiction between "one" and "many". "Water" is a visual angle Thales adopted in order to interpret the world. This visual angle can only be "one", while "all things" opposite to it is undoubtedly "many". Noticeably, the "water" here is also one of the "all things", but here it obtains a special position for interpreting other things. We may say this is almost the common characteristic of all early philosophers, i.e.: the intuitive characteristic. This has to do with the thinking level of the people in that time. It was the period in which human society was moving from barbarism to civilization and people's thinking was being transferred from representative thinking or pre-logical thinking to conceptual thinking or logical thinking. In that period, human's thinking had possessed the ability of abstraction, but this ability was still very low, far from the level of pure logical thinking, so when thinking, general and particular were still entangled. General things are completely beyond representation of sensibility and cannot be perceived by sense and can be grasped only through thinking, but in this stage of human thinking, they could only be expressed through representation of sensibility. Therefore, although Hegel considered Thales's "water" was a thing with pure universality or general flowability,[1] in a sense of alleged exaggeration, just as Deng Xiaomang said:

> Due to the "flowability", water may permeate and dissolve the perceptual particularities of many tangible special things, while it itself remains unchanged. This is consistent with the universality of concept. Water does not have color, odor and fixed shape and is very simple in perceptual particularity. This feature is close to the abstractness of concept, too.[2]

In this sense, it is inevitable that the people in this thinking stage chose a concrete thing as the archee to interpret the world, but the thing chosen is accidental to a large extent, because it is highly subjective to interpret the world with a concrete thing, and the situation varies with people and is affected by the natural environment and social environment where people live.

In fact, after Thales, natural philosophers also chose other matters as the archee of the world, for example, Anaximander's "Apeiron", i.e.: "infinite" or formless thing", Anaximenes' "gas", Heraclitus' "fire", Empedocles' "four elements" and Anaxagoras' "seed". Without question, a natural philosopher chooses a thing as the principle to interpret the world all because they think this thing has more explanatory power. However, this explanatory power is rather limited. As indicated by us when we discuss ancient materialism, natural philosophers explain the nature only

---

1 [German] Hegel: Lectures on the History of Philosophy, Vol.1, p.184.
2 Deng Xiaomang: Tension of Speculation, p.13.

from the aspect of quantity. In the words of Aristotle, they discuss the world only from the aspect of ulee. When the motions of things must be explained, archee will become powerless. In fact, when natural philosophers study the motive of things, they usually search bases outside archee. For example, "love and hatred" and "nous" cannot be explained by primary substance.[1] Below we will see movement is relevant with "many". In early natural philosophers, "many" also means a pre-theory state, but in the later Eleatic school, "many" has become a theoretical visual angle. In this way, we may easily understand why Zeno negated "many" through negating movement to advocate and follow Parmenides' notion of "being is the 'one'".

Apparently, in the initial stage of dialectic, i.e. the intuitive stage, contradictions existed at least in two aspects: one is the contradiction between the intuitive of archee (a concrete thing) and the abstractness "one" as a single visual angle should possess; the other is the contradiction between archee as a visual angle and other visual angles (movement in particular). The contradiction in the first aspect was transcended by Heraclitus and Democritus to some extent. The Logos put forth by Heraclitus has very high abstractness and has come down till present as a philosophical category, while the latter's atom is also an abstract product of thinking. However they were unable to transcend the contradiction in the second aspect. They were not aware of the unity of multiple visual angles.

Typical ancient dialectics

Windelband said: A single cosmic material or the origin of the world is the foundation of the change process of the whole nature; according to ancient legends, this seems to be the self-evident supposition of Ionian school. The only problem is to determine what this primary material is.[2] In fact, this assertion can be applied to all intuitive dialecticians. Following the improvement of human's abstract thinking, these far-fetched ex-

---

1 Aristotle had first seen the difference between the two and included them into "material cause" and "efficient cause". ([Ancient Greek] Aristotle: Metaphysics, p.19)
2 [German] Windelband: A History of Philosophy, Vol.1, p.49~50.

planations were gradually discarded, and intuitive proofing was also considered subjective and unreal. Parmenides had differentiated between the "way of truth" and the "way of opinion". The way of truth is a way of pure thought and transcends all perceptual sensations; on the contrary, the way of opinion is a way of perceptual sensation and a way of illusion.[1] This notion of Parmenides is indeed the negation of previous natural philosophers, but it is also a continuation of intuitive dialectic logic. The difference is that, the "being" and "one" generated by pure thought, owing to its high abstractness, avoid intuitive dialecticians' far-fetched analogy; moreover, "many" has been consciously recognized. Although its status may be still completely negative, it is evident that the contradiction between "one" and "many" had obtained a conscious form for the first time. Hegel has given a high comment on it: real philosophical thought starts from Parmenides. Here we can see philosophy is raised to the sphere of thought.[2] On this basis, Hegel also regards Parmenides' "being" as the first category of his The Logic of Hegel system, because logic in fact starts where the history of real philosophy starts.[3]

In the Eleatic school, the contradiction between "one" and "many" had been fully recognized, but it did not have a positive meaning and the communication between the two edges of that contradiction had not been realized – in fact, in Zeno, this "communication" is unidirectional. The aim that Zeno introduced paradox is to uphold the basic notion of Eleatic school that "being is the 'one'" and "being" is immobile and invariable. His basic approach is to prove the notion that "being" is the "one" and is immobile and invariable when he tries to disclose the proposition that "being" is numerous, mobile and variable is, self-contradictory. The actual situation seems so. "Many" as a category of philosophy was recognized because the philosophers of Eleatic school thought it was necessary to prove and announce the opposite of the "one" is an illusory thing. But how high is this necessity? If the notion of Eleatic school can be reasoned only in this way, then undoubtedly it indicates there is an

1 Huang Yusheng: Truth and Freedom, p.5.
2 [German] Hegel: Lectures on the History of Philosophy, Vol.1, p.267.
3 [German] Hegel: The Logic of Hegel, p.191.

essential relativity between "many" and "one". The fact is so. The proposition of the Eleatic school cannot be proved in a direct way. Therefore, Zeno's dialectic aims to use the inherent contradiction of "many" to prove only the "one" is being, but this proof per se indicates that in terms of "one", "many" is haunting. We see even if the theoretical visual angle of natural philosophers is developed into a pure concept here, the finity of this visual angle as manifested from the very beginning is still not overcome and on the contrary, is brought into the openness.

Generally it is believed that the method adopted by Zeno, i.e.: the method to prove his own view through disclosing the contradiction of its opposite, is dialectic. Apparently, it is in a negatory sense. However, the significance of Zeno's "negative" dialectic is not limited to this. We would rather say its negativity is to disclose the finity of a theoretical visual angle. In fact, if our vision is not limited to the theoretical system of Eleatic school, or in other words, if we adopt an approach by combining Eleatic school and the later Sophist school, this finity will become obvious. In the opinion of Hegel, the thesis of Eleatics that only "'being' is, and 'non-being' is not at all" is identical to Sophist thesis in essence. By Sophists, this thesis means that negative is not at all, for only: what has being is, there is nothing false; what has being – everything – is something true. In other words, everything that we perceive or imagine, the purposes we espouse, are purely affirmative determinations and, as such, are all something true and not something false.[1] In fact, it is "to give him the dose of his own medicine". Sophists used a method similar to Zeno's, but the conclusion was the contrary. Zeno's dialectic aims to obtain the truth of "One", whereas what Sophists obtain here is "many". In Eleatics, "many" is recognized only in a "negatory" way, while in Sophists, "many" has become a visual angle.

Aristotle said when people used dialectic, they did not delve into the essence of the things they have researched but only involved the form of dialectic. Aristotle even thinks dialectic is only an empty form. However, we have seen that even in Sophists, we cannot say dialectic is a sheer empty form. If we conceive dialectic as a pure formal method only, then

---

1 [German] Hegel: Lectures on the History of Philosophy, Vol.2, p.210~211.

the generation of this method will seem sudden and lose its continuity with previous philosophy. Only when we understand dialectic from the perspective of "content", can Eleatics and Sophists be easily understood in the whole history of Greek philosophy. The "negative" dialectic in this period laid a foundation for later "positive" dialectic. In fact, Platonic dialectic emerged exactly from the critique of the two.

Plato's critique on the dialectic of Eleatics and Sophists is roughly divided into two aspects: one is to point to their negativity and subjectivity; the other is to unify their theoretical visual angles. Plato has seen that there is sharp antagonism between "one" and "many" in Eleatics, and although Zeno and other persons did not avoid "many" when they discussed "one", the result is the negation of "many" only; whereas in Sophists, "one" and "many" are optionally and even dramatically "unified". If the unity between these two concepts can be announced ad arbitrium, it certainly indicates this "unity" is essentially "many". Plato's task here is to realize the intrinsic and objective unity of these concepts. In Parmenides, whether "opposites" are combined or not, this primitive issue is solved in its two polarized modalities. Meanwhile a new idea about "form" is generated. The issues of opposition and separation automatically disappear. The issue of Teilhabe (ger. share) becomes the issue of the connection of forms and has been solved in a few groups of deductions, i.e.: "form" is neither opposite to nor separated from things, things "are" only in the connection of form, and the being of things rests with the assembly of "forms".[1] In the end Plato arrives such a conclusion: "One", whether is being or non-being, same or different, moving or still, generated or ruined, is and is not. In other words, unity and all these pure ideas are: being and are non-being, and "one" is both "one" and "many".[2] It seems that this conclusion is negative, too, but Plato obviously regards the unity and movement of these concepts as the stipulation inside idea. In fact, Plato has realized the synthesis of the standpoints of Eleatics and Sophists. Their theoretical visual angles find reasonable positions in the Platonic theory of idea.

---

1 [Ancient Greek] Plato: Parmenides, p.404 and 410. Here "form" is equal to idea.
2 [German] Hegel: Lectures on the History of Philosophy, Vol.2, p.219.

We may say that Plato's thought of conceiving things as the assembly of "forms" or "ideas" reveals the essence of the dialectic in theoretical philosophy. Theoretical philosophy wants to reduce the world or things to abstract "ideas" or "forms", but in real life, the complexity and concreteness of the real things do not allow reducing them to abstract things. A philosopher may smear at real life, but he is unable to get rid of the real life and moreover it is unavoidable that his theoretical conception will have some inherent connection with real life, and even when he is smearing at the real life, his premise is still the acceptance of the real life. In fact, it is those issues in real life which push philosophers' thinking, and without real life and the issues in it, there would not be philosophical thinking. Therefore, every philosopher who is yet to lose the sense of reality will inevitably give explanation on real life, other than simply reduce it to falsehood or untruth. If we are to give convincing explanation on the things in real life from the approach of abstract concepts, it seems that we cannot find any other method except conceiving concrete things as the integration of many abstract stipulations in a specific way. Therefore, we may say that this concept has an immeasurable influence on Western philosophy. Not only the philosophers have argued that dialecticians had all tried to explain things in a diversified and unified way, and we can also find the sign of this thought from the traditional philosophers who had vehemently opposed Plato. If we carefully analyze Berkeley's thesis that being is the perceived, Maher's thesis that thing is the composition of sensation, and other theses, we can obtain the above conclusion without difficulty.

This achievement of Platonic dialectic was inherited by Aristotle at first, although Aristotle absolutely does not admit that he is a dialectician. Above we have mentioned that Aristotle excludes dialectic from philosophy, but if we correct the concept of negative dialectic, we may easily find out that; Aristotle is also a typical dialectician. In fact, the stipulation of Aristotle's concept of substance is much richer than Plato's idea. As put by Gadamer, Aristotle is an expert at bringing extremely different stipulations to a concept,[1] while these different stipulations are exactly

---

1 [German] Gadamer: Gadamer on Hegel, p.6.

the bases on which the philosophers establish different theoretical visual angles. In this aspect, Aristotle is successful, but his concept obviously does not have the flowability of Plato's concept, and his stipulations on substance are always irrelevant. Usually, Aristotle observes the stipulations one by one, rather than to organize them in a connective system; whereas this flowability and connectivity are necessary for a dialectician to reach a concrete unity. The previous philosophers either regarded it as a reason why they denied Aristotle as a dialectician, or did they not talk of it and instead they looked for "dialectic" elements from "metaphysics" (such as: potential and reality). I think it does not constitute a reason to regard that Aristotle is not a dialectician, to say nothing of that Aristotle has improved Platonic dialectic. I would rather say that Aristotle saw the finity of the Platonic dialectic. Aristotle criticized Plato and said idea was inane.[1] Besides, he also negates the concept that a thing is mutually generated from opposite thing (including creating something out of nothing).[2] Today, it seems that it is not difficult to refute Aristotle's critique, but in the scope of substantial philosophy, the refutation was not so easy. In fact, Aristotle had pointed to the fundamental issue of the dialectic of ancient substantial philosophy – what is the basis for the relation and flowability between concepts? If no proper basis is found, no doubt dialectic can only be a form. Although Plato criticized the inanition of Sophist dialectic in the very beginning, he was unable to give response to a similar criticism. In the sense of Hegel, this connection and flowability are objective because they are completely in the sphere of pure idea. Unfortunately, the premise of this sphere is the development of the components of subjectivity. This is what Plato and the whole ancient philosophy lacks. Therefore, although Hegel found a resonance in Plato, he had to admit that the Platonic dialectic was unconscious and imperfect. In this way it will not be difficult to understand the introduction of subjectivity and the historical principle in the early-modern dialectic, because it was a way to overcome the limitation of ancient dialectic.

---

1 Here Aristotle reveals the limitation of idea mainly through material cause.
2 [Ancient Greek] Aristotle: Metaphysics, p.260~263.

Early-modern age dialectic

The theory of ancient dialectic was unprecedentedly enriched by Plato and Aristotle, but this richness is extremely limited and not guaranteed. On the one hand, from today's point of view, ancient dialectic belongs to the substantialist philosophy and its richness is within that scope of sub- stantialist philosophy; on the other hand, it seems that the relation and unity of the concepts of typical ancient dialecticians such as Plato are groundless. Metaphysicians emphasize that concepts belong to the sphere of pure idea and thus are objective, but if this sphere is ultimately under- stood as a pure substance, then the discussion of this objectivity must be a dogmatic act. Ancient dialectic could only go so far, because we may say it had included all kinds of concepts into substance, while substance is also a theoretical visual angle (of course this was discovered after early modern times). If it goes even farther, the sphere of subjectivity will be involved.

From the concept of dialectic as indicated by us above, the emergence of early-modern subjective philosophy has the nature of dialectic, because the self-consciousness of subjectivity itself has indicated the finity of the visual angle of substance in ancient philosophy. In addition, in the sense of early-modern dialecticians, subjectivity provides a basis and principle for concept, thus dialectic bids farewell to the randomness and arbitrari- ness of ancient dialectic. Therefore, early-modern dialectic is subjective dialectic and the major contradiction it faces is the contradiction between subjectivity and its object.

As a whole, medieval age dialectic does not go beyond the vision of Plato and Aristotle. Its basic form has been established as early as in neo-Platon- ism; and the inane formal dialectic was popular in a time, too.[1] However, it seems that these did not make much contribution to later early-modern dialectic. The subjective spirit gradually developed in later Middle Ages and the historical concept brought by Christian tradition constituted two major factors of early-modern dialectic. In early-modern dialecticians, these two factors brought about huge changes on ancient Greek dialectic. Of course, all these were summarized into the Hegelian system.

---

1 [German] Hegel: Lectures on the History of Philosophy, Vol.3, p.314~319.

Through the efforts of Francis Bacon and Rene Descartes, subjective phi-losophy was generated. However, only by Kant, the category of concept was consciously conceived as subjectivity. Kant thinks that concepts should be classified into two types: intellectual concept and rational con-cept. The two are completely different in nature and source. Kant has a hidden premise – every concept or idea is the product of subjectivity or belongs to subject. This premise corresponds to the "being-in-self" nature of Plato and Aristotle's idea and category. While formulating his category list, Kant directly criticized Aristotle's category list and thought that Ar-istotle "pieced together" ten basic concepts only and named them as cat-egories, but this category list did not distinguish sensuous pure idea (from space and time), to say nothing it distinguished rational concept. Most importantly, Aristotle's category list does not have a consistent principle, which links these categories into a system. Kant thinks it is the system-atical-ness of his category system that distinguishes it from the old un-principled piece-together, while the soul of the systematical-ness is its subjectivity because intellectual concept is by no means a concept gen-erated from an object-in-itself and needs to take sensuous intuition as its basis.[1] Intellectual concept is only used to functionally stipulate em-pirical judgment and makes it a general empirical judgment, but all these are based on finite experience. If intellectual concept is content with this finity, no problem will be generated. However, human's reason is never content with it.

> Every single experience is only a part of the whole sphere of its domain, but the absolute totality of all possible experience is itself not experience. Yet it is a necessary [concrete] problem for reason, the mere representation of which requires concepts quite different from the categories.[2]

This is rational idea. Idea is inherent in the nature of reason. Moreover, if we say category has a delusive falsehood, then this falsehood will be unavoidable in idea, because the totality of all experience is not an expe-rience. In the sense of Kant, if knowledge is not "empirical", it will in-evitably be falsehood. This falsehood is the dialectic called by Kant. Here,

---

1 [German] Kant: Prolegomena to Any Future Metaphysics, p.97~102.
2 The same book as above, p.104.

the situation similar to Zeno's paradox occurs: the contradiction of time and space between finity and infinity and the contradiction between "one" and "many" which was revealed by Zeno appear (antinomy) again. Hegel thinks that Kant's "rational contradiction" does not go much farther when compared with Zeno's paradox.[1] It is not fair enough. Kant's philosophy and Zeno's philosophy belong to different paradigms. Zeno only directly points out that contradiction is unreal, while Kant proves that contradiction is generated from the transcendental use of reason. Later we will indicate that this is extremely important for the Hegelian dialectic to include dialectic into subject and the sphere of reason. It distinguishes Hegelian dialectic from ancient dialectic. First of all, it should be attributed to Kant.

But, since Kant thinks dialectic is a transcendental illusion, it should be avoided. It seems to run in the opposite direction with Zeno. Zeno's dialectic aims to indicate that only the metaphysical sphere is real, while Kant's dialectic wants to negate it. Here exists the difference between "ancient and present", i.e.: the difference between substantial philosophy and subjective philosophy. Zeno had denied the authenticity of "many" in the very beginning, but we cannot say that the core of Kant's argumentation is to affirm the authenticity of "many". Otherwise Kant would have no difference from "Sophists". Kant's intellectual sphere is not in disorder. On the contrary, from the very beginning his aims were : unity, objectivity and systematical-ness ; he wanted to reach those aims through the establishment of subject,, only that this subjectivity is humbler than Hegel's.

Kantian philosophy always has dual meanings. On the one hand, it makes subjective philosophy shake off the dogmatic and non-critical state and become more "unquestionable"; On the other hand, it also indicates in an equally convincing way the finity of subject and indicates that "thing-in-itself" is inaccessible for man's reason. Kant's "negative" dialectic essentially reveals the finity of the subjective visual angle of the early-modern philosophy since Rene Descartes, but later dialecticians

---

1 [German] Hegel: Lectures on the History of Philosophy, Vol.2, p.45.

could not accept this finity. Therefore, the later German classical philosophy can be evaluated as a process in which people try to overcome this finity, i.e.: the process in which the "unquestionable" character of intellectual sphere is extended towards rational sphere. Owing to the subjective particularity of early-modern philosophy, this process is also the process in which "thing-in-itself" is included into an even more powerful subjectivity.

Concretely speaking, this process was realized through the introduction of the historical principle. If subjectivity is to "fight in enemy's territory" (by words of Hegel), it must involve subjective activity, while subjective activity will certainly constitute history. The concept of history will certainly involve the tradition of Christianity. Above we have indicated that ancient Greek people did not have a sense of history, while the concept of history is not necessary for the dialectic of substantialist philosophy. In the sense of ancient Greek, the two are even repulsive. Only after Christianity assumed a ruling position, the concept of history in the Hebrewist tradition started to influence the spirit of European people. In the early-modern philosophy, Vico is the first person upholding the banner of Historicism. Contrary to the early-modern non-historical and abstract rationalist spirit represented by Rene Descartes' philosophy, Vico wants to discover an ideal and eternal historical pattern every nation will experience in different historical periods.[1] Kant conceives experience as a thought that intellectuality has concealed a process for the comprehensive activities of sensuous materials, but Kant does not unfold this thought and is content to let each category stay parallel extrinsically. Deducing categories with the principle of logical evolution started by Johann Fichte. This deduction process in fact is the process in which subject takes "action". History receives equal stress in Schelling's philosophy. Some people even say freedom and history are always the dominant concepts in Schelling's 50-year philosophical activities.[2] The unity between logic and history really became a principle only in the Hegelian philosophy. As a result of this principle, historicist principle was intro-

---

1 [Italian] Vico: New Science, p.7, Beijing, People's Literature Publishing House, 1987.
2 Ni Liangkang: Self-knowledge and Reflection, p.238.

duced into dialectic or contemplative logic and became a fundamental stipulation of the dialectic system; and logical principle was introduced into the understanding on history and history therefore was understood as the unfolding process of logic. Thus, the consciousness of history originating from the Hebrew civilization and the consciousness of reason originating from Greek civilization realized a kind of intrinsic fusion.

No doubt, Hegel's principle of history serves subjectivity. In the historical process of mental activity, i.e.: the course of logical deduction, different stipulations were ultimately included into absolute spirit. In view of the small aspect, in his book "Logic", Hegel proceeds from the most abstract "being", "non-being" and "change" of "ontology", realizes the full grasp of phenomenal level in "standard", enter the contradictory evolution of phenomenal level and essential level in "essentialism" and in the end grasps the concreteness of absolute idea in "conceptualism". In view of the large aspect, from Logic via Natural Philosophy and in the end in his Spirit Philosophy, he reaches the absolute spirit as the highest concreteness, i.e.: develops the useful of all finite stipulations and discard the useless in them. In this way, an unprecedented system was completed. In the sense of Hegel, all the theories of the philosophers in the history may find out their suitable positions in his system, just like they may find their positions in history. Hegelian dialectic system echoes with the Platonic system and Aristotelian system in ancient Greece. In Plato and Aristotle, we see that the dialectic of substantial philosophy was completed, while in Hegel, subjective dialectic is given utmost play. Gadamer has made the following comment:

> Through an extremely different later methodological concept, the excellent monologue of his own philosophical dialectic realizes the ideal which self presents its ideology. This methodological concept more relies on Rene Descartes' methodological principle, relies on the learning of catechism and relies on the Holy Bible.[1]

According to Hegel's concept, the history of philosophy should be completed in his system, but the history of later philosophy indicates that

---

1 [German] Gadamer: Gadamer on Hegel, p.5.

the fact is absolutely not so. In fact, Hegel in the end only obtained an abstract theoretical visual angle; although this visual angle is better than any visual angle of the previous theoretical philosophy, it, as an abstract theoretical visual angle, has no essential difference from previous philosophical theories. Later on, Marx's sphere of life practice, and his discovery on the superiority of theory and the generation of practical dialectics indicate that Hegel's absolute spirit is not comprehensive and far from being concrete, and the real concreteness lies in human's life practice.

CHAPTER TWO

Marxist Practical Dialectic

Introduction

Our above discussion on the essence of dialectic has consciously set foothold at the standpoint of Marxist practical philosophy, but it is only a conceptually logical analysis. It is necessary to present Marxisit thought of dialectic in its historical evolution. Although Marx's dialectic will become easily understood after a study of various kinds of abstract dialectics in the history, the uniqueness of Marx's dialectic is still an issue that should be further stipulated, because people usually do not carefully differentiate Marx's dialectic from previous dialectic and often confuse Marx's dialectic with ancient dialectic or Hegelian dialectic or confuse it with the two. Below our main task is to differentiate Marx's dialectic from the dialectic of any of the previous theoretical philosophies and elucidate dialectic as practical philosophy.

Critique and inheritance of previous dialectics, particularly Hegelian dialectic

Revolutionary element in Hegelian dialectic

As mentioned above, the single visual angle of Hegelian dialectic and the entire early-modern dialectic was ultimately established through the introduction of the principle of history, but the introduction of the principle of history has reated problems for this visual angle. These problems also indicate the finity of this visual angle. Firstly if history is understood as the history of the formation of a spiritual entity, then Hegel would certainly declare the termination of history when this spiritual entity is completed, whereas it goes against the essence of history. Engels clearly saw this point:

> Hegel, especially in his book Logic, emphasized that this eternal truth is nothing but the logical, or, the historical, process itself, he nevertheless finds himself compelled to supply this process with an end, just because he has to bring his system to a termination at some point or other. In his Logic, he can make this end a beginning again, since here the point of the conclusion, the absolute idea -which is only absolute insofar as he has absolutely nothing to say about it- "alienates", that is, transforms, itself into nature and comes to itself again later in the mind, that is, in thought and in history. But at the end of the whole philosophy, a similar return to the beginning is possible only in one way. Namely, by conceiving of the end of history as follows: mankind arrives at the cognition of the self-same absolute idea, and declares that this cognition of the absolute idea is reached in Hegelian philosophy.[1]

Firstly, Hegel had not only declared the end of the history of philosophy but also declared the end of human's world history. In the sense of Hegel's "rational vision": World history had begun from the Orient and ended in the West. It started in the Oriental empires of China, India and Persia. Following the decisive victory of Greek over Persian, the reasonable generation procedure was moved to Med countries and completed in Western Christianity – German empires. Europe absolutely is the end point of history.[2] However, neither the history of philosophy

---

1 Marx & Engels Selected Works, Edition 2, Vol.4, p.218.
2 [German] Karl Lowith: World History and Salvation History, p.68~69.

nor the history of world will be terminated due to Hegel's declaration. Why did Hegel declare the termination of history? Engels thinks "this, indeed, for the simple reason that he was compelled to make a system and, in accordance with traditional requirements, a system of philosophy must conclude with some sort of absolute truth."[1] According to our above discussion on Hegelian dialectic, this reason can be conceived as that Hegelian dialectic ultimately will resort to an eternal supporting point, i.e.: ultimately come to a theoretical visual angle, whereas every theoretical visual angle is finite. The end point of history declared by Hegel is essentially the boundary of his theoretical visual angle. If philosophy and history do not come to the end point as declared by Hegel, then it certainly implies the existence of the spheres outside Hegelian history and absolute spirit, or implies the existence of the sphere outside the scope of other theories.

Secondly, when German classical philosophy had evolved to Hegelian philosophy, the essential relation between history and subject was finally established. But while providing a powerful "medium" force for subjectivity, history also discloses the characteristics of subject in another aspect, i.e.: its finity and concreteness. If we conceive history from the perspective of timeliness, it will undoubtedly reveal the possibility of discussing subject in another way, i.e.: the possibility of regarding subject as a real individual person. Later on when Martin Heidegger discussed Hegelian concept of time and view of history, he also gave a positive comment on it. In a word, the principle of history may help Hegel establish his colossal dialectic system and meanwhile provided the possibility for later generations "explode" this system. Marx's dialectic was generated under the premise of this possibility.

No doubt, the theoretical resources of Marx's dialectic are the dialectic thoughts of previous theoretical philosophies, the Hegelian dialectic thought in particular. Since Hegelian dialectic is the maturest form of the previous dialectics, the establishment of the dialectic of Marx's practice has to begin with the critique and reform on the Hegelian dialectic. Marx ever said that Hegelian dialectic was inverted, so it must be re-

---

1 Marx & Engels Selected Works, Edition 2, Vol.4, p.217~218.

versed, i.e.: critically reformed. Nevertheless here we must not simplify this reversal. If this critical reform were simply understood as changing the "absolute spirit" of Hegelian dialectic into "matter", it would have no difference from a play game, anyone with a little common knowledge could complete and there would be no need of a philosophical revolution. In this simple understanding, it is not a surprise that Marx's dialectic is deemed as a thing which has no much difference from ancient dialectics and at most is more exquisite. As a result, Marx's dialectic is interpreted as a strange mixture. On the one hand, in terms of that ordinary "matter" is considered as a moving subject, it is the re-publication of ancient dialectics; on the other hand, in terms of that Hegelian categories are directly included, it is also non-critical acceptance of Hegelian dialectic. The result becomes a mixture of Heraclitus and Hegel. Such a mixture can be by no means called a philosophical revolution. Therefore, we must seek the true meaning of Marx's dialectic and the real significance of Marx's critique on Hegelian dialectic. In the sense of Marx, it is very easy to point out the unreality of Hegelian philosophy by proceeding from human's common sense. This has been done by Feuerbach brilliantly. However, we would rather say that Feuerbach's job is tactful than say that it is profound (by words of Engels).When talking on religion, Marx ever said with deep wisdom: "in fact, it is much easier to seek unreligious core from the illusion of religion through analysis than,on the contrary to educe its heaven form from the then real life relations. This method is the only materialist method and also the only scientific method.[1] The spirit of this remark by Marx fits well the critique on Hegelian dialectic. Therefore, the important is not to pull down Hegelian "absolute spirit" from the heaven and declare it is the reversal of the dialectic movement of "matter" but to proceed from real life practice, reveal the essence of Hegelian dialectic and keep its "reasonable inner core" in a new type of dialectic.

Above we have indicated the two categories of Marx's philosophy, i.e.: modern practical philosophy and materialism. Here, if we are not content with the "theoretical" dialectic and its extrinsic combination with

---

1 Marx: Capital, Vol.1, p.410, Beijing, People's Publishing House, 1975.

materialism, then we must reveal the intrinsic connection between Marx's dialectic and these two categories. As described above, Hegelian dialectic system has contained the elements which breaks his system. In other words, his dialectic indicates the element of the finity of this absolute spirit as a single theoretical visual angle. Thus, if the standpoint of Hegelian theoretical philosophy is transcended, the vision sphere of modern practical philosophy will be opened. Marx did it so. This transcendence process was linked with materialism in the very beginning: Feuerbach's materialism always plays an important role in Marx's critique on Hegel. We may say it is Feuerbach's materialism that enabled Marx to see the spheres outside Hegelian idealism; although later on Marx also gave equally profound critique on Feuerbach, anyway Marx became a materialist since then. Of course, this transcendence process cannot be explained clearly with such a few sentences. Below we will present it in light of the formation process of Marx's thought.

Formation process of Marx's dialectic

In his *Economic and Philosophical Manuscripts of 1844,* Marx tries to criticize "Hegelian dialectic and whole philosophy". It is not difficult to understand that Marx firstly should get hold of the rips of Hegelian dialectic system – the finity and abstractness of this system was implied by the principle of history. But here, Marx has to seek help from Feuerbach and even sometimes has to use Feuerbach-style language. When people, such as: Strauss and Bruno Bauer, were still repeating word for word and uncritically accepting Hegelian dialectic, Feuerbach had carried out critique on the idealism of Hegelian dialectic. Marx thinks "Feuerbach is the only one who has a serious, critical attitude to the Hegelian dialectic and who has made genuine discoveries in this sphere. Feuerbach is in fact the true conqueror of the old philosophy."[1] Marx thinks Feuerbach's great achievement is:

---

1 Collected Works of Karl Marx and Frederick Engels, Chinese version 1,
   Vol.42, p.157~158.

(1) The proof that philosophy is nothing else but religion rendered into thought and expounded by thought, i.e., another form and manner of existence of the estrangement of the essence of man; hence should equally to be condemned;

(2) The establishment of true materialism and of real science, by making the social relationship of "man to man" the basic principle of the theory;

(3) His opposition to the negation of the negation, which claims to be the absolute positive, the self-supporting positive, positively based on itself.[1]

Feuerbach equates the essence of Hegelian philosophy with religion and antagonizes it with "real" man (affirmation based on itself and actively taking itself as the basis) and absolute spirit (the negation of the negation as absolute affirmation). In fact he tries to discover the spheres outside the Hegelian system and seek a theoretical visual angle opposite to the Hegelian absolute spirit. This no doubt is a positive attempt to overcome the abstractness of Hegelian dialectic, but this sublation by no means was successful. He did not see through the essence of such concepts as "actuality", "sensuousness" and "reality". In addition, his understanding on Hegelian dialectic was not profound enough. "Feuerbach thus conceives the negation of the negation only as a contradiction of philosophy with itself – as the philosophy which affirms theology (the transcendent, etc.) after having denied it, and which it therefore affirms in opposition to itself."[2] Therefore, his sublation only makes the self contradictions of Hegelian dialectic public, so we cannot say it is profound but it is "tactful" indeed. Here Marx says that Feuerbach transcends old philosophy. Obviously Marx overstates him. However, no doubt Feuerbach pointed out to a direction for sublation – the direction of sensuousness and reality. The critical point of this theoretical direction is to stress that same as religion, Hegelian abstract system is nothing but the alienation of the sensuous and real men.

We may say that Marx has criticized Hegel exactly along this direction from the very beginning, but different from Feuerbach, Marx tries to capture Hegelian system from its inside. This requires Marx to find the

---

1 Collected Works of Karl Marx and Frederick Engels, Chinese version 1, Vol.42, p.158.
2 Collected Works of Karl Marx and Frederick Engels, Chinese version 1, Vol.42, p.158.

positive elements of Hegelian dialectic. In the words of Marx, it is to explain "the critical form of this in Hegel still uncritical process". Marx had discovered:

> The outstanding achievement of Hegel's Phänomenologie and of its final outcome, the dialectic of negativity as the moving and generating principle, is thus first that Hegel conceives the self-creation of man as a process, conceives objectification as loss of the object, as alienation and as transcendence of this alienation; that he thus grasps the essence of labour and comprehends objective man – true, because real man – as the outcome of man's own labour.[1]

"The only labour which Hegel knows and recognizes is abstractly mental labour",[2] because "for Hegel the *human being – man – equals self-consciousness*".[3] Therefore, the key to rescuing the "reasonable inner core" of Hegelian dialectic is to reverse the relation between self-consciousness and the men alive and disclose the absurdity that Hegel equates self-consciousness with man and the essence of man. The result of this critique or "reversal" is that the essence of man is conceived as "the free and conscious activity"[4] that reforms objective world. This sensuous activity as human essence is completely opposite to the abstractness of self-consciousness. When Hegel equates man with self-consciousness, "all estrangement of the human being is therefore nothing but estrangement of self-consciousness.",[5] "his objective essence, or thinghood", "equals alienated self-consciousness, and thinghood is thus posited through this alienation".[6] As a result, everything is reversed.

> The estrangement of self-consciousness is not regarded as an expression – reflected in the realm of knowledge and thought – of the real estrangement of the human being. Instead, the actual estrangement – that which appears real – is according to its inner-most, hidden nature (which is only brought to light by philosophy) nothing but the manifestation of the estrangement of the real human essence, of self-consciousness.[7]

---

1 Collected Works of Karl Marx and Frederick Engels, Chinese version 1, Vol.42, p.163.
2 The same book as above, p.163.
3 The same book as above, p.165.
4 he same book as above, p.96.
5 The same book as above, p.165.
6 The same book as above, p.166.
7 The same book as above, p.165.

When Marx regards man as the unity of "directly a natural being" and "a human natural being", conceives the essence of man as productive labour, "abstracts from the Hegelian abstraction and puts the self-consciousness of man instead of self-consciousness",[1] thus the "reasonable inner core" of Hegelian dialectic obtains a real foundation. Now, the alienation of human essence is no longer purely spiritual alienation of self-consciousness, rather it is the real alienation of the productive labour that "reforms objective world", and the supersession of alienation is no longer only the supersession of the dogmatics, jurisprudence, political science and natural science "already as an object of knowledge", but the supersession of real religion, the real state or real nature.[2] This "self-alienation and self-estrangement" and "objective movement of retracting the alienation into self" are no longer a "divine process" and absolute spirit's "pure, incessant revolving within itself" but "the actual realisation for man of man's essence and of his essence as something real".[3]

Here we discover that the direct influence of Feuerbach's dialectic and Hegelian dialectic on Marx is still very obvious. Same as Feuerbach, Marx tries to find a sphere outside Hegelian absolute spirit and antagonize them. No doubt the sphere is the sensuous and real man. Here we do not discuss whether Marx had really grasped the real man for the moment, but without doubt, Marx obtains a route to overcome the abstractness of Hegelian dialectic. In his book, Marx speaks highly of Feuerbach and he also talks in a way of Feuerbach from time to time. Feuerbach defines the essence of man as the consciousness or reason which regards his own species and own essentiality as objects and is fundamentally different from animal's sensation which regards individual as object.[4] The essence of man in the sense of Feuerbach is such consciousness. Although Marx does not conceive the essence of man in this sense, he still defined the species essence of man in another way – defined it as a kind of "free and conscious activity" – the material productive labour that "reforms

---

1　The same book as above, p.171.
2　Collected Works of Karl Marx and Frederick Engels, Chinese version 1, Vol.42, p.174.
3　The same book as above, p.175~176.
4　[German] Feuerbach: Feuerbach, Selected Philosophical Works, Vol.2, p.26~27, Beijing, Commercial Press, 1984.

objective world". He said: just in changing the objective world, man really proves that it itself is a species being. The production is man's active species-life.[1] Apparently, at the points where Marx and Feuerbach diverge, Hegel plays a decisive role. The labour stressed by Marx is exactly what Hegel had carefully observed in his phenomenology of spirit. As Marx's species essence of man is a kind of existing being, the labour of man in fact is still a process similar to the exteriorization of spirit. This process starts from the species essence of man and in the end returns to this species essence.

It appears that Marx has not achieved the real transcendence of the Hegelian dialectic here, because although he had realized that he must look for a position of his own philosophy from outside of Hegelian abstract theory – Feuerbach's philosophy has offered him some inspiration – he still cannot be considered successful and species essence is still highly risky to slip to another kind of abstractness. Anyway, the two categories of Marx's dialectic have been unveiled here. The species essence and labour of man are the first step for Marx to go to the concreteness of practice. Its significance rests with the sphere where philosophy is led to human activity. This sphere cannot be covered by Hegelian theory in the end. In addition, productive labour hence became the focus and center of Marx's theory. Below we will indicate this central position means that productive labour becomes a priority visual angle of the multiple visual angles of Marx's dialectic. This is exactly the materialist characteristic of Marx's dialectic.

In Economic and Philosophical Manuscripts of 1884, Marx does not succeed in transcending the abstractness of Hegelian dialectic and the result is to achieve a kind of existing and abstract species essence and ideal labour. In the book The Holy Family, Marx adopts another angle to probe into reality. This angle enables Marx to have a deeper understanding on the worldly stipulations on human life. Here French materialism generates great effect. In a sense, Marx uses the approach of French materialism to carry out a new critique on Hegelian dialectic. Auguste Cornu said:

---

1 Collected Works of Karl Marx and Frederick Engels, Chinese version 1, Vol.42, p.97.

In the development stage of Marxist thought, he was mainly influenced by the materialism and French socialism in the 18th century. Marx comprehensively studied the doctrines and views of the materialist and French socialist theorists in the 18th century and obtained such a conclusion: circumstances play a decisive role on the formation of man.[1]

Through the research of French materialism, Marx formed a new opinion on the role of nature and material interests in human life: "Therefore, it is natural necessity, essential human properties, however alienated they may seem to be, and interests that hold the members of civil society together; civil, not political life is their real link. [...] Therefore [...] they are not divine individualists but individualist men"[2] Apparently, the species essence with idealistic notion and the labour process defined in Economic and Philosophical Manuscripts of 1884 were overcome, and the men in the visual sphere of Marx's theory are sensuous individuals who are in various kinds of material interest relations and restricted everywhere.

Along the train of thought of French materialism, Marx discloses the secret of contemplative Hegelian structure as follows:

"If from real apples, pears, strawberries and almonds I form the general idea 'Fruit', if I go further and imagine that my abstract idea 'Fruit', is derived from real fruit, is an entity existing outside me, is indeed the true essence of the pear, the apple, etc., then in the language of speculative philosophy — I am declaring that 'Fruit' is the 'Substance' of the pear, the apple, the almond, etc. I am saying, therefore, that to be a pear is not essential to the pear, that to be an apple is not essential to the apple; that what is essential to these things is not their real existence, perceptible to the senses, but the essence that I have abstracted from them and then foisted on them, the essence of my idea — 'Fruit'. I therefore declare apples, pears, almonds, etc., to be mere forms of existence, modi, of 'Fruit'"[3] Obviously, Marx's critique on Hegelian idealist dialectic is con-

---

1 [French] Auguste Cornu: Origins of Marxian Thought , p.79, Beijing, China Renmin University Press, 1987.
2 Marx and Engels: The Holy Family, p.154, Beijing, People's Publishing House, 1958.
3 The same book as above, p.71~72.

sistent with the train of thought of French materialists and British materialist pioneers. In view of this train of thought, the true reality is the existence of individuals other than their abstract essence. Hobbes' view as described by Marx most clearly indicates this point:

> If all human knowledge is furnished by the senses, then our concepts, notions, and ideas are but the phantoms of the real world, more or less divested of its sensual form. [...] It would imply a contradiction if, on the one hand, we maintained that all ideas had their origin in the world of sensation, and, on the other, that a word was more than a word; that besides the beings known to us by our senses, beings which are one and all individuals, there existed also beings of a general. [1]

Needless to say, this train of thought by Marx contains a strong nominalist factor – only admit the reality of sensuous individuals and deny the significance of their universality. In this train of thought, the dimension of the ideality of human being is completely ignored and only the dimension of naturalness and the dimension of common custom are left. To accord to this idea, in the critique on the abstract species essence, the reality of human communication relation is ignored, too.

In this way, it seems that Marx has gone to the opposite of Economic and Philosophical Manuscripts of 1884 and man's initiative and freedom were reduced to an extremely lower position, while the human restriction by the relation between environment and various "things" was unprecedentedly emphasized. On the surface, it seems that the "individualist man" in this materialistic interest relation really realizes the "reversal" to Hegelian absolute spirit. But are they the so-called concreteness and reality? But apparently they were not. Although Marx has seen the correrelativity between material interest relation and human essence, but this human essence was still a ready-made essence and subject to ambience. This ambience is not the life-world mentioned by us above. The activity and effect of man do not become factors constituting environment. Marx tries to introduce the theoretical visual angle of modern materialism as a supporting point to surpass the dialectic of Hegelian theory, but he does not successfully incorporate this visual angle into an even

---

1 The same book as above, p.164.

broader visual sphere; on the contrary, it seems that Marx's mode of discourse was more obviously influenced by this visual angle and thus generated the contradictions similar to French materialism's. These contradictions were reviewed only in Theses on Feuerbach.

It seems that Marx's transcendence to Hegelian dialectic also needed to experience a dialectic process. In Economic and Philosophical Manuscripts of 1884 and The Holy Family, Marx adopts two obviously different theoretical approaches and these two approaches in fact have been embodied in the theoretical visual angles of early-modern materialism and idealism. In this case, the antagonism and contradiction of different theoretical visual angles in early-modern philosophy are reflected in different stages of Marx's dialectic. Since the contradiction has come to light, the synthesis and sublation of this contradiction will become imperative and once this synthesis is successful, a brand new philosophical visual angle will be generated and Hegelian dialectic will be transcended indeed.

The transcendence on Hegelian dialectic reveals the finity of Hegelian dialectic on the basis of an even broader philosophical visual sphere and regard it as a visual angle among the many visual angles in this visual sphere. In Theses on Feuerbach and The German Ideology, this transcendence is finally realized.

Although Theses on Feuerbach mainly talks about Feuerbach, its hidden premise is the critique on idealism. In other words, the theses are the critique on the two dominant logics of early-modern philosophy and the synthesis of these two visual angles. In the first thesis, Marx clearly points out to the defect of old materialism and idealism. The defect of the former is "that the thing, reality, sensuousness, is conceived only in the form of the object or of contemplation", while the defect of the latter is that the active side "was developed abstractly". In the third thesis, Marx proceeds from circumstances and upbringing, criticizes the theoretical stance of old materialism and points out the doctrine which holds that men are the products of circumstances and education doctrine forgets that circumstances are changed by men and educators should be educated.

Though it is still the materialism that is criticized directly here, it also implies the criticism on idealist rational voluntarism. The former believes men are determined by circumstances and the latter disregards the influence of human circumstances on human activities. In the sense of Marx, the changing of circumstances is consistent with human activities or self changes and can only be regarded and reasonably conceived as revolutionary practice. Practice is the medium synthesizing these two antagonistic visual angles. We can see without difficulty that the finity of the materialism and idealism in old philosophy and the two stages which was explored in Marx's previous theory was superseded and they are regarded as some factors and links of practice. By now, Marx no longer has to seek help from the discourse of another school and instead he speaks in his own discourse.

Practice is the result of Marx's critique on old philosophy, Hegelian dialectic in particular. However, if this critique is conceived in the way of Hegel, it will certainly be a category more comprehensive and concrete than absolute spirit – we may also say it is a more superior theoretical visual angle. In this case, the revolutionary feature of Marx's philosophy will be greatly underestimated. Above we have indicated the revolutionary significance of Marx's philosophy is absolutely not to obtain an even more superior theoretical philosophy, but to transcend the paradigm of the whole theoretical philosophy. Therefore, here practice absolutely cannot be understood as a category in the sense of theoretical philosophy. Essentially, the total social life is practical. The transcendence to Hegelian philosophy and even the whole theoretical philosophy means that these theories are only a kind of modality of practice, i.e.: human's theoretical activities, while these theoretical activities essentially not only stem from practice and ultimately they will go to practice. The problems of theory can be finally solved only in practice. It seems that the process from different visual angles of early-modern theoretical philosophy to the unfolding of the visual sphere of practical philosophy is also a dialectic process. Above, we have indicated it is a process from theory to practice.

However, by this point, Marx only takes the first step to transcend Hegelian dialectic, because here Marx only discloses that the dialectic of previous theoretical philosophy will certainly go to practice, and does not yet exhibit the dialectic of his theory of practice in these theses. Marx does not re-present this process in the visual sphere of practical philosophy. Dialectic is a process in which theory moves towards practice, while theory is also a specific human practical activity. Therefore, Marx's dialectic can only be presented through the observation of this activity, while the premise is the personal grasp on the subject of this activity – concrete reality.

Based on the visual sphere of practical philosophy, the previous prescriptive abstractness of human essence will become more easily understood. "Species" or "interest" relation, once it is a supporting point of a theory, it will repulse practice; while a real subject must be the man under the background of extrinsic life practice. Just as Marx said: "The human essence is no abstraction inherent in each individual. In its reality it is the ensemble of the social relations."[1] Different from the "individualist" individual who is in various kinds of material interest relations as described in The Holy Family, here the men who are in various kinds of social relations have certain initiative. These social relations are not apriori and invariable. They are formed by men during their activities. Here Marx draws a clear demarcation line with old materialism: "The standpoint of the old materialism is civil society; the standpoint of the new is human society, or social humanity."[2] In The German Ideology, Marx defines social relation as "communicative relation" and observes the immanent relation between man's productive activities and this communicative relation. Marx had observed the corresponding relation between communicative form and productive force and had revealed the isomorphism of all kinds of human activities.

By now, Marx completes the transcendence of theoretical dialectic, particularly Hegelian dialectic. In Theses on Feuerbach and The German Ideology, the vision sphere of practical philosophy is established and the real subject and its activities are properly positioned. These lay a foundation for our understanding on dialectic as a specific process of theoretical activity.

---

1 Marx & Engels Selected Works, Edition 2, Vol.1, p.56.
2 The same book as above, p.57.

The abstractness and dialectic nature of subjective activities

The dialectic structure of productive and communicative activities

Marx's critique and successful transcendence to Hegelian dialectic is essentially to open the visual sphere for practical philosophy and make the generation of the dialectic of a practical theory possible. In fact, it was very reasonable that Hegel conceived dialectic as the "immanent transcendence" to intellectuality, but only his cause was limited to the scope of theory only; now we may say that dialectic is the "immanent transcendence" process of theoretical activity. In the sense of Hegel, the reason why intellectuality conceals contradictions and must generate a kind of "immanent transcendence" is the finity of intellectual concept; today we see that the finity of intellectuality is subordinate to the finity of theory. The failure of Hegelian dialectic has indicated that this finity cannot be overcome in the scope of theory. Therefore, the most fundamental task of dialectic is to complete the "immanent transcendence" of theory itself. It is the dialectics of practical theory.

Although we usually say dialectic is a theory, but if we want to understand its essence, we should not stay in the scope of theory only. The essence of dialectic stems from the finity of theory. Above, we have indicated that theory is a way of practice, or a way of human activity, so the finity of theory is certainly inherent in the subject of this activity and the existence of this subject. In this way, we naturally trace the essence of dialectic to the finite existence of subject or a finite subjectivity. The "see" and "perceiving" of theory contains the separation and opposition between "the seeing" and "the seen". This opposition is essentially a basic form of the subject-object opposition. If we extend this observation range to other spheres of human activities, we will discover without difficulty that this opposition is the premise of any specific subjective activity. We think it was infeasible to preach the subject-object opposition before early modern times. It is in fact in the sense of philosophical concept only, while in the real life, if we do not admit the subject-object opposition, any concrete human activity will become out of question. In fact, in ancient society, subjectivity was not wakened, but a being of unconscious subjectivity had been supposed. This subjectivity was concealed in all objective activities of ancient people. It was the initial condition for man's separation from the direct identity with the nature.

If subjectivity could only be reflected in the separation and opposition between subject and object in the very beginning, then this will undoubtedly imply the predestination of the finity of subject, firstly because of the existence of object as its opposite. This is fully revealed in Kant. Even in later Hegelian dialectic system, the absorption of object by subject was not successful; in addition, today we have known that before the opposition between subject and object, a more primordial practical sphere had existed. As far as this sphere was concerned, subject and its activity were always abstract. Thus we may conclude that all concrete human activities have the nature of dialectic. This nature originates from the finity and abstractness of these activities. After knowing this dialectical nature, we may easily understand the isomorphism and intrinsic consistency of the multiple modes of human activities, while the prototype of dialectic practice as we have often talked on ; can be understood only in this sense. Below we will mainly review the dialectic structure of three activities, namely: productive activity, communicative activity and theoretical activity. Above we have mentioned that productive activity assumes a priority position among human's specific activities and is also a sphere to which Marx pays the most attention, while the dialectic structure in theoretical activity is the dialectic we are continuing to review here.

Since ancient Greece, people have been used to completely separate all kinds of activities (theory, practice and production), whereas the position and importance of activities have varied with historical conditions. The theoretical growth point of many philosophers is often the emphasis and elucidation on the importance of one activity type. The philosophers we mentioned above such as: Habermas and Hannah Arendt did in this way. They were also accustomed to apply this train of thought to Marx. Hannah Arendt said:

> The spectacular rise of labour from the lowest, most despised to the highest rank and most esteemed of all human activities, had began with Locke, who

discovered that labour is the source of all properties. It was followed by Adam Smith who asserted that labour was the source of all wealth, and found its climax in Marx, who contended that labour became the source of all productivity and the expression of the very humanity of man.[1]

Hannah Arendt regards Marx and other people's high regard on labour as a manifestation that labour suppresses "action" sphere in modern society. It is true that since his youth, Marx had perceived and insisted on the essential correlation between productive labour and man, but Hannah Arendt has applied this Aristotelian trichotomy to Marx. In essence, she has simplified Marx. In fact she did not realize labour was not only related to man's physiological process,[2] more crucially, labour had an inherent consistency with politics, theory and other activity types. This point was not seen by ordinary theorists, including many ancient and early-modern practical philosophers. If this point is not understood, it will be impossible to understand Marx. As mentioned above, the consistency among various kinds of human activities share a common life-world background. Besides, in view of the internal consequence of an activity, they also show consistency or isomorphism in certain sense. This isomorphism stems from the common undertaker of these activities – real and finite subjectivity.

The basic structure of productive labour is the opposition between man and nature. The former is the subject of labour. The latter is the object of labour. In the process of labour, the subject of labour and the object of labour constitute the two poles. The subject of labour holds a tool or a tool system and enters activities for a purpose. As purpose is owned by man only, while nature does not have a purposiveness of human purpose, since the very beginning human activity has been observed as the opposition between purpose and nature. The nature itself does not conform to the human purpose in terms of direct modality. Human activity is to reshape the nature in a form conforming to the human purpose. This opposite relation with external nature makes man break away from the direct identity with nature and separates man from the external world.

---

1 [American] Hannah Arendt: The Human Condition, p.93.
2 The same book as above, p.1.

In this way, this relation between man and his labour object reflects its original subjectivity. Marx said: "The animal does not enter into "relations" with anything, it does not enter into any relation at all. For the animal, its relation to others does not exist as a relation."[1] Whereas man is different, owing to subjectivity and independence, the relation between man and others is true and constitutes the original essence of man.

In the relation between labour subject and labour object, labour tool acts as a medium. We used to limit ourselves considering it as the extension of human limbs. Its significance to labour process had not been fully revealed all the time. In fact, we can say that the tool reflects the essential structure of human labour process.

Man and tools

Firstly, the tool is a means through which human purpose acts upon the labour object. The tool shows an identity with both purpose and object. On the one hand, labour tool as the extension of human limbs conforms to human purpose, or in other words, it is embodied with a form that conforms to purpose and shows identity with purpose; on the other hand, tool itself is a material object and shows identity with labour object. Therefore, tool can, under the control of purpose, interact with labour object in form of its material objectivity and endow labour object with a form that conforms to purpose. This process in which the tool is used to achieve the purpose is the "cunning of reason"[2] as called by Hegel and Marx.

Secondly, the labour tool is the manifestation of subjective abstraction and men's abstracting power. This abstraction has a certain consistency with the abstraction of theory. The reason why labour tool is different from ordinary things is that man uses it to fulfill a task or it carries a function; while the quality of a tool is decided by how much its attributes

---

1 Marx & Engels Selected Works, Edition 2, Vol.1, p.81.
2 [German] Hegel: The Logic, Vol.2, p.437, Beijing, Commercial Press, 1976;
   Marx: Capital, Vol.1, p.203.

are competent with this task and play this function. Therefore, theoretically a tool should possess a special attribute or a special form to better adapt to its function. Initially, the special attributes and forms of tools were found occasionally and showed randomness in application, but when a tool is shaped up, these characteristics will be fixed and labour subjects will familiarize with them. When a tool is used as this tool, it always acts upon all objects through its unique characteristics; these objects are showed as all the things which can accept it. In this way, the tool may govern all objects, while this governance is exactly based on its characteristics. Here we can easily find a contradiction – between the oneness of the tool and the multiplicity of the objects it governs. Here tool represents a kind of universality. When Hegel said tools were more precious than products, he wanted to express that a product is only a thing with a special use, while a tool shows universality and generality and a thing with universal use for man.[1] In labour, the opposition between purpose and object is further reflected as the opposition between tool as universality or "oneness" and the multiplicate things as labour objects.

Apparently, there is a paradoxical nature between universality and particularity, and "one" and "many". The reason why tool as universality or "one" is possible is : its outstanding characteristics in an aspect as well as the unitary function it executes and man's unitary purpose, whereas these are exactly particular or "one" among "many". This particularity with universal function, this "one" which can govern "many" in the final analysis is man's subjectivity and the abstractness of this subjectivity. In this way, the situation of dialectic in the theoretical sphere similar to the above discussion appears. There, the things acting as generality are nothing but man's some special visual angles. The finity of theoretical visual angle is consistent with the finity of activity subjects here. Originally, theory is also a kind of human activity.

Although this paradoxical nature has a deep root in the essence of subject, the growth process of this subjectivity is often seen as the "sublation" of

---

1 [German] Hegel: The Logic, Vol.2, p.438; Zhang Shiying: On Hegel's Philosophy of Mind, p.51, Shanghai, ShanghaiPeople's Publishing House, 1986.

it in a sense. If we say that a paradox always means difference, then this sublation means synthesizing the things with difference. We may say the development process from ancient simple tools to modern technical system is exactly such a process. In the ancient times, the oneness and finity of tools were obvious, therefore certainly craftsmen should have all kinds of tools; following the development of technology, various kinds of tools and the functions they perform were converted and connected by a more general means, thus realizing the "sublation" of the finity of simple tools. This "sublation" has laid the foundation for the modern technical system. The emergence of the technical system created an illusion – the general principle in the system has overcome the finity of human activities and become an irresistible generality. But for the real human being, this irresistible generality is seen as an alien force. Marx has disclosed this technical alienation to some degree. By the time when Weber put forth the concept of rationalization, the critique on this technical alienation formed an important task for contemporary philosophy. Whereas, the critique in the final analysis will return to the finity of human subject and the paradoxical nature of human activities. This is undoubtedly also the basic direction for the solution of technical problems.

The communicative activity of man and its dialectic

The one corresponding to productive labour is the dialectic nature of communicative activity. Marx's discussion on communicative activity is concentrated directly in The German Ideology where Marx does not give a definite definition for communicative activity, but in view of the content of the discussion, communicative activity constitutes the interaction and social activity of men. Later on, this content was mainly discussed as production relations. According to the **ethics – conduct paradigm** of practice as we have reviewed in the book, this is undoubtedly the sphere of practice and this sphere is essentially different and comprehensively separated from the sphere of production. In the sense of Marx, human's communicative activities take different forms in different historical eras. These forms are closely related with productive labour, so communism as the result of the production of communication forms has an economic nature in essence.[1] Habermas has commented on this: In the sense of Marx, "production" is an activity, while the instrumental activity and institutional framework in this activity, i.e.: "productive activity" and "production relations" are only different elements in the same process.[2] Habermas thinks that this is essentially to reduce communicative activity to productive labour, and the inevitable consequence of this approach is the recession of positivism. For this reason, Habermas has clearly declared that the starting point of his theory is the fundamental difference between labour and interaction.[3] Behind such a thorough differentiation between these two activities made by Habermas and other thinkers, there is another differentiation – it is between dialectic and non-dialectic. Here productive labour is reduced into instrumental activity. Instrumental activity is carried out as per technical principle, while technical principle must be established on the basis of experiential knowledge. Experiential knowledge is in no way reckoned as dialectic sphere. In essence, the communicative activity is dialectic, because it is conceived as the interaction and dialogue of subjects under certain context. This is undoubtedly consistent with the Logos tradition of ancient Greek in essence. In this way, productive labour is repulsed again. Above we have pointed out the illegality of this thorough differentiation. Our task here is to point out the consistency of these two activities in internal structure, in other words, indicate that there is a dialectic structure in both productive labour and communicative activity. It is not to reduce one activity to another activity but to try to reveal the unity between the two activities. Below we will indicate that this unity is not only equally valid to the theoretical activity but also critical for our understanding of dialectic.

Habermas conceives society as a life-world constructed by signs. If his conception is correct, the formation and regeneration of society will indeed only rely on the communicative act.[4] The dialectic and finity reflected by communicative acts are relative to life-world, while life-world

---

1 Marx & Engels Selected Works, Edition 2, Vol.1, p.122.
2 [German] Habermas: Erkenntnis und Interesse, p.47.
3 [German] Habermas: Technology and Science as "Ideology", p.48~49.
4 [German] Habermas: Post-Metaphysical Thinking, p.83.

is constructed by these activities. Without doubt, the dialectic of any activity comes from its own finity and abstractness, but the finity and abstractness of communicative activity can not be explained based on itself. It seems that Habermas hands over the dialectic of communicative act to lansign, while language has the "transcendency" similar to life-world. In any case it is an ideal premise. On the contrary, Marx's analysis on communicative activity is completely based on a real foundation. This reality lies in the fact that communicative activity is not conceived as a "pre-economy" fact but the finite activity belonging to finite subject like productive labour. Owing to Marx's materialist standpoint, Marx's research on communicative activity is always closely related to productive labour and economic activity, but this does not denote a reductive relationship or essential precedence relationship. This research method is also the choice by a theoretical visual angle.

The starting point of Marx's research on communication is the social division of labour. In productive activity, similar to the finity and unicity(singleness) of tools, the finity of individuals is also manifested. The manifestation of this finity is that an individual usually can only act as a specific role or link in the realization process of a purpose. And, moreover these roles or links often need to be undertaken by a specific group. In this way, the polarization in labour process is also manifested in the organizational form of the human groups. This polarization stems from the finity of concrete activity subject. Since polarization has been formed, the communication and cooperation of roles and links will become necessary. This is the communicative sphere of human life. Obviously, different from productive labour which involves the relation between man and nature, the communication sphere involves the relation between man and man. The direct purpose of communication is to transcend the finity of a single individual or a single group, while the realization of this purpose needs social cooperation. Social cooperation may have two basic forms: direct social cooperation and indirect social cooperation. In direct social cooperation, many individuals cooperate directly with each other in labour and jointly complete the plan of an activity. Indirect social cooperation stays outside direct social cooperation and is realized through exchanging labour fruits. Since labour fruits are the results of direct activities, the exchange of products should be also the exchange of activities, and is the indirect exchange of direct activities. In this sense, direct social cooperation in essence may also be deemed as direct exchange of activities. All in all, all social co-operations can be deemed as the exchange of activities. However, since social cooperation is the exchange of direct activities, it must be restricted by the direct activities in a specific form and form normalized and institutionalized exchange mode or communicative relation.

Normalized and institutionalized social relation is the result of communicative activities and is also the transcendence to the finity of a specific subject. On the one hand, it is seen as the result of a specific subjective activity. On the other hand, in terms of a concrete individual, it is also seen as a criterion the activity subject must accept. The opposite relation between "one" and "many", and abstraction and concretion is presented between social relation or social system and individuals. This is the dialectic structure of interpersonal interaction or inter-subject communicative activity.

The dialectic structure and dialectic of theoretical activity

The dialectic structure of the above productive and communicative activities indicates the structure of dialectic has its root in the finity and abstractness of the activity subject. In this case, we may conclude without difficulty that regarding theory as a specific activity, its structure must be "dialectic", too.[1] Therefore, if the fundament of theory is involved or theory is conceived as the "perspective" structure, the generation of dialectic will become unavoidable. The above discussion on the essence and history of dialectic has indicated that the origin of the dialectic of the theories in various forms is the dialectic structure of theoretical activity. Of course, it is the result of our observation which is consciously

---

1 The third part of this section will discuss in depth the difference of abstractness between these two activities.

based on the standpoint of practical philosophy, but in terms of theoretical philosophy, the fact is not like this.

There used to be the following two views on theoretical dialectics : one is to reduce theoretical dialectic to its object – the self structure of natural substance. This view matches with the thinking paradigm of ancient philosophy. Our previous interpretation on Marx's dialectic in essence had combined this concept with early-modern age materialism. The other view thinks that theoretical dialectic stems from the inherent structure of a "reason" or "spirit" which rules the world and governs all things. No doubt, it is the dialectic concept of early-modern subjective philosophy. Young Lukacs' dialectic was essentially generated under this concept.

Now, we attribute dialectic to the structure of theoretical activity. In this case, what it involves is not a being-in-itself object or an abstract subject but the real activity of a real subject. Of course, in addition to theoretical activity, the understanding on productive labour, communicative activity and their dialectic structures is also a necessary premise for our understanding of the dialectic as a theoretical process.

If theory is understood as a kind of specific human activity, it will not be difficult to understand the relation between the dialectic structure of theoretical activity and the dialectic structure of the previous two activities. Above we have traced the "dialectic" of the two activities back to the finity of the activity subject, while this subject-man- is also the subject of theoretical activity. Then theoretical activity should undoubtedly have a similar structure. In fact we may easily find the contradiction between "one" and "many" and man's governing behavior in productive activity, social communication and theoretical activity. The tools, social organizations and class division in productive activity and the logical classification and categories in theoretical activity all display this governing behavior and the dialectic nature in theoretical activity. The similarity among these activity spheres has been discovered by some sociologists and anthropologists though they could not clearly express the essence of this relation. For example, Frazier thinks that the social relations of human should be based on the logical relations of things, whereas Emile Durkheim, thinks contrarily that people classify things in this way just because they are divided by clans. "The first logical categories were social categories; the first classes of things were classes of men, into which these things were integrated."[1] Therefore, the logical classes as conceptual classes which were finally formed after a long forging. Neither Frazier nor Emile Durkheim could correctly reveal the essence of this isomorphic mechanism. The former adopted approximately the concept of early-modern philosophy. The latter could not fully justify his conclusion, regardless of the confirmation of facts or the attestation of logic. In fact, the view of Emile Durkheim also has the risk of obliterating the independence of theoretical activity. Anyway, they have both discovered the isomorphic relation between theoretical logic and social organization. From another aspect, we can say that, if Emile Durkheim also had thought over the isomorphism between theoretical activity and productive labour, he would not have included logical classes into social classes, because for the same reason, we may include logical classes into the tool classes of productive activity.

In fact, the dialectic structure of all kinds of activities should be reduced into the finity and abstractness of the activity subject. Just because, a specific subjective activity must have a specific foothold, it also must have a persistent principle. Any persistent principle is the result of the abstracting power of man. To adapt to the complexity of the world around us, it is necessary to transcend this abstractness on the basis of abstraction. This transcendence is dialectical. After studying various activities, we may understand the true basis of this isomorphism and meanwhile ensure the "essential" independency of each kind of activity. However, we should not equate all kinds of activities and must find a cut-in point for the entry of theory. According to the principle of Marx's materialism, this cut-in point is productive activity. Therefore, Marx's research on theoretical dialectic always proceeds from productive activity or economic activity. This does not indicate Marx reduces theoretical dialectic to the dialectic structure of productive activity because these two activi-

---

1 [French] Emile Durkheim and Marcel Mauss: Primitive Classification, p.89. .

ties must be traced back to general human activity. In The Poverty of Philosophy, Marx criticizes that Proudhon had applied Hegelian method to political economy and "everything being reduced to a logical categories, and every movement, every act of production to method, it naturally follows that all masses of products and of production, of objects and of movement, are reduced to an applied metaphysic."[1] The fact should be that "the economic categories are only the theoretical expression, the abstractions, of the social relations of production".[2] "The same men who establish social relations conformably with their material productivity, produce also the principles, the ideas, the categories, conformably with their social relations."[3] Here Marx mainly criticizes the ideas of theoretical philosophy and aims to reset theoretical activity on the basis of reality, i.e.: human activity. Of course, Marx's dissertation here indeed may mislead people to think that his purpose is to reduce social relations and theoretical categories to productive labour – in fact it is people's most popular misunderstanding on Marx's materialism and dialectic. If this misunderstanding were correct, Marx's critique on theoretical philosophy would become contradictory and it would be possible to think that he is criticizing theoretical philosophy based on a firm standpoint of theoretical philosophy. Obviously, if theoretical philosophy is aimed as a criticized object, it can be impossible that this critique is a critic of theoretical philosophy. We would rather say that Marx observes other two activities from a visual angle of productive activity. Due to the isomorphism of various activities, this observation is undoubtedly legal. The selection of this angle of vision by Marx's philosophy essentially reflects its finity as a philosophical theory, but this will not hamper our understanding on facts.

After we understand the relation between theoretical activity and productive and communicative activities, it will not be difficult to understand the generation of dialectic as a theoretical process. Same as productive and communicative activities, human's theoretical activity is

---

1 Marx & Engels Selected Works, Edition 2, Vol.1, p.140.
2 The same book as above, p.141.
3 The same book as above, p.142.

also a process in which multiplicate things are governed and integrated. Different from the labour tool system from which productive activity seeks help; and also the help of normative system in communicative activity, the medium from which theoretical activity seeks help is the conceptual system of logic. This system is expressed with lansigns. Same as productive activity and communicative activity, the medium that the subject possesses in theoretical activity is also "one", universality, while the object is "many" or particularity. Through theoretical activity, "one" governs "many", grasps "many" and integrates "many" into an integral body. This process is the process in which thinking integrates sensations with language. Through activity, words unify sensations, supersede their multiplicity and reduce non-orderly sensations to the examples of "generality" symbolized by words.[1]

In human language, the non-logical image language was first developed, so the opposition and unity between "one" and "many" were first manifested in form of image. In the beginning, in myth, a god corresponds to a kind of activity and the god as "one" is the administrator and controller of this kind of activity as "many". On the occasion when myth declined and logical language was not mature, a semi-image way of expression emerged, i.e.: intuitive dialectic way. In Western countries, the natural philosophy in ancient Greece tried to replace the previous god with "water", "gas", "fire" and other concrete and meanwhile abstract things to describe the unity of the world.[2] "Water", "fire", "gas" and so on of course are not qualified rulers, but this indicates the certainty that the essence of thinking manifests itself under the restriction of lansigns in a specific development form. In ancient China, people attempted to grasp the world with the images of Yi. "Yi has three meanings: simplicity, variability and invariability."[3] Therefore, Yi is the attempt to control multiplicity and variability with invariable "simplicity". Only when the

---

1 [German] Ernst Cassirer: Language and Myth, p.78, Beijing, Sanlian Bookstore, 1988.

2 Ye Xiushan: Research of Pre-Socratic Philosophy, p.45, Beijing, People's Publishing House, 1982.

3 Yi Wei Qian Zao Du, Refer to Qian Zhongshu Literary Selection, Vol.1, p.1, Guangzhou, Flower City Publishing House, 1990; Zhu Bokun: History of the Philosophy of Changes, vol.1, p.155, Beijing, Peking University Press, 1986.

logical function of lansigns was strengthened, this internal structure of thinking which uses "one" to control "many" could achieve a reliable language expression and a conceptual system could be formed. Thus the thinking level of pure idea was achieved and manifested as a conceptual dialectic – a dialectic in a pure theoretical form.

After this concept system was formed, it seems that the subject retreated from activity and theoretical activity had emerged as an independent and "objective" movement. From the perspective of today's practical philosophy, no matter how abstract concepts are and how their objectivity is stressed, the relations of these concepts can be ultimately traced back to concrete subjective activity. **Concept**, as "one" in theoretical activity is a visual angle from which subject "sees" the world. The "one" which acts by this visual angle, will certainly be a concept which can govern all the other concepts. In this way, dialectic is first manifested as the relation of concepts, the highest concept is "one" and the concepts below it is : "many". From the paradoxical nature of the concrete activities revealed above, we can see the highest concept as "one" is essentially only a visual angle of subject, while as far as "a" visual angle is concerned, it must be abstract. In this way, it seems that the direction of theoretical activity appears as a trend of "return" -- from a theoretical sphere to a non-theoretical sphere, because when we discover that the final result that theory pursues is the concreteness in a unique way is nothing but exposing its own abstractness, a non-theoretical sphere appears before us. In the end, theoretical activity goes back into its essence again. This process is dialectical or dialectic. Apparently, the two ends of this activity are thoroughly different: before theory is a totally unconscious chaos and after theory is a true concretion. Thus, we may deem the process of a theory as a process, which starts from the generation of an abstract visual angle and aims to the sublate the abstractness of the visual angle.

Two layers of dialectic

Two types of "concretion" and the important leap in dialectic process

In the first chapter, we have seen, Marx thinks that there are two types of concretion at the two ends of a theory. One is life practice as the "real" starting point of the theory. The other is thinking concretion as the outcome of the theory. The former is a sphere beyond and before theory. The latter is inside the theory. Owing to the essential abstractness of theory, the latter type of concretion cannot be reckoned as true concretion. To realize a true concretion, it must walk out of the scope of theory, i.e.: decompose theory. Marx's dissertation advocates that theoretical activity is different from "real" activities like productive activity and social communication. We should not "thoroughly" separate productive activity and social communicative activity from life-world just because of their abstractness, but for theoretical activity, if we do not separate it in this way, the abstraction of theory will become impossible. Therefore, the differentiation between two types of concretion indicates the differentiation between theoretical activity and productive and communicative activities, while this differentiation also embodies the differentiation of their abstraction ways. We can say that,the reason why concretion is concrete is that it is the integration of multiple categories and aims the unity of diversity; while the reason why abstraction is abstract is that it highlights a category and abandons other categories. When illustrating the concepts of economics, Marx points out that, production in general is an abstraction, but as a sensible and reasonable abstraction, as far as it actually emphasizes and defines the common aspects of a process this abstraction avoids repetition. Yet, this general concept, or the common aspect which is brought to light by comparison, is itself a multifarious compound including divergent categories. Although theory should pay constant attention to the existence of other different categories, if theory cannot abandon these categories, it will be unable to become a theory. In fact, it is the thinking mode of conception that makes the simplification of theory possible. In comparison, it is impossible that productive activity and social communication possess such simplicity, or it is impossible to reach such degree of abstraction. In these "real" activities, when a category is highlighted, other categories will be hidden only temporarily, but it is impossible to completely draw them out. In fact, in actual activities, these hidden categories often must be considered. For example, when man uses an attribute of a tool, other attributes must be accepted in the same time. The concepts constituting a theory can be simplified. That is to say, when concept depicts the category of an aspect of a thing, it may give up other categories. Since the nature of theory is abstract, then the concretion within the scope of theory will be very finite. If we say that any theory must have a visual angle from which it "sees" the world, then concrete theory should be a more inclusive visual angle. Nevertheless, a more inclusive visual angle is still a single visual angle, so theory in the end is still abstract. If theory is to grasp the whole world through a visual angle, i.e.: aim to realize the ultimate concretion within the scope of theory, it will just be the pretence of theory. In this sense, the previous theoretical philosophy is essentially the theory of pretence.

Concretion of practice and the finite concretion of theory

It is not difficult for us to see the two types of concretion put forth by Marx are essentially the concretion of practice and the finite concretion of theory. But here Marx seems to ignore a critical point and this directly results a serious misunderstanding on him – how do people grasp the concretion of life-world? Marx, had criticized that Hegel equated the process of thinking with the process of reality and thus regarded the concretion in thinking as real concretion. He pointed out, this absolutely is not the generation process of concretion. Marx also said that,the method to elevate from abstract to concrete was only a way in which thinking grasps concretion and reproduces it as spiritual concretion.[1] It is not difficult to understand his criticism at Hegel, but to say thinking is a way to reproduce concretion may mislead people: The spirit and thinking which Marx here refers to, are in the sense of theoretical activity. From this sentence, many people usually conclude,- without thinking- that theoretical

---

1 Marx & Engels Selected Works, Edition 2, Vol.2, p.19.

activity can completely "reproduce" concretion. This is a fatal misunder-standing. This misunderstanding is even below the thinking level of Hegel. Because, Hegel had definitely cognized the finity of subject-object opposition and tried to transcend this finity, but this above misunder-standing is even not aware of this finity. In essence, it is to conceive Marx as simple reflectionism. We admit that the concretion of theory and the concretion of practice have a qualitative difference, but their relation is by no means the relation between the reflecting and the reflected, and theory can in no way completely reproduce the concretion of practice. The first direct result of this misunderstanding, is to conceive dialectic as the dialectic which is within the scope of theory only and that it is only the reflection of real concretion.

We may affirm that the dialectic process will certainly go beyond the scope of theory because one of the necessary results of dialectic process is the decomposition of theory; in addition, the relation between theo-retical dialectic and life practice is not the relation between the reflecting and the reflected. We should remain conscious all the time that we are discussing theoretical activity in an ontological sense and theoretical ac-tivity itself must be deemed as a part of concrete life-world, so it will be impossible that theory's overall reflection on life-world is similar to pro-ductive activity, and the true relation between theory and life-world should be the concreteness of the life-world formed through activities. Of course, inside theory there is an inherent objective structure, i.e.: a reflectionist structure, but its object is only an extruded thing. This thing itself is the result of abstract activity. To go to concretion, theory should break through the finity of "reflection" other than reflect concretion. In the end, theory's return to the concretion of practice is the decomposi-tion of theory. After the decomposition of theory, will it achieve identity with life practice, i.e.: the first type of practice described by Marx. If we are limited to the differentiation of these two types of concretion, it will seem to be unavoidable, but it will inevitably lead us to the incompre-hension of dialectic. How can we understand theoretical activity's move-ment to complete identity with life-world? We know that theoretical activity belongs to life-world. If theory disappears in life -world, is the result of theoretical activity not to return to zero? In fact, the result after disappearance of theory can only be the grasp of the world- but no longer in a way of theoretical "see" and a reflective way. Since it appears as the result of the decomposition of theory, then this grasp may get rid of the restriction of theoretical abstractness and a concrete grasping can be truly realized. Hence we may easily find that although Marx pointed out the two ends of dialectic, and the two types of concretion have hinted that dialectic process must contain a leap, Marx did not clearly point out the part after this leap. Of course, it is not the fault of Marx, because this part is not necessary for his discussion on economic method. However, this part is the most important for our study on dialectic in this book.

It goes without saying that, dialectic process is not a continuous process and experiences a leap. Since it is a leap, it implies the difference of meaning before and after the leap. It is necessary for us to think over the meaning of dialectic in two layers. The first layer is certainly within the scope of theoretical activity. The second layer is after the decomposition of theory. On the first layer, i.e.: the dialectic within the scope of theory, our predecessors have made much research. Plato and Hegel's theoretical dialectics are typical models. However their visual spheres are limited to the scope of theory, exactly speaking, they were limited to a single theoretical visual angle. If it combines the meaning of dialectic in the second layer, the dialectic within the scope of theory still needs to be re-comprehended. Is the meaning of dialectic in the second layer a brand new thing? No, it is not. In fact, as early as the ancient times, a non-theoretical grasp on the world had been recognized, discussed and applied. However, it did not happen in the tradition of theoretical philosophy but in the tradition of practical philosophy. This non-theoretical grasp has been called "practical wisdom" for a long time. In the history of the previous philosophy, the two stages of dialectic and its meanings in the two layers were separated and had belonged to different traditions, while now we need to integrate them. This integration needs to explain the reasonableness, connotation and the boundary between the two.

Inclusive visual angle and practical wisdom

Dialectic process is divided into two stages. In fact this division is distinguished by the two existence ways and states of dialectic – theoretical state and "practical" state. We should say that this understanding on dialectic itself is the result of the practical philosophy approach. The theoretical philosophy's understanding on its own dialectic will not consider practical wisdom. If we are to investigate on the "practical" state of dialectic, we have to think about the finity of theory at first– which is also the finity of theoretical dialectic.

We have said, dialectic is a concrete process from the abstraction of theory to the concretion of practice. The driving force in this process is the tension between abstraction and concretion. This tension originates from the fact that the subject of theoretical activity belongs to life-world. Therefore, any abstraction of theory needs to move to the concretion of practice. Of course, the move is not to return to the state before the occurrence of theory, but to grasp concretion by means of dialectic. Since the abstraction by theory is the starting point of dialectic, then its theoretical process will be its first stage.

Dialectic is a process of overcoming abstraction and moving to concretion. To overcome abstraction is to overcome the unicity(singleness) of a visual angle and take other visual angles into consideration. Then, can it mean that the dialectic within the scope of theory is a theory with multiple visual angles? In fact it was the aim, the dialecticians of theoretical philosophy have tried to realize since the ancient times, but this effort was doomed to failure from the very beginning. We know theory by nature is the perspective to objects, while a perspective can only be a single visual angle. Multiple visual angles and theory are a pair of contradictory concepts. The previous theoretical philosophers tried to take hold of all aspects of the world and include all aspects of the world into vision. Their result was to create a view point going beyond the world, but this view point was unable to obtain an explanation on itself. Below, we will indicate that the essence of this view point is inherent in the world. This inherent nature indicates that no transcendent perspective is possible.

But how should we look at the dialectic system in history? It goes without saying that, the dialectic of any theoretical philosophy is the extreme manifestation of theoretical pretence. Plato and Hegel are the most typical examples. However, if we do not put the ultimate visual angle aside,without discussing on it for the time being, we may find without difficulty that their theories, in fact all were established in consideration of previous theories. In their theories, the contents of previous theories was taken into consideration to different extent, i.e.: the contents from different visual angles was considered to some extent. Of course, this absolutely does not mean that such a theory may contain more than one visual angle, but comparing with previous theories, it is true that their visual angles have been broken. This is the positive significance of the dialectic of theoretical philosophy approach. But, because it had still aimed to a single visual angle at the ultimate level and does not see the finity of this single visual angle, it is not only the dialectic in the scope of theory but also the dialectic of theoretical philosophy approach.

The dialectic in the scope of theory and the dialectic of theoretical philosophy approach are two concepts. We should say that the first concept caters for the dialectic outside the scope of theory in general, while this dialectic is unreasonable to the dialectic of theoretical philosophy, because the visual sphere of theoretical philosophy has never gone beyond the scope of theory. If these two concepts are not differentiated, the dialectic of theoretical philosophy will directly equal to the first stage of dialectic or its meaning at the first level. In fact, the consciousness of the being on the practical sphere determines the nature of this kind of dialectic. If, the being of practical sphere is perceived, it equals to the perception of the finity of theoretical activity, thus dialectic process must contain the decomposition of theory itself. This second as its nature belongs to the dialectic of practical philosophy; if I express it conversely, it means substitution of an absolute theoretical visual angle for other visual angles, or substation of the realization of an absolute rule of a single visual angle. This is the difference between the theoretical dialectic of practical philosophy and the dialectic of theoretical philosophy approach.

Since the generation of dialectic aims to break through the finity of a theoretical visual angle, then we may say that dialectic should happen between theories. The content outside the single visual angle can be perceived only when different theories collide with each other. When other contents are perceived, the original single visual angle will be either revised or thoroughly abandoned. In both cases, a more inclusive visual angle will be generated. This process is similar to the "fusion of horizons" in Hermeneutics, but as long as it is still within the scope of theory, the result of this fusion will be still a theory, i.e.: a more inclusive visual angle.

Although dialectic is not thorough or complete in the scope of theory or dialectic process in the end should or will surpass the theoretical sphere, it does not that mean the dialectic in the scope of theory is meaningless. Although theory and the dialectic of theory cannot comprehensively grasp the world and the concreteness of the world, the way theory grasps the world is absolutely necessary, and we may even say it is decided by man's objective survival and must exist. Theory must systematically grasp the beings as its objects. The dialectic in this scope is to achieve a grasp as concrete and rich as possible. Although the dialectic within the scope of theory cannot thoroughly overcome the finity of theoretical activity, comparing with the dialectic of previous theoretical philosophy, it obviously tries to introduce a "tolerant principle" other than stick to the "dogmatic principle" of theoretical philosophy. Of course, this "tolerant principle" cannot be thoroughly realized within the scope of theory, but the consciousness on the finity of theoretical activity is the beginning of this principle.

Practical wisdom and practical dialectic

Since the richer grasp within the scope of theory is still abstract after all, then the course of dialectic will certainly break through the finity of the whole theory. It is practical dialectic. We may also call it practical wisdom or practical knowledge. Practical dialectic breaks through the finity of single theoretical visual angle, so this dialectic allows the co-existence of multiple visual angles and these visual angles may be integrated into an integral body. Of course, this integration has an essential difference from the integration in the scope of theory. The integration in the scope of theory is to eliminate the independence of each visual angle and constitute them as a part of an absolute visual angle. This in fact is to use another visual angle to substitute multiple visual angles and integrate them into one. By contrast, the integration of practice wisdom is not to unify all visual angles into one but to compromise and balance them and incorporate their reasonable elements into them, but due to the circumstances and concreteness of practical knowledge, the certainty will not therefore be lost. Of course, the certainty of practical knowledge resulting from practical integration is based on the certainty of concrete life circumstances, other than the general certainty of theoretical knowledge, which is abstract and divorced from any concrete conditions. Anyway, as long as there is certainty, it will be valid knowledge. For this reason, the multiple visual angles or multiple meanings which are illegal and vehemently repulsed in theoretical knowledge find legality in practical knowledge. Here the tolerant principle of dialectic is carried through. In this way, many things which used to be excluded from the scope of knowledge, and ideas such as: "Golden Mean" and "Harmony Together With Differences" put forth by Chinese ancient Confucians may be appropriately understood. Indeed, these cannot be called theoretical knowledge, but they are consistent with practical wisdom and practical dialectic.

Here, we put practical wisdom behind theoretical dialectic and conceive it as the sublation and transcendence of the unicity(singleness) of theoretical visual angle. It does not mean that practical wisdom must exist "behind" the theory. As a matter of fact, practical wisdom is often considered "pre-" theory, or in other words people often discover practical wisdom in the state of pre-theory. We should say that, this understanding on practical dialectic contains two meanings or aspects. Firstly, practical wisdom deals with things and grasps concrete life-world in a multi-angle way. This is consistent with the true living state of human in the world. Before the abstraction of theory had emerged, people had existed in a "dialectic" way, so practical wisdom was often manifested as discoveries on human's real living state. Therefore, today's practical dialectic does not only manifest itself as a transcendence to theoretical abstractness but also manifests itself as the return to "pre-"theoretical state. Differently, in those days, the state before theory was an unconscious state in essence, whereas the practical wisdom after the development process of theory is conscious. Secondly, the tracing of the state "before" theory is essentially an effective way to discover men's real survival and understand practical dialectic. The typical one is Martin Heidegger's existentialist analysis. In fact, Martin Heidegger's approach is to "put aside" the objective existence of theory and man and deem it as an "issue" to be solved, thus he has opened a "pre"-theory visual sphere. Heidegger also thinks that this sphere is prior to theory, but in terms of the process of operation of his thought, it is "posterior to" theory. In this sense, Martin Heidegger's phenomenological method is very much similar to Lao Tzu's "in the pursuit of Tao, every day something is dropped" method. The process of forward pursuit here is essentially a transcending process. Therefore, forward and backward here must be conceived as the same process.

The integration of the dialectic within the scope of theory and practical wisdom is the dialectic of practical philosophy. In fact, the two cannot be separated. When we observe the dialectic within the scope of theory, the factors of practical wisdom have been perceived; while the practical wisdom in the conscious form is a result of the development of theoretical dialectic. When we understand dialectic in this way, we will also open a realistic sphere of dialogue with Chinese ancient philosophy and also create an opportunity to revive Chinese practical philosophy. In fact the Chinese ancient philosophy as we call is a non-theory practical wisdom. The revival of this practical wisdom is not to simply return to ancient practical philosophy. Instead, it must be modernized and converted into a modern practical wisdom. This is because the life-world we are faced in modern practice is fundamentally different from the world ancient people were faced. The corresponding practical wisdom or the way to obtain practical knowledge is needed. One of the ways to realize this conversion is based on the circumstance of the real life practice in modern China. On the one hand, it is in dialogue with the ancient practical philosophy and on the other hand it dialogues with the Western modern practical philosophy. Through dialogue, it extends its own theoretical visual angle and realizes the fusion of horizons. It itself is a dialectic process as practical wisdom.

PICTURE OF THE LIFE-WORLD OF FINITE SUBJECT

Introduction

In fact, the presupposition of the essence and existence condition of man often contains a "preconditional" attitude towards philosophy. From the above discussion, we can see the key to the differentiation between Marx's philosophy and previous philosophy, and between this interpretation on Marx's philosophy and the previous interpretations is whether it consciously sets foothold on real individual life practice and on the finite survival of man. Although we have deeply investigated the reality and finity of human existence and regarded it as the starting point of theoretical elucidation, this existence condition, the human essence it constitutes and the relation between man and the world where man lives were not directly described. This is exactly the content this chapter wants to complete. In the history of philosophy, many dissertations were made on man and its existence condition. We will mainly set our foothold on Marx's dissertations on man and at the same time give necessary remarks on previous views.

CHAPTER ONE

Marx's Two Propositions On Man

For man and its existence condition, we were used to express Marx's view with two propositions. One proposition thinks man is a conscious animal. His essence is free and self-conscious activity. Man is what he manifests himself; the other proposition regards men as "the ensemble of the social relations" and as real individuals in a specific historical circumstance. The former underlines man's active side, while the latter stresses on man's finite and given side. We should say these two propositions are not contradictory, and only when we combine the two, we can truly and comprehensively understand Marx's thought. But in fact, none of the previous interpretations on Marx's philosophy inherently connected these two propositions, so none of them had considered this issue at a height of Marx. The result is the regress to various kinds of "pre-"Marx "anthropology". Here we are going to reinterpret these two as a preparation for the description of man's existence condition.

Marx and the contradiction between "active" and "passive"

The fundamental reason why previous interpretations on Marx were unable to inherently unify these two propositions is that the two propositions were differentiated and simplified into the contradiction between active and passive and the contradiction between free and decisive, thus equating these contradictions with the contradictions between early-modern materialism and idealism. Things seem like this, Marx could include the two parties of each contradiction into his own theory, thus providing a superior answer to this fundamental issue of early-modern philosophy – even solve this issue. His understanding seems rather reasonable and has nothing improper. However, the place which seems to have no problem often conceals fatal danger. In fact, the "unity" people refer to is only a category in form, whereas it is this formal category that stops people from further inquiring its essential content. Although, here the critical secrete which distinguishes Marx's philosophy from early-modern philosophy is embodied, we have to admit people have talked nothing of it.

In fact, the problem is not that we cannot say these contradictions are united in Marx's philosophy, but that how to understand these contradictions and how to understand this unity. If, we equate these contradictions with some contradictions in early-modern philosophy, we will inevitably think in the way of early-modern philosophy, and once we think about these issues in the way of early-modern philosophy, these issues will become unsolvable. Above, we have mentioned that early-modern theoretical philosophy essentially is a theory with an absolute single visual angle, and just because of this absolute single visual angle, these contradictions are ultimately manifested as the contradictions between different theories. If we adopt the thinking mode of early-modern philosophy, in the end we will certainly choose a "point" as the ultimate visual angle of theory and this will have no difference from theoretical philosophy. In fact, the past interpretations on Marx are like this – either stay at the simple amalgamation of the two parties of the contradiction in early-modern philosophy or choose one party as its standpoint. In essence, they both return to "pre-" Marx state in their own ways.

No doubt, the key here is how to understand the significance of the revolution by Marx's philosophy. We say, Marx has transcended early-modern philosophy and became the founder of modern philosophy. Does it mean that Marx had satisfactorily solved the fundamental issues of early-modern philosophy? Obviously not. If the issues are still "issues of early-modern philosophy", Marx will be unable to solve them; if we say Marx has really solved some issues, then they must not be the "issues of early-modern philosophy" but the reconstructed issues, though they are very similar to the issues of early-modern philosophy and even Marx himself had also used the terms of early-modern philosophy to express them. Therefore, the issues of early-modern philosophy are not "solved" but was "decomposed". We admit the difference of the two propositions about man and his existence condition inside Marxist theory, but we must not equate them with the contradiction in early-modern philosophy and we must abandon the structure of the issues of early-modern philosophy and re-understand the issues Marx had faced.

In fact, Marx's critique on early-modern philosophy was to try his utmost to avoid raising and solving problems in the way of early-modern philosophy. For example, when Marx talks about the relation between man and his circumstances in Theses on Feuerbach, Marx directs at materialist determinism and idealist rational voluntarism in early-modern philosophy, but he neither choose any of the two standpoints nor combine them. Instead, he thinks the change in circumstances is consistent with human activity or self changes and can only be regarded as and reasonably conceived as revolutionary practice. Conceiving an issue as the issue of "revolutionary practice" is to re-construct the issue itself, because this contradiction is theoretical opposition only, while theoretical opposition can be solved only in a practical way and with the help of the power of practice; therefore, the solution of this opposition is by no means the task of recognition but a task of real life. The failure of philosophy to solve this task is because philosophy regards it as a theoretical task only. The process from theory to practice indicates that Marx speaks not in the framework of early-modern philosophy. It should be stressed that the practice here is in the broad-sense meaning of practice as we have mentioned above, and it is not a volitive activity of any early-modern philosophy but a real and concrete sphere. Just in this sense, we say social life essentially is practical. This sphere is beyond the visual sphere of early-modern philosophy, so what Marx puts forth, based on this sphere is no longer an issue in the sense of early-modern philosophy. Therefore, it looks as if the two parties of the contradiction in early-modern philosophy were unified by Marx, but certainly it is not understandable in the thinking mode of early-modern philosophy. The past interpretations are to replace the issues inside Marx's theory with the issues which have been decomposed by Marx. Their illegality is self-evident.

Then, how should we understand the difference and unity between the two propositions inside Marx's philosophy? This will again involve the understanding on dialectic. We say dialectic as a "quasi theory" is the transcendence of the absolute single visual angle of theory. This transcendence does not mean establishing a higher single visual angle above many single visual angles. If so, there will be no fundamental difference between Marx and Hegel. What makes Marx's dialectic distinguish itself and surpass ancient and early-modern dialectics is that, it really goes beyond the sphere of theory. Therefore, if we take the single visual angle of theory and monism as reference, then Marx's dialectic will be displayed as a multi-angle and plural determinism. The so-called plural decision refers to that the parties or edges of a contradiction have certain independency and cannot be reduced to others. These "non-reducible" aspects form the totality of dialectic. We should not perceive this totality in a theoretical way – because it appears paradoxical before any theoretical perception – it can only be exhibited and this exhibition is negative in most cases. The two propositions mentioned above can be deemed as two non-reducible aspects. The only reasonable method to study them is dialectic method. Of course, this method is legal only when it is based on life practice. Below we will study Marx's relevant dissertations on this basis.

Generally speaking, the first proposition – the essence of man rests with his free and conscious activity – is mainly reflected in Marx's Economic and Philosophical Manuscripts of 1884. Here Marx stresses that, it is human activity and it is the objective relation between man and external world that constitutes human essence. Marx said:

> It is, therefore, in his fashioning of the objective that man really proves himself to be a species-being. Such production is his active species-life. Through it, nature appears as his work and his reality. The object of labour is, therefore, the objectification of the species-life of man: for man produces himself not only intellectually, in his consciousness, but actively and actually, and he can therefore contemplate himself in a world he himself has created.[1]

> The entire so-called history of the world, is nothing but the creation of man through human labour, nothing but the emergence of nature for man, so he has the visible, irrefutable proof of his birth through himself, of his genesis. Since the real existence of man and nature has become evident in practice, through sense experience, because man has thus become evident for man as the being of nature, and nature for man as the being of man, the question about an alien being, about a being above nature and man – a question which implies the admission of the unreality of nature and of man – has become impossible in practice.

We may say the inherent connection between Human's objective activity and human essence is the dominating thought in the the manuscripts. Marx takes it as a starting point to study both philosophical issues and the issues of whole economics. Here the striking structure of the opposition between man and external world as well as "objectification", "species-being", "visible" and other concepts used by early-modern philosophy and also used by Marx often make people interpret the content of the manuscripts naturally in the way of early-modern philosophy, concretely speaking, in the way of Hegel or Feuerbach. The result of this interpretation is no doubt Hegel-style Marxism or Feuerbach-style Marxism. The fact is so. For a time after the Manuscripts was discovered, it was reckoned as the "testimony" of Lukacs's Hegel-style Marxist philosophy and became the main object elucidated by the so-called "humanistic" Marxism. We should say the confrontation of the Western Marxism founded by Lukacs and other people against the orthodox Marxism of the former Soviet Union and the Second International is a

---

1   Collected Works of Karl Marx and Frederick Engels, Chinese version 1, Vol.42, p.131.

matter of great significance in the development of Marxist philosophy, but the tenability of this confrontation exposes an unfortunate issue: "orthodox" Marxism obviously only holds to the argumentations of early-modern and even ancient materialism. The tenability of this confrontation indicates people including Lukacs could not really reach the philosophical vision opened by Marx and we even may say that they still stay at the level of early-modern idealism. We know that the opposition between early-modern materialism and idealism is what Marx wants to surpass. In addition, people like Louis Althusser who had regarded the Manuscripts as a lower development "stage" of Marx's philosophy also thinks that the Manuscripts still belongs to a philosophy which bears a deep impression of Feuerbach's way of questioning and is influenced by Feuerbach's hesitation and retrogression to Hegel.[1] Therefore, the Manuscripts reflect Marx's both triumphant and failing thought. We have to admit Louis Althusser's comment is rather intelligent and the Manuscripts indeed bears the impression of Hegel and Feuerbach, but we should not therefore interpret it in the way of early-modern philosophy. We should re-understand the content of the Manuscripts based on the visual sphere opened by itself. In fact, this was the way closer to Marx, because the Manuscripts embodies the "secrete" of new philosophy.

In fact, the key of the issue is, whether we should deem the labour discussed by Marx as the rational and spiritual activity in the sense of early-modern philosophy, Hegel in particular, whether its objectification equals the exteriorization of spirit and further whether the structure of subject-object opposition forms the ultimate structure of Marx's philosophy and whether subjectivity is the ultimate visual angle of Marx's philosophy. If the answers are positive, the following statement by Marx will become incomprehensible.

> Man is directly a natural being. As a natural being and as a living natural being he is on the one hand endowed with natural powers, vital powers – he is an active natural being. These forces exist in him as tendencies and abilities

---

1 [French] Louis Althusser: For Marx, excerpt from [French] P. Rodrigo: Marx and Phenomenology, Philosophical Translation, 1993(3).

– as instincts. On the other hand, as a natural, corporeal, sensuous objective being he is in a suffering, conditioned and limited creature, like animals and plants. That is to say, the objects of his instincts exist outside him, as objects independent of him; yet these objects are objects that he needs – essential objects, indispensable to the manifestation and confirmation of his essential powers. To say that man is a corporeal, living, real, sensuous, objective being full of natural vigor is to say that he has real, sensuous objects as the object of his being or of his life, or that he can only express his life in real, sensuous objects.[1]

In fact, in the Manuscripts, Marx intensely criticizes Hegelian philosophy of spirit. The core content of this critique is to reveal the abstractness of Hegelian philosophy. In the sense of Hegel, the essence of man is equal to his self-consciousness, while the so-called subjective activity is the exteriorization of self-consciousness. Hegel had also observed labour and confirmed the inherent association between labour and human essence, but the labour in the sense of Hegel "is man's coming-to-be for himself within alienation, or as alienated man. The only labour which Hegel knows and recognises is abstract mental labour."[2] If the outside world is only the exteriorization of spirit, then this spirit should be non-objective being in the very beginning and Marx calls this being "Unwesen".

Comparing with Hegel's "Unwesen", Marx thinks, man is real, sensuous and concrete. Then what do Marx's sensuousness and reality mean? Is it to stick to Feuerbach's standpoint and oppose Hegel? Indeed, Marx gives very high remark on Feuerbach and even cites many terms from Feuerbach, but the ideas released from them are not understood by Feuerbach. In fact, Marx's citation of Feuerbach's terms aims to indicate man has his life-world, and the so-called objective activity can only be the activity in his life-world. In this sense, man is "suffering", "conditioned". This suffering stems, to a large extent, from man's "natural" or biological attribute. At this point, Marx and Feuerbach are very close, but Marx does not stop here. Therefore, the sensuous world called by Marx absolutely does not mean a biological environment only. It refers to all things a concrete man accepts as the precondition of his survival. Marx stresses

---

1 Collected Works of Karl Marx and Frederick Engels, Chinese version 1, Vol.42, p.167~168.
2 The same book as above, p.163

that all abstract oppositions can be solved only in society, in man's practical activity. We know society represents a sphere constituted by men, and the labour which forms man's "species-essence" must be carried out in a social way and meanwhile constitutes the society. In this way, we may perceive without difficulty the difference between Marx and Feuerbach. In Economic and Philosophical Manuscripts of 1844, this difference is not manifested explicitly, but after all, Marx uses the discourse of Feuerbach to reveal to us a new philosophy in an unclever way.

Later on, when Marx criticized Feuerbach in a focused way, he pointed out straightforward this new philosophy as well as its difference from Feuerbach:

> Feuerbach, not satisfied with abstract thinking, wants contemplation; but he does not conceive sensuousness as practical, human-sensuous activity.
>
> Feuerbach resolves the religious essence into the human essence. But the human essence is no abstraction inherent in each single individual. In its reality it is the ensemble of the social relations.
>
> Feuerbach, consequently, does not see that the "religious sentiment" is itself a social product, and that the abstract individual whom he analyses belongs to a particular form of society. [1]

Here, we turn to Marx's second proposition about man. In fact, in the sense of Marx, although Feuerbach is not satisfied with Hegel's abstract self-consciousness, attempts to resort to "sensuousness" and "contemplation", Feuerbach's sensuous man does not have a world, so is still abstract. Marx also recognizes man's "natural" attribute, but does not directly conceive this attribute as man's "species-essence". Instead, he thinks man as "a living natural being", as an "active" being, who can constitute his essence only through activity, but man's such activity can be regarded as real "man's sensuous activity" and also man's practical activity only when "in a particular form of society". We should say, in Theses on Feuerbach, Marx, only stresses man and his practical activity belong to a concrete form of society, but he was unable to give positive description on this form of society. In addition, how does the claim that

---

1 Marx & Engels Selected Works, Edition 2, Vol.1, p.56.

man belongs to a particular form of society, achieve a unity with Marx's above claim that man is a "natural" being? It seems that this question is not consciously put forth. Of course, it was impossible to fulfill such a task in these same theses, but in the direct critique on Feuerbach, the prospect of real men and their life-world has been vividly portrayed by Marx.

In *The German Ideology*, the picture of this life-world is clearly visible. Here, Marx again criticizes German ideology. Though, Hegel and Feuerbach are the most important objects and "dialoguers", Marx's ideological platform is mature and he does not need to seek help from other people's ways of discourse, so here Marx indicates his standpoint in a straightforward way. Here Marx discusses the activity of "real individual" as well as his relation with the world in which he acts. We should first clarify that here Marx discusses the relation between man and "world", other than the relation between man and "circumstances". We know that in Theses on Feuerbach, Marx explores the relation between man and circumstances. In essence, it was an issue of early-modern philosophy, because it only studied which of the two came first, and was unaware of their essential inseparability, to say nothing of the precondition for discussion. Marx tries to use this issue to disclose its paradoxical nature. This was the irreconcilable contradiction between rational voluntarism and determinism as we see. Through this contradiction, the sphere of practice emerges, and merely emerges. The relation between man and world represents a brand new way of question and narration. The precondition of this relation is not the separation of the two but the inseparability of the two. We may even say this relation itself represents the essential association between man and his world. Marx had said: "Where there exists a relationship, it exists for me". "Consciousness is, therefore, from the very beginning a social product, and remains so as long as men exist at all".[1] Old materialism explores the relation between man and circumstances. This relation essentially might be equal to the relation between animals and circumstances. Originally, man's natural essence considered by early-modern materialism was man's biological attributes,

---

1 Marx & Engels Selected Works, Edition 2, Vol.1, p.81.

even physical attributes. It seems that early-modern idealism does not have this issue on its agenda, because for it, circumstances are the object of consciousness, while the object of consciousness is the exteriorization of consciousness. However, its opposition with materialism indicates that this issue was unshakably there. The only way to solve this issue is the structural conversion of the issue itself, i.e.: the change in the way of questioning. The result of this conversion is the introduction of the relation between man and his sensuous world. Marx had pointed out, circumstances make men just as much as men make circumstances. This expression has used old terms, but the way "contradiction" was revealed and the issue Marx focuses is a brand new issue : the issue of man and the world he lives in:

> The individuals here are not as they may appear in their own or other people's imagination, but as they really are; i.e. as they operate, produce materially, and hence as they work under definite material limits, pre-suppositions and conditions independent of their will.[1]

As described above, Marx also points out, this sum of productive forces, capital funds and social forms of intercourse, which every individual and generation find in existence as something given, is the real basis of what the philosophers have conceived as "substance" and "essence of man," and what they had deified and attacked; but the real basis which is not in the least disturbed, in its effect and influence on the development of men, although that these philosophers revolt against it as "self-consciousness" and the "Unique". Only the individuals in the world are real individuals, while the world must be a world of men. Here, the significance that the essence of man called by Marx is the "ensemble of the social relations" in "reality" was substantiated and world as the real premise of human essence was also formally established.

---

1 The same book as above, p.71~72.

Constitution of the world and human essence

Above we obtain the following rough conclusion from our reinterpretation on Marx's two propositions about the essence of man: Marx converts the issue of the essence of man into the issue of the relation between real individual and his sensuous world, or coverts it into the observation on the real individuals, those who act and live in the sensuous world. Obviously, the world is vitally important to the constitution of the essence of man. Concretely speaking, it serves as a precondition. Then how to understand this precondition? In terms of form, this precondition indicates a kind of finite subjectivity, but we still need to separate it from ancient practical philosophy and old materialist concepts regarding to its content, even need to distinguish it from Kantian "finite subjectivity".

We should say that the most important object of Marx's philosophical revolution is Hegel, while Hegel was the culminant figure of German classical idealism. Today, our finite subjectivity mainly corresponds to early-modern idealism's subjectivity without finity and precondition. May we say all that has passed beyond early modern-idealism is finite subjectivity? Apparently not. Our descriptions on finite subject, and its world may be said to be similar to ancient practical philosophy in some aspects. But it is apparently improper to talk about subjectivity in ancient philosophy; and the "non"-subjectivity of early-modern materialism is only a shadow of idealism, which obtains its significance only from the absolute subjectivity of idealism, and could even be developed into a disguised absolute subjectivity in the end. On the other side, Kantian "finite subjectivity" cannot be regarded as the transcendence of early-modern philosophy, and should be regarded as an immature state of its absolute subjectivity. However, all these aspects are "resources" of our understanding on Marx's finite subjectivity. Since it is a "finite" subject, we should proceed from observing the restrictions on this subject. Of course, this finity directs and opposes at the infinite subject of early modern-idealism. According to common sense, when we talk of restriction on a thing, it is inevitable that we should involve the relation between the restrictor and the restricted. For man, his restrictor is his object. Marx clearly expresses this point in Economic and Philosophical Manuscripts of 1844. He thinks man is an objective being and manifests his "species being" through his objective activity, while even if Hegelian "self-consciousness" also has an object, and its object is formed from its exteriorization, so in the final analysis is a non-object "monster". Here, Marx expresses finity more as objectivity. However, if our understanding stops here, it will be unable to get rid of the framework of early-modern philosophy. In fact, if we understand early-modern idealism as the recognition on subjectivity, then materialism can be understood as the recognition of the object of this subject. If only subject and its object's reality are recognized, then it will be nothing but only concisely expresses, the basic framework of the whole early-modern philosophy. Therefore, if the Manuscripts opens a brand new philosophical visual sphere, then the "finity" of the finite subject cannot be understood as an external restriction by its object. In fact, from Marx's objective restriction, we may also see the meaning of finity in another layer.

According to Marx's analysis, human activity is an objective activity, this activity will certainly change its object, but the existence of the object must be accepted by subject. The acceptance mentioned here corresponds to creation, exteriorization and other concepts. If subject must accept its object, it must accept the existence of the object, too. At least we may say this acceptance must also involve object as object. But for infinite subjectivity, the acceptance of object as object is incomprehensible, because it is obviously illogical that a subject accepts itself. Acceptance must be acceptance to the sphere outside or beyond the accepter. We may easily understand the acceptance of an object. The accepter and the accepted are at a same level. However, it is not so easy to understand the acceptance to an object as object, because it involves a more essential level. In fact, object as object and subject as subject are two aspects of the same issue. Therefore, the acceptance of the object as object essentially is also the acceptance of subject as subject. In this way, a brand new thought is revealed: subject as subject or the origin of subject's essence is accepted. This is the deeper meaning on the "finity" of finite subjectivity.

But perhaps somebody may say, we are going to the opposite of Marx, because Marx had ever explicitly said: "A being only considers himself independent when he stands on his own feet; and he only stands on his own feet when he owes his existence to himself. A man who lives by the grace of another regards himself as a dependent being. But, I live completely by the grace **of another**, if I owe him not only the maintenance of my life, but if he has, moreover, created my life – if he is the *source of my life.*"[1] Can we say that Marx, here means to say that, the source of the essence of subject is accepted equal to "living by the grace of another"? No, it isn't. In fact, here Marx mainly targets theism. If we make careful analysis, we may discover without difficulty this acceptance is really problematic. The "another" here in this passage, undoubtedly should be conceived as a completely alien being, just this complete alienation indicates the accepter has existed before acceptance and giving. If the accepter exists in advance, we cannot say its essence was given here. Therefore, at the two ends as acceptance and giving, there must be a thing with a special association. If we admit this special association, this giving will be no longer the giving by "another". Hence, we cannot say that the acceptance is contradictory with Marx's "standing on his own feet".

Then, how should we understand this giving is not by "another" and how to realize the acceptance of it? The giver of the essence of subject and its object must be in the sphere where subject and object come from, i.e.: the sphere "before" the opposition between subject and object. This sphere is not the "other" of subject. Obviously, it is life-world. Above we have mentioned, the opposition between subject and its object essentially is the excrescence of the two from life-world, while life-world is the giver of the essence of subject and its object. From the perspective of subject, the generation of any subject in fact is the excrescence from life-world and meanwhile is also manifested as the acceptance by this specific life-world. As Martin Heidegger said, man is "thrown" into this world and can obtain its essence only in this world.

By now, we may very naturally associate some ideas of ancient practical philosophy. In Aristotelian practical philosophy, the essence of man is

---

1 Collected Works of Karl Marx and Frederick Engels, Chinese version 1, Vol.42, p.129.

given by the "world" where he lives. This "world" is the state. We should say that it is improper to use the concept of subjectivity in the era of Aristotle even if it is finite subjectivity. However, we may see here the "primitive" form of finite subjectivity. In Aristotle, the conditions for the free man are, whether he lives in the state and whether he engages in political activity. The state is a community and represents a mode of life. The people in the state accept this mode and act according to its rules, thus becoming men. In contrast, the people outside the state – the slaves and barbarians, do not possess this mode of life and are not regarded to possess the "conditions" for man. Therefore, Aristotle said, "man is by nature a political animal" and "he who by nature and not by mere accident is without a state, is either a bad man or above humanity".[1] Obviously, here the essence of man is given by state where he lives. Aristotelian state is absolutely prior to individuals, because by nature totality must come before part. Because individual's effect on state was not fully perceived. More importantly, although Aristotle perceived and attempted to describe a "world", i.e.: state, the meaning of the state here is a narrow-sense political "world", much different from the life-world we have tried to define.

The state represents a definite mode of life. The acceptance to this mode of life is the condition for the formation of man. As described in the second chapter, Marx also gave similar expression. He had pointed out: "the mode of production must not be considered simply as being the production of the physical existence of the individuals. Rather it is a definite form of activity of these individuals, a definite form of expressing their life, a definite mode of life on their part. As individuals express their life, so they are. What they are, therefore, coincides with their production, both with what they produce and with how they produce. The nature of individuals thus depends on the material conditions determining their production". Marxist mode of life and Aristotelian state differs mainly in two aspects. Firstly, Aristotelian state is a specific political life at first, while Marxist mode of life must consider productive activity and material condition at first. Marx said:

---

1 [Ancient Greek] Aristotle: Politics, p.7.

The fact is, therefore, that definite individuals who are productively active, in a definite way enter,into these definite social and political relations. Empirical observation must in each separate instance bring out empirically, and without any mystification and speculation.[1]

Social relations and political relations belong to the sphere of interpersonal communication. Generally speaking, Marx observes this sphere from production, but the "contradictory" relation between the two affirms communication is independent of production. Marx on the one hand says the "form of communication" is decided by production but on the other hand says the premise of production is the communication Verkehr(germ. exchange) among individuals. This approach essentially affirms the non-reduction approach. Aristotle limits the mode of individual life to political life only. In comparison, Marxian life-world is much richer. In addition, in the era of Aristotle, individual's effect on the community where he lived was negligible. Therefore, Aristotle naturally neglected the effect of individual activity in the state. This negligence is not "illegal". However, by the era of Marx, any negligence of it had become impossible: "Artificial articles" have become the most prominent and most noticeable part of life-world. Those days some people even asserted that all the external objects were created by subject. Thus, the restriction on subject becomes a necessary link for a reasonable evaluation on its role. As known to all, Marx conceives subject as "an individual in reality", on the one hand he is a subject and he creates world and history; on the other hand this subject "must be in a position to live" in order to make history. "But life involves before everything else eating and drinking, a habitation, clothing and many other things."[2] What defined by this contradiction was the real individual, the real subject. For this subject, creation also means acceptance, or in other words his way to accept the world is his activity, and his creation.

Accepting the real world is a critical link for man's formation of his essence. This is the essential meaning of the finite subjectivity. This finity is different from Kantian finity as: transcendental subjectivity. Although

---

1 Marx & Engels Selected Works, Edition 2, Vol.1, p.71.
2 Marx & Engels Selected Works, Edition 2, Vol.1, p.79.

Kantian finite subjectivity bears form resemblance with Marxist real individual in form, Kantian finite subjectivity mainly targets against the absolute subjectivity of Hegel, Edmund Husserl and other people. A key difference between them is enough to divide them into different eras. That is, Kantian finite subject does not have a world, while Marxian finite subject has. In the sense of Kant, it is thing-in-itself, that sets a boundary for subject, and the reason why this boundary is possible is that thing-in-itself is Anderssein in relation to subject and subject does not have any knowledge about, it except confirming its existence; while the finity of the Marxist finite subject means it is a being in the world and it must accept a definite world at first, so subject is inseparable from the giver of its finity, i.e.: the world.

Since the world is so important to the constitution of the essence of man, then the best way for us here, to understand the finite subject, will be to depict the life-world where it acts. In Marx's works, The German Ideology in particular, we see those effort in this aspect. However, we have to admit that there it is an outline only and a complete picture of life-world is yet to be depicted.

CHAPTER TWO

Material World and Human Activity

Introduction

We should say man's life-world is an integral body, but we have to divide it during theoretical our descriptions. In fact, in *The German Ideology,* Marx roughly divides the relation of men and the world around them into two: the relation between man and natural objects and the relation between man and man. Here we will use his division to depict the world of man, from two aspects: the relation between man and things and the relation between man and man. This section mainly discusses the relation between man and material and discusses how the nature becomes a part of man's life-world and what role does **the tool** play in constituting the essence of man.

Instrumental activity and human world

Firstly, we will explore "material" world. Generally, it is thought that the ultimate attribute of material is its nature of occupying space, i.e.: extendability. However, as far as material as a part of life-world is concerned, extendability is not a factor of its essentiality. We say man must live in a definite material world. It does not mainly mean that man must live in a definite physical space. Of course, man must be a corporeal being at first. This being certainly takes up some space and must form a physical relation with other beings. But if such spatial relation was enough to form the reason for the existence of man in material world, we would be unable to separate man from animals and even non-living beings. Obviously, spatiality is far from covering man's material world and is unable to play an essential role in the formation of human world, too. Whereas, previous materialists conceived the relation between man and material just in this sense, so they could only explore the issue of man and its world as the problem of the relation between "man and circumstances". Above we have indicated this exploration was based on the thinking mode of early-modern philosophy, and under this mode of thinking, there was no result. Marx had expressed this view on many occasions. But, undeniably, the spatial relation between man and material is indeed a necessary part of man's life-world. Here, what we need to do is not to exclude space from the world but conceive it based on the totality of the world and grasp it based on a more essential level.

The key of the issue is, how does this spatial relation become the spatial relation between "man" and his material world and why does this relation always "belong to man"? Marx points out, for animal, external thing is a completely alien and unassailable opposite, it is impossible to form a relation between animal and external object; while man is different. In the world of man, external object has the character of "belonging to me" from the very beginning, so the relation between man and external object becomes possible. For man, external object does not mean a complete alienage but means an inherent association with man.

Then, how to understand this inherent association? The ordinary understanding is that it is man's consciousness and spirit that distinguish man from animal, this intrinsic association covers the meaning of the relation between man's consciousness and "external object" – the object of this consciousness. In this approach, we may conclude that man obtains his essence from the opposition with external object, that is to say, man and his opposite can be defined as : "opposite and yet being complementary".

Indeed, this interpretation may separate man from animal, but it cannot explain this relation is an "intrinsic" relation and such a definition indicates that it is exactly an "extrinsic" relation. Besides, the relation between consciousness and material needs to be explained, too. Above, we have indicated that this intrinsic association between man and his world is prior to the constitution of his essence. If this intrinsic association is conceived, as an objective relation between man and external object, then the situation will be just the opposite – the essence of man happens before any relation. But, if the essence of man happens before any relation, these relations can only be "extrinsic" relations – either negative acceptance or his active reformation efforts. Of course, we cannot deny the existence of such relation, but it should be deemed as a derivative state only. The sphere "before" it, i.e.: the sphere as the cause of this objective relation is where the essence of the problem lies.

Therefore, seeking the intrinsic association between man and the material in the world and tracing the origin of the objective relation between man and external object are the same issue. In terms of the sphere where man and material are inherently associated, the objective relation between man and material is derivative, but our investigation on the former must start from the latter. Concretely speaking, we must start from a real objective activity. Among man's real activities, obviously instrumental (tool using) activity is the first thing which links man and external objects. Before, our understanding on instrumental activity used to stay at the level of tha objectivity, in other words, we have been only admitting that it was a "world—reshaping" activity. The basic structure in this activity is the opposite relation between man and his object, but we did not make a deep research on what this relation implies or what we can see from this relation. Now, our task is to display, from this objective activity, the non-objective level of the relation between man and his material world.

The view of non-objective association between man and material seems contradictory, because ordinary people cannot understand the material or that the material in human world also has other ways of existence in addition to be man's object. In other words, material will become meaningless if it is not the object of human activity. But, how will material become man's object and how does this objective relation happen? This question is often ignored. In fact, if we try to analyze man's instrumental activity by using the framework of objective relation, we may discover without difficulty that the explanatory power of this framework is rather finite, or in other words, this framework can explain the world, only in a finite way. Beyond this specific range, this framework will lose its explanatory power, while it itself needs explanation.

We say instrumental activity is a typical activity linking man and external object, but we do not say instrumental activity is a kind of objective activity only. They are different. If, instrumental activity is only a kind of objective activity, the tool which links man and his object will become an awkward sphere. In the past, we usually called this sphere a medium of the interaction between man and his object, but as far as the clear differentiation between man and its object is concerned, the identity of medium is no doubt ambiguous. Our question is, is tool also an object of man? If we carry our analysis through the objectivity approach framework, all things outside subject may become its objects, while the material which forms a relation with man will be his real object. Tool is certainly a material which forms a relation with man, but if we consider tool as man's object, another medium will be needed between man and tool, whereas the identity of this medium is also unclear. If we consider tool as a special object – an object with the function of medium, it is equal to say that the tool has the characteristics of both subject and object, thus transcending objective framework in a sense. In the past, we seldom noticed that the tool had the nature of transcending objective framework. Marx had said: "tool is the extension of human organs". In fact, he also conceived the tool as a special object, thus evading the problem. In fact, the special identity of the tool just implies a sphere which is to be disclosed and which transcends objective framework.

The essence of the issue is that we should not equate material with object. Material not only greatly outdoes the object in terms of scope but also can accommodate much more meaning than object can. In human world, material may not necessarily be an object, but man's object must be a material in the world. Thus, tool marks the boundary of objective thinking framework and meanwhile also marks the categorial boundary of the object. In instrumental activity, the objective relation between man and material can be easily understood, but beyond the sphere of this objective framework, it can be revealed only through an analysis on the tool. Here we want to ask, in addition to being a link between man and his object, what else can a tool link with man? If we discuss man's object in a sense of general material, what role does tool play? If we can disclose from the tool, how general material forms an association with man in the very beginning, we may understand how human world is constructed.

On this issue, Martin Heidegger's analysis is rather illuminating. He divides the relation between man and material, and particularly man and the tool, into two states: ready-to-hand and present-at-hand. The former is the derivative state of the latter. Martin Heidegger has explained itt with an example:

> Hammering with a hammer, for example, but in such dealings an entity of this kind is not grasped thematicaly as an occurring Thing, nor is the equipment-structure known as such even in the using. The hammering does not simply have knowledge about the hammer's character as equipment, but it has appropriated this equipment in a way which could not possibly be more suitable. ......The less we just stare at the hammer-Thing and the more we seize hold of it and use it, the more primordial does our relationship to it become, and the more unveiledly is it encountered as that which it is – as equipment. The hammering itself uncovers the specific "manipulability" ["Handlichkeit"] of the hammer. The kind of Being which equipment possesses – in which it manifests itself in its own right – we call it "readiness-to-hand" [Zuhandenheit].[1]

Readiness-to-hand does not regard presence-at-hand as its premise. On the contrary, readiness-to-hand is more primordial in any way because presence-at-hand happens only when what is ready-to-hand becomes not "ready-to-hand", comes into people's sight and is "seen". Presence-at-hand is a still state that confronts with man. The relation between man

---

1 [German] Martin Heidegger: Being and Time, p.81.

and material in this state is an objective relation or directly called the relation between man and its object. In this relation, object is thematized and stands out from environment. Therefore, the relation between man and object is stressed as a relation independent of environment. In readiness-to-hand, the relation of man and material is a dynamic relation and material does not stand out from environment, so the relation between man and material here can be conceived only when it is put in the world – in this totality. "Taken strictly, there 'is' no such thing as equipment. To the Being of any equipment there always belongs a totality of equipment, which it can be this equipment that it is"[1] That is to say, what is brought from the relation of equipment with man is a world other than mere equipment itself.

In fact, the readiness-to-hand and presence-at-hand defined by Martin Heidegger are not limited to equipment or tools. The relations between man and the things in the nature which can be made, such as: iron, stone and wood also include readiness-to-hand and presence-at-hand. The two states may also be conceived as the objective relation and non-objective relation between man and material. In the objective relation, the world to which material and man belong is hidden. It seems that this relation is only a relation between two beings and can be understood only when they are extracted from the world; while in non-objective relation, we must think about a totality, and the thorough separation of man from tools and objects is cancelled. Strictly speaking, this separation is yet to happen. Through instrumental activity, life-world becomes accessible as far as our exploration is concerned. Above we have discussed life-world. It can be conceived only when it serves as a background compared with concrete objective activity. In other words, it is conceived in a negatory way. Now we have disclosed the non-objective layer of instrumental activity, thus obtaining a positive route to enter life-world, while instrumental activity becomes an entrance door from which we enter life-world.

Tools are extension of human limbs. This view breaks through traditional division of organism and inorganics. In a sense, it also wavers the sepa-

---

1 [German] Martin Heidegger: Being and Time, p.80.

ration of spirit and matter. In terms of this issue, it is the thorough separation of man and his object. Why? Because it seems that we may separate man as a being with spirit and consciousness from his object, even
from tools, but we can hardly separate man as a spiritual substance from
his flesh. Of course, we do not deny the existence of this differentiation
and opposition. We want to indicate that the validity range of this separation is extremely finite and only after this range is broken, can it help us
solve problems. This indicates that man and the things in his world, tools
in particular are integral. The reason why a thing is the thing in the world
of human is that it has a specific relation with man. Of course, this relation
is firstly conceived as the readiness-to-hand as said by Martin Heidegger.
The spatial relation between man and material can be reasonably conceived
as belonging to man, only when it is based on this relation.

Marx on the one hand stresses that the existence of man must accept a
material world and must have a certain material foundation and on the
other hand also stresses that man should be an individual in a specific
real world, but he does not give more detailed description on the state
of the man who lives in this world. This cannot be deemed as a theoretical failure, because this existence condition has been hidden in the first
insight. In fact, Marx regards productive activity as human's primary activity. This idea implies the primary position of this activity, in the construction of life-world and the understanding on life-world. Here we
consider this activity as the entrance to the understanding and description of life-world. In fact it is only a supplementary investigation on the
premise established by Marx.

Nature as a part of life-world

Talking on material world, we have to take a particular look at nature,
because nature is often considered the most "typical" part of material
world. Above we have indicated how material world becomes the material world of "men". Our task here is to indicate how nature becomes a
part of the world. We know the world of men mentioned here has a
meaning different from before. Nature as a part of the world deserves to

be conceived in a way different from the previous concept of nature. We know each philosophical paradigm has a concept of nature corresponding to it. These concepts may become either obstacles to our re-understanding of the nature or ladders us to this understanding.

In fact, same as other basic philosophical concepts, "nature" (or phusis) has extremely complex meaning. It is researched by scholars that "nature" has tens of meanings and used in ancient literature.[1] In Metaphysics, Aristotle lists many meanings of the "nature" and thinks "nature in the primary and strict sense is the essence of things which have in themselves, as such, a source of movement; for the matter is called the nature because it is qualified to receive this, and processes of becoming and growing are called nature because they are movements proceeding from this. And nature in this sense is the source of the movement of natural objects, being present in them somehow, either potentially or in complete reality."[2] Without doubt, nature is a research object of metaphysics. If we do not look at metaphysics only, we may discover without difficulty that nature is different from the spheres of social life and art. According to the differentiation method in Aristotelian practical philosophy, nature can only be the object of theoretical activity. In addition to theoretical activity, there are also political practical activity and artistic activity in the Aristotelian state. Apparently, the latter two do not involve nature. Martin Heidegger also said: "Encompassing what we, although not the Greeks, regard as the opposition between the living or psychic and the physical, phusis is contrast with thesis and nomos, with ordinance and law, rule in the sense of the ethical", and "phuisis is narrowed by contrast with thechnee".[3] Aristotle,also stresses the difference between natural things and art or artificially produced things and he thinks "art is a principle of movement in something other than the thing moved, nature is a principle in the thing itself".[4] Obviously, from the very beginning nature was distinguished from "artificial" sphere. According to common understanding, the knowledge for research on nature should be "physics" (ta

1 American scholar Lovejoy for example, refer to Wu Guosheng Editor-in Chief:
  Natural Philosophy, Vol.2, p.567~580, Beijing, China Social Sciences Press, 1996.
2 [Ancient Greek] Aristotle: Metaphysics, p.91.
3 Martin Heidegger: An Introduction to Metaphysics, p.17-18, Beijing, Commercial Prs, 1996.
4 [Ancient Greek] Aristotle: Metaphysics, p.239.

phusika), while, philosophy should be "metaphysics" (ta meta ta phusika) which is above "nature". However, in ancient Greece, this differentiation was not very obvious, because we may even call Platonic and Aristotelian metaphysics as a kind of natural concept in a broad sense. Obviously this was determined by the substantialistic paradigm of ancient philosophy.

Ancient theoretical philosophers had conceived the entire world in an ontological way. No doubt they had also conceived natural things in the same way. The substance we mention here is not Aristotle's strict concept of substance. Instead, he emphasizes a thinking mode different from early-modern subjective philosophy and contemporary theory of practice. In general, it is a thinking mode under which the world is conceived as an uncaused being. To explore natural things in this thinking mode is certainly to explore the inherent and eternal nature of the things and explore what the things really are, what is behind them. In fact, ancient Greek philosophers used the word "nature" exactly in this sense. That is to say, nature is conceived as a fundamental, prime and eternal substance.

Since nature is conceived as an eternal and invariable substance, it must exist outside human life. It does not mean there is no nature in human life or nature cannot be talked about in human life. In fact, in the sense of ancient philosophers, everything has its nature, so do men and their activities. Aristotle thinks the state "is a creation of nature and that man is by nature a political animal".[1] Nature means a kind of self-rooted and invariable being. This being is fundamentally contradictory with making and planning, while making and planning are often the fundamental content of real life. Aristotle thinks that the essential activity of man is political and ethical activity. That is to say, man essentially tends to political and ethical activity, i.e.: the activity of "planning", but the nature of man cannot be planned. In the sense of ancient philosophers, the nature of man and his activities is as the same kind of things, as the natural things in external world and even the spirit and soul of man can be conceived as this kind of things.

---

1 [Ancient Greek] Aristotle: Politics, p.7.

Apparently, in the beginning, the concept of nature did not only refer to the Nature as we usually call. It had generally referred to all the spheres that human activity is inaccessible to, but must accept. It is noteworthy that the acceptance here is different from the abovementioned acceptance of human life to a specific world stated by Marx. In the sense of ancient philosophers, acceptance can only be the acceptance to a substance. The accepted is the absolute prior. Hence this acceptance can only be passive acceptance. An example of this accepted substance is a natural object. In the sense of ancient people, natural thing is outside real life and can only be an object to be watched or admired. Therefore, these accepted substances as the objects of theory stand high as the sun, moon and stars. Even if they are the nature of man and its life, it is absolutely repulsive to man's role of constitution. In the sense of Aristotle, the state as the totality of human life is also a "creation of nature". Above we have indicated that Aristotle did not think about the role of human activity in constituting the state. From the perspective of the individuals in real life, the absolute priority of the state as totality is as undisputable as the "objectivity" of natural objects. But, human's acceptance to the world in our sense is not so. Because, firstly, world is absolutely not a substance. The reason why we stress that, men can only live in a "specific" world and in a "specific" historical circumstance is that we want to indicate that a world which never changes does not exist. From the perspective of real individuals, the specific world is undoubtedly a "fact" that must be accepted, but this "fact" is constituted by all kinds of human activities, only this constituting activity is often outside individual's visual sphere. The nature in the sense of ancient philosophy is a typical substance. This substance in the end can only be the object perceived by theory, so its "communication" with man's real activity is impossible. Secondly, the way that men accept the world is man's activity. Only when we understand this special acceptance way ancient age, can we understand the essence of man is structural and acceptant. Man's activity can do nothing to substance.

We should say ancient philosophers' passive acceptance to nature had an intrinsic reason. We know ancient people were not aware of subjective consciousness, and the effect of human activity on environment was not obvious, so the environment was seen as an eternal substance. Nature is exactly this substance. Therefore, ancient philosophers were not really aware of the life-world as we described above, or in other words, they conceived life-world as a substance, i.e.: as nature. Although ancient people's understanding on the world has a remarkable difference from our concept of life practice, it still plays an enlightening role, compared with the concept of nature in early-modern philosophy.

Following the deepening of the change of external world by human activity and the wake of subjective consciousness, the independency and mystery of nature has gradually disappeared. In the sense of early-modern philosophers, nature is a reasonable being only when it is the object of subjective consciousness. Along with the development of scientific spirit in early modern times, this object appeared with the following changes, compared to ancient substantial philosophy: on the one hand, nature was no longer conceived as nature in a broad sense. It was directly defined as the Nature, or the totality of natural things; on the other hand, nature was the object perceived by subjective theory and was also the object of subjective "practice", so it became a controllable "resource" of subject. This role change of nature is obviously reflected in the philosophy of Francis Bacon and Rene Descartes. Francis Bacon had said:

> Man, being the servant and interpreter of Nature, can do and understand so much and so much only as he has observed in fact or in thought of the course of nature. Beyond this he neither knows anything nor can do anything.[1] Human knowledge and human power meet in one; because where the cause is not known the effect cannot be produced. Nature to be commanded must be obeyed; and that which in contemplation is as the cause is in operation as the rule.[2]

"The happy match between human understanding and the nature of things that Francis Bacon envisaged is a patriarchal one: the mind, conquering superstition, is to rule over disenchanted nature. Knowledge, which is power, knows no limits, either in its enslavement of creation or

---

1 [British] Francis Bacon: The New Organon, p.7.
2 The same book as above, p.8.

in its deference to worldly masters."[1] Francis Bacon had often compared nature to female, while the era of science is a "male era", an era of conquest of the nature. Rene Descartes also said: "Through the understanding of craftsmen's craftsmanship and the power of objects, we may rule and own nature."[2] We may say that ruling and conquering the nature is the tendency in the whole early modern times. This tendency is even affecting the life of contemporary people to a great extent. It has deep conceptual foundation – the concept that "man establishes laws for nature". The conquest and control of nature was intrinsically united with the notion of conceiving nature as a constructed object. In other words, if the law of nature is established through proceeding from man, then fundamentally speaking, this nature will be controllable.

Although "man establishes laws for nature" was officially put forth by Kant, its sign can be seen from Rene Descartes. The "Archimedean point" of Rene Descartes' theoretical system is "ego cogito", while the existence of "ego", the existence of "things" and the existence of God all can be deducted from this "Archimedean point". Nature no doubt is the existence of "things". Generally, Rene Descartes is thought to be a dualist. As Martin Heidegger said, Rene Descartes differentiated ego cogito as res cogitans from res orporea. Later on this differentiation was defined as the differentiation between "nature and spirit" in ontology.[3] In fact, this differentiation does not constitute a sufficient reason to judge Rene Descartes as a dualist, because in no way, the existence of things enjoys an equal position as the existence of ego or spirit does. On the one hand, ego and cogito are inseparable, "ego cogito" is both "ego" and "cogito", while the existence of things can be deducted only from "ego cogito"; on the other hand, Rene Descartes thinks that extension is the true existence of things, but the definition of extension in length, width and height is an universal mathematical principle other than the principle from thing itself. It is the principle from subject or "ego cogito". In this way, we can easily understand that the existence of things is "constructed" in the philosophy of Rene Descartes.

---

1 [German] Max Horkheimer and Theodor W. Adorno: Dialectic of Enlightenment, p.2, Shanghai, Shanghai People's Publishing House, 2003.
2 Wu Guosheng Editor-in Chief: Natural Philosophy, Vol.2, p.502.
3 [German] Martin Heidegger: Being and Time, p.105.

This notion can be clearly seen from Kantian concept of nature. Kant said: "Nature is the existence of things, so far as it is determined according to universal law."[1] "The formal [aspect] of nature in this narrower sense is therefore the conformity to law of all the objects of experience, and so far as it is cognised a priori, their necessary conformity."[2] Kant clearly linked the existence of nature with a universal law, but did not discuss the "thing-in-itself" outside this law. Although, Kant took this approach due to his clear awareness on the finity of subject, it could, in a certain scope, complete the "legal" construction of nature. In the sense of Kant, at least within the scope of experience, this "construction" was undisputable.

This notion of Rene Descartes and Kant was further developed by later German classical philosophy and Edmund Husserl. After Hegel and Edmund Husserl confirmed the elimination of thing-in-itself, the whole nature was declared as the exteriorization or construction of the subjective spirit. In this way, it seems that early-modern philosophy had gone to the opposite of ancient philosophy. Ancient philosophers had conceived nature as an uncaused substance, and human activity could do nothing but passively accept it; whereas in the sense of early-modern philosophers, nature in a sense could be conceived as the "product" of subjective consciousness. If we think over this issue further, we may discover that the two approach share some common points. We know, the nature in ancient philosophy can be used as the object of theoretical perception, but the perceiver is always invisible. Therefore, although we cannot say the opposition between nature and man or man's activity is formally tenable, the precondition of our understanding on the relation between nature and man has to include it into an opposite framework. In other words, ancient concept of nature could be reasonably observed only under the framework of the opposition between subject and object in most cases. We know, the opposition between subject and object is the ultimate structure of early-modern theoretical philosophy. The concept of nature in early-modern philosophy is a typical manifestation of

---

1 [German] Kant: Prolegomena to Any Future Metaphysics, p.57.
2 The same book as above, p.60~61.

the opposition between subject and object. In a sense we can say that the substantialist concept of nature in ancient philosophy can be conceived as an immature state of the opposition between subject and object in early-modern philosophy.

As mentioned above, the nature in the sense of ancient philosophers is outside man's real life. Early-modern philosophy had conceived nature as a "construction" of the subject, but can we say this nature was inside man's real life? After taking a brief look at the concepts of practice and life-world we have described above, we can easily negate this conclusion. The reason is very simple: the subject in early-modern philosophy is not a real subject and moreover the "constructive activity" of this subject is absolutely not real life. In fact, this subject and its constructive function are only the abstraction of some aspects of real subject and its real activity. One of the results of this abstraction was to conceive nature as the product of the subject and the object it controls. Obviously, this is widely divergent from our understanding of nature as a part of the world, because the relation between a real subject and world should be acceptance at first other than construction.

Then, how to understand real man's acceptance to nature? Apparently we should proceed from the understanding of man's acceptance to environment, because we have known that nature is the most important part of man's material world. The acceptance by ancient philosophy to nature is only passive acceptance, because it has no construction but pure acceptance; while early-modern philosophy only had the pure construction and no acceptance. Our work here is to dialectically unify construction and acceptance, these two processes. Of course, the knowledge of dialectic tells us this unification is not the compromise of the two, but the opening of a brand new visual sphere –the visual sphere of life-world.

How to understand the nature in the visual sphere of life-world? It involves a brand new concept of nature, i.e.: the view of nature in Marx's theory of practice. Marx's view of nature is a fundamental part of his view of world, so Marx's philosophical reform certainly contains the reform of old view of the nature. We cannot imagine how a view of world can be transformed without the reform on view of nature. We may say Theses on Feuerbach is a programmatic document for the establishment of Marx's new view of world. In this frequently cited article, Marx puts forth the basic starting point of his new view of nature, i.e.: "the thing, reality, sensuousness", cannot be "conceived only in form of the object or of contemplation", but "as sensuous human activity, practice", and should be conceived from the aspects of both subject and object in a unified way. In other words, nature cannot be conceived in the form of contemplation which abstracts it into a pure object, but it should be conceived in the active relation between man and nature; cannot be conceived simply from its thing-in-itself, but should be conceived from its personalized form. In a word, the thing-in-itself nature must be conceived after elevating it to the level of personalized nature. Fundamentally speaking, the foundation of this personalized form or active relation is a material practical relation, other than the spiritual relation as conceived by idealism; spiritual active relation is only an abstract reflection of material active relation, and itself is non-foundation. Therefore, Marx suggests the prime task of the new view of nature is to supersede the intuitive and passivity adhered to by old materialism and the activeness to which idealism gives that role abstractly, or in other words, for Marx, it was necessary to import man's activeness to which idealism gives play abstractly into materialism, and turn it into real activeness.

The key reason why this activeness is real is that it must be in real world, while on the other side nature is a part of this real world. From the perspective of another aspect, observing nature in the world is to observe nature in its relations with human activities. Thus nature is no longer an alien being completely outside life as conceived by ancient philosophers and no longer the pure construction of subject but is the totality of things brought before the eyes of human by instrumental activity. Our above analysis on instrumental activity has already indicated that this activity is not merely an objective activity, and from that we may unfold the non-objective relation between man and things. Here we should conceive the instrumental activity from non-objective layer. Only in this way, can the thing it brings before the eyes of human be an integral body, other than mere the "object" of subject. Otherwise, nature will be conceived as the totality of all objects of the subject, just like early-modern philosophers did. Since nature and man are integral in a primitive sense, we may say nature is a part of human essence, and meanwhile must be a part of the world man must accept.

CHAPTER THREE

Social Life and Human Essence

Generally speaking, it seems inexplicable to say nature is a part of human life-world, while it is undisputable to affirm that society is a part of human life-world. This does not mean that we have completely understood the relation between man and society and there is no need for further inquiry. The fact is the other way round. In the history of philosophy, the relation between man and society was seldom described as the relation between man and the world where man lives. The past theoretical philosophy approach had considered society either as a substance similar to thing-in-itself characteristic or as a pure "artificial thing". Apparently, the relation between man and world is not like this. The basic starting point of Marx's philosophy's observation on society is real individuals, the individuals in specific social and historical circumstances and in a specific social relation. Only proceeding from this basic starting point, can we obtain a concrete description on social life.

Drawing the Picture of the social life of human

Contradictions of sociality concept in the theoretical philosophy approach

Marx's descriptions on world and social history have a premise. It is "men, not in any fantastic isolation and rigidity, but in their actual, empirically perceptible process of development under definite conditions. Why are real men stressed by Marx? The reason is very simple: the premise of theories of previous philosophers usually is not real men, and is either abstract substance or abstract men. However in the sense of Marx, society itself is true and real, because real individuals in fact are the "ensemble of the social relations". Obviously, the premise that Marx observes society is real individuals and the premise that he observes real individuals is society. It is not a simple tautology. It indicates essential inseparability between real individuals and the society, where they are active. Men are born social. Men are social animals. Society is an aspect of man's life-world. Our observation on society meanwhile can be conceived as the observation on human essence. Below we will indicate that, only and only in this way, will the observation on society be possible and the society be understandable. Of course, the observation here is thoroughly different from previous philosophers' theoretical observation on society.

Here we need to draw a demarcation line from such a concept: we must regard men as the premise to observe society, so the essence of society can be reduced to man or man's essential attribute. It is certainly a concept of early-modern philosophy. The most typical ones are Hegelian social concept and the atomism of social contract. We know the starting point of Hegel's observation on society is man's self-consciousness or absolute spirit. He deems man's essence as self-consciousness. Marx pointed had out in Economic and Philosophical Manuscripts of 1844, that, man's essence and man equals self-consciousness in the sense of Hegel. If starting from absolute spirit, society can only be conceived as extrinsic manifestation of spirit. "The State is the march of God through the World".[1] If we say Hegel conceives human society as a kind of abstract spirit, a kind of construction of abstract subject, then the supporters of

---

1 [German] Hegel: Philosophy of Right, p.259, Beijing, Commercial Press, 1961.

social contract theory are to conceive it as a kind of construction of abstract natural persons. Social contract was the social origin theory in the beginning. Its general concept is that mankind was in a natural state before the formation of state and society, in this state everybody enjoyed natural rights and there were no other laws except the law of nature, later on for some reason, the safety of individuals' life and properties was not guaranteed, so people came to a consensus to enter into a contract with each other and in the end society was "formed" and proceeded from natural state to a rational rule. It seems that the theoretical logics of these two social concepts are contrary – they are holist social concept and atomist social concept, but they share a critical common point: deny the authenticity and essentiality of real social life, or try to seek the essence of society from more real substance outside the society. Moreover all the real substances they find are men. The difference is that the former conceives man as a kind of self-consciousness, while the latter conceives man as a natural being similar to animal. Here essentially what is constructed is the uni-directional naturalization relation between society and man. If we conceive society as a part of human's life-world, then this naturalization will be illegal. Let's look at this issue from another angle, the concepts both have such a difficulty: since starting point is defined as self-consciousness or atom-like individuals, then how is social relation generated? Because obviously the aggregate sum of atoms is not a society.

Apparently the notion of naturalizing social essence towards man is inseparable from the tradition of Western theoretical philosophy. Theoretical philosophy essentially is to interpret and construct the world by proceeding from an "Archimedean point" that is above the world. Real life is considered untrue or not real enough. Without the support of a real world, it will become meaningless. As early as ancient Greece, Plato had believed, "reality was to be found, not in worldly or human immortality but in the eternal, something extra-worldly or super-human, the object of philosophical contemplation".[1] No doubt, this real world is ideal world. Plato's concept has consequences at least in two aspects: in terms of theory, real world can be understood only from an angle outside

---

1 [British] Michael H. Lessnoff: Political Philosophers of the Twentieth Century, p.86, Beijing, Commercial Press, 2001.

the world; while in terms of "practice", theoretical activity is established as the highest life of man. Just as what Hannah Arendt believed, "the contemplative life of the philosopher, therefore, was elevated above the active life of the citizen –bios theoretikos was elevated above bios politikos".[1] Generally speaking, contemplation is an individual activity, while politics can happen only among people. In medieval theological system, the results of these two aspects are manifested in another way. For Christians, worldly life is untrue, or it is meaningful only because of God's world. Here the God's world is equivalent to Platonic ideal world and is the "Archimedean point" for understanding of real life. In addition, just like Plato's contemplative activity as the highest activity, that faces ideal world, Christians' highest activity is the belief in God. This activity is also an individual activity. We can easily discover that interpersonal relation and real social life are not seriously treated in both ancient theoretical philosophy and medieval thoughts, or in other words it is impossible to get reasonable observation, because in essence, society conflicts with their theoretical starting points.

After knowing the awkward position of society in ancient theoretical philosophy and medieval thoughts, we may easily understand the difficulty of social theory in early-modern philosophy. In early-modern philosophy, the abovementioned results of Platonic concept in two aspects were merged and were all reflected on early-modern people's concept of subject. Subjectivity, became the "Archimedean point" through which early-modern philosophy had interpreted the world. Of course, society should be interpreted through it. The result of this interpretation is that society essentially is the creation of subject and the reflection of subjective consciousness. But, how to guarantee the reasonableness of this interpretation? To answer this question, we must think over subjective activity. In the sense of early-modern philosophy, society is artifact or in other words the product of subjective activities. In terms of its difference from the communicative activity between man and man or subject, this constructive activity has no essential difference from ancient people's contemplative activity and Christians' belief activity. They were all separate

---

1 [British] Michael H. Lessnoff: Political Philosophers of the Twentieth Century, p.86.

individual's activities. This separate individual is repulsive to others in essence. By now, we may conclude the issue of society or human communication cannot be reasonably treated and solved within the standpoint of the whole theoretical philosophy. To solve this issue within the standpoint of theoretical philosophy, one question should be answered: From a separate subject, how to generate another subject? The constructed subject is not a thing but a unique subject same as the previous subject. The contradiction has been very obvious.

In fact, this contradiction is typically reflected in Edmund Husserl's philosophy. Apparently, once another subject is involved, it has no longer been a simple issue of subjectivity but an inter-subjective issue or an issue of inter-subjectivity. "In early days, Edmund Husserl had realized that he was facing the issue of inter-subjectivity. And in the latter development process of his thought, he had studied this issue all the time."[1] No doubt, Edmund Husserl deeply felt this fundamental problem of theoretical philosophy, but he handled this issue in the way of typical theoretical philosophy. That is to say, he was committed all the time to deducing other subjects from a separate subject, thus forming a picture of the world of inter-active subjects.

> In Edmund Husserl's phenomenology, the concept of "inter-subjectivity" is used to identify all of the interactive forms among multiple transcendental egos or multiple worldly egos. The foundation of any interaction is the community formed by proceeding from the transcendental ego of me. The prototype form of this community is unfamiliar experience, i.e.: the construction of ego of which itself is primary -- stranger.[2]

In the sense of Edmund Husserl, numerous transcendental subjects are the numerous "monads" in the world, "every monad, as long as it intentionally 'constructs' other monads in its existence (just like every monad constructs the past), it will be unable to exist without other monads",[3] such monads constitute a "monad community". The monad community essentially is an intersubjective world. If we roughly equate inter-subjec-

---

1 Ni Liangkang: Explanation on the Concepts of Edmund Husserl's Phenomenology, p.256.
2 Ni Liangkang: Explanation on the Concepts of Edmund Husserl's Phenomenology, p.255.
3 The same book as above, p.299.

tivity with sociality, then no doubt what Edmund Husserl tries to construct here will be a picture of society.

Apparently, Edmund Husserl had realized that the truth of inter-subjectivity and subject's sociality must be affirmed, but is his construction of sociality successful or legal? It is really a problem. The key of this problem is that since other is constructed by previous transcendental ego, then his "primacy" will become incomprehensive. In fact, Edmund Husserl reduces the other and related interactive relation to a separate transcendental individual. This decides that his method has no essential difference from previous theoretical philosophy. Nevertheless, Edmund Husserl gave prominence to the issue of inter-subjectivity and sociality and tried to solve it in a typical way of theoretical philosophy. The significance is not the proposition of this issue only. His failure tells us the impotence of theoretical philosophy in this issue.

If the failure of Edmund Husserl is a matter concerning the whole theoretical philosophy, then we can look for a solution from outside the standpoint of theoretical philosophy. It looked as if theoretical philosophy was to interpret society, this objective being, but essentially it had theoretically constructed it from a specific starting point. For example, after we realize the conflict between society and the single visual angle of theoretical philosophy, naturally we will give up the attempt of theoretically constructing social relations. In fact, Marx and many philosophers in the 20th century had gradually realized that the real understanding on society just because they gave up the attempt of theoretically constructing society.

The picture of social life in practical philosophy

If society is not theoretically constructed, then how do we understand society? Here we have to go back to "real individual" - a premise given by Marx. In fact, real individual contains the element of society in Marx's interpretation, because men are "the ensemble of the social relations". If we proceed from this premise, isn't it to conceive society by proceeding from society? From the perspective of theoretical philosophy, it is no doubt ridiculous. However, if we do not limit ourselves to the standpoint of theoretical philosophy, we may find the reasonable elements without difficulty. Under the understanding model of theoretical philosophy, society first of all is an object that needs to be interpreted, but if we regard society as a premise of understanding, it will impossibly be an object that theory observes, but a thing that provides possibility for this observation. In other words, Marx thinks society first of all that it is not an object that needs to be theoretically observed, but a premise that must be accepted at first. In view of our observation on the world, we may easily find that Marx thinks society itself has the nature of world and this is a premise that the concrete individuals who live in this world must accept.

According to the method proposed by Marx, we can easily educe a society-understanding method that is thoroughly different from the method employed by theoretical philosophy and may easily draw a picture of society that is completely different from the former. It proceeds from real individuals, so it is the picture of real social life. The primary feature of this social picture is that for man, society must be accepted, and man may become man only when he accepts a specific social form. This relation between society and man is subordinate to the above observed relation between man and his world. By many contemporary philosophers after Edmund Husserl, this relation was also affirmed in different ways. Martin Heidegger said: "The world of Dasein is a with-world [Mitwelt]. Being-in is Being-with Others. Their Being-in-themselves within-the-world is Dasein-with [Mit- daseiri]."[1] Different from Edmund Husserl, Martin Heidegger does not think others are constructed by transcendental ego. At first, he recognizes the existence of Dasein and others. Moreover, this being-with, is different from Edmund Husserl's nomad community, because Dasein is not equal to transcendental ego.

> It is not the case that one's own subject is proximally present-at-hand and
> that the rest of the subjects, which are likewise occurrents, get discriminated

---

1 [German] Martin Heidegger: Being and Time, p.138.

beforehand and then apprehended; nor are they encountered by a primary act of looking at oneself in such a way that the opposite pole of a distinction first gets ascertained. They are encountered from out of the world, in which concernfully circumspective Dasein essentially dwells.[1]

This sentence in fact can be used to refute Edmund Husserl. Fundamentally speaking, Edmund Husserl's transcendental subject is a kind of "self-being", while in the sense of Martin Heidegger, "Dasein's Being-alone is the Being-with in the world". "Being-alone is a deficient mode of Being-with; its very possibility is the proof of this".[2] Here, the view of Martin Heidegger is the reversal of Edmund Husserl's.

However, although "Heidegger had thus recognized, correctly, the worldly and social (or plural) condition of human life, but had later immediately shifted to devalue it. For Heidegger, interpretation of existence in terms of Umwelt or Mitwelt is inauthentic thus misleading. The shared Umwelt appears objective, universal, durable; while the reality of human existence is subjective, singular and – above all – finite. Death – human mortality or finitude – is for Heidegger the ultimate reality".[3] As far as this point is concerned, Martin Heidegger went back to Platonic tradition, so he is contradictory in this issue. On the one hand, men's social state is recognized at first; while on the other hand, men's real existential state is repulsive to this social state, because Dasein ultimately will have to face its death alone, while the being-with others is conceived as a way to evade this painful real state.

Apparently, Martin Heidegger's critique on Edmund Husserl and the traditional social concept of the whole theoretical philosophy is not thorough. The thoroughness of this critique not only needs recognize the priority of society to individuals but also to fully recognize the reality of this priority. Hence, we are closer to Marx's standpoint. Marx said: "The human essence is no abstraction inherent in each individual. In its reality it is the ensemble of the social relations." "The standpoint of the old materialism is civil society; the standpoint of the new is human society, or

---

1 German] Martin Heidegger: Being and Time, 138.
2 The same book as above, 140.
3 [British] Michael H. Lessnoff: Political Philosophers of the Twentieth Century, 83.

social humanity." In the sense of Marx, human essence contains sociality, man who can live in the world as a man has implied his acceptance to a specific social relation, being an individual of the society. This social individual is different from the atom-like individual in old philosophy. He is not an alone individual regarding his own interest as the starting point but has been in a specific social relation from the very beginning. Of course, the "standpoint" of Marx's philosophy is "human society, or social humanity", so absolutely Marx is not like Martin Heideger who thinks society as the existential state of men is which is inauthentic.

The relation between productive labour and social communication

Nevertheless, Marx was still misunderstood by Hannah Arendt, Habermas and other people. As mentioned above, these misunderstandings essentially are to think Marx reduces the social relation between man and man to productive activity, and to the relation between man and nature. Hannah Arendt criticized that Marx's doctrine is "anti-politics". Of course, politics she talks about here is the politics in the sense of Aristotle, i.e.: the social activity in public sphere, which is believed to be human's most essential activity mode. "Anti-politics" here means suppressing or replacing political activity with other activities. Generally, Marx is believed to suppress political activity with productive labour. At this point, Habermas shares the same idea with Hannah Arendt. He also thinks Marx uses "the framework of production category" to suppress "social theory". They think the consequence of this suppression is that Marx was unable to thoroughly distinguish his philosophy from previous theoretical philosophers' philosophy. In fact, Hannah Arendt and Habermas represent a very popular attitude towards Marx. The question is: does this critique hold water? Here we might as well think it from two aspects: one is whether the thorough separation even antagonism between productive labour and social communication is legal. The other is whether productive labour constitutes suppression on social communicative activities within the standpoint of Marx's philosophy. Our above analysis on human's practical activity has indicated that all kinds of human activities possess inherent unity, and it is illegal to thoroughly separate even antagonise them; besides, although Marx stresses the importance and priority of productive labour, we have no reason to think that it paves the way to tha suppression of the sphere of social communication by productive labour activity. In fact, it contradicts with the fundamental standpoint of Marx's practical philosophy. Marx had ever said: "In turn this presupposes the intercourse [Verkehr] of individuals with one another. The form of this intercourse is again determined by production."[1] Marx, here in fact underlines the inseparability between productive activity and social communication. To think Marx stresses the uni-directional determination of communication by production apparently does not conform to Marx's original intention. Of course, it should be noted that Marx gives more stress on the determinant role of production mode on the communication mode, and indeed pays less attention to communication, particularly the independence of communication in political and ethical layers. This is because on the one hand other contemporary theorists had given too much stress on other visual angles, and on the other hand, a theory is limited to a single visual angle and cannot proceed from multiple visual angles at the same time. In Marx's works, the theme of politics cover such a large part that some people think Marxist philosophy is principally a political philosophy, but in terms of its theoretical structure, the restriction by the "incompleteness" of theoretical visual angle exists indeed. In fact, the stress of Hannah Arendt and other people on social communicative activity neglects the significance of productive activity in modern society. At this point, their theories are much less "realistic" than Marx's philosophy.

Marx has stressed many times that human activity must be carried on under certain social condition. This in no way should be merely understood that, if a man wants to live in this world, he must deal with others and form social relations. More essentially, the society here refers to the background and possible conditions of these activities. As Friedrich Hayek put it:

---

1 Marx & Engels Selected Works, Edition 2, Vol.1, p.68.

> The reason why we can understand and communicate with each other and successfully act according to our plan is that in most time, the members of our civilized society follow some unintentionally established behavioral models, thus showing a kind of regularity in their actions; here it needs to be stressed that this regularity of actions is not the result of order or coercion but the result from firmly established habit and tradition. The universal observation of these conventions is the necessary condition for the orderliness of the world where we live, though we do not know their importance or even are not aware of their existence very much.[1]

Society as a part of life-world was unconsciously accepted at first, so any attempt of theoretically penetrating to it had doomed to failure. In this way we may easily understand why previous theoretical philosophy had failed in theoretical construction of society.

If we know society is a premise of human activity, we may reasonably understand human activity's role in "creating" the society. That is to say, it is impossible for us to understand society as the construction of abstract subjects as early-modern subjective philosophy did.

This creation is not go-as-you-please but has a premise, a boundary and conditions, so it is not a creation without foundation but the interaction between man and objective social structure. On this issue, Hayek also reached to the roughly same conclusion: between our effort to realize our task and the utility that system, tradition and habit possess, there exists a non-stop interaction; here it should be noted that system, tradition and habit are often mingled together and take effect together, and generate something far from the goal when we want to realize.[2] Although Marx stresses society is the creation of men, concrete human activity, i.e.: real human activity is bound to be restricted by this "creature". This is consistent with Hayek's stress that human behaviors are restricted by "non-rational" factors.

By now, we have obtained a kind of understanding on society that is different from the version of theoretical philosophy, and depicted a picture of interaction between human activity and objective social structure. Of course, it is also an aspect of the understanding on the finity of finite subjects.

---

1 [British] Friedrich Hayek: The Constitution of Liberty, p.71~72.

Ethics and the constitution of human essence

Ethic as a sphere of philosophical study

When talking on society, we must talk on ethic and moral, because ethics and the concepttion on society are closely related. In ancient Greece, the spheres involving interpersonal relations could even be included into ethical sphere. Above we have completed the theoretical description of societal being. Below we will further study the ethic which corresponds to it. Similar to the concept of society, there are many views on ethic and moral. We will investigate the ethics that corresponds with the concept of society in Marx's materialism on the basis of critique on past concepts.

Apparently, the content we discuss here belongs to ethical or moral philosophy, but our aim is not to obtain some moral criteria, but to probe into the essence of this sphere. We should say that ethic and moral are two distinct concepts. The joint use of these terms here implies that: they have similar content and immanent unity, and sometimes can even be interchangeable. However, they still have some subtle difference, and their joint use points to complementation between them. In fact, Chinese habit in wording exactly reveals the relation of these two concepts: "In Western languages, 'moral' and 'ethic' on the one hand have connected etymological meaning and on the other hand have different philosophical interpretations. In Chinese language, the two have close association and subtle difference."[1] Generally speaking, moral mainly refers to individual's objective self-cultivation in social activity, while ethic mainly refers to the value principles and criteria that regulate the relations between man and man, and man and society. No matter how different people define and understand these two concepts, two points are universally accepted:

(1) "Moral and ethic both have to do with human life, the good and evil in human behaviors and the criteria of value;

---

1 Wan Junren: Search for Universal Ethics, p.47, Beijing, Commercial Press, 2001.

(2) They both have the function of value criteria that regulate human behaviors and relations".[1] Then what sphere does human life, the good and evil in behaviors and the relations between individuals and group or society belong to? What is its position in the modes of man's life practice? Firstly let's see how our predecessors have studied this sphere.

Kant said: "Two things fill the mind with ever new and increasing admiration and awe, the oftener and the more steadily we reflect on them: the starry heavens above and the moral law within."[2] In fact, nature and moral have become two major spheres and themes of human exploration since ancient Greece other than by the days of Kant. However, in view of the history of ancient philosophy, these two spheres had not entered the visual sphere of philosophy in the same time. We know the philosophers before the emergence of Sophists mainly studied the issue of "nature (phusis)". Many moral proverbs appeared as early as the era of the "Seven Sages" in ancient Greece, but it cannot be reckoned as philosophical study; later on the schools of Heraclitus and Pythagoras published some articles about moral conducts, but they aimed to declare that the general principles obtained from their "natural" philosophy also play a role of criterion in the sphere of human behaviors, so they cannot be reckoned as the real theoretical study on moral sphere. With the rise of Greek Enlightenment, the conviction in these two preconditions wavered, thus moral became an issue to be researched.[3] In the past nobody questioned the legality of law or nomos. Following the turbulences in the society and the frequent changes in law, its authority was challenged. This raised such a question to the then Sophists: Is there such thing which is valid in any time and anywhere and is there such law which has no discrimination over nations, states and times, so has authority over everything? This authority is similar to the eternity and invariability of "nature". The opposites of it are all prevailing statues which are valid in a specific time and a limited area. They are specified and established by man made nomos or man made decrees. Here we can find without diffi-

---

1 Wan Junren: Search for Universal Ethics, p.48, Beijing, Commercial Press, 2001.
2 [German] Kant: Critique of Practical Reason, p.177, Beijing, Commercial Press, 1999.
3 [German] Windelband: A History of Philosophy, Vol.1, p.103.

culty that this issue in moral sphere has a structure similar to that of the basic issue of early natural philosophy. The former explores the invariable behind the multiplicate phenomena, while the latter studies the universally valid "nature" in the opposite of man made nomos and law.

Ethic as a research sphere of philosophy is different from nature. It is an artificial sphere, but here a questioning method similar to natural philosophy must be adopted. In other words, the issue of ethic also regards the contradiction between "one" and "many" as its basic framework in the beginning. Windelband said: the contradiction between nature and nomos or statue is the most representative conceptual structure in the era of Greek Enlightenment. [1] No doubt, nature, this concept was carried down from early natural philosophy. Here it stands for the pursuit to an eternal and invariable principle for human behaviors, but we cannot say it is a concept sheer in the sphere of "human affairs". It is not thoroughly differentiated from the nature of natural philosophers. This objectively indicates moral sphere was yet to become independent, and Sophists were yet to form a set of concepts and methodology which thoroughly distinguish themselves from natural philosophy.

Above we have mentioned that Sophists regarded sensuous individual as the only real existence way of men, then human nature, emotional impulsion was naturally announced as the law of nature – the ultimate and supreme guideline of human behaviors. The inevitable outcome is that "interest" is the "nature" in social behaviors, while the moral sphere as we generally call is excluded from "nature". This on the one hand means the separation between moral and nature, and on the other hand means no universally valid things exist in moral sphere. This undoubtedly is the relativism and skepticism in ethics. Therefore, Sophists only put forth a question, but the result of their research was negative.

We may say Socrates inherited the issue of Sophists, but did not accept their conclusions. Socrates also studied the universally valid things in the sphere of human behaviors, but he shifted his sight out of the sphere of

---

1 [German] Windelband: A History of Philosophy, Vol.1, p.104.

nature and looked for answer from inside of "man". Socrates thinks the "objective" standard for evaluation of human behaviors is his "insight", the "insight" into good. The knowledge about good is virtue. The knowledge here is not empirical knowledge as generally called and even not natural philosophers' philosophical cognition to nature, but is the knowledge of practice. This knowledge is neither like empirical knowledge which needs to be applied in "practice", nor like philosophical knowledge which is completely separated from action. Instead, it directly and inevitably causes action. The inevitable result of this virtue based on knowledge about good is happiness. We can easily find that Socrates sets the foothold of his thought at a sphere greatly different from nature, and moreover, his concepts and way to study issues are different from those adopted by previous philosophy. Therefore, we may say that only in the thought of Socrates, ethic and moral really became a unique sphere of philosophy. All content of Socrates' philosophy as we know belongs to this sphere, but his student Plato, a "systematic" philosopher, thinks ethics is only a part of his system and must maintain consistence with other parts. Although Socrates discussed good and regarded the knowledge about good as the core of his ethics, he gave little stipulation on good; whereas Platonic ethics mainly discusses good – the idea of good. Socrates only thinks good is the highest idea and highest goal, while Plato corresponds good to real society. Plato's Republic is a worldly hierarchy, and meanwhile it also reflects the good at different layers, so it is also the hierarchy of ideas. In such hierarchy, different levels correspond to different virtues. The behavior that complies with this moral is virtue.

We may say the process from Sophists to Plato is exactly the process in which ethics gradually gained independence and formed a peculiar concept centering on good and virtue. In this stage, as long as we make clear the difference between nature and nomos, we can grasp the main content by and large. In Aristotle, what the ethical and moral sphere faces is not the sphere of nature only. It must be clearly separated from art. Although Aristotle's way to discuss issues – particularly within the scope of ethics – is remarkably different from his predecessors', in terms of the stipulations on ethical and moral sphere we may consider he introduced the **sphere of art** on the basis of differentiating nature and nomos.

In Aristotle's "ethics" and "politics", nature, moral and the art are studied in connection with human activity. With these three as a frame system, Aristotle systematically studied the different ways of human activity. They are commonly referred to as "trichotomy" of human activity. Here it is necessary to differentiate the meanings of Aristotelian ethic in two layers: on the one hand, in terms of the differentiation between nature and nomos, the discussion of the activities of the men in the state shall belong to ethics, so his Politics should also be a work on "ethics"; on the other hand, Aristotle's this discussion involves different activity types. Moral activity and political activity involve the relations between man and man, and man and state. Comparing with science that involves nature, and art that involves the creation, this sphere is "ethical" indeed. The meaning in the first layer indicates any kind of human activity shall have ethical significance. This is the key of Aristotelian practical philosophy. However, it did not attract enough attention from the later generations; the meaning in the second layer indicates Aristotle put forth another important stipulation on ethical and moral sphere, i.e.: its differentiation from artistic activity.

Aristotle's differentiation between nature and moral, and science and practice has no much difference from his predecessors': Nature is eternal and necessary being, which man cannot change but comply; while moral sphere is artificial and practicable. In terms of activity type, both science and practice are free, while in terms of object, nature is necessary and invariable, man does not have "freedom", but moral is free in every sense. This is not only because practical activity takes itself as its end but also because its objects are variable. Aristotle also emphatically differentiated moral practice and artistic activity. This differentiation highlights freedom, a characteristic of moral practice. Comparing with moral practical activity, artistic activity is not free because its end is not in itself, but outside it. It appears that Aristotelian concept of freedom is different from today's understanding. This differentiation between freedom and non-freedom is also reflected by the classification of activity subjects -- classes: Slaves are non-free and their actions are non-free, so they are not the research objects of ethics; the activities of craftsmen are non-free, so their citizenship was questioned. Therefore, Aristotle said men were "political" animals. Men here, are free men. "Politics", the symbol of free men, belongs to ethical sphere.

The realm of freedom and realm of necessity

In the sense of Aristotle, ethic has the significance of a "paradigm". Every activity has the significance of ethic, pursues its good and ultimately forms the good in the state, as totality. After the life style in state community became history, this "paradigm" became unrealistic to later philosophies. Therefore, Aristotelian ethic in a broad sense was not accepted by later generations. Instead, his differentiation on the three kinds of activities, particularly the differentiation between moral/ethic and other two spheres were widely accepted. Following the establishment of the subject-object dual frame in early-modern philosophy, nature was conceived as the object of subject and this differentiation was simplified into the differentiation between man and nature, and as necessity and freedom. Nature is the object of both theoretical activity and artistic activity and they belong to the realm of necessity, while the object of moral and ethic is man's willpower, so they belong to the realm of freedom. In this way, Aristotelian concept was rewritten. Nevertheless, moral was still considered a realm of freedom. This is typically reflected in Kantian ethics. As mentioned above, in the sense of Kant, "now there are but two kinds of concepts, and these yield a corresponding number of distinct principles of the possibility of their objects."[1] The former makes cognition's compliance to apriori principles possible. The latter establishes the fundamental principles which enlarge the scope of will activities. The development belonging to the former is natural philosophy and that belonging to the latter is moral philosophy. Kant said in the preface of his Critique of Practical Reason:

> Inasmuch as the reality of the concept of freedom is proved by an apodeictic law of practical reason, it is the keystone of the whole system of pure reason,

---

1 [German] Kant: Critique of Judgment, Vol.1, p.8.

even the speculative, and all other concepts (those of God and immortality) which, as being mere ideas, remain in it unsupported, now attach themselves to this concept, and by it obtain consistence and objective reality; that is to say, their possibility is proved by the fact that freedom actually exists, for this idea is revealed by the moral law.[1]

No doubt, freedom is not only a core concept of Kantian moral philosophy but also is "real" and a "fact". It is also the premise of Kantian ethics. Unfortunately, this fact is not Kant's research object. Here he does not study free behaviors, but conducts purely conceptual analysis and construction. In fact, the freedom here refers to the independence of subjective reason, while this fact reflects the expansion of subjectivity in early modern times.

The subjectivity developed by Kant reached its peak in Hegelian philosophy, but it brought about an ethics different from "critique of practical reason". Hegel talks about ethic and moral in philosophy of law and his state doctrine. They are the last two stages of objective spirit. Moral comes from the transcendence of abstract law and is the truth of law. Free will, realized in the heart of man is moral, and that realized outside is abstract law. The former is subjective, while the latter is objective. Only the unity of subject and object realized through both external objects and innermost being is the real reflection of objective spirit. This unity between this subjective good and the objective and "An sich und für sich sein" good is ethic. In this way, it seems that Hegel gets close to Plato and Aristotle's holist notion. The difference is that Hegel adopts a historical approach, and the totality in the sense of Hegel is constructed by subjectivity. Therefore, Hegel does not stress Aristotelian classification of activities. Instead, he puts everything under absolute spirit.

In any case, all philosophers in the history conceived ethic and moral as the sphere of men's social behaviors. The symbolic characteristic of this sphere is defined as freedom in general. People differ greatly in the definition of freedom, but freedom may be roughly expressed as the alternatives in behaviors or the independence enjoyed by the subjects of actions.

---

1 German] Kant: Critique of Practical Reason, p.1~2.

Position of ethic and moral in Marx's philosophy

Above we have studied the essence and position of ethic and moral in the visual spheres of the philosophers before Marx. Now the question is: What is the position of ethic and moral in Marx's philosophy? Many people feel that Marx thinks little of this aspect, and some people even think Marx has "discarded" the things in moral and ethical aspect. Compared with "ethical" socialists and compared with Feuerbach and Bauer, ethics is indeed not the focus of Marx's philosophy and Marx has never conceived practice as a moral and ethical behavior. Nevertheless, we cannot say Marx has "discarded" ethics, because in view of Marx's practical philosophy, moral and ethic are undoubtedly a sphere belonging to human's concrete activities, while real activities can by no means be discarded by theory. In fact, although Marx does not have a separate ethics, we can easily find his assertions on ethic and moral, and explain his ethical thought, just like Marx did not write any works on dialectic, but it does not prevent Marx from having extremely rich dialectic thought.

So, the question is how we understand and enunciate Marx's ethical thought. Above we have indicated Marx's reform in philosophy. Based on this philosophical reform, certainly Marx's ethical thought will have a great difference from previous ethics. This may be an important reason why many people do not understand or even misunderstand Marx's ethical thought, but it is also our key to understanding Marx's ethical thought. Through above study, we may discover without difficulty that ethic and moral as a sphere of men's free behaviors and related interpersonal relations are the practice conceived by the above mentioned **"ethic – conduct paradigm"**. This sphere was separated from nature in the beginning after it had entered the visual sphere of philosophy. In Aristotle, ethic and moral were differentiated from artistic activity. People after Aristotle had all accepted Aristotle's differentiation. Even in the 20th century, some philosophers were still dedicated to reviving Aristotelian concept of practice. Besides, freedom was considered a symbolic characteristic of this sphere in general, but it seems that since Sophists, people have tried to discover something similar to "nature" from this sphere and regard it as the unity in all kinds of moral behaviors. The "interest" insisted by Sophists, and the "good" in the state as advocated by Plato and Aristotle as well as the will 'freedom" of subject proposed in early-modern philosophy are all the "nature" that governs all moral behaviors. These two aspects can be considered as the main characteristics of the ethics before Marx. Our study on Marx's ethical thought has to take them as reference.

Firstly, in terms of the relation between ethic/moral and other activity types, Marx is fundamentally different from Aristotelian tradition. Above we have mentioned that Marx's understanding on practice belongs to **"production – technology paradigm"**, so it is impossible for him to conceive moral activity as "the primary activity" and it is even more impossible to thoroughly separate moral activity from productive labour and theoretical activity and even repulse productive activity. On the contrary, Marx thinks moral activity is usually restricted and affected by the productive labour in a specific period. In The German Ideology, Marx and Engels pointed out:

> This conception of history depends on our ability to expound the real process of production, starting out from the material production of life itself, and to comprehend the form of intercourse connected with this and created by this mode of production (i.e. civil society in its various stages of societal development), as the basis of all history; and to show it in its action on the State, to explain all the different theoretical products and forms of consciousness, religion, philosophy, ethics, etc. and trace their origins and growth from that basis.[1]

Here, Marx starts from the standpoint of historical materialism and establishes the priority of productive activity to moral activity and meanwhile also forms the relationship of the two types of activitity. In this way, Marx draws a demarcation line from the practice that completely separates all kinds of activities or does not look into the unity of the activities. In fact, Aristotle had ever stressed the unity of all types of activities, for example, at the beginning of Nicomachean Ethics, Aristotle

---

1 Collected Works of Karl Marx and Frederick Engels, Chinese version 1, Vol.3, p.42, Beijing, People's Publishing House, 1960.

writes, every concrete activity has its end, for example: the end of the medical art is health, that of strategy victory, and etc., but certainly, "Every art and every inquiry, and similarly every action and pursuit, is thought to aim at some good" and "all things aim at good".[1] State as totality pursues the highest and broadest good. Aristotle's this insight did not gain much attention later on. People usually only stressed Aristotle's "trichotomy" of human activities. In fact, the relations between moral activity and production/theory are not only reflected by their mutual influence and moreover they are reflected as the isomorphism and common background of all kinds of activities. We know social communicative activity is exactly from the finity of men. Below we will indicate moral activity exactly is such kind of a communicative activity, and moral activity is also the result of those numerous real individuals' dialogue and exchange with each other, based on a standpoint. This result forms a part of the social reality. In a word, while recognizing the primary position of productive activity, Marx also thought of the reasonable position for moral and ethical activity and thought about the immanent unity between moral and ethical activity and other activities. This alone is enough to distinguish Marx from previous ethicists and early-modern practical philosophers including Gadamer.

Secondly, as far as the meaning of freedom is concerned, it is necessary for us to distinguish Marx from other ethicists. Generally, it is believed that the separation of ethical and moral sphere from nature indicates its attribute of "artificialness" and "independent choice", i.e.: the attribute of freedom. Socrates' link between moral behaviors and knowledge about good also underlines the voluntariness and self-consciousness of men as manifested in this sphere. Aristotle thinks that comparing with compulsory actions and ignorant and unconscious actions, the starting point of voluntary actions are in itself (themselves), and he recognizes the environment and conditions of actions one by one.[2] However here we discover the freedom and self-consciousness proposed by people including Aristotle are both the initiative identification of good that is similar to

---

1 [Ancient Greek] Aristotle: Nicomachean Ethics, p.1~2.
2 [Ancient Greek] Aristotle: Nicomachean Ethics, p.48.

"nature". In Socrates, the meaning of this good is not very clear, but in Plato and Aristotle, no doubt the good corresponds to the state. Therefore, the so-called self-consciousness is initiative identification of the state order, though this order is often Utopian. Therefore, the freedom talked by ancient Greek is often to study the relation between man and totality, but in fact, both individuals and totality are not very clear in their concepts. Comparing with the concept of subject in early modern times, here "free, voluntary, conscious and independent" do not mean the self of the own activity or mental activity. Behind them, there are always reason, good, reality, justice and other non-inherent backgrounds.[1] In the sense of early-modern age ethicists, freedom is the freedom of subject's will. The freedom of subject plays a role as an "Archimedean point" in Kantian ethics and Hegelian ethics. Therefore, although ethics studies human behaviors as well as its relations with the society and other people, but in early-modern age philosophy, these issues were all reduced to the "relation" between abstract subject and it-itself. In the sense of Marx's philosophy, the freedom in the moral and ethical activities in ancient and early modern times is abstract, because of the abstractness of their subjects. In Aristotle, the subject of action is yet to become independent, while in Kant and Hegel, subject becomes the final basis of every activity. None of them are concrete and real subjects, so the freedom of such subjects is not concrete freedom. The foothold of Marx's practical philosophy is the real individuals under specific historical background, so on the one hand it needs to give up the concept of absolute subject in early-modern age philosophy, i.e.: give up the absoluteness of abstract freedom, and on the other hand it needs to stress on the significance of historical background to individual activities. In this way, it seems that Marx has gone back to Aristotelian practical philosophy in form. However, the historical background, here in Marx, is constituted by subjective actions, and the relation between individuals and totality is a two-way interactive relation, it is not like the view of Aristotle who thinks "citizens" disappear in the totality of the state.

---

1 Ni Liangkang: Self-knowledge and Reflection, p.30.

Seemingly, Marx's practical philosophy can only conceive ethical and moral activity as a kind of social communication activity affected and restricted by productive activity under a specific historical situation. On the one hand, it is the abstractness, finity and uniqueness of individual activities that make communication and community life necessary or make the rule of conduct of a specific group necessary. On the other hand, the commonness of the concrete life situations of numerous individuals makes this communicative activity realizable. In this communicative activity, individual is a free and self-conscious subject and can independently choose his way of act, but the act of the individual will immediately take effect on others. What is more, this effect will be fed back to the actor through moral evaluation, and influences actor's act. Hence, between individual and other(s), and between individual and the group he belongs to, a two-way interactive relation is generated. It is exactly the interweaving of such countless relations that constitute a specific moral community. This community is supported by a relatively stable frame of moral standard. This framework is manifested as an apriori and compulsory rule for the subject in concrete activity.

Good and placing human essence in ethics

Talking of an apriori rule that must be accepted and observed, we must involve our above stipulations on world. Without question, same as the material world as we have discussed above, ethics plays a role in constituting man's essence. But how to understand that this "manmade" sphere constitutes the essence of man? To answer this question, we must understand the meaning of this rule in a brand new way. In social life, this rule is "good". Our mission here is to re-understand "good" as well as its effect on man.

Ethic constituting man's essence and the "good"

The most fundamental value pursuit of ethical and moral activity is "good". It is different from the "truth" pursued by man's cognitive activity. Any ethics, regardless of its standpoint, must be unfolded by centering on the issue of "good". It is even believed that how to define "good" is the most fundamental issue of the whole ethics.[1] That the definition of "good" became such an "issue" which indicates that people were yet to reach a consensus on the understanding of "good". In the history, owing to different theoretical standpoints and visual angles, philosophers and ethicists have understood "good" differently.

In fact, when the issue of moral was put forth, the concept of good was not put forth directly, whereas this way of questioning is consistent with the later problematic on good. In ancient Greece, people initially searched for the eternal and invariable "nature" in all kinds of nomos and laws. In the sphere of social behaviors, this "nature" no doubt is the rule that people "should" observe. From today's point of view, if this rule should be observed, it should be "Good". Sophists had conceived this "nature" as individual interest and man's inborn impulsion to this interest. Socrates vehemently opposed Sophist conclusion, but he accepted the issue raised by sophists. Not like Sophists, Socrates did not seek nature from human emotion and impulsion. Instead, he thought over the knowledge and insight of man. The object of this special knowledge is "Good".

Socrates interpreted **the virtue** (a basic ethical concept) as insight, while insight is the cognition of good; but he did not give universal content to the concept of good and in some aspects, he opened its (the concept of good) door. This created the possibility that the colorful outlook on life in relation to life. **telos** enters the conceptual void of Socrates.[2]

In fact, according to Xenophon's exposition, this good always tallies with the favorable or useful. If it is the case, we may say, Socrates did not keep a sufficient distance from Sophists, but we can hardly explain the self-control virtue advocated by Socrates, because it is exactly the contrary to the pursuit for interest. Anyway, Socrates put forth the concept of good though the meaning of this concept is still not very clear.[3] Plato defines good from the perspective of idealism. He thinks the idea of good

---

1 [British] G. E. Moore: Principles of Ethics, Wang Haiming: New Ethics, p.27, Beijing, Commercial Press, 2001.
2 [German] Windelband: A History of Philosophy, Vol.1, p.115.
3 The same book as above, p.110~111.

is a duty that people must fulfill and a goal that people pursue in social life. This good as an idea is not a finite but an ultimate goal pursued by an action. All of the other ideas are subordinate to the idea of good, so it is divine. If Platonic idea of good is inaccessible, then we may say Aristotle pays more attention to the concrete content of good, because he thinks good is not a name. "If there is an end for all that we do, this will be the good achievable by action, and if there is more than one, these will be the goods achievable by action." "Goods must be spoken of in two ways, and some must be good in themselves, the others by reason of these."[1] It is also about "intrinsic good" and "good as a means". The latter is not the highest and ultimate, while the former is the ultimate good. The intrinsic and ultimate good is "autarkeia". Autarkeia here is not about individual, but about community life, i.e.: the life in the state, because Aristotle thinks man by nature is political. Therefore, the state as a reasonable life style of the totality is the highest good -- happiness.[2]

All in all, the reason why "good is good" is that it is the direction of all ends. We can easily differentiate the two extremities of an action. One is good and the other is the act of good, i.e.: virtue, but in Aristotelian philosophy, the two are inseparable, because the ultimate good is in itself. Here we may conceive individual life and the state life are integrated.

Comparing with ancient philosophers, the later ethicists paid more attention to subjective action when they discussed on good. When talking of subjective action, the motive of the actor and the effect of the action must be involved. We know, people including Aristotle think these two cannot or should not be separated. Once they are separated, there will be such possibility: We may discuss good or the act of good based on either the former or the latter. Kant is a typical person based on motive of actor. He said, "Nothing can possibly be conceived in the world, or even out of it, which can be called good without qualification, except a Good Will".[3] "A good will is good not because of what it performs or effects,

---

1 [Ancient Greek] Aristotle: Nicomachean Ethics, p.12 & 10.
2 [Ancient Greek] Aristotle: Nicomachean Ethics, p.12~13.
3 [German] Kant: Fundamental Principles of the Metaphysics of Morals, [American] Tom L Beauchamp: Philosophical Ethics, p.175, Beijing, China Social Sciences Press, 1990.

not by its aptness for the attainment of some proposed end, but simply by virtue of the volition, that is, it is good in itself."[1] Then, how to understand the "good" of will? The law in that case determines the will directly; "the action conformed to it is good in itself; a will whose maxim always conforms to this law is good absolutely in every respect and is the supreme condition of all good."[2] Good will's conformity to the law of morals is direct because, it itself is "categorical imperative". "Categorical imperative" is absolute "Sollen (should)", that is to say, an action is good only because it is required and imperative. Categorical imperative is categorical, direct, objective and necessary. It is different from all hypothetical imperatives. That is to say, it is not for any end or an act as any means. Kant said:

> If now the action is good only as a means to something else, then the imperative is hypothetical; if it is conceived as good is itself and consequently as being necessarily the principle of a will which of itself conforms to reason, then it is categorical.... The former represents the practical necessity of a possible action as means to something else that is willed (or at least which one might possibly will).[3]

Apparently, Kant's categorical imperative as a rule observed by the action of good considers neither other ends nor the contents of the action, so Kantian definition of good is purely formal, too. Kant is also called a moral formalist.

If good is manifested in form as something required and deemed to be Sollen(should), according to general thinking, there must be a "demander" and a "commander", while Kantian "categorical imperative" has no commander, because if the action of good has another driver, inevitably it will become a means of this driver. Since action is divided into such two ends, Kant will be unable to stop other people from thinking over this issue from another angle. In other words, people may look at good from the effects of action. And this is moral utilitarianism. In the sense

---

1 The same book as above, p.176.
2 [German] Kant: The Critique of Practical Reason, p.67.
3 [German] Kant: Fundamental Principles of the Metaphysics of Morals, [American] Tom L Beauchamp: Philosophical Ethics, p.182.

of utilitarianist, if an action produces the most likely good results or the least likely bad results in the whole world, then this action is moral and good. The starting point of utilitarian theory is interest, although this interest is not longer as simple as Sophists' private interest. We should say utilitarianism is different from the so-called pure individualism or self-preservation. Utilitarians, coordinate individual with society or other individuals and try to achieve the consistence between individual's maximum interest and the overall interest of the society. Jeremy Bentham said, the happiness which constitutes the utilitarian standard of morally correct action is not the happiness of the actor alone but the happiness of all the people relevant with this action. "Utilitarians, require the actor strictly and fairly treats his own happiness and other people's happiness, like a benevolent onlooker who has nothing to do with this matter."[1] Comparing with Kantian good, utilitarians are much more "realistic", but even the most likely interest and happiness are also very abstract. In fact, there are many deviations among utilitarians. These deviations are mainly seen in the understanding and calculation of interest. As a matter of fact, it is often impossible for actors to make such calculations in real life, and to a large extent, it is similar to the drive of "categorical imperative" as proposed by Kant. Obviously, utilitarians indeed simplify society and the relation between individual and society into a pure interest relation, while they are not aware of the part that cannot be calculated in social life.

The understandings and definitions on good are all based on respective social concepts and ethics. If we are based on the social concept and ethics of Marxist theory of communicative practice, we will be unable to unconditionally accept any understanding. The ancient concept of good represented by Plato and Aristotle corresponds to the state life and ontological social concept. The aim of their ethics is to search for a reasonable life style in the state. Although good is the end and pursuit of men's "free" activity, men have no effect on the good itself. Instead, men can do nothing but realize or approach this end, while ultimately this end is "natural" and even supernatural. Men's practical activities will nei-

---

1 [American] Tom L Beauchamp: Philosophical Ethics, p.114.

ther increase nor decrease the content of good. In fact, the relation between good and virtue, the two basic concepts of Aristotelian ethics is
enough to address this issue. Good is the ultimate end of practical action,
while virtue is the character with which individuals can approach and
realize man's peculiar end.[1] The effect of the two is uni-directional other
than bi-directional. This notion is inappropriate in today's society. The
most principal and most realistic reason is that state-type community
life has disappeared for a long time, while the activities of individuals as
subjects are playing increasingly remarkable role in constituting the mode
of social life. Under this condition, it is apparently inappropriate not to
consider the role of subjective activity in constituting the mode of social
life and in constituting the ends of the activity.

Can we accept the above mentioned good determined, based on the subjective actions? Apparently not. Both Kant's good will and Jeremy Bentham's most likely interest and happiness give full consideration to the
dynamic behaviors and rational capacity of the subject, but they neglect
the "non-rational" sphere in human's social life. Kant's categorical imperative as the law of morals has no "commander". In fact it stresses the
self-consciousness of practical reason; whereas the interest of utilitarians
is directly the result of subjective actions. Moreover, they think this result
can be used as a standard judging good and evil through rational calculation. Apparently, no matter how much the two schools differ in the
meaning of good, they both believe that "good – "Sollen" (should) action
is under the complete control of reason. The "rational" being is the basic
assumption of the above two types of ethics. Kant's rational being is such
a concept: a being that can envisage necessary links, make deductive inference or probable inference and form an apriori concept.[2] When criticizing Kant, Broad said:

> When the concept of a "rational being" is brought into the common light
> of day and analysed, as we have done to it, we see that one can no more infer
> that a rational being would recognise any principle as right than that it would

---

1 American] McIntyre: After Virtue, p.234, Beijing, China Social Sciences Press, 1995.
2 [British] Charlie Dunbar Broad: Five Types of Ethical Theory, p.104, Beijing,
   China Social Sciences Press, 2002.

recognise any end as desirable. Still less could we infer from the concept of a rational being that it would accept all those principles and only those which answered to a certain formal condition.[1]

Utilitarians' "rational being" had also met with many difficulties. This "rational being" essentially is the being performing interest calculation. We can imagine without difficulty that if the differentiation between good and evil must be determined through calculation, then essentially it will turn the qualitative differentiation into quantitative differentiation. Not to say that the dimension cannot be grasped, even the legality of the quantization of social behaviors and their effect is questionable.

From the above we may grasp that, Aristotelian good does not give full consideration to subjective activity, while the good in the version of Kant and Jeremy Bentham is based on a kind of abstract subject, so all these concepts of good are abstract. No doubt, if we are to seek a concrete concept of the good and essence of good, we must set our foothold at concrete subject and the concrete life of this subject.

To study the good in human's moral activities, we might as well start with Kantian pure form. In terms of pure form, good is manifested as "Sollen", that is to say, the behavior that regulates man should be like this other than like that, and is the standard of moral behavior. As Feng Youlan put it: "The so-called good refers to the act that conforms to a standard ... the so-called evil refers to the act, that goes against this standard."[2] In fact, it reveals the characteristic of good only in form. The reason why this standard or criterion can guide man's moral behaviors and make them good is that the actors consider it as a universally valid criterion, i.e.: a criterion that shall be observed under the same situations. In terms of specific individuals, this criterion has existed since ancient times and needs to be observed and accepted. If Kant is right, then when people accept these rules and do good, they usually are not for any other end and just think it is what they "should" do. But does this indicate

---

1 The same book as above, p.105.

2 Feng Youlan: Collection of Sansongtang, p.98, Zhengzhou, Henan People's Publishing House, 1986.

that the acceptance to these rules is out of the reason of man? In fact, our moral behavior usually does not have the self-consciousness of Kantian "rational being", and is only a "performative formula". On the contrary, when we have definite consciousness on these rules and attempt to study them, their validity becomes doubtful. At this point, moral behavior is like Ludwig Wittgenstein's "language game": If an actor wants to enter the "game", he must accept the rules of this game and this acceptance is unconditional. In this way, the rules accepted constitute a part of man's life-world. In a sense, the acceptance of them becomes one of the conditions for the existence of man in the world. Therefore, this acceptance can be conceived as man's acceptance to its essence. Let's talk of it, from another angle, the good as a criterion can be conceived as one of the shapers of man's essence.

But, cannot actor do anything on these rules and are these rules invariable? It seems so as far as separate individual actions are concerned. If the truth is so, these rules will have two ways of existence only: either the "nature" insisted by Sophists, i.e.: reducing the basis of moral activity to some "natural attribute", or "supernatural", i.e.: the "highest good" with divinity or God.

Above we have indicated these are all abstract goods. Although good as a rule of moral behaviors in all cases shall be universally valid and stable to some extent, and it is the earliest viewpoint of ethics, do this universality and validity mean the eternity and invariability of nature? Obviously not. Above we have indicated that the possible independent existence of ethical and moral sphere rests with its separation from nature. Nature and moral have always been thought to be two different realms. In addition, how to explain the historical change and regional differences in moral and ethic? As far as, the static "highest good" is concerned, it is always an unsolvable question. The only reasonable explanation of this phenomenon is that the good as a moral behavior is "artificial". As for how to understand the meaning of "artificial", it is indeed another issue.

Marxist communicative practice and the good

Above we have indicated that both Kantian "artificial" and utilitarian "artificial" are abstract. Kantian "man" is a purely formalized will, while utilitarian "man" is atom-like interest pursuer. If we set our foothold at the social concept of Marxist communicative practice, we may easily understand that "man" in fact is the individual who associates with others under specific social conditions just as Marx said, "the ensemble of the social relations". Conceiving actor as an individual in social relations on the one hand stresses that the "ensemble of the social relations" serves as a background for individual. The good we discuss here as a rule of conduct is a part of this background; but on the other hand, this background in fact is constituted by many individuals and their behaviors. In this way, we can integrate the above mentioned versions of the concept of good. We may say, the previous versions of the concept of good are all the products of uni-directional thinking, while here we realize the bi-directional interaction of the two aspects: firstly it is the interaction between the subject and rule of action. This interaction is realized through the interaction of different subjects, i.e.: subjects "constituting" the rule of activity in fact is the process in which many subjects communicate with each other and reach a "consensus". By now, we can understand without difficulty that, the result of the "artificial" nature of good was inevitably the communicative activity approach.

PRACTICE AND
HUMAN KNOWLEDGE

PRACTICE AND
HUMAN KNOWLEDGE

Introduction

Cognitive activity is no doubt an important aspect of human activity. Human engages in cognitive activities in order to obtain knowledge. Though, we may say human possessed some knowledge in the very beginning, the theoretical reflection on knowledge was not possessed. It was generated after human knowledge was developed to some extent and people had raised doubts on the knowledge. Since early modern times, the observation on knowledge has become an important part of philosophy and even thought to be the most important part. In Marx's works, there is no systematic dissertation on the issue of knowledge, but this issue is unavoidable for Marxist philosophy. Epistemology should also be an important part of Marxist philosophy. As the interpretative system of college or university textbooks often remain at the level of early-modern materialism, the previous understanding on Marx's knowledge theory has remained at the level of early-modern materialist empiricism, too. More and less we have involved the issue of knowledge in the discussion of the relation between theory and practice in Chapter 1 and Chapter 2. Here we will set foothold at modern practical philosophy to systematically enunciate Marx's knowledge theory.

CHAPTER ONE

Epistemological Issues and Their Way out

Epistemology is a branch of philosophy that studies the nature, scope, preconditions, basis and general reliability of knowledge.[1] This definition reflects the general view of Western philosophical community. According to this definition, much of the content which used to be discussed as epistemology by Chinese academic philosophical community does not belong to this discipline, or at least it cannot be called philosophical epistemology and can only be appropriately called cognitive psychology or something alike. Therefore, when we study cognitive activity as a modality of human activity as well as the development of traditional epistemology in the name of traditional epistemology, the study is limited to the scope defined above and does not involve the content that belongs to cognitive psychology. In this section, we will disclose the theoretical predicament of traditional epistemology and indicate its only way out as quasi epistemology.

---

1 [British] D.W. Hamlyn: A Brief History of Western Epistemology, p.1.

Ancient and early-modern age epistemology and its problems

In the history of philosophy, epistemology as a relatively independent philosophical branch has emerged in the seventeenth and eighteenth centuries. Though it achieved certain development in ancient philosophy, in ancient times the study on human knowledge activity or theoretical activity still belonged to the study on the world. That is to say, the phenomenon of cognition was studied as one of the existing spheres only, while the theories about cognition or knowledge were subordinate to ontology. Therefore, the research of ancient philosophy on cognitive activity cannot be reckoned as epistemology in a strict sense.

Epistemology began with the thorough reflective study on existing objective knowledge. It is not for obtaining the knowledge of related objects, but for determining the reliability and possibility of objective knowledge. Of course, such study does not occur without reason. It stems from the doubts on knowledge. This doubt is not any special doubt on specific knowledge but the ordinary doubt on man's possibility to obtain reliable knowledge. It is this doubt that makes the study on the authenticity of human cognition necessary, thus leading to the defense for or limitation to man's cognitive ability. Like Hamlyn said: When a philosopher asks whether a thing is possible, his question must direct at the view of thinking this thing is impossible and must direct at common skeptical attitude towards this thing.[1] Therefore, the necessity of epistemology rests with the existence of skepticism. Skepticism was the earliest way to reflect upon human knowledge. It reflects upon human knowledge in a negative way, whereas epistemology reflects upon human knowledge basically in an affirmative way, though this affirmation is no longer a direct affirmation but one after full consideration on the negation of skepticism. Therefore, in view of the original and un-reflected, direct affirmation, epistemological affirmation is a higher-level affirmation, a negation of the negation. At this point, epistemological affirmation is temperate and finite affirmation. In this way, epistemology has established an indissoluble bond with skepticism since the very begin-

---

1 [British] D.W. Hamlyn: A Brief History of Western Epistemology, p.4.

ning. It always keeps company of the latter and the latter is always a necessary precondition for its existence. We may say that, they are the two facets of a thing, one is the affirmative side and the other is the negative side. Skepticism can be called special epistemology, negative epistemology and the sinfonia of epistemology.

The epistemology of ancient philosophy had sprouted in 4th century BC. Before that, i.e. in 5th century BC, human habit and system were critically examinedfor the first time. Numerous things which used to be considered a part of the nature were treated differently. As a result, people universally compared nature with human nomos or conventions and questioned their demarcation line.[1] Sophists are the first people who had doubted on human knowledge. The famous maxim of Protagoras is, "man is the measure of all things". It means that everything is, what it presents itself to a man. Therefore, true or not, it depends on man. Gorgias went one step further. He claimed: "Nothing exists; even if something exists, nothing can be known about it; and even if something can be known about it, knowledge about it cannot be communicated with others"[2] These skeptical views caused people's disbelief in the things they used to firmly believe. If people want to claim any convincing knowledge, they must provide reason to defend this possibility. Therefore, epistemology sprouted.

The first philosophers who thought about how to distinguish real knowledge from false things are Parmenides, Heraclitus, Democritus and Plato. For example, Parmenides had differentiated the "way of truth" and the "way of opinion", and Democritus had differentiated two kinds of properties of things. One was what conventional is, such as: color; the other was what truly belonging to the thing, such as: volume, shape and others from atom. Only the latter constitutes the true knowledge. Plato also differentiates knowledge and sensory perception. He thinks true knowledge comes from ideal world, and the so-called cognition is only the memory of the ideal world where the spirit comes from, while senses can only provide some uncertain opinions. Neither Democritus nor Plato's

---

1 The same book as above, p.1.
2 Ancient Greek and Roman Philosophy, p.138.

dissertations on knowledge can be reckoned as the epistemology in a strict early-modern age sense, because they all rely on or are subordinate to ontology.

The epistemology in a strict sense has emerged in early modern times and began with the introduction of the concept of mind or ego by Rene Descartes. In the Middle Ages, Christian Culture superseded Greek Culture, belief superseded reason, and philosophy was descended to the maid of theology. In theology, belief enjoys priority, while reason-based suspicion is neither possible nor necessary. However, since Renaissance in early modern times, the doubt on religious doctrines sprung up. In Renaissance, many famous thinkers held a skeptical attitude. The most typical one is Michel de Montaigne.

> He made universal and so general suspicion on things that this suspicion drags itself in, i.e.: if he suspects and even suspects suspicion itself, his sense of uncertainty rotates around a nonstop circle towards the sense of uncertainty itself; he gives equal opposition to the people who are certain everything is uncertain and the people who are certain nothing is uncertain, because he wants to be certain of nothing and his opinion essentially is the suspicion that even suspects itself and the ignorance that even is ignorant of itself. He calls it is the primary form. He is unable to express this opinion with any affirmative words. Because he said he suspects, he should at least determine he suspects and betray himself. This in form goes against his intention. He can only express himself with doubt. Therefore, as he does not want to say "I do not know", he only says "what do I know"? This is his motto. He put it under the balance that weighs contradiction. This balance is completely balanced: that is to say, he was a pure Pyrrhonist.[1]

Just as Marx put it, this skepticism is an extremely powerful weapon that smashes hackneyed dogma.[2] However, Montaigne's example above indicates skepticism is a double-edged sword. When he stabs others, he will hurt himself, too. In terms of man's fundamental purpose, suspicion does not aim to suspect itself, but aims to destroy the old world through suspicion and establish a new world. Therefore, after skepticism, it is necessary to save reason so as to establish an edifice of scientific knowl-

---

1 [French] Blaise Pascal: Talks with Mr. Desargues, excerpt from Rationalist, p.23, Chengdu, Sichuan People's Publishing House, 1988.
2 Collected Works of Karl Marx and Frederick Engels, Chinese version 1, Vol.2, p.162.

edge by taking reason as the highest authority or the most fundamental foundation. On this premise, epistemology will unavoidably thrive. Rorty had said correctly, "the 'epistemological turn' taken by Descartes might not have captured Europe's imagination, had it not been for a crisis of confidence against established institutions, the crisis was expressed paradigmatically in Montaigne."[1]

Early-modern age skepticism has a major difference from ancient skepticism or traditional skepticism: "Traditional skepticism had been troubled principally by the 'problem of the criterion' – the problem of validating procedures of inquiry while avoiding either circularity or dogmatism. This problem, which Descartes thought he had solved by 'the method of clear and distinct ideas,' had little to do with the problem of getting from inner space to outer space – the 'problem of the external world' which became a paradigm for modern philosophy. The idea of a 'theory of knowledge' grew up around this latter problem – the problem of knowing whether our inner representations were accurate. The idea of a discipline devoted to 'the nature, origin, and limits of human knowledge – required a sphere of study called 'the human mind,' and that sphere of study that, what Descartes had created."[2] Hegel also ever underlined the difference between ancient skepticism and early-modern age skepticism.[3] Generally speaking, as ancient philosophy is not conscious of the effect of "ego cogito", ancient skepticism is only to hold a suspicious attitude towards the certainty of knowledge, while as early-modern age philosophy is aware of this effect, it shows general doubt on man's ability in acquiring knowledge. It goes without saying that, the latter is a suspicion in a deeper layer. Due to different direction of suspicion, the early-modern epistemology thoroughly different from the dissertation of ancient philosophy on knowledge, was born.

Early-modern skepticism suspects man's cognitive ability, so in order to refute this suspicion, certainly early-modern philosophy regards demon-

---

1 [American] Richard Rorty: Philosophy and Mirror of Nature, p.120, Beijing, Sanlian Bookstore, 1987.
2 The same book as above, p.120.
3 [German] Hegel: Lectures on the History of Philosophy, Vol.3, p.108~111.

strating man's ability in acquiring knowledge as their prime task. As a necessary result, "mind" or "ego" was considered the main content of philosophical research. Following the introduction of the concept of "mind", the issue of the relation between mind and external world had emerged, too, i.e.: the famous issue of "the relation between thought and being" as called by the tradition of German philosophy. The thriving of epistemology thus possessed a basic precondition.

The relation between thought and being

We know the issue of the relation between thought and being is a basic issue of early-modern philosophy. It decided epistemology's dominant role in early-modern philosophy. In a word, the fundamental reason why early-modern philosophy turned to epistemology is the wake of reflective spirit and the discovery of ego. On the one hand, skepticism is based on self and subjectivity and thinks my mind is the last thing for me;[1] on the other hand, epistemology as the opposite of skepticism also starts with objectivity and ego. However, epistemology is not fully aware of this basis. In Rene Descartes, – founder of early-modern philosophy as well as Locke and other people behind Rene Descartes, the residue of old metaphysics can still be seen. Epistemology did not achieve true self-consciousness until Kant. Since then, philosophy was truly separated from all subjects of empirical science.

Now, by early-modern age the philosophy, with epistemology as its core is not the "highest" science as thought by ancient philosophers. On the contrary, it is the "foundation" of all sciences. Philosophical epistemology should not unrealistically pursue the solutions of metaphysical issues like God and spirit again. Instead, it should be devoted to the study on "how our knowledge is possible" and other epistemological issues, thus laying a foundation for other disciplines. Kant asked himself a question: "how is the synthetic judgment a priori possible?" Kant's solution to this question is to try to combine rationalism and empiricism's solutions to

---

1 [German] Hegel: Lectures on the History of Philosophy, Vol.3, p.109

"how knowledge is possible". He thinks true knowledge must constitute two factors: sense representations and apriori conceptual categories that link these representations together. He criticized rationalism as trying to reduce sense to concept, while empiricism tried to reduce concept to the sense (Leibniz's intelligentizing of phenomena corresponds to Locke's sensitizing of all wise concepts).[1] Kant on the one hand agrees with empiricism and thinks all knowledge is inseparable from perceptual experience; on the other hand, he agrees with rationalism and thinks universal necessity must come from concept and intellectuality. Therefore, the question is how intellectual concept turns perceptual perception into a universally and necessarily valid knowledge form. Kant here negates old metaphysics' concept of mind or ego which exists as a substance, and substitutes it with a concept of functional transcendental subject. Transcendental subject is something that regards intellectual categories as activity modes and performs the function of synthetic sensuous material. It is not a substance. By contrast, thing-in-itself and mind substance are nothing but extreme concepts. They are "non-phenomenal" negative, other than positive concepts. In this way, the transcendental subject that performs synthetic sensuous and perceptual material essentially is only the unity of intellectual concepts. Therefore, the question of "how is the synthetic judgment a priori possible" is also the question of "how does the transcendental subject, as the unity of intellectual concepts use sensuous materials to construct knowledge object. It is also the basic issue of standard epistemology. Kant adopts a phenomenalist way. His final conclusion is that object is only a phenomenon other than a being-in-itself substance. Thus the world, mind or God as substance have no possibility to become the objects of knowledge. All these are the necessary results of the development of epistemology, i.e.: the necessary results from the introduction of the concept of mind or inner space and its role as the foundation of epistemology.

Kant's this train of thought was inherited and developed by Edmund Husserl. Edmund Husserl's phenomenology is always closely related to epistemology. We may say, cognitive behavior is its most central task for him. Edmund Husserl said: Kant tried to find, from subjectivity or the

---

1 [German] Kant: Critique of Pure Reason, p.229.

relation between subjectivity and object, the final definition of objectivity which is recognized through cognition. At this point, we are consistent with Kant.[1] As mentioned above, early-modern epistemology must take the inner space of subject as its foundation, so it has to solve the issue of the unity between the subject of cognition and its object. Kant's approach is to limit the object of cognition to the scope of experience through the concept of limit. If subject goes beyond this scope and reaches the thing-in-itself, it will become illegal. How does subject go beyond itself and reach its object? It is a basic issue of epistemology. Kant's solution to it is ; to make necessary limitation to object and isolate it from the thing-in-itself. Edmund Husserl clearly knew this fundamental issue of traditional epistemology. Same as Kant, he also strictly limits epistemology to the scope of subjective consciousness and thinks "inherence is the necessary characteristic of all cognitions in epistemology".[2] The difference is that Edmund Husserl, does not allow the existence of the sphere of the thing-in-itself. What Edmund Husserl uses to eliminate the thing-in-itself is transcendental subjectivity. In fact, the reason why Kant's transcendental synthetic proposition is possible is that : subject constructs its object. In the sense of Edmund Husserl, the reason why objective knowledge is possible is also the transcendental subjectivity constructing its object, i.e.: the construction of objective world. In this construction, Kantian the thing-in-itself disappears. If, Edmund Husserl was successful, this epistemological issue would be solved, but the fact is not so -- Edmund Husserl's transcendental subjectivity itself ran into trouble. Above, we have pointed out the cycle of transcendental ego and reduction. The other problem is that cognitive objectivity must involve the validity on multiple subjects, i.e.: inter-subjective validity. Kantian concept of objectivity in fact is used in this sense, but now Edmund Husserl must enunciate this validity and it must be the enunciation based on transcendental subjectivity. Edmund Husserl also thinks each transcendental ego may surpass itself and be conceived as an interactive subject, but the contradiction in this idea is obvious. Singular transcendental subject can by no means construct "plural" subject. Even if it is constructed, absolutely it cannot be

---

1 Ni Liangkang: Explanation on the Concepts of Edmund Husserl's Phenomenology, 458.
2 The same book as above, p.460.

called a subject. Therefore, Edmund Husserl's inter-subjectivity is an "awkward expression" (commented by words of Luhmann).

Edmund Husserl moves largely along Kantian direction, but in the end the difficulty of theoretical direction was exposed. In fact, Edmund Husserl's "inter-subjectivity", "life-world" and other concepts indicate his philosophy has exceeded the scope of epistemology. However, Edmund Husserl introduced these concepts only for "theoretical purposes", i.e.: serving his core theme -- epistemology. This implies that the epistemology in the sense of Kant, also presents itself as similar to traditional epistemology -- the dependent relationship of the traditional epistemology on the spheres outside it--, or we can say it implies traditional epistemology itself, and possesses unsolvable problems. In fact, Martin Heidegger, Habermas and other people's criticism and development of Edmund Husserl's approach are exactly based on these spheres outside epistemology and they have given up the basic framework and questioning method of traditional epistemology. Does this mean the possibility of cognition and the objectivity of knowledge are built on "quicksand"? We will discuss this question in next section. Here we want to say that the traditional epistemology represented by Kant has run into predicament.

Modern analytical philosophy

In the another major trend in contemporary philosophy, i.e.: in analytical philosophy, this predicament manifests itself in another way. Analytical philosophy has opposed Hegelian rational contemplation from the very beginning and gradually deepened the opposition to all basic principles of early-modern age epistemological philosophy. The common tendency of early-modern epistemology is the opposition between subject and object, i.e.: the opposition between the cognizing mind and the external world it faces and tries to cognize.[1] The modern analytical philosophy was good pictured in Moonitaz's statement:

---

1 [American] Moonitaz: Contemporary Analytical Philosophy, p.4, Shanghai, Fudan University Press, 1986.

All have a notable characteristic that is to try to abandon the issue of epistemology and all the solutions to this issue as envisaged by early-modern philosophy......These philosophies do not consider how mind is like or whether
it can truly cognize the external world. Instead they assume in advance that
we have acquired knowledge by various means and we can cognize the world
under any circumstance. If skepticism or a doctrine which considers the
world essentially unknowable is deducted from our starting point, then the
model, paradigm or a complete set of advance assumption which causes such
result must be abandoned. Such skepticism indicates that we are not certain
of such a world or (as another view may claim) and we can never know its
structure, then there will be no such issue of external world, though we may
claim we know its existence.[1]

In this way, the issue of skepticism is put aside, but not solved. It is considered to be the result of a wrong way of questioning. Rene Descartes
and Kant used that to establish the foundation of their philosophical systems. But now it is believed as false and it is not necessary to deal with
skepticism with all energy. The above attitude of modern analytical philosophy is simple. It has straightly abandoned the opposition between
subject and object or mind and external thing – the preconditions for
the tenability of skepticism and early-modern age epistemology. Therefore, all theories about this opposition and theories on the solution of
this opposition are considered the false issues of "Metaphysics" and thus
are abandoned.

Modern analytical philosophy values the significance of linguistic statements. It thinks thought is the application of language. Therefore, our
study on knowledge should certainly turn to linguistic analysis. From
the perspective of linguistic analysis, many epistemological propositions
were only meaningless statements resulting from wrong linguistic application and do not deserve careful handling. Now, before linguistic analysis, the most serious criticism at a statement is not to say it is wrong or
false, but is to say it is meaningless. According to the view of analytical
philosophy, all propositions can be classified into "analytical propositions" and "empirical propositions". The former can be demonstrated
logically, while the latter could be demonstrated by experience in prin-

---

1 The same book as above, p.17.

ciple. According to this classification, the basic premise of Kantian phi-losophy was defined as follows : – existing "another permissible statement – transcendental synthetic statement - therefore this is a statement which advises; truth can be clearly determined by us, although for such knowl-edge, on the one hand, the ways of formal logic is not enough; on the other hand, in order to obtain such knowledge, observation is not un-necessary-- in addition to apriori analytical statement (equivalent to the analytical proposition of analytical philosophy) and posterior synthetic statement (equivalent to the empirical proposition of analytical philos-ophy) will not be tenable.[1]

Therefore, the core issue of the entire Kantian philosophy – how is apri-ori synthetic judgment or statement possible – is evaluated as a mean-ingless issue. According to this view, in neither mathematics nor natural sciences, we can meet such statements; all examples given by Kant are wrong.[2] Since transcendental synthetic statement does not exist, the core issue of Kantian critical philosophy and its questioning is: "how is this issue possible?" becomes redundant. It is even more unreasonable to es-tablish a cognitive theory on this basis to answer this question.

Here, what negated is the entire early-modern philosophy other than Kantian philosophy alone because from every aspect, we can say that Kantian philosophy is a model of early-modern philosophy, it not only sticks to the general premises of early-modern epistemological philoso-phy but also tries to integrate the most profound insights into the major tendencies of early-modern epistemology, namely: rationalism and em-piricism.

Therefore, the negation of Kantian philosophy is the negation of the en-tire early-modern epistemological philosophy. Kantian critical philoso-phy had ever declared that the old metaphysics was meaningless, whereas today the weapon of critique targets at critical philosophy itself and de-clares it is meaningless. It is really a joke of the history. Under the attack

---

1 [German] Wolfgang Stegmuller: Mainstream of Contemporary Philosophy, Vol.1, p.373, Beijing, Commercial Press, 1986.
2 The same book as above, p.375.

of modern analytical philosophy, early-modern epistemological philosophy gets into unprecedented predicament and is unable to defend its survival. Philosophy itself turns to linguistic analysis, i.e.: no longer cares for whether we can acquire knowledge but concentrates its attention on probing into logical issues and clarifying the language with which we discuss knowledge and belief. This is the so-called "linguistic direction change" in modern philosophy.

However, just when modern analytical philosophy won a sweeping victory over traditional epistemology, it has faced a crisis of survival. Moreover, this crisis was not from an external critique. It was generated from its own development. Analytical philosophy was established by negating the basic premise of epistemological philosophy. This premise is the assumption of the opposition between subject and object or between man's inner space and outer space. In Kantian philosophy, this opposition is the opposition between transcendental subject's intellectual category which possesses universal necessity and the sensuous material which is caused by external objects and only possesses contingency, i.e.: the opposition between form and content. Analytical philosophy negates Kant's premise ; "the existence of apriori synthetic statement", negates the premise of the opposition between subject and object, but retains the differentiation between their form and content. That is to say, for modern analytical philosophy, this differentiation is still considered meaningful. This differentiation is regarded as the differentiation between analytical proposition and empirical proposition. The falseness or trueness of the former is purely in a sense of logical form, while the falseness or trueness of the latter relies on the content of experience. This differentiation has also suffered constant internal attack during the development of analytical philosophy. Among the attacks, the most decisive one is the Quine's article as; Two Dogmas of Empiricism. In this article, Quine put it bluntly: "Modern empiricism has been conditioned largely by two dogmas. One is a belief in some fundamental cleavage between truths which are analytic, or grounded in meanings independent from matters of fact and truths which are synthetic, or grounded on facts. The other dogma is reductionism: the belief that each meaningful statement is equivalent to some logical construction upon terms which refer to immediate experience. Both dogmas, I shall argue, are ill founded."[1] Therefore, in the sense of Quine, many analytical philosophers are still incarcerated in the dogmas of traditional epistemology and unable to set themselves free from them. What they need to do is to abandon these dogmas (of course, from a more thorough point of view, Quine is not thorough, either) and completely moves to pragmatism. Quine, has indicated this point in his above article. He thinks, one effect of abandoning the two dogmas of empiricism is "a blurring of the supposed boundary between speculative metaphysics and natural science. Another effect is a shift towards pragmatism".[2]

Shift towards pragmatism is indeed a general development trend in analytical philosophy. This trend is more dramatic in the development and changes relating to scientific methodology. The earliest is the "positivism" of logical empiricism, followed by Popper's "falsification-ist" critical rationalism, Kuhn's historicist "paradigm", and Feyerabend's "anarchism" that has ended up with thorough relativism. In addition, in the "language game" theory put forth by Ludwig Wittgenstein in his old days, in Lyle's analysis on Rene Descartes-type concept of "mind" and in the works of Austin, Sellars and other people, this trend can be seen clearly. Analytical philosophy once developed to this new step, became remarkably different from its original look. This development on the one hand is the thoroughness of its anti-epistemology attitude, but on the other hand also thoroughly ruins its original intention of pursuing philosophy as an accurate science. The inevitable result of this shift towards pragmatism is the thorough relativity on knowledge, and the objectivity of knowledge becomes an issue of validity in life. In this case, analytical philosophy has moved to its opposite and the legality of the existence of epistemology was more questionable. How to deal with the issues of philosophy? can epistemology be reconstructed? If yes, then what is its premise? These are the questions we must answer before we discuss the concrete content of epistemology.

---

1 [American] Quine: From a Logical Point of View, p.19, Shanghai, Shanghai Translation
   Publishing House, 1987.
2 The same book as above, p.19.

Reasonableness of "quasi epistemology"

Traditional epistemology runs into predicament. Is pragmatism a way out of this predicament? To a great extent, the answer is negative. For traditional rationalist epistemological philosophy and those scientist analytical philosophy, pragmatism no doubt is an "antidote". However, another "toxicity" this antidote contains results in another form of ideological "poisoning". This "toxicity" is thorough relativism. The negation by pragmatism against epistemology, first of all, is the opposition between the mind and external things as the premise of epistemology, the opposition between concept and intuition, and the opposition between universal item and particular item, or in a word, negating the opposition between subject and object. After this opposition is negated, the issue of the relation between thought and external world will naturally become a meaningless falsehood issue. The issue of the objectivity or truth of cognition essentially is meaningless, too. If we say these terms still have some realistic significance, the significance can only be the eulogy on the conviction that validity will bring about good effect. In this way, we come to the standpoints of pragmatists - Dewey and James as follows : "Knowledge is only a tool, truth is only a tool that can achieve success and effect". We may also cite a sentence by Ludwig Wittgenstein in his old days as comparison: "My experience indicates, this (and not others) assumption can simply express my this experience and future experience. If it is proved that another assumption may more simply express this empirical material, I will choose this simpler method. ... we give up an assumption only for a greater interest.[1]

Relativism and Pragmatism

This thorough relativism is more typically shown in Kuhn's scientific methodology. Kuhn reduces scientific revolution to the conversion of scientific research "paradigm". Between these paradigms, no commensurability exists. Therefore, the conversion is not a knowledge develop-

---

1 [Austrian] Ludwig Wittgenstein: The Philosophical Review, [American] Moonitaz: Contemporary Analytical Philosophy, p.273.

ment process that conforms to reason, and is only a conversion to approximate "belief". In this case, not only Copernicus' theory is incompatible with Ptolemy's, and Newton's theory is incompatible with Rene Descartes', even Einstein's theory from which Newtonian formula was deduced is incompatible with the latter. Once relativism comes to this phase, there will be no space for objectivity.

However, relativism thinks so much on the discontinuity of human knowledge that it fundamentally neglects the continuity of cognition. A result of the continuity of cognition is the cumulative character of knowledge. Without this cumulative character, the development of science and technology, and the subsequent development of the entire human society will become unimaginable. Relativism exactly neglects this point and cannot explain this point. Besides, the negation by thorough pragmatism against the opposition between subject and object or between inner space and outer space is also rather doubtful. Of course, the epistemological explanation on this opposition is rather problematic, but can we completely negate these differentiations? If a true statement does not possess universality, in any sense, then what is the sense of calling it knowledge? Moreover, the thorough negation to universality will inevitably lead to skepticism and the untenability of the issue of "meaning". The issue of meaning is established on the basis of the communicability among subjects, but the negation to universality will lead to the loss of communicability. Communicability cannot be explained as "conventionalism", because "convention" in fact has assumed communicability in advance. Therefore, the negation by pragmatism against epistemology goes to skepticism – a premise on which epistemology was established, though it is a moderate skepticism.

Nevertheless, our negation on pragmatism does not mean we must go back to the standpoint of traditional epistemology. It was the difficulty of traditional epistemology that finally paved the way to pragmatist standpoint, so if we return to the standpoint of traditional epistemology, it will be like starting a new round of cycle, while it will have nothing good for the solution of the problem. In fact, the difficulty of traditional epistemology also lies in the difficulty in reasonably solving the problem of communicability, except the abovementioned attacked points. The problem area in the meaning of a proposition, in the final analysis, is the issue of the communicability among subjects, i.e.: the issue of meaningful communication among subjects. The attack of modern analytical philosophy against traditional epistemology firstly directs at the incommunicability of its propositions, i.e.: meaninglessness. According to modern analytical philosophy; same as the language of metaphysics, the language of traditional epistemology is vague, ambiguous and lacks objective verifiability. Stegmuller, gives an example; A typical or thorough epistemological standpoint is the standpoint of transcendental philosophy; the transcendental philosophy originating from Kant or Edmund Husserl's transcendental phenomenology, but when they cite the transcendental view to prove the reasonableness of their viewpoints, they will inevitably face the problem of lack of communicability and verifiability among subjects. This lack will unavoidably lead to the contrary to the scientificalness as they require initially.[1] In this case, although the standpoint of traditional epistemology is opposite to the standpoint of pragmatism, they both run into predicament in the communicability and verifiability among subjects.

Gorgias' three questions

It appears that the three suspicions Gorgias put forth on human knowledge more than two thousand years ago all come true. When Gorgias put forth these questions, perhaps he did not expect they would puzzle countless philosophers in the next thousands of years. His three questions have become the core questions of philosophy by turn. Ancient philosophy was dedicated to the question: how is existence possible. It is a non-reflective direct attitude, early-modern age philosophy as the reflective philosophy was dedicated to the question of how knowledge is possible, modern philosophy cares more about the publicity or communicability

---

1 [German] Wolfgang Stegmuller: Contemporary Analytical Philosophy, Vol.1, p.123~124、364~365.

of knowledge. It seems that the mission of philosophy is to solve these three major questions in a sense. However, these three questions are not irrelevant and separate questions. They are three aspects of the same issue. Though the question of existence is fundamental, if the question of how knowledge is possible is not solved, the question of existence as the question of knowledge will be unable to be solved, while if the question of how knowledge is possible is not solved, the question of the publicity or communicability of the knowledge or the question of universal validity of knowledge will be a question that can hardly be solved. Therefore, I think, if we are to solve this time-honored issue of suspicion fundamentally, we must change our visual angle and solve it as a whole. If we cannot find a way to solve it as a whole, none of the questions will be reasonably solved. One of the reasons for the failure of ancient ontology, early-modern age epistemology and modern linguistic analysis philosophy is that they only grasp one question, respectively and try to solve it in a separated way. The result can only be the unsurmountable dualism or pragmatism and skepticism.

To get rid of this predicament, we must take a standpoint that is different from both traditional epistemology and pragmatism. This standpoint should be able to reasonably solve the question of knowledge objectivity and the question of communicability among subjects as a necessary condition of knowledge objectivity. Of course, this standpoint should certainly absorb the reasonable stuff in traditional epistemology and pragmatism and unify them on a new basis.

The scope of "quasi epistemology"

This new standpoint is the standpoint of "quasi epistemology". Richard Rorty, had mentioned this quasi epistemology in his; Philosophy and Mirror of Nature. He thinks "most philosophers who see Marx and Freud or both of them, as figures who needed to be drawn into 'mainstream' philosophy have tried to develop quasi-epistemological systems which centers around the phenomenon which both Marx and Freud throw into relief; that is the change in behaviors which results from the change in self-description."[1] For the moment we do not discuss whether it is reasonable that Rorty lists two of them in parallel. Rorty opposes this attempt because he holds a pragmatist standpoint and thoroughly negates any attempt that is similar to epistemology. In view of many difficulties in the pragmatist standpoint, it seems that choosing a standpoint of "quasi-epistemology" is reasonable. This new standpoint certainly opposes the thorough and relativist knowledge-based view of older pragmatism and meanwhile also opposes the non-historical absolutist standpoint in traditional epistemology. The core of this absolutist standpoint was the absolutization of human's sensible activities and regards it as the most basic form of all human activities. The standpoint of quasi-epistemology, that is probably based on Marx's epistemological standpoint is the standpoint of Marx's practical philosophy which is advocated in this book. This standpoint is not to regard all cognitive activities or theoretical activities of human, as the foundation of all human activities but to regard them as one of the modalities of human activities. Therefore, for the study on cognitive activity, we cannot adopt traditional epistemological standpoint, and regard cognitive activity as the most fundamental activity and merge it with other modalities of activities. Quasi-epistemology, does not adopt the pragmatist standpoint, reduce the cognitive activity to pure practical activity, rely everything on their validity in practice or disregard the relative independency of theoretical activity, thus it studies cognitive activity only in the mutual relations of many modes. It only regards cognitive activity as a part of human activity and does not incline to one pole – as traditional epistemology or pragmatism.

Then is it possible that such "quasi-epistemology" holds water? It is a question we must demonstrate. The precondition for the tenability of epistemology is the tenability of the opposition between subject and object or between mind and material. Only when this opposition is tenable, the epistemological question of how subject or mind reaches external world is tenable. In view of reality, the opposition between man as subject and natural world as object is self-evident. The opposition between

---

1 [American] Richard Rorty: Philosophy and Mirror of Nature, p.330.

the conformity of human activity to aim and the non-conformity of external nature to aim is the premise of human existence. However, this opposition is different from the opposition envisaged by traditional philosophy. The opposition between subject and object set by traditional epistemology is a kind of opposition that can be called as absolute opposition. The prototype of this opposition is the opposition between ego and external object set by Rene Descartes. Ego is a kind of self-consciousness and a pure thought without extension, while external object is a kind of pure extension. Under such an absolute opposition, it is impossible to achieve the unity between subject and object. Therefore, the epistemological philosophers after Rene Descartes could only choose one of them, mind or material as their starting point and regard the other as a derivative. This was the fundamental reason for the opposition between modern idealism and materialism in early modern times. However, from modern practical philosophy's point of view, the opposition between subject and object is not that kind of an absolute opposition. Here the opposition between subject and object is a derivative state of the life-world which does not separate object and subject, so it is an opposition on the basis of a kind of unity. Therefore, in cognitive activity, the opposition between subject and object is non-absolute or finite opposition in a dual sense.

Firstly, the opposition between man as the subject and external nature as the object is not like the opposition abstractly conceived by old philosophy. It is the opposition between the mind substance without extension and the material substance (which is the extension of essence). Man and external nature are not completely different beings, so this opposition can only be a kind of finite opposition.

Secondly, the opposition between subject and object in theoretical activity or cognitive activity is only one aspect of the opposition between man and nature other than the all-round opposition as conceived by old philosophy. Therefore, this opposition between the subject of theory and object of theory is only a more finite opposition.

Thirdly, although the opposition between subject and object in cognitive activity is manifested as the opposition between "mind" and "material" due to the abstractness of cognitive activity, the opposition between "mind" and "material" is only the abstraction of the concrete relation between subject and object. Therefore, the "mind" or "consciousness" here is only a functional term other than a kind of absolute being. The only real is human subject and its activity rather than abstract "mind". Therefore, in quasi-epistemology, the finite opposition between "mind" and "material" will not lead us to the metaphysical problem: ambiguous meanings. Thus, will not lead to the traditional approach that departs from man's real activity and uses fantastic abstract principle to solve the other equally abstract issues. In this way, we may say the finite opposition between subject and object as a premise of this quasi-epistemology is tenable.

Then, what is the research object of this quasi-epistemology? Or what content should it contain? By nature, epistemology, no doubt, should be the study on the nature and premise of knowledge as well as the basis of the objective validity of the knowledge. However as cognitive activity is only one of the modes in human practice or in life totality, usually the so-called mode of theoretical reason or theoretical activity is not an original thing. Therefore, although this quasi-epistemology seems to have the same content with traditional epistemology, in fact there is a great difference between them. Concretely speaking, under certain historical background, quasi-epistemology should research two questions. First the reason why the scientific knowledge possessing quasi universal necessity and validity is possible; and secondly, the nature and finity of this scientific knowledge. Certainly, the question of why the scientific knowledge with quasi universal necessity and validity is possible within historical scope or under historical background should not lead us to study the form of the abstract, or the historical and transcendental reason constituted by knowledge, but should historically study the "forms" or previsions" in which human acquires scientific knowledge in cognitive activity under historical background and reveal the nature of scientific knowledge which serves as the foundation of knowledge. The "historicalness" here does not mean "relativism" or no persistent laws, but means developing and unfixed. These "quasi-transcendental forms" or "previsions" that constitute the ground for acquiring universally necessary knowledge normally are not directly manifested as knowledge patterns. These "quasi-transcendental forms" or "previsions" are rather, forms of knowledge background or basic structures. Therefore, they can be clearly presented only in man's critical study. To clearly present such historical "previsions" or "quasi-transcendental forms" should be the main premise of this quasi-epistemology. And on this premise quasi-epistemology should analyze their general composition method, i.e.: the foundation of validity, draw the scope of knowledge based on this analysis and reveal the nature of knowledge. It goes without saying, the foundation of the objective validity of knowledge is still the core issue of this quasi-epistemology. The scope of knowledge can be drawn only on this basis. The issue of the objective validity of knowledge is the issue of the truth of knowledge as we usually refer to.

CHAPTER TWO

Quasi-Epistemological View on Truth

Difficulties in traditional epistemology's view on truth

It goes without saying, the pursuit for truth is the fundamental goal of human's cognitive activity. Hegel's words speak out this fact: "Truth is a noble word, and the thing is nobler still. So long as man is sound at heart and in spirit, the search for truth must awake all the enthusiasm of his nature."[1] Therefore, inevitably the issue of truth becomes the core issue in the entire epistemology. Is our knowledge subjectively valid? If yes, what is the ground? These are questions that epistemology should solve at first. In view of history, epistemology emerged out of the suspicion on our ability in acquiring objectively valid knowledge, so it certainly puts the issue of the objective validity of knowledge in the first place. This issue is also closely related to the issue of the sources of knowledge, so the two issues are consistent. On how to solve the issue of the objective validity of knowledge, traditional epistemology had two trends -- rationalism and pragmatism, as well as the efforts to reconcile these two trends. Empiricism is inclined to propose; the correspondence theory

---

1 [German] Hegel: The Logic of Hegel, p.64.

on truth. It thinks, the truth of knowledge or proposition lies in its correspondence with facts; rationalism generally is inclined to propose; the coherence theory on truth. It thinks, the standard of truth lies in truth itself and does not need to seek help from others and truth itself can guarantee its objective validity.

Empiricism and Rationalism

The fundamental premise for the tenability of epistemology is to set the opposition between mind and external object. Rationalism, suspects the reliability of sense perceptions, so it attributes the reliability of knowledge, only to reason, itself. Rene Descartes regards the clearness of the concept itself, as the symbol of the truth in the concept. Spinoza had also declared: "By an adequate idea, I mean an idea which, in so far as it is considered in itself, without relation to the object, has all the properties or intrinsic marks of a true idea."[1] "Even as light displays both itself and the darkness, so is the truth; a standard both for itself and for falsity".[2] Therefore, same as Rene Descartes, Spinoza also thinks whether an idea is true or not can be judged by reason itself. The judgment standard is clearness, or concretely speaking, should not contain contradictions. "Necessary, when its non-existence would imply a contradiction; possible, when neither its existence nor its non-existence implies a contradiction ......"[3] Obviously, in formal logic the standard of truth is based on the principle of non-contradiction. This point is more clearly illustrated in Leibniz's theory of truth. He classifies truth into two types, namely: necessary truth and contingent truth. Necessary truth is identified with the principle of contradiction, while the latter resorts to the law of sufficient reason.

However, the truth determined in this way is still a thing inside the truth itself, that is to say, the truth determined according to the principle of non-contradiction still does not exceed idea itself and its objective validity is still questionable. Since rationalism generally suspects the relia-

1 [Dutch] Spinoza: The Ethics, p.44.
2 The same book as above, p.82.
3 [Dutch] Spinoza: On the Improvement of the Understanding, p.36, Beijing, Commercial Press, 1960.

bility of sense perceptions, it certainly seeks another way out. This is the doctrine of "innate ideas" and various kinds of other similar doctrines. Innate idea is inborn idea. It is not made up by man but implanted into man's consciousness by God, because the omniscience and omnipotence of God guarantee the authenticity and validity of the innate ideas. Rene Descartes said: "I noticed certain laws which God has established in nature. Since He has imprinted the ideas of these laws in our souls, after we have reflected on them sufficiently, we cannot doubt that they are precisely observed in everything which exists or which acts in the world."[1] Spinoza thoroughly spurns interactionism and sticks to a strict psycho-physical parallelism. As a result, the issue of the objective validity of knowledge becomes more heavily dependent on the settings of God. As God simultaneously possesses two attributes: thought and extension, "the order and connection of ideas are the same as the order and connection of things", and "a true idea must correspond with its ideate or object".[2] Therefore, we may hence induce "God's power of thinking is equal to his realized power of action, that is, whatsoever from the infinite nature of God in the world of extension, follows without exception in the same order and connection from the idea of God in the world of thought".[3] Later, Leibniz also relied on "pre-determinate harmony" theory, to solve the issue of the objective validity of thought. However, all these rationalist solutions were full of contradictions. In order to ensure our knowledge is objectively valid, and guarantee the identity between thought and being, we should seek help from the omnipotent God. In addition, in order to obtain those objectively valid concepts of truth, man must surpass rational knowledge and seek help from "intuition". In this way, for rationalists, rational knowledge inevitably descends to the second place, while the mysterious intuition takes the highest place. Therefore, the rationalist solution to the issue of the objective validity of knowledge was unsuccessful and can hardly be accepted.

---

1 [French] Rene Descartes: Discourse on Method, See Philosophies in the Countries of Western Europe from Sixteenth Century to Eighteenth Century, p.152, Beijing, Commercial Press, 1961.
2 [Dutch] Spinoza: The Ethics, p.4.
3 The same book as above, p.49.

Rationalism runs into predicament in the issue of the objective validity of knowledge. Then what about empiricism? Empiricism thinks all of our knowledge is from sensual experience. At this point, it is different from rationalism. Besides, empiricism and rationalism are opposite in the issue of the relation between body and mind. In most cases, rationalism denies the role of human body in cognition and holds a view of psycho-physical parallelism, while empiricism, as it affirms sensual experience, must affirm the role of human body in cognition. As human body has the duality: "ego" and object, seemingly the body may act as a bridge or a medium between mind and external object. For this reason, empiricism negates psycho-physical parallelism. According to its principle, empiricism is incompatible with the doctrine of innate ideas. Therefore, the only channel between consciousness and external object is perceptual experience.

But can we determine the objective validity of knowledge simply by relying on sensual experience? At the first sight, it seems not a problem at all, but after careful analysis, we will discover it is rather difficult, and we almost cannot find any method to determine the objective validity of knowledge. Firstly, from the perspective of empiricism, we cannot find a reliable criterion to judge whether our sensual experience or simple idea tallies with external object or not. Our knowledge about external object always needs sensual experience, so we are unable to compare an idea with the external object it reflects, and what we can compare is still an idea. In this case, it has no reliable basis to say an idea is the same as an external object. Secondly, more importantly, the so-called knowledge in general is not the experience about the existence or non-existence of a thing. Pure simple ideas cannot constitute the knowledge in a strict sense. Knowledge is always a complex system of ideas. Complex idea is the composite of simple ideas. What mind can directly feel is simple ideas only. Complex ideas are coupled through the action of mind. Therefore, the relation between ideas is added on ideas by mind. It is unknowable whether the principle of mind activity tallies with external objects, because what mind directly feels is simple ideas only. It is very clear that by the standpoint of empiricism, the issue of the objective validity of knowledge was also unsolvable.

Owing to these difficulties, when empiricism had developed to Hume, he thoroughly abandoned the issue of the objective validity of knowledge and only considered the issue of the correspondence between ideas and impressions. He argued: "Now, since nothing is ever present to the mind but perceptions, and since all ideas are derived from something antecedently present to the mind; it follows, that it is impossible for us, so much as to conceive or form an idea of any thing specifically different from ideas and impressions. Let us fix our attention out of ourselves as much as possible: Let us chase our imagination to the heavens, or to the utmost limits of the universe; we never really advance a step beyond ourselves, nor can conceive any kind of existence, but those perceptions, which have appeared in that narrow compass."[1] Hence, the so-called relation between perception and external object does not go beyond consciousness, while the necessity and cause-effect relation of knowledge as believed by men, in fact are determined by the customs of mind only because "in the operations of nature, where similar objects are constantly conjoined together, and the mind is determined by customs which infer the one from the appearance of the other. These two circumstances form the whole of that necessity, which we ascribe to matter. Beyond the constant conjunction of similar objects, and the resulting inference from one to the other, we have no notion of any necessity or connexion."[2] While carrying the principle of empiricism through, empiricist Hume also abandons it and turns to pragmatism, or as Mr. Zuo Huazheng said, turns to "irrationalist nativism", i.e.: "the nativism based on the practical instinct that can no longer be analyzed by mind".[3] This destroys the principle of empiricism.

---

1 [British] David Hume: An Enquiry Concerning Human Understanding, p.75, Beijing, Commercial Press, 1957.

2 Zou Huazheng: Study on "An Essay Concerning Human Understanding", p.7, Beijing, People's Publishing House, 1987.

Kantian revolution

The failure of rationalism and empiricism in their attempt to solve the issue of the objective validity of knowledge has led to Kant's philosophical revolution. As an inevitable result of this revolution, a very distinctive view of truth in Kantian philosophy was formed. Generally speaking, the solution of pre-Kant epistemology to the issue of the objective validity of knowledge had always focused on the correspondence of thought to external object and the correspondence of thought to being. Obviously, empiricism defines the standard of objectivity as the correspondence of the initiative of mind to the passivity of the accepted idea. And, although rationalism assumes God as the guarantee of the objective validity of knowledge, it still requires that the ideas in mind should conform to external objects. Considering the failure of the above solutions, Kant completely reversed the issue. Since the old methods were unfeasible, why not try the reversal? Kant said:

> It has hitherto been assumed that our cognition must conform to the objects; but all attempts to ascertain anything about these objects a priori, by means of conceptions, and thus to extend the range of our knowledge, have been rendered abortive by this assumption. Let us then make the experiment, whether we may not be more successful in metaphysics, and assume that the objects must conform to our cognition. This appears, at all events, to accord better with the possibility of our gaining the end we have in view, that is to say, to arrive at the cognition of objects a priori, of determining something with respect to these objects, before they are given to us. We, here propose to do just what Copernicus did in attempting to explain the celestial movements. ... If, the intuition must conform to the nature of the objects, I do not see, how we can know anything on them a priori. But if, on the other hand, the object conforms to the nature of our faculty of intuition, I can then easily conceive the possibility of such an a priori knowledge.[1]

It is really remarkably original and forceful remark! It was contrary to the established mind-set and has opened a new visual sphere. Through this revolutionary move, we may say that in a sense, Kant has theoretically solved the difficulties of rationalism and empiricism. Of course this

---

1 [German] Kant: Critique of Pure Reason, p.12.

solution is on the basis of idealism, but this idealism is different from Berkeley's idealism of "being is the perceived", and Leibniz's idealism. Kant, distinguishes the phenomenon from the thing-in-itself. He thinks, only cognition can reach phenomenon and cannot reach the thing-in-itself. Thus, the so-called object can only be the phenomenon other than the thing-in-itself. However, because the phenomenon is formed on the premise that the subject accepts the action of thing-in-itself, then the laws or structure of phenomenon will certainly be same compared with the laws or categories of thought. In this way, the objective validity of knowledge does not rest with the correspondence of knowledge or thought to external object. On the contrary, knowledge is based on the correspondence of the external object,- as phenomenon- to thought. As the thing-in-itself is inaccessible for knowledge, the objectivity here, can only be the objectivity of phenomenal world. In addition, because Kant's subject or ego is different from the "whiteboard"-type, individual mind as advocated by empiricists. Then, it is the synthesis of the innate transcendental ego in form of thought and the self-consciousness, which is able to accept external stimulation, or the synthesis of "large ego" and "small ego" as proposed by Mr. Xie Xialing.[1] For this reason, Kant does not have to seek help from Rene Descartes' God or Berkeley's God to guarantee the objective validity of knowledge. Thus, the objective validity of knowledge only rests with the correspondence of the empirical object to the knowledge. This in fact is the synthesis of the "small ego" which belongs to "self-consciousness" with the "large ego" which is a pure thinking form.

In Kantian theory about the objective validity of knowledge, what is noticeable is Kant's view on objectivity. Kant spurns old metaphysics' view of considering objectivity as the thing-in-itself, opposes Berkeley's subjective idealist view of "being is the perceived", and defines the objectivity with universal validity. In Kantian philosophy, universal validity is in fact an issue of vindicability or publicity, or as Hamlyn said, Kantian standard for objectivity is always the standard for inter-subjectivity, i.e.:

---

1 Xie Xialing: Kant's Supersession to Ontology, p.143, Changsha, Hunan Education Publishing House, 1987.

valid to everybody".[1] Therefore, Kantian concept of universal validity is publicity or inter-subjectivity.

Before Kant, in early modern times, man's study on knowledge had mostly concentrated on necessity and objectivity, while they had considered the publicity of knowledge as an implicit assumption only and never paid much attention to it. Rationalism gave particular attention to necessity. In a sense, necessity is the intrinsic nature of true knowledge just as stressed by Spinoza. The premise of knowledge must be the possession of a certain degree of necessity (absolute necessity is not needed), because only a certain degree of necessity can provide a basis for certain correctness of human behavior, while pure contingency does not deserve the good name of knowledge. As defined by Spinoza, we may also say the objectivity of knowledge is the external symbol of true knowledge. However, if the guarantee of God is withdrawn, then this "external symbol" will become a necessary condition. Nothing without objective validity deserves the name of knowledge. While, how to connect the internal standard and external standard of knowledge? This connection was impossible in rationalism and empiricism. Kant unifies the two with the medium of publicity or inter-subjectivity. This in a sense, which can be regarded as Kant's answer to the very old philosophical question-- Gorgias' doubt on the communicability of knowledge. The necessity of the knowledge is guaranteed by the internal links of the categories offered by pure thinking forms, but cognition is performed by individuals. It is inevitable that individual's self-consciousness may be wrong, while the transcendental ego as a pure thinking form must correct it under the help of publicity or inter-subject communicability and vindicability. What acts upon communicability acts upon pure thinking form, thus possessing objective validity. That is to say, Kant highlights the publicity and inter-subject vindicability of true knowledge. This is the major significance of Kantian view on truth.

Nevertheless, same as the old metaphysics criticized by him, Kant did not really solve the issue of the objective validity of knowledge. He reduced objectivity to publicity or inter-subjectivity. In fact, he did not

---

1 [British] D.W. Hamlyn: A Brief History of Western Epistemology, p.65.

walk out of the scope of subject and his solution was still a special subjectivity or non-objectivity. In his system, objectivity is still extrinsic the thing-in-itself. His objectivity in fact only distinguishes the "small ego" as individual's self-consciousness and the "large ego" as a pure thinking form and is unable to differentiate subjectivity and objectivity. His definition on objectivity of course is much higher than those given by empiricism and rationalism, but fundamentally speaking, Kant also could not sublate the hard nut of the objective validity left by earlier generation. In our opinion, the main reason is Kantian rationalism.

The difficulty of Kantian transcendental philosophy also lies in the inability to explain the development and changes in human knowledge. Since the laws of nature is put in by intellectuality, and while intellectual form is innate, then the picture of the nature before us should be eternal and invariable, neglecting that there are different scientific world prospects in different scientific times. If intellectual form is not changed according to the changeing world prospect, it will become meaningless to say intellectuality establishes the laws for nature. Therefore, in order to understand the varying world prospects, we must go into the history and observe human's cognitive ability by revealing it in the historical process. In this way, we will certainly walk out of the standpoint of pure epistemology and also walk out of rationalism. Of course, we say Kant is a rationalist. It does not mean Kant only pays attention to rational activity and never thinks of other activity modes – on the contrary, Kant pays great attention to man's moral life and thinks practical reason is higher than theoretical reason. We want to say that Kant thoroughly separates theoretical activity and practical activity. On the one hand, he tries to solve the issues of epistemology in the range of pure theoretical activity; on the other hand, he conceives practical activity as pure moral life only; or although he admits a kind of technical practice, he also regards it as something irrelevant with moral life. In this way, in Kant it will be impossible that there is any realistic link between theory and practice. Therefore, the difficulties in Kantian philosophy, including the difficulties in the view on truth, can be dialectically sublated only when it breaks through rationalism and joins historicity.

---

1 [British] D.W. Hamlyn: A Brief History of Western Epistemology, p.65.

Marx, exploring a new view on the truth

The difficulties of Kantian transcendental philosophy indicate the issue on the truth of cognition is unsolvable in pure epistemology. Therefore, we should transcend the sphere of pure cognitive activity, while this transcendence will break the standpoint of rationalism. After Kant, Marx became the first person who transcended rationalism. Marx has two well-known sayings. One is "the question whether objective truth can be attributed to human thinking is not a question of theory but is a practical question. Man must prove the truth - i.e. the reality and power, the this-sidedness of his thinking in practice. The dispute over the reality or non-reality of thinking which is isolated from practice is a purely scholastic question."[1] The other is "the philosophers have only interpreted the world, in various ways; the point is to change it." Marx spoke these words to address German classical philosophy. Here, he hints a brand new train of thought for the solution to the issue of the objective validity of knowledge, but this train of thought is not groundless. It is based on the difficulties in the view on truth in traditional epistemology. Therefore, we must conceive this hint under this background and should never look at it in an isolated way. Unfortunately, Marx's new train of thought was not conceived and investigated under its background. Instead, Marx's new train of thought, is directly included into an empirical epistemological system. As a result, it completely loses its original power and becomes a pure adornment of empirical view of truth. By this mistaken understanding, "practical standard" not only cannot sublate the difficulties left by Kantian philosophy but on the contrary, it falls into pre-Kantian obsolete empirical doctrines and goes even farther from the real solution to this problem. On the premise of empiricism (a kind of metaphysical materialism, which has no other choice except empirical standpoint), the so-called "practical standard" will be either the same essentially with the empirical "correspondence theory" or modern empirical "verification standard" or will be the same as pragmatic standard that what is useful is truth. If such, the universal necessity of knowledge cannot be verified, so it is difficult to achieve true objectivity. Therefore,

---

1 Marx & Engels Selected Works, Edition 2, Vol.1, p.55.

we must re-conceive Marx's hints on the new view on truth, and regard these hints as a response to the difficulties in Kantian philosophy and also faced by successors, i.e.: the attempt to sublate the difficulties, other than go back to empiricism or go to pragmatism from empiricism.

After Kant, philosophers tried many methods to sublate the difficulties of Kantian transcendental philosophy. In the German classical idealism movement after him, people including Hegel attempted to introduce historical method to solve issues. However, as Hegelian philosophy still set foothold at rationalism and was still based on reason, its historicism is only a fictitious historicism and only a thing with history as its shell and the logic of absolute idea constituting its kernel. In a word, Hegelian historicism is established on the basis of rationalism and is still a derivative or external manifestation of the latter. Therefore, Hegelianism cannot really sublate the predicament of Kantian philosophy. Instead, it blurs issues. Among the schools of modern age philosophy, analytical philosophy either sticks to a rationalist standpoint or turns to pragmatism, so it cannot sublate and has not sublated any difficulty of Kantian philosophy and only simply discards the premise of Kantian philosophy. As commented by Stegmuller, Edmund Husserl's transcendental phenomenology shows an increasingly obvious trend towards Kantian idealism,[1] so fundamentally speaking, Edmund Husserl could not solve the difficulties of Kantian philosophy. What can really enlighten us on our solutions to the issues is the "pre-structure theory" on interpretation in Martin Heidegger's hermeneutics, and the "world-picture" doctrine in Ludwig Wittgenstein's "language game" theory. These two doctrines both fundamentally goes beyond the standpoint of rationalism.

Martin Heidegger and his "pre-structure theory"

Martin Heidegger thinks man as "Dasein" which is not in a position opposite to the world in the beginning. At first man was "a being in the world". Later the subject was polarized and object had developed. Therefore, the question of "how does subject cognize object" was raised later,

---

1 [German] Ludwig Wittgenstein: Mainstream of Contemporary Philosophy, Vol.1, p.86.

while at first it was only Dasein's understanding on its being. The understanding is a way of the being of Dasein other than a way of cognition of subject. "Knowing is a mode of Dasein as a Being-in-the-world, and is founded ontically based on this state of Being".[1] That is to say, knowing is based on understanding and rooted in understanding. In such understanding, "we have deprived pure intuition [Anschauen] of its priority, which corresponds noetically to the priority of the present-at-hand in traditional ontology. 'Intuition' and 'thinking' are both derivatives of understanding, and already rather remote ones".[2] "The understanding has in itself the existential structure which we call "projection".......The character of understanding as projection is constitutive for Being-in-the-world".[3] Through lowering knowing to a derivative of understanding on the way of existence of Dasein, Martin Heidegger gives his solution to the difficulties of rationalism as represented by Kantian transcendental philosophy. No doubt, Martin Heidegger's train of thought is rather enlightening, though we cannot completely agree with his solution.

The "world-picture" doctrine put forth by Ludwig Wittgenstein in his old days is very inspiring for our exploration to a new view on truth. In some of the works written by Ludwig Wittgenstein in his old days, he introduced the concept of "world picture". He thinks a world picture is a complete language system or a set of convictions. With regard to the much conditioned and limited language games as well as our activity rules in these games, it serves as a background and all-inclusive conceptual framework. "Those things just give our way of looking at things, and offer our researches, their form. Maybe they were once disputed, but perhaps, for unthinkable ages, it has belonged to the scaffolding of our thoughts."[4] The ground for the existence of world pictures is that "the questions that we raise and our doubts depend on the fact that some propositions are exempt from doubt, were like they were hinges on which

---

1 [German] Martin Heidegger: Being and Time, p.75.
2 The same book as above, p.180.
3 The same book as above, p.177.
4 [Austrian] Ludwig Wittgenstein: On Certainty, Section 211, [American] Moonitaz: Contemporary Analytical Philosophy, p.398.

those turn."[1] This is because "we just cannot investigate everything, and for that reason we are forced to rest content with assumption. If I want the door to turn, the hinges must stay put."[2] That is to say, the convictions and propositions as world pictures play a special logical role in human cognition. These propositions are affirmed by us without special inspection; they are propositions which play a special logical role in our system of empirical propositions.[3] We inspect an ordinary proposition by checking whether it tallies with reality and by seeking help from practice, but "tallying with reality" and "seeking help from experience" themselves, should be decided by the world picture we use and they are not applicable to the convictions that constitute world picture. As long as people use and accept a world picture, they will no longer ask whether this world picture as a complex whole or the convictions constituting it "tally with reality" and whether experience verifies it. We may as well say, it is a world picture that provides a criterion, standard and rule to inspect other propositions and decide whether they are tallying with reality. If a real thing has a ground, then this ground will be neither true nor false.[4] Therefore, just as Moonitaz put it, Ludwig Wittgenstein's use of world picture, this expression formula, wants to stress that world picture and its components like "concepts", "convictions", "rules" and "propositions" form a system. This system is not only a transcendent and not only a purely rational structure, but accurately speaking, is interwoven with our daily practice in countless ways and in countless times. Like every kind of other finite language games, world picture is based on life form and "practice".[5]

Obviously, Ludwig Wittgenstein's „world picture theory" goes beyond the rationalist framework of traditional epistemology and attempts to find a premise or foundation for theoretical activity, beyond human's theoretical activity. Thus aims to sublate the theoretical difficulties which can hardly be sublated by rationalist epistemology. However, Ludwig

---

1 [American] Moonitaz: Contemporary Analytical Philosophy, p.398.
2 The same book as above, p.398.
3 [American] Moonitaz: Contemporary Analytical Philosophy, p.400.
4 The same book as above, p.401.
5 The same book as above, p.404.

Wittgenstein has interpreted the source of "world picture" as accordance with authority and did not make deep investigation on many facts. As a result, while he negated rationalism, he shifted to something similar to relativism or pragmatism.

Without doubt, Martin Heidegger's "pre-structure theory" about cognition and Ludwig Wittgenstein's "world picture theory" are rather illuminating for our correct understanding on Marx's sublation to the difficulties brought by the rationalist tendency in traditional epistemology. Marx, Martin Heidegger and Ludwig Wittgenstein are all the modern philosophers after Kant. They have all attempted to get rid of the rationalist framework of epistemology to sublate its difficulties. This common tendency is by no means accidental, and rather it is decided by the predicament of traditional epistemology. Therefore, we may say, to break through rationalism and go to a broader sphere of human activity should be a general direction of the re-birth and development of traditional epistemology. More convincingly, these three philosophers as well as many other modern philosophers have very different basic philosophical tendencies, but they all chose the direction of transcending rationalism. This also indicates that Marx's view on truth still has vitality today. The key is how to understand it. If we still interpret Marx's concept of practice from the standpoint of traditional rationalism, it will be impossible for us to surpass the standpoint of empiricism, and the so-called practical standard can only be an empirical standard or verification standard. Unfortunately, people conceive the concept of practice, exactly in a rationalist way. And by large, people's interpretation on the concept of practice originates from Hegelian interpretation, while they are not aware that Marx has transcended rationalism including Hegel. Hegelian concept of practice is only a link of the rationalist progress in Hegel's logical system, so it has not gone beyond theoretical activity. Concretely speaking, in his Conceptualism, Hegel puts practical idea behind epistemology. Therefore, in principle, practical idea is developed from cognitive idea. This does little harm to the "logic first" principle in the Hegelian philosophical system, but this idea is directly applied to the interpretation on a real cognitive process, problem will arise. It will just lead to people's common definition on the concept of practice: practice is a sensuous material activity under the guidance of theory. This kind of definition sets in advance the priority of theoretical activity. Therefore, when people again require that practice should provide "transcendental" foundation for cognition, they will inevitably get into Alfred Schmidt's dilemma cycle.[1] This practice of which its premise is cognition certainly cannot provide a foundation for cognition. Therefore, where will the epistemology without "transcendental" form be reduced to if not to empiricism?

Two types of practice and life-practice

Where is the root of problem? Marx had said: "Man must prove the truth of his thinking in practice". Does not he mean thinking as cognition comes before the inspection in practice? We think it is a wrong understanding. It is true that, in real life, cognition and practice are interwoven and people cannot tell which comes earlier. Moreover, in terms of a concrete activity process, there is a plan, scheme and other things which are part of the theoretical activity at first, while real implementation comes after them, but it is only a superficial phenomenon.

If we ask; what are the plan and other thinking activities before practical activity, based on, problem will arise. If the answer is the previous practice, it will not be a real explanation, because the previous practice is also guided by the even earlier theoretical activity. By parity of reasoning, there will be no end and it will make the problem even remoter from solution. If we say the foundation effect of practice, has nothing to do with time and argue that whether the cognition is true or not will be determined by post-verification, then the post-verification cannot be called the foundation of cognition. Moreover, the argument of post-verification, makes the pre-verification type of cognitive activity lose its "transcendental" premise, thus cognition itself becomes a thing without real

1 [German] Alfred Schmidt: The Concept of Nature in Marx, p.116, Beijing, Commercial Press, 1988.

foundation. In this case, the objective validity of cognition can only be reduced to either whiteboard reflection or sheer coincidence. The former is a typical empirical attitude. The latter is the skeptical attitude, worse than empiricism. Obviously, the rationalist understanding on the concept of practice is unfeasible.

Then, what does "prove the reality of its own thinking in practice" mean?

People often overlook an issue: thinking can prove its reality only when it has a premise of reality. If thinking itself does not possess this foundation, the post-verification will become an animal-type trial and error only. Now the question is: where does this reality prior to cognitive activity or "transcendental" reality come from? If we say it comes from practice, we will run into the above mentioned cycle. In order to cut off this cycle, we must turn back again to the understanding on the concept of practice with two meanings or two layers which we have proposed before as practical philosophy view. On the one hand, we can understand the narrow-sense practice as a concept which is similar to the empirical senseous experience. This concept of practice or experience refers to those particular sensuous activities. When we say practice inspects a special proposition, in fact it means verification with practice. On the other hand, we can understand the broad-sense practice as the practice which can provide a realistic premise for our cognition or thinking. The practice in this broad-sense meaning, is not a special or particular sensuous activity but the totality of human's sensuous activities or it is life-world. This practice is the reality foundation used for the cognition. It is neither to provide post-verification on cognition nor provide post-confirmation based on some thinking forms or logical categories. But just to provide a basis for the objective validity of thinking form, as the essential structure of cognitive activity, thus providing a basis for the objective validity of all cognitive activities. The key to provide a basis for the objective validity of cognition is to provide a basis for the objective validity of thinking form as the essential structure of cognitive activity. This is because in terms of concrete cognition, transcendental thinking form or the law of cognitive activity essentially is isomorphic with the activity form or law of the totality of practical activities. In other words, proving-- prior to particular cognition or "transcendental" --the objective validity of cognitive form or law is decided by the fact that cognitive activity is a practical activity and subordinate to life practice, to this totality. We know that, the finity of cognitive activity as a kind of theoretical activity, is relative to life practice, and theory should need to "open" to practice in the end. The objective validity we discuss here addresses cognitive activity other than particular activity. With respect to particular cognitive activity, we may resort to some standards and check whether it meets the standards, so as to judge its authenticity; whereas with respect to cognitive activity, we should not seek its truth from itself. Instead, we should seek its truth, in life practice outside the scope of theory. In Marx's words, "It is not a question of theory but is a practical question". With respect to theoretical activity, life practice is really objective and real. We may say, this objectivity and reality exist "congenitally". Life practice, as totality is the existence of the whole mankind. This directly proves the objective validity of the essential structural form of human activity, thus proving the objective validity of the essential structure, or thinking law or thinking form of cognitive activity as a modality of the essential structure of human activity. This proof directly uses the valid existence of human. But, the essential structure of human activity as a form or law, inevitably and only exists in the totality of human activity, and unnecessarily exists in particular practical activity or theoretical activity. Therefore, only the totality of human practice can provide direct proof for the objective validity of the law of human activity including the law of cognitive activity, while particular practice can not. The thinking form or the law of cognitive activity as a modality of the essential structure of human activity which can be directly proved by the totality of practical activity constitutes the "transcendental" framework which enables theoretical activity, and constitutes the "transcendental" category that grasps sensuous material.

Between a particular practical activity and a particular theoretical activity, we cannot see the above relation, but we can see a relation of mutual premise and mutual infiltration. Therefore, we can only say particular practice is carried on under the guidance of theory, but for the totality of practice, it is not that case.

After distinguishing the meanings of total practice (holistic practice) and particular practice, we can say that total practice provides a "transcendental form" for theoretical activity and enables theoretical activity. Owing to the evidence of direct existence of man, this "transcendental form" possesses the character of reality or objective validity. Therefore, the knowledge formed on the basis of this "transcendental form" may possess reality or objective validity. Merely by accident or coincidence, the objective validity of human knowledge will become unimaginable.

However, this "transcendental form" only provides the possibility of objective validity other than reality because this "transcendental form" is decided by the totality of human practice or the totality of human's direct existence, while on the other side, concrete cognition is executed by particular persons. The totality of human activity transcends particular individual's changeable activity and possesses an invariance. Therefore, the "transcendental form" or thinking form as the foundation of theoretical activity also possesses invariance, while individual's cognitive activity that executes theoretical activity does not naturally possess this invariance.

This is because individual's thinking organs and sensory organs are all affected by corporeal state. Therefore, there is the question: how to enable individual's cognitive activity conform to human's total thinking form. Thinking form as a basic form of human activity is not an isolated abstract being, but is a profound thing that is embodied in the cultural system based on lansign. Meanwhile as the operation of tools and the application of lansigns must take the existence of inter-subjective social structure as a condition, the structure of human society naturally possesses a kind of epistemological significance. Just in the social structure, human cognitive activity solves the problem of the transition from the possibility of pure thinking form to the real knowledge with objective validity.

Language and knowledge

This problem is solved in two ways. Firstly, it is the output of thinking form from society to individuals. This output is performed mainly through language. Language learning is certainly not a purely intellectual process. It is carried out in cooperation with other kinds of activities. We may say it is a kind of "language game". This development process of child's intelligence is the research object of genetic epistemology. Through language learning, children gradually grasp the thinking forms embodied in language and possess the ability to apply these forms to form knowledge. Nevertheless, in the process that individual forms knowledge, he may still make mistakes in two aspects, thus may be unable to form real knowledge. Firstly, he may make mistake in the use of thinking forms. Secondly, he may make mistake in sensuous materials. The mistake in the first aspect can be prevented by requiring sentence (proposition) must possess inter-subjective vindicability, communicability or publicity. This is to require individual must state a sentence (proposition) in a way conforming to thinking forms. In this way, the publicity of knowledge form, i.e.: public verifiability or vindicability is guaranteed. For this reason, publicity or communicability becomes a necessary element of knowledge. Without it, nothing can be called knowledge. In his Philosophical Investigations, Ludwig Wittgenstein convincingly proves the impossibility of private language,[1] therefore also proves the impossibility of the incommunicable private knowledge as well as the necessity of social structure or inter-subjective structure to knowledge because knowledge certainly takes a language form, while language is certainly inter-subjective or social. The mistake in the second aspect can be prevented through ordinary repetitive experience and practice – this repetition can be completed by others or himself, but mainly by others, while repeatable experience probably must take the communicability or publicity of the sentence (proposition) as a premise and cannot be repeated

---

1 [American] Moonitaz: Contemporary Analytical Philosophy, p.366~367.

by others, even cannot be repeated by himself in principle, either.

That is to say, in human's cognitive activity, not only thinking form is public and is inter-subjectively communicable and universally valid, but also the perceptual facts as the raw material of knowledge are public and universally valid, too. In knowledge, a real fact cannot be a special thing which is only and unrepeatable and appears only for a particular subject, rather it must possess the universality which is valid to every subject in principle. In principle, the unrepeatable things cannot be recognized as the real facts in knowledge. Therefore, science only recognizes the publicly observable phenomena as real facts and does not accept those unrepeatable anecdotes as objects. In this sense, we may say that in cognitive activity, human's sensory organs as the tools or channels of knowledge are also publicized and socialized.

After the basis for the objective validity of total practice or human's basic activity structure (including pure thinking forms) provided by human's direct existence is obtained, society inputs these form into individuals, and the inter-subjective communicability, vindicability and repeatable experience of propositions are required, the issue of the objective validity of knowledge will be solved. Thinking form regards the totality of practice as the basis of its objective validity. This totality of practice is directly associated with nature and takes human's direct survival as evidence. Such objective validity effectively guarantees the true objective validity of knowledge.

We see that, the issue of the objective validity of knowledge is not simply an issue of fact verification but a complex structure containing many links. As knowledge, its inherent character possesses a certain degree of necessity and universality. This is decided by the thinking form that reflects the basic structure of human activity. However, to turn this inherent character into a real thing, publicity or inter-subjective communicability must be used as an intermediate link. The publicity or communicability of knowledge is not its external symbol. It is also decided by the nature of knowledge. Knowledge is no more than man's reflection on his activity, while the inter-subjectivity of human activity decides the inter-subjectivity of knowledge. The publicity or intersubjectivity of knowledge is not extrinsic to its objective validity. It itself constitutes a necessary link for objective validity. Owing to this point, it is not difficult to understand why Kant defined publicity as objectivity. This point is the flaw of Kantian view of truth, but also reflects its profoundness. Without publicity, there will be no way to seek objective validity. It is also the reason why modern analytical philosophy pays great attention to the meaning of a proposition. The meaning of a proposition is nothing but the meaningful communicability between subjects of the proposition. What analytical philosophy strives to explore is exactly this link of the objective validity of knowledge. Of course, the limitations and achievements of analytical philosophy are all at this link. Besides, true knowledge is often compared to currency which has purchasing power, by James for instance.[1] Certainly, it emphasizes the publicity and communicability of knowledge. However, only publicity cannot form the objective validity of knowledge. Therefore, I can say that Rorty, by antagonizing cooperativity (he means publicity in fact) and objectivity loses his way. He advocates that cooperativity(publicity) should educate and correct objectivity; and on the other side he opposes realism education of cooperativity from objectivity, thus he cuts off the links of true knowledge and regards the publicity as the only stipulation, so inevitably he shifts to relativism.[2] Therefore, we should comprehensively grasp the links for true knowledge and avoid to block those links.

By now, we have preliminarily demonstrated a new view on truth. This view on truth is based on Marx's transcendence to rationalism and meanwhile interprets and develops it at a modern age standpoint. This view on truth treats the issue of the objective validity of knowledge based on the totality of human practice or the evidence of human's direct existence.

---

1 [American] James: Pragmatism, p.106, Beijing, Commercial Press, 1960.
2 [American] Richard Rorty: Philosophy and Mirror of Nature, p.407~422.

PART VI

HISTORY AND HUMAN IDEAL

HISTORY AND HUMAN IDEAL

Introduction

In Chapter 4, we have described the picture of the life-world of finite subject, but on the one hand, it is the basic existence condition of real subject outlined in a static way. We did not directly investigate into the time dimension and history of human life; on the other hand, we did not further discuss the profound existence contradiction embodied in the finity of finite subject as well as philosophy's numerous efforts to solve this contradiction. Therefore, in this chapter, it is necessary to investigate study the basic status of human life from the perspective of history. We will try to indicate that in Marx's thought, the finity of human existence is intrinsically contained in the dimension of ideality. The immanent contradiction between this finity and ideality constitutes the essence or basic structure of human existence, while human's effort to solve this immanent contradiction constitutes human history, while philosophy is inlaid in this history in a special way, i.e.: pursuit of philosophy to grasp and solve to this contradiction constitutes its own history. The significance of Marx's philosophy is to give its own interpretation and solution to this basic contradiction of human existence in a realistic way.

CHAPTER ONE

The Most Fundamental Contradiction in Human Existence

Finity and ideality in the existence of man

In Chapter 4, we have indicated the finity of human life rests with the fact that men must belong to a specific world. Meanwhile we also make general description on this world. Here we will further describe each aspect of the finity. On this basis, we will reveal its intrinsic relation with the realm of ideality. In essence, we are engaging in a finite anthropology, for all analyses and dissertations proceed from man's finite existence. However, the work here is mostly descriptive because finite existence cannot be used as a starting "point" of theoretical reasoning in a general sense.

Man's real life essentially is finite, but man can never leave ideals or give up the pursuit to ideal at any moment. Above we have roughly studied the significance of the finity of human existence. Here we will mainly study the realm of man's ideality. Of course, firstly we will make clear that the ideal we are to discuss here is not the concrete goal pursued in daily life but the ideal of the whole mankind and an ultimate ideal. Generally speaking, ultimate ideal is the provider of the meaning of this world. Without it, all finite pursuits will become meaningless. But, how do we understand this ultimate ideal and who gives the meaning of its existence? This seems to be a pseudo question, or a self-contradictory question, because "ultimate" means the end of pursuit to reason in general, thus the meaning of ultimate being is not given, on the contrary, the meaning of other beings is given by it. If we adopt the thinking mode of theoretical philosophy, this understanding will become reasonable, because ultimate ideal is the "Archimedean point" of theoretical philosophy in most cases. However, above we have criticized this thinking mode and transcended it. The result of this transcendence is the opening of the visual sphere of practical philosophy. If we think over questions under the thinking paradigm of practical philosophy established by us, ultimate ideal must be put in life-world. Reasonable understanding can be obtained only based on human's finite existence. As Marx said, all mysteries which lead theory to mysticism find their rational solution in human practice and in the comprehension of this practice. Therefore, our question here is no longer whether the meaning of ultimate ideal is given or not, but is how to understand this meaning on the basis of life practice.

To understand an ideal on the basis of real life in fact is to understand the reality of the ideal. This reality not only refers to the possibility to realize an ideal as commonly thought but also refers to the reality of the existence of the ideal. In other words, it refers to how to intrinsically associate the ultimacy of an ideal with the finity of human existence. We may as well read Marx's two paragraphs of words at first:

> Feuerbach starts out from the fact of religious self-alienation, of the duplication of the world into a religious world and a secular one. His work consists in resolving the religious world into its secular basis. But, that the secular basis detaches itself from itself and establishes itself as an independent realm in the clouds can only be explained by the cleavages and self-contradictions within this secular basis. The latter must, therefore, in itself be both understood in its contradiction and revolutionized in practice.[1]

---

1 Marx & Engels Selected Works, Edition 2, Vol.1, p.55.

Feuerbach, consequently, does not see that the "religious sentiment" is itself a social product, and that the abstract individual whom he analyses belongs to a particular form of society.[1]

Obviously, religion is an ideal world. Marx's critique on Feuerbach here aims to show the necessity of a reform in secular world, but he offers two aspects: on the one hand, Marx agrees with Feuerbach's reason for seeking religious world on secular basis; on the other hand, Marx's understanding on secular basis is thoroughly different from Feuerbach's. Feuerbach resolves the religious essence into the human essence, but the human essence is only the abstraction inherent in each single individual, so essentially he resolves an abstract world into another abstract world. To break through Feuerbach's thinking limit, the key is to conceive the secular basis of religion in real human life practice and in finite human existence; and conceive man as the individual in reality and as "the ensemble of the social relations".

Marx, stresses that ideal should be understood in secular world, but if the essence of ideal is reduced to finite real life, will an ideal still be an ideal? In fact, Marx's critique on Feuerbach aims to "reform" and "revolutionize" real world, but anyway it does not mean cancellation of ideals, on the contrary, Marx puts forth another kind of ideal – communism; which will be involved below (of course, in the sense of Marx, communism is not only an ideal. Its reality lies in its realizability). But, since human existence is finite in essence, then how is ideal as an infinite appeal generated ? ; and how does it reasonably exist ? Or in other words, how to concretely describe the general relation between ideal and real life? In fact, when we speak of the finity of a thing, certainly we compare it with an infinite or a perfect thing. This is a thinking habit or thinking rule. Common people will not dig into the root of this thinking rule, but here it is particularly important for us to dig into this root, because if this thinking rule is reasonable, it may reveal the information of "deep structure" inherent in real life. That is to say, the treatment of finity and infinity perhaps already exists in real life. We may basically confirm this

---

1 The same book as above, p.56.

judgment from the isomorphism of various kinds of human activities as described above. The following words of German socialist Karl Mannheim are rather illuminating:

> Wishful thinking always appears in the things of men. When imagnation can be satisfied in reality, it will try to hide in the ivory tower built with wishes. Fables, fairy stories, religious commitments to the other world, humanistic illusions and travel legends have always been changing the expressions on the things absent in real life. Comparing with the Utopias which oppose reality and break down current status, they are closer to supplemented colors of the picture of real being.[1]

The fables, fairy stories and other things mentioned by Mannheim construct an ideal world in a way of imagination to overcome the imperfection of real world. This can be deemed as a special function of art in human life in general. Broadly speaking, the artistic activity here does not only refer to activity of artists' artistic creation but generally refers to all aesthetic activities of mankind, of course also including artists' creative activities and common people's aesthetic activities. Furthermore, the Utopia used by Mannheim is not a derogatory term. It generally refers to the ideal world, people establish in order to make up or transcend the finity and imperfection of real life. If a thinking state is inconsistent with the reality it belongs to, it will be utopia.[2] We cannot evaluate this ideal world simply with positivity or passivity, because people may either hide in themselves an ideal world, to passively deal with reality or regard an ideal as a value orientation to change the reality positively. Here our task is not to evaluate the effect of ideal but to study its inherent relation with reality. Mannheim thinks, man's thinking activity universally has the structure of antagonism between finity and infinity. In our opinion, without this structure, man's any value pursuing activity will become impossible, because although the value pursued by particular activity is certainly finite, certainly it also takes an assumption of infinite value as its premise. In this way, we can understand without difficulty ideal is a necessary part in man's real activity. This is the reality of ideal

---

1 [German] Karl Mannheim: Ideology and Utopia, p.209, Beijing, Commercial Press, 2000
2 [German] Karl Mannheim: Ideology and Utopia, p.196.

sphere in the sense of being. We say the finity of the pursuit to finite value is that, such activity must face a specific object and must be inherent in a specific life-world, but ideal as an infinite appeal does not mean, it may be divorced from a specific life-world though it always exists in a form that transcends real being.

Therefore, the tension or contradiction between this finity and ideality in human existence inevitably constitutes the most fundamental contradiction in human existence. On the one hand, real man cannot get rid of the finity, otherwise man will become god; on the other hand, man cannot live without an ideal, otherwise man will fall back to ordinary creature and have no difference from birds and beasts. Man will inevitably live in such a contradiction, so this contradiction also constitutes man's essence. Moreover, the very reason why man is man is, that he possesses such a contradiction and can incorporate this contradiction. If man does not have this contradiction and cannot incorporate this contradiction, the unique essence of man will be lost. Seemingly, it is man's mission to set foothold at real world, to pursue an ideal world and build the ideal paradise on the earth. If man is to exist as a man, he must take this mission as his vocation and must eternally pursue and work on the earth. The continuity of this pursuit and work constitute the human history.

Contradiction of human existence in philosophy

People have long realized or known this fundamental contradiction in human existence and tried to solve it in a way. People's grasp and solution to this problem initially adopted a divine or religious conceptual form and later on adopted a philosophical form. In different development stages of philosophy, different expressions were adopted. Although philosophy is often thought as pure contemplation that is divorced from reality, from the perspective of the visual sphere of practical philosophy, philosophy has never been divorced from life and cannot be divorced from life. Just in the grasp and solution to the fundamental contradiction of human existence, philosophy most profoundly demonstrates its inseparability from real life. Every philosophy has a highest category. Generally speaking, this highest category constitutes this philosophy's grasp or expression of human ideals. In this way, no matter how abstract a philosophy is, as long as we seize hold of its highest category, we may discover its association with real life. Of course, different philosophies have different expressions of their highest category, some are directly manifested in their systems and some not. No matter what cases they are, it is unquestionable that every philosophy certainly logically contains a highest category. In principle, the highest category of each philosophy is unique to some extent, but in a same era, there is much similarity among the highest categories of philosophical systems, so we may study by era philosophy's grasp and solution to the contradiction of human existence by certain era. Generally, people classify philosophy into ancient philosophy, early-modern philosophy and modern philosophy. These three types of philosophies have remarkable differences in the way to grasp and solve the contradiction of human existence.

Generally speaking, the highest category of ancient philosophy can be roughly reduced to the realization of human essence, so in ancient philosophy, the solution to the contradiction of human existence generally means man's existence state of self-realization, self-sufficiency and perfection. Although Socrates did not leave any works for later generations, from the memory of Plato and other people, we know his life-long inquiry is: How should a man live to make his life valuable, thus perfect and happy. His answer is, the value of life is the realization of good: The good is the end of all our actions, and it is for its sake that all other things should be done, and not it for theirs."[1] Plato inherited his teacher's philosophical standpoint and directly defined the "good" as the highest category of his philosophy. In Platonic philosophy, the world is divided into two spheres, namely: an eternal ideal world and rheological visible world or perceptual world, just like sun is the imperator of the visible sphere, "good" is the imperator of ideal world. Therefore, good also constitutes the inherent essence of human spirit. In real life, the deviation

---

1 [Ancient Greek] Plato: Plato Complete Works, Vol.1, p.392, Beijing, People's Publishing House, 2002.

between ideal and reality is caused by the entanglement of spirit by perceptual world. The path to ideal world is to know the nature of your spirit, return to ego and directly reach the idea of pure good through education. In the process to virtue, the ideal state (republic) where philosopher is the king is a social form most helpful to the realization of this goal.

The highest category of Aristotelian ethics is happiness. He said, happiness is the highest good; considering that he regarded contemplation as the greatest happiness, we may also think that the happiness is the highest category of his philosophy. Happiness is nothing but the realization of human essence. Aristotle said: "there are three prominent types of life – the life of enjoyment, the political and thirdly the contemplative life."[1] Among these three types of life, the life of enjoyment is vulgar; political life pursues honour and virtue, so inevitably shallow; only contemplative life is the greatest happiness. This is because "contemplative activity is the best (since not only is reason the best thing in us, but the objects of reason are the best of knowable objects); and secondly, it is the most continuous, since we can contemplate truth more continuously than we can do anything."[2] Moreover, contemplation is the most self-sufficing activity, "a wise man can contemplate by himself", while other activities need the involvement of other people. Furthermore, contemplative activity has "no end beyond itself, and has its pleasure proper to itself".[3] Aristotle thinks this contemplative life "would be too high for man; for it is not in so far as he is man that he will live so, but in so far as something divine is present in him", because "if reason is divine, then, in comparison with man, the life according to it is divine in comparison with human life".[4] Such divine life is certainly the first degree, or the first position and is what we should try to pursue, but it is possible for minority people only and is inaccessible for majority people. For this reason, he also points out: "in a secondary degree the life in accordance with the other kind of virtues as happiness; for the activities in accordance with

1 [Ancient Greek] Aristotle: Nicomachean Ethics, p.6.
2 The same book as above, p.225.
3 The same book as above.
4 The same book as above, p.226.

this, befit our human estate. Just and brave acts, and other virtuous acts, we do in relation to each other, observing our respective duties with regard to contracts and services and all manner of actions and with regard to passions; and all of these seem to be typically human."[1] Apparently, this happiness in the second degree can be achieved by majority people through effort.

We see that, although Greek philosophy has got on the track of theoretical philosophy in the era of Plato and Aristotle, but as a whole, it still maintained an association with real life when it comes to the ideality of human existence, and did not thoroughly antagonise real life with ideal. Particularly in Aristotelian practical philosophy, we can still feel the great care for reality, while ideal life is established on the basis of real life. That is to say, the world in the sense of ancient people is still a finite and affirmative world, a simple totality, without full consciousness of the antagonism between man and nature. As ancient people were not conscious of this finity, their existence is a relatively rich and perfect existence in a finite sense. Schiller said, ancient people were great due to finity, while modern people are great due to infinity.[2] Just because of the finity of ancient people's consciousness, they deemed the realization of perfect personality, i.e.: freedom as the process they were put in this affirmative world. Ancient people were childhood men, who were still in the age of innocence, a state in which the antagonism between subject and object had not occured.

Finite perfection is something which cannot stand long. Human's further development will inevitably lead to its breach and lead to the consciousness on the immanent contradiction of human existence. However, initially man did not realize this antagonism in a realistic way. Instead, man became conscious of this antagonism in an illusory way and with the help of religion and myths.

---

1 The same book as above, p.227.
2 [British] Bernard Bosanquet: A History of Aesthetic, p.388.

Christianity and its ideal

It is what reflected in genesis of Christianity and in infralapsarianism. Here the basic contradiction of human existence is expressed with God's genesis, an illusory form. Nature is no longer considered an ultimate and divine being, but as a creation of God, a thing lower than man. In the sense of Christianity, only God is the ruler of man, while nature is something created by God to provide service for man's interest. In this sense, man's subjective status to nature is expressed in an illusory form, so this subjectivity is a kind of extremely abstract subjectivity. It thinks "the self must also merge itself in another self, but in one beyond, and only there does self have its value".[1] That is to say, it melts man's subjectivity down to the admiration to the Absolute, while natural things are absolutely repulsed. It thinks "man is not by nature what he ought to be. The animal is by nature what it ought to be. The misfortune in natural things is that they get no further. To this spiritual unity pertains the negation of nature, of the flesh, as that in which man must not rest; because nature is from the beginning, evil. Man is likewise naturally evil, for all the wickedness that man does proceed from a natural desire."[2] Therefore, if we say ancient people had basically affirmed secular life or secular world, then Christianity in principle negates secular world. It considers all natural powers and desires of man worthless. What is more, it is contemptuous to rational knowledge. It only pursues the eternal life in other world, and considers this world as the tribulation Christians must endure. Therefore, the only route to man's real ego, i.e.: return to God's divinity is the direct negation of man's nature, i.e.: renounce his natural will, knowledge, and existence.[3]

Since man is the creature of God, and the direct existence of man is natural, then how can man give up evil and pick up good? If man is naturally evil, then in order to assume responsibility for evil and make God's salvation necessary, man must have responsibility, i.e.: have the freedom to choose. However, if man has the freedom to choose, God will not be

---

1 [German] Hegel: Lectures on the History of Philosophy, Vol.3, p.284.
2 [German] Hegel: Lectures on the History of Philosophy, Vol.3, p.263.
3 The same book as above, p.264.

omnipotent. How can the God which is not omnipotent create the whole world and how can it save mankind? If man is defined no freedom and as a natural thing without responsibility, his behaviors are all out of necessity and he is not responsible for his evil, then God, the creator of man should be responsible for all evils done by man. This contradicts with God's Perfection. If God is the root of human evils other than the being of supreme good, then how will he save mankind to supreme good? The profound contradiction that puzzles Christian theology indicates the illusoriness of the basic principle of Christianity and indicates that starting by this principle, it will be impossible to reasonably solve the contradiction of human existence.

Christianity had put forth the principle of subjectivity in an illusory form, but it is the subjectivity that loses ancient finite integrity and points at abstract infinity. Engels commented:

> Antiquity, which as yet knew nothing of the rights of the individual, whose whole outlook was essentially abstract, universal and material, could therefore not exist without slavery. The Christian-Germanic view of the world, by contrast with antiquity, set up abstract subjectivity, and hence arbitrariness, inwardness and spiritualism, as the basic principle. However this subjectivity, precisely because, it was abstract and one-sided, was bound to turn at once into its opposite and to engender, not the freedom of the individual, but the enslavement of the individual. Abstract inwardness became abstract outwardness, the rejection and alienation of man.[1]

That is to say, God as absolute subject set by Christianity, due to its abstractness and one-sidedness, in fact becomes an external fetter of true subject and external necessity. This opposition between the absolute subject inside Christianity and individual's free will was manifested as the opposition between realism and nominalism in the Middle Ages. Realism advocates universal is reality and is the confirmation of God as absolute subject; while nominalism advocates individual is reality, and is the confirmation on individual's free will. Of course, the two sides discuss within the scope of ethology and their premise is to recognize the existence of

---

1 Collected Works of Karl Marx and Frederick Engels, Chinese version 1, Vol.1, p.662, Beijing, People's Publishing House, 1956.

God. Therefore, nominalism only stresses individual's free will and is not an introducer of a new principle. Anyway, the battle between nominalism and realism has, in a sense, revealed a sign of transition towards modern philosophy. All in all, Christian philosophy expresses, in an illusory way, the principle of abstract subjectivity or negatory principle which is different from ancient philosophy. It expresses in an illusory way that the process of man's self-realization or a tortuous process of negation of negation is a historical process. This has generated far-reaching effect on later philosophies.

Only in early-modern philosophy, particularly German classical philosophy, the contradiction of human existence was most strikingly expressed, i.e.: generally expressed as the relation between freedom and necessity. Early-modern philosophy's such grasp and solution to the basic contradiction of human existence obviously were based on the framework of subjective philosophy with opposition between subject and object. As described above, the basic issue of early-modern philosophy was the issue of the relation between thought and being. The whole early-modern philosophy centers on the solution to this issue. Hence in the framework of early-modern philosophy, we may say, the basic issue of philosophy was the issue of the relation between thought and being, while the issue of the relation between freedom and necessity as the fundamental issue of human existence became the ultimate issue or the highest issue. In other words, in philosophy these two issues had inherent logical links. One is premise and the other is conclusion: the relation between thought and being here becomes the most abstract expression of the contradiction of human existence and also constitutes the logical starting point of the issue of freedom and necessity in a philosophical system, thus decides the solution to the issue of the relation between freedom and necessity in logical possibility. Premise decides conclusion; while the conclusion itself also restricts the solution of premise. Therefore, for a complete philosophical system, on its objective logical structure, it is certain that the issue of the relation between thought and being constitutes the logical starting point, while the issue of the relation between freedom and necessity constitutes the logical end point. No matter how many intermediate links there are between the two logical ends of a system, the bipolar relation must exists on the objective logical structure. In the framework of early-modern philosophy, no matter how it is expressed, a philosophy must give a solution to the issue of the relation between thought and being and should give a solution to the issue of the relation between freedom and necessity. After the issue of the relation between freedom and necessity is solved, logically a philosophical system was completed. Therefore, once philosophy solves this issue in a way, it also symbolically solves the fundamental issue of human existence in an ultimate sense and fulfills philosophical mission (whether true of not).

Of course, just as we have pointed out above, the issue of the relation between thought and being is only a basic issue of early-modern philosophy, so the issue of the relation between freedom and necessity which is based on the framework of early-modern philosophy is only a special way to grasp the contradiction between the finity and ideality of human existence in early-modern philosophy. In this special way, the understanding on the concept of freedom could only be limited to the framework of subjective philosophy with opposition between subject and object. Here the realization of freedom as the ultimate solution to the contradiction of human existence could only mean the unity of subject and object and the governance and dominance of subject over object.

Different from the directness of ancient philosophy, early-modern philosophy is a philosophy dominated by a reflective spirit. This stems from the self-knowledge of self-consciousness in early-modern age spirit. The self-knowledge of self-consciousness was first manifested in the literature and art in Renaissance in a sensuous form. Jacob Burchkhardt said: "In the Middle Ages. ... Man was conscious of himself only as a member of a race, people, party, family, or corporation--only through some general category."[1]Compared with the sensitivity of writers and artists, philosophical theory was no doubt much greyer. In philosophy, this self-knowledge of self-consciousness was not explicitly expressed until Rene

---

1 [Swiss] Jacob Burckhardt: The Civilization of the Renaissance in Italy, p.125, Beijing, Commercial Press, 1979. .

Descartes' philosophy. This is the epoch-making significance contained in the proposition of "ego cogito ergo sum". Early-modern philosophy broke ancient philosophy's naïve and direct attitude and had also surpassed the abstract and subjective attitude of medieval philosophy. It was aware of the opposition between human's spiritual activity and material activity in an abstract way and had expressed this opposition as the opposition between thought and being. Hegel had pointed out, this opposition though is embodied in the ancient scholars' scientific objects, they were not conscious of it,[1] so "The principle of modern philosophy is hence not a free and natural thought, because it has the opposition of thought and nature",[2] "the interest is then altogether found in grasping the reconciliation of this opposition in its highest existence, i.e. in the most abstract extremes".[3] Hence, early-modern philosophy elevated the issue of the relation between general being and particular being in the basic issue of ancient philosophy to the issue of the relation between thought and being, and solved the issue of the relation between freedom and necessity by proceeding from the issue of the relation between thought and being.

Rene Descartes' philosophy is the beginning of early-modern philosophy. In Rene Descartes' philosophy, the authenticity of the existence of God and external world is deduced from ego cogito ergo sum, but the mind/ego and external world are completely antagonised. Therefore, in Rene Descartes' system, there are three substances: God, matter and mind. The ideas in mind about the laws of external world come from God. He said, "I noticed certain laws which God has established in nature. Since He has imprinted ideas of these laws in our souls, after we have reflected on them sufficiently, we cannot doubt that they are precisely observed in everything which exists or which acts in the world".[4] The existence of God guarantees the objective necessity of human's rational knowledge. Therefore, observing reason is to observe objective ne-

---

1 [German] Hegel: Lectures on the History of Philosophy, Vol.4, p.4.
2 The same book as above, p.7.
3 The same book as above, p.11.
4 [French] Rene Descartes: Discourse on Method, Refer to Philosophies in the Countries of Western Europe from Sixteenth Century to Eighteenth Century, p.152.

cessity. Reason is the reflection of objectivity on mind. But on the other hand, self-consciousness exists without doubt. It is a premise that enables man to choose freely. In other words, self-consciousness makes the freedom of man possible, but once this free will oversteps reason, it will lead to a mistake. In Rene Descartes, the issue of the relation between freedom and necessity is dual and disordered, like the solution to the basic issue of philosophy.

Rene Descartes' philosophy contains a profound contradiction. In his system, mind has the ability to think and no extension, matter has extension but does not have the ability to think, self-consciousness or ego cogito and external world are completely opposite and not communicable. The unity between the two must obtain help from the guaranteeing role of God. But the guaranteeing role of God only ensures human reason's acquisition of truth, so this knowledge is pure theoretical inference by the right of innate ideas. Geometry is a typical model of this cognition. In this cognition, the standard of truth is self-evident – not self-contradictory. But the idea, grasped in this way is at most the law of a thing and the essence of the thing, other than the real being of the thing. Generally speaking, the essence of a thing does not contain being, and even if an idea is clear, we are still unable to affirm that it certainly has an object in the world. That is to say, the dualism in Rene Descartes' system results in the division of essence and being in cognition. Therefore, the successors of Rene Descartes' philosophy was to solve this issue on the precondition of adhering to his basic rationalist principle.

Spinoza's solution to this contradiction was to perpetuate substance – God or nature and make it an eternal being which is timeless other than in-time. In this way, substance itself is invariable spatial being and its attribute can only be timeless spatial being. Therefore, in substance, idea and its object or thought and extension correspond to each other, one to one. Such being is a necessary being and its essence and being are absolutely identical. Since essence and being are identical, an inevitable conclusion will be that God as substance also has no possibility of choice, i.e.: in substance, possibility is completely the same as reality, and no possibility priori to and greater than reality is available to God for selection. Therefore, God is a necessary being, but this necessary being is decided by itself. It is freedom. Of course, necessary being is only an eternal, thus immobile substance, while quatenus modificatum is concrete thing, and the negation to substance is timely. Therefore, here in the mind of man, idea and object are not necessarily consistent. This is because human body always leads mind to direct material object. This interferes in the cognition on truth and makes man enslaved by emotions. This is the root of mistake and also the root of non-freedom of man, so the only way to truth and freedom is to improve self condition, eliminate the influence of emotion, subdue desires and generate rational love for God.[1] Relying on the love for god, we can return to the arms of god and enjoy the freedom of god. Freedom is not the freedom to choose a will but rational obedience. If mind can completely submit to reason and obey necessity, the majestic height of freedom will be reached. "The will and the intellect are one and the same".[2] Submission to reason is the love for God. Even God has no choice, not to mention man. In summary, Spinoza's conclusion is that freedom is necessary cognition and submission.

For God or nature, there will be no problem with the freedom as necessary submission, but man after all is a finite modality, and the existence of human flesh is also insurmountable, so one more step over Spinoza's philosophy may infer the conclusion that everything is necessary and there is no contingence and no possibility of freedom. This step was made by French materialists. They inherited the principle that substance is the identity of essence and being in Spinoza's system, but they changed Spinoza's premise – in French materialism, the substance is nature, but nature is the moving matter and the direct sensuous being. In this way, the necessity of substance being, that is deduced from the identity of essence and being in Spinoza's philosophy becomes the identity of the essence and being of direct sensuous natural things. In this case, the being of contingency is thoroughly negated and contingence is reckoned as the

---

1 Dutch] Spinoza: The Ethics, p.259.
2 The same book as above, p.189.

pronoun of ignorance. As a result, "every thing in nature is necessary, that nothing to be found in it can act otherwise than it does."[1] Matter is the only substance, while ideas are only the results of human body's perception on things and have no independent existence. In this way, the accordance of ideas and objects does not need the action of god. There are no innate ideas. Everything in man's mind is human body's own activities generated,when it accepts external movements. These activities are a part of all activities of nature, so are necessary. "The actions of man are never free; they are always the necessary consequence of his temperament, of the received ideas, and of the notions, either true or false, which he has formed to himself of happiness; of his opinions, strengthened by example, by education, and by daily experience," so "man, then, is not a free agent in any one instant of his life; he is necessarily guided in each step by those advantages, whether real or fictitious".[2] In other words, "the necessity that governs the physical, governs also the moral world, where every thing is also subject to the same law."[3] There is no freedom and everything submits to necessity. This was the conclusion of French materialism. It is an absolute mechanicalism and fatalism. But, if everything is necessary, all actions of man are decided and there is no freedom, then how is moral life possible?

The solutions of early-modern rationalist and mechanistic materialism to the issue of the relation between thought and being and to the issue of the relation between freedom and necessity as studied above, apparently all run into trouble due to their distinctive metaphysical thinking mode. Early-modern rationalism is such a typical metaphysics that, its distinctive thinking mode obtains the name of metaphysical method. The characteristic of this thinking mode is abstraction. The abstraction here mainly refers to two aspects: unreality and non-historicity. Unreality means it only starts from abstract and infinite God or nature, sets its essence as reason and attempts to rationally deduce the stipulation on finite human existence. This is theological residue which was inherited by metaphysics from the Middle Ages. The materialism in the 18th cen-

---

1 [French] Holbach: The System of Nature, Vol.1, p.53, Beijing, Commercial Press, 1964.
2 The same book as above, p.177.
3 The same book as above, p.191.

tury only regarded nature as an absolute thing to replace Christian God and antagonize it with man. Non-historicity means, it starts from God or nature as eternal being, regards the relation between thought and being as an unchanged thing and does not think about the possibility of change of this relation in time and neglects the association between this relation and world history.

The defects of these two metaphysical methods were what the philosophical movement from Kant to Hegel in German classical philosophy had tried to sublate. The problem Kant faced was to explore a new basic principle to solve the issue of the relation between thought and being and then solve the issue of the relation between freedom and necessity. In Kantian philosophy, this issue first appears as "how is apriori synthetic judgment possible?" In the sense of Kant, it is exactly this issue that makes all previous philosophies run into mistake. None of the previous philosophies, rationalism or empiricism, could conceive knowledge as the consequence of the constitutive activity of subject other than the passive acceptance to existing concept, whether this concept is rational as believed by rationalism or perceptual as believed by empiricism. As cognition is a process in which subject – with a complete set of apriori conceptual framework synthetizes sensuous material and endows it with a rational form. The formation of knowledge, scientific knowledge in particular, is not the conformity of knowledge to object. On the contrary, it is the conformity of object to knowledge. But Kantian philosophy channels essentiality back to self-consciousness,[1] i.e.: only regards essence as our thought other than the objective being outside thought, so in the sense of Kant, the knowledge formed in this way is only the knowledge of phenomenal world, i.e.: the objects of knowledge are phenomena only other than things themselves. "Things in themselves" as transcended being are not the objects of man's intellectuality. The apriori concept of intellectuality is legal and valid only in phenomenal world and in all possible experience. Any attempt to go beyond phenomena and the finite range of possible experience and target at "transcendental thing-in-itself" will certainly run into paradox. In this way, on the one hand, Kant had

---

1 [German] Hegel: Lectures on the History of Philosophy, Vol.4, p.257.

declared the impossibility that old metaphysics regards God, nature or any other transcendental thing as object, and negated the identity of essence and being in a metaphysical sense, and had only recognized their identity in phenomenal sense. On the other hand, Kant thinks he also has in the same time sublated the prejudices of empiricism and provided a reasonable philosophical foundation for empirical natural sciences.

But the sphere where theoretical reason is invalid is exactly the sphere where practical reason is legal and valid. This is so-called noumenal world, which is different from phenomenal world. In phenomenal world, as essence (i.e.: intellectual concept) and being (perceptual experience) are identical, it is a realm of necessity where there is no possibility of freedom. Man as a natural being also belongs to this realm and governed by the necessity of nature. But in noumenal world, essence is no longer readily identical to being. Here man is the initiator of action and the decider of his actions, and man itself is the end and by no means is a tool of an external end. Therefore, when man turns an action into real being according to internal moral imperative, he is free and he observes internal moral imperative other than external compulsion. That is to say, moral is a kind of autonomy other than heteronomy, so only under the condition of freedom of subject, moral can be talked, whereas all heteronomy as the forced submission of necessity does not contain moral. This also indicates moral's precondition is the ability to undertake the responsibility of moral, while the premise of the ability to assume responsibility is the ability to choose freedom. Responsibility is proportional to freedom. No freedom, no responsibility. Responsibility is as much as freedom.

In this way, Kant solved in a unique way the basic issue of philosophy and the issue of the relation between freedom and necessity. He negated rationalism and empiricism's solutions to the issue of the relation between thought and being, and divided the identity of thought and being into two ways: in phenomenal world, theoretical reason achieves the identity of thought and being through grasping sensuous material. This grasp is the spontaneous action of theoretical reason, so this sphere does not have freedom, but it is a realm of necessity; when the legal use scope of theoretical reason is surpassed, antinomic noumenal world will become inevitable. Practical reason achieves another type of identity through regulating man's own behaviors, but this regulation is a kind of conscious autonomy, so this sphere is a realm of freedom. Now, necessity and freedom are assigned to different spheres and do not do harm each other, and it seems that the antinomy of freedom and necessity that puzzles metaphysicians has been solved. Man, now is a dual being. As a natural being, he is unable to get rid of the manipulation of natural necessity, while as a rational being, he is also a free being and transcends the being of natural necessity. What is man? One half is beast and one half is angel! This ancient proverb is thus explained in philosophy. Is man really such a mutually irrelevant dual being? Although Kant himself did not say theoretical reason could not reach the sphere of moral life, practical reason must act upon empirical sphere, otherwise moral imperative will become meaningless to man. In view of this contradiction, after Kant thoroughly separated theory and practice, these two spheres, he tried to find a bridge to connect them together. This was the issue he wants to solve in the third critique, i.e.: Critique of Judgment. Kant pointed out:

> Albeit, then, between the realm of the natural concept, as the sensible, and the realm of the concept of freedom, as the supersensible, there is a great gulf fixed, so that it is not possible to pass from the former to the latter (by means of the theoretical employment of reason), just as if they were so many separate worlds, the first of which is powerless to exercise influence on the second: still the latter is meant to influence the former-that is to say, the concept of freedom is meant to actualize in the sensible world the end proposed by its laws; and nature must consequently also be capable of being regarded in such a way that in the conformity to law of its form it at least harmonizes with the possibility of the ends to be effectuated in it according to the laws of freedom. There must, therefore, be a ground of the unity of the supersensible that lies at the basis of nature, with what the concept of freedom contains in a practical way, and although the concept of this ground neither theoretically nor practically attains to a knowledge of it, and so has no peculiar realm of its own, still it renders possible the transition from the mode of thought according to the principles of the one to that according to the principles of the other.[1]

---

1 [German] Kant: Critique of Judgment, Vol.1, p.13.

That is to say, in his third critique, Kant wants to solve the opposition and contradiction between abstract mind and nature and make them unified,[1] and link and unify nature with spirit, and freedom with necessity. The medium of this transition is the judgment which is between intellectuality and reason, "it will effect a transition from the faculty of pure knowledge, i.e., from the realm of concepts of nature, to that of the concept of freedom".[2]

The judgment mentioned here by Kant refers to the "reflective judgment"[3] that looks for generality from given particularity. The object of this judgment is "the product of art and the product of organic nature". When applied to the former, it is called aesthetic judgment, and what is manifested is subjective conformity to end; when applied to the latter, it is called end judgment (here we adopt the translation of Mr. Zhu Guangqian).[4]

It shows the objective purposiveness of the organism in the nature. Hegel pointed out, in the sense of Kant, the products of art and the products of organic nature all tell us the unity between the concept of nature and the concept of freedom. The appreciation of these products lets us see the unity between intellect and special things.[5]

Kant thinks that through setting a transcendental principle of natural purposiveness of judgment, the issue of the unity between spirit and nature, and between freedom and necessity will be solved. However this unity is not objective real unity but subjective unity. This principle of natural purposiveness is only the objective principle of judgment and only our subjective way to observe object. We only observe those things according to unified principle, but it itself is not like that; what it itself is like is not achievable by knowledge.[6] Hence in fact the issue of the

---

1 [German] Hegel: Aesthetics, Vol.1, p.70.
2 [German] Kant: Critique of Judgment, Vol.1, p.16.
3 The same book as above, p.17.
4 Zhu Guangqian: History of Western Aesthetics, Vol.2, p.356, Beijing, People's Literature Publishing House, 1979.
5 [German] Hegel: Lectures on the History of Philosophy, Vol.4, p.296.
6 The same book as above, p.296

unity between spirit and nature and between freedom and necessity is not solved. For this reason, German philosophy after Kant launched an ideological expedition aiming to sublate the dualism of Kantian philosophy and unify it.

But since opposition exists and has been deduced by Kant to a very sharp limit,[1] this opposition will become unavoidable, and people must look for a way to sublate it on the precondition of recognizing it, while this is possible only through a process. Johann Fichte attempted to realize the unity between thought and being through the dialectic movement of self-consciousness, but he deleted Kantian "thing-in-itself," so this unity is subjective only.

In this regard, Schelling directly sets the indistinctive primitive identity between subject and object and thinks freedom only lies in the grasp of this unity through artistic creation by intellectual intuition. These progresses certainly are very important, but only Hegel consciously conceived the identity between thought and being as a historical process of dialectic.

Not satisfied with Schelling's direct setting of the primitive identity between thought and being, Hegel wants to conceive the identity between thought and being as a concrete identity and a concrete universal containing many categories other than a kind of abstract identity. For this reason, Hegel particularly stresses the negativity, particularity or infinity of thought.

He said: The one who is fed up with finity can in no way reach reality but indulge himself in abstraction and end up with depression in his whole life.[2] If thought is indifferent to particularity, it will be indifferent to its own development, too.[3] Therefore, Hegel pays particular attention to the process of history. Just in the process of history, consciousness has walked step by step to absolute knowledge from abstract sensuous certainty. The finally reached absolute knowledge is not an existing thing

---

1 [German] Hegel: Aesthetics, Vol.1, p.70.
2 [German] Hegel: The Logic of Hegel, p.53.
3 [German] Hegel: Phenomenology of Spirit, Vol.1, p.59.

which can be directly obtained through intellectual intuition, but the labour process of spirit itself. In this way, Hegel includes the whole human history into the process of spiritual historical development. History is reckoned as "the detailed history of the process of consciousness training and educating itself up to the level of science".[1] Expressing these contents in concepts will constitute the logical science of concepts. This is the dialectic system Hegel explains in his The Logic of Hegel. This system wants to exhibit the links of truth, i.e.: absolute ideas in the pure inference of concept, thus achieving the integration of subject and object, identity of thought and being, and absolute idea.

Logical idea is still an abstract thing and a thing not realizing itself. Therefore, it will certainly be exteriorized into its opposite, i.e.: nature. Nature can be reckoned as the spirit that descends to the world and roams in the world. However, nature itself is something rigid without reason and self-consciousness, so during development, spirit will certainly want to get rid of the fetter of matter and return to spirit itself. This is achieved through the emergence of man. Man is a concrete form through which spirit returns to itself.

To ultimately realize the absolute return and reach absolute spirit, man as a real form of spirit must undergo a development process, too. Here firstly it is the development of the subjective spirit as the form of individual consciousness and the objective spirit as the form of law, moral and ethic in antagonism. But subjective spirit is manifested as soul, sense, reason, desire and so on, is still a kind of internality, and yet to realize real being, while objective spirit is manifested as property, family, society, state and so on, objective spirit lacks consciousness though it is an objective being, so subjective spirit and objective spirit are two mutually restricted finite beings. To reach infinity, spirit must go ahead continuously and eliminate the opposition between subject and object in absolute spirit; while the self-recognition of absolute spirit also experiences three forms: art, religion and philosophy. Art, religion and philosophy are same in content and essence. Their objects are all absolute spirit, but

---

1 [German] Hegel: Aesthetics, Vol.1, p.129.

their ways of cognition are different. The first form of cognition is a direct and perceptual cognition, the cognition on the form and shape of sensuous objective things. In this cognition, absolute idea becomes the object of contemplation and sense. The second form is imaginative (or presentative) consciousness. The third form is the free thinking of the absolute mind.[1] In the sense of Hegel, beauty is the sensuous presentation of idea.[2] But art as the contemplation of idea is always restricted by its sensuous form. From "symbolic art" to "classical art" and to "romantic art", art is getting rid of materiality and externality and tending to spirituality and internality, but even its highest stage "romantic art" is still unable to get rid of its sensuous form. This indicates that art is still not enough to represent absolute idea, and must give place to the higher representation form – religious and philosophical forms.

We see, on how to reach "absolute", Hegel differs from Kant, Schelling and Fichte. Fichte only resorts to unconscious intellectual intuition and infinite historical process, and Kant and Schelling seek help from aesthetic activity; but Kant thinks the unity achieved with the help of the medium of judgment is only a subjective unity, while Schelling shows the least hesitation in making art into the highest form of the subjective and objective unity between subject and object. Hegel had praised that, only by Schelling, the true concept and scientific status of art was discovered and men started understanding the true and highest task of art, but he also thinks Schelling's understanding is not correct.[3] Hegel gives a low position to art in his system. He opposes to give art the highest position. This on the one hand has to do with his great sense of history", i.e.: he wants to sublate opposition through historical dialectic movement, and on the other hand has a close relation with his standpoint of more thoroughly spurning all sensuous forms of idealism. Hegel thinks the transition from art to religion is necessary. Why religion is above art is that religion eliminates objectivity and turns to the inner life of subject. However, religion still contains the externality of art and represents truth

---

1 [German] Hegel: Aesthetics, Vol.1, p.129.

2 The same book as above, p.142.

3 The same book as above, p.78.

in a symbolic way, so although the content of religion is true, this truth is a guarantee without understanding. This understanding is philosophy, absolute knowledge, --same as the content of religion, but adopting a conceptual form.[1] In philosophy, spirit really returns to itself; when man's spirit reaches philosophical cognition, it will merge with absolute spirit and reach the extreme realm of man's spirit and the highest realm of freedom.

Hegelian philosophy solves the issue of the relation between thought and being in a way of absolute idealism. What it does is to dissolve being into thought and reduce reality to spirit, so this absolute identity is not real identity and is still the identity of spirit itself, while being is still outside it. Different from Schelling, Hegel returns to Fichte in a sense. He regards nature as a thing without development and spirit. In this case, nature becomes a being just because of the exteriorization of spirit. But how does this exteriorization become possible?

Marx had said, when absolute idea "lets nature emerge from itself, it has really let emerge only this abstract nature, only nature as a thought-entity".[2] Therefore, the root cause for the fundamental difficulty of Hegelian philosophy is that it has not really achieved the identity of thought and being and the real nature still exists externally and independently. Fundamentally speaking, the whole system is illusory, while opposition still exists. The false solution to the identity of thought and being results in the false solution to the issue of freedom and necessity. Hegel is not satisfied with Schelling's philosophy which directly sets absolute identity and resorts to unlogical intellectual intuition. He tries to use the dialectic progress of consciousness in history to unify intellect and intuition, and unify thought and being, i.e.: thus regards intellectual intuition as a process with a historical medium. This idea has, to a great extent, promoted philosophy's solution to its issues. However, as it negates the independency of nature, it is a regression, too. It recedes to a more illusory solution. Kant's finite ego and Fichte's dual ego are thoroughly converted into absolute subject in Hegelian philosophy, i.e.: the

---

1 Hegel: Jenenser Real-Philosophie, Zhang Shiying: On Hegel's Philosophy of Mind, p.261
2 Collected Works of Karl Marx and Frederick Engels, Chinese version 1, Vol.42, p.179.

subject of dialectic movement and history is no longer the man as finite ego but is absolute idea itself, so absolute identity is only the identity of absolute idea itself, freedom as the grasp and transcendence of necessity is only absolute idea's cognition on its own necessity, thus freedom is only the freedom of absolute idea itself other than the freedom of real man.

Hegel's conclusion: real individuals are insignificant, and individual's freedom is to submit to the logos or Providence extrinsic to himself. This is the thought of "cunning of reason" created by Hegel through inheriting and developing Kant's "Plan of Nature" and Fichte and Schelling's "Cosmos Plan". He said:

> Reason is as cunning as it is powerful. Cunning may be said to lie in the inter-mediative action which, while it permits the objects to follow their own bent and act upon one another till they waste away, and does not itself directly interfere in the process, is nevertheless only working out its own aims. With this explanation, Divine Providence may be said to stand to the world and its process in the capacity of absolute cunning. God lets men do as they please with their particular passions and interests; but the result is the accomplishment of--not their plans, but His, and these differ decidedly from the ends primarily sought by those whom He employs.[1]

Just as Wang Fuzhi said, "God uses its partiality to realize impartiality". In the history of the world, "God governs the world. The actual working of His government, the carrying out of His plan is the history of the world."[2] In this hidden plan, "it sets the passions to work for itself, while that through which it develops itself pays the penalty and suffers the loss."[3] Apparently, in this kind of theory, real individuals are only tools or means by which "Providence" or God's "World Plan" is realized. Hegel talks in an irony tone: the "rationality" that ordinary people are fiddled with by reason, while he endows the "world-historical individuals" who represent "Providence" with the privilege that "may treat other great and even sacred interests inconsiderately", because "so mighty a

---

1 [German] Hegel: The Logic of Hegel, p.394.

2 [German] Hegel: Philosophy of History, p.37, Shanghai, Shanghai Bookstore Publishing House, 2001.

3 The same book as above, p.33.

figure must trample down many an innocent flower, crush to pieces many things in its path".[1] Therefore, the realization of such freedom is irrelevant with real ordinary individuals, and they can obtain the meaning of existence only under the submission to Providence. Hegel further infers his conservative view of state. He said "the state is mind on earth" and "the state is the march of god through the world".[2] He completely deified the state. Hence, Hegelian philosophy, this colossal system, owing to the wrong solution of absolute idealism to the issue of the relation between subject and object, educes a totally illusory solution to the issue of freedom and necessity. Therefore, just as Engels said, the failure of Hegelian philosophy is a huge abortion. The issue of philosophy was still outstanding and waiting for a new solution.

Then, how can this issue be solved? In fact, the failure of early-modern philosophy has indicated that to solve this issue, we should not be limited to the framework of abstract opposition between subject and object. The solution to the issue of freedom and necessity in early modern times is to achieve the unity between subject and object through a specific way, but no matter what way is adopted, a powerful subject must be resorted to. If the solution is still a kind of abstract subjectivity, then this solution will not be successful, because subjectivity by no means is a concept that can transcend the opposition between subject and object. Moreover, once the framework of the opposition between subject and object is overstepped, the issue of freedom and necessity will become incomprehensible. Accurately speaking, it cannot be conceived as the issue of the relation between subject and object only.

The overstepping of the framework of the opposition between subject and object means the opening of an even broader visual sphere of philosophy, i.e.: starting from "real individuals" other than from abstract opposition between subject and object. Starting from real individuals is to start from the individuals who are in a specific historical circumstance and a specific life-world. In this way, we can conceive the opposite rela-

1 [German] Hegel: Philosophy of History, p.33.
2 [German] Hegel: Philosophy of Right, p.259.

tion between subject and object as a derivative form, a special state of the relation between concrete individual and his world. While, the issue of freedom and necessity as conceived by previous theoretical philosophy, early-modern philosophy in particular, essentially can be conceived as a derivative form of the issue of the relation between man's finite existence and infinite value pursuit, or a special existent form under the paradigm of theoretical philosophy. Thus, the solution to the issue of freedom and necessity in previous theoretical philosophy essentially is not to directly give an answer, but to deepen the understanding on the issue and convert it into a more profound issue.

Though, Marx's modern practical philosophy also continues to use the terms of early-modern philosophy, such as: freedom and necessity, their meanings are very much different. In a sense, Marx's concept of freedom is closer to Aristotle's concept of self-realization. Of course, they both belong to practical philosophy, this tradition, so their similarity is nothing surprised. The issue of freedom and necessity discussed by Marx should not be like the issue of man and external object as conceived by theoretical philosophy in ancient and early modern times. It should be the contradiction between the finity of man' real life and the infinite value pursuit. In Marx's philosophy, this infinite value pursuit is expressed as communism. The question now is: how to realize communism? If we say the solution of previous philosophy to the issue of freedom and necessity is illusory because of the abstractness of their understanding on this issue, then after concrete understanding on this issue, Marx should be able to find a road leading to ideal reality. In this case, we have to involve Marx's way to ideal. This way is history.

CHAPTER TWO

History and Ideal

Meaning of the history

Before Marx, history had been deemed as a process to ideal. We know ancient Greek's view of the world is still, they did not have a strong sense of history and it was impossible for them to think history is a medium leading to ideal. In Christian tradition, the meaning of history has been linked with an ideal sphere and had an ultimate orientation since the very beginning. Generally, history is conceived as a process from original sin to atonement and from tribulation to redemption. This ideal existence of history itself has its reality, but it will never be realized. Of course, Marxist history is not the meaningless occurrence of events. In terms of concrete individual, it is a process with value orientation. Differently, Marx not only was aware of the reality of the ideal existence of history but also was always dedicated to finding a road to ideal reality.

Here we may classify the ways to approach ideal into two types, namely: non-historical way and historical way. The most typical non-historical way is ancient Greek's way to approach ideal. Ancient Greek looked at the world with still eyes as a whole. Their way to reach ideal was still, too. In the sense of ancient Greek, the being of supreme truth and supreme good is the universe noumenon. The being of this noumenon is timeless. Man's way to approach this noumenon is belief and is not the effort in reality but the exploration of reason or philosophy's theoretical activity. This case was most typically manifested in Platonic and Aristotelian philosophy. In the sense of Plato, world is divided into real world and ideal world, and man is the being between the two worlds, because man as a member of the real world, meanwhile he can approach ideal world through a special channel. In the sense of Aristotle, philosophical activity is also a way to approach the celestial bodies and god, thus is the happiest and freest life mode. It seems that Greek did not pay much attention to the "process" of these activities. We may obtain formal concept of these activities, but we can hardly conceive them as a concrete process. Ancient Greek's description on the state life is still, too, and the state and the eternal and invariable substance explored by theoretical philosophy are same by nature, so it does not have the process of generation or development.

To sum up, ancient Greek seldom thought over the process of the ideal-approaching action, so they adopted a non-historical way. However, we do not mean ancient Greece did not have history or historiography. We mean the history in the sense of ancient Greek has essential difference from the process with value orientation as conceived by us today. The history of ancient Greek is more about the record of real events, while the aim of this record is to keep the memory of valuable events from the destructive impact of time.[1] Hegel also said, Herodotus and other historians' "descriptions are for the most part limited to deeds, events, and states of society, which they had before their eyes, and whose spirit they shared." They only "bind together the fleeting elements of story, and treasure them up for immortality in the Temple of Mnemosyne".[2] Therefore, ancient Greek had had certain experience of time, but their attention was concentrated on how to seize eternal thing to exclude the effect

---

1 [American] Donald R. Kelley: Faces of History, p.21, Beijing, Sanlian Bookstore, 2003.
2 [German] Hegel: Philosophy of History, p.1.

of time, or exclude temporal things out of essential realm. Under this circumstance, it becomes unimaginable for them to add the factor of timeliness.

Different from ancient Greek, Hebrew's experience on history is positive. In other words, Hebrew is not like ancient Greek who equated time and historical things with multiplicity and phenomena, thus excluding them from the essence of the world. Instead, they conceived history as an essential process, a process closely related to worldly tribulation and redemption. This is the history of Christianity. This history is conceived as "interim", one end is man's original sin and tribulation, while the other end is redemption. As Karl Lowith, put it, In this theological perspective "the pattern of history is a movement progressing, and at the same time returning from alienation to reconciliation, a great detour to reach in the end the beginning through ever repeated acts of rebellion and self-surrender. Man's sin and God's saving purpose – they alone require and justify history as such, and historical time. Without original sin and final redemption the historical interim would be unnecessary and unintelligible".[1] "To experience history as an 'interim' means to live in a supreme tension between conflicting wills, running a 'race', the goal of which is neither an airy ideal nor a massive reality but the promise of salvation".[2] History always starts with an event. This start is that due to some reason, the existence of human loses the past perfect state and becomes finite and incomplete existence. Likewise, history ends with an event, too. This end is the sublation to this finity and incompletion, in a sense, is to return to pre-historical perfect state. With respect to human existence, both ends of history are very decisive events, but only interim state is most clearly experienced. In other words, only the interim state is real, but the two ends of the history are ideal. However, if without the decisive events at two ends, the interim process will not be tenable: the history without a start and the history without an end are unimaginable for Christianity. Because for Christians, in real life, the end of the history is more important, because all interim activities will become meaningless,

---

1 [German] Karl Lowith: World History and Salvation History, p.218.
2 [German] Karl Lowith: World History and Salvation History, p.219.

if they are without final settlement and judgment. Thus, the "Millennium" after the end of the history will become the ultimate goal of belief activity, while history in a sense will also become a route to reach or approach this goal.

Original sin and redemption become the two extremities of the history and are also the conditions for the existence of history. Through its religious form, we may easily discover what original sin expresses is a fact – the finity of human existence, while redemption no doubt is man's ideal. We may say that this concept is the source of the whole Western concept of history. It has essential difference from the concept of ancient Greek. The history in the sense of Greek is a circular motion at most, while the history in the sense of Christianity is a line segment with an unknown length, nobody knows its end, but the existence of this end is certain. The history in the sense of ancient Greek has no orientation, while in the history in the sense of Christianity, only the existence of the ultimate goal is meaningful.

We may say that Christian concept of history is the source and internal structure of the whole Western concept of history. This structure exists implicitly or explicitly in various worldly concepts of history, no matter whether these concepts of history are "anti-Christ" or not, because firstly Christianity has an important position and influence in Western civilization, and secondly Christian concept of history, indeed reveals some truth of human existence. Karl Lowith said: "The view most commonly held in antiquity was that: Hope is an illusion which helps man to endure in life, but, which in the last resort, is an **ignis fatuus.** On the other hand, St. Paul's verdict about pagan society was that is had no Hope, he meant that, a hope is the substance and assurance of which is faith instead of an illusion."[1] Indeed, all the ideality spheres are relative to the finity and incompleteness of reality, thus all idealities are manifested as "unreality" in form, while the expectation on this ideal often falls into phantasy and illusion. But on the other hand, ideal is also realistic. Its reality rests with the fact that all ideals are based on the finity and incompletion of reality.

---

1 [German] Karl Lowith: World History and Salvation History, p.244.

Moreover, for finite being, this effect of ideal is irreplaceable. Christian belief can be conceived as a way to pursue ideal, while the history in the sense of Christianity can be conceived as a way to reach ideal. Of course, in the sense of Marx, this way to approach ideal, even the ideal of Christianity per se, is identical to illusion, so Marx thinks religion is the "opium" that poisons people. This does not mean Marx negates the reality of religious belief in any sense. Below we will indicate Marxist theory of history also contains something similar to Christian concept of history. Differently, although Christians believe in their ideal, the precondition of the existence of this ideal is people's ignorance of the fact that, it has its roots in real being, whereas Marx on the contrary, not only perceived the secular nature of ideal sphere, but also explored, on this basis, a "real" road from real world to ideality realm. Christians only think the worldly life without ideal realm and for them hope is meaningless, but they do not know or do not think that the realm of ideality without finite secular world is meaningless, too. Therefore, we may conceive Christian ideology based on the finity of real life, while Christians can conceive real life only based on ideal. This is the abstractness of Christian ideology and is also the root of the abstractness of its theory on history.

The internal structure of Christian concept of history – history as a process from secular world to ideal – exists in the concepts of most of the later historical thinkers. What is more, before Marx, the abstractness of Christian concept of history had been widely inherited. It does not mean Christian belief was widely accepted, but it means that Christian concept of history was re-written by different thinkers in different secular ways. The key to the re-writing of Christian concept of history is to use a secular ideal to replace the belief in God's salvaging the world. We should say, in the beginning, the thinkers since early modern times rewrote Christian concept of history in aim to go to reality and go to the secular world from heaven, i.e.: oppose Providence through progress. However, this aim was only partially realized, because various worldly ideals often became the substitutes of the belief in God in the end. Same as Christian ideology, the realm of ideality became the starting point of early-modern age theory on history. This ideal can be a forthcoming event, not like final judgment, but it is always used as a perfect aim to terminate history although this termination is not like Millennium which expresses the termination with a concrete time. Therefore, "the philosophy of history in the Enlightenment movement, far from having enlarged the theological pattern, has narrowed it by secularizing divine providence into human prevision and progress".[1]

The most typical concept of history in early modern times is Hegel's philosophy on history. If we say the history in the sense of Christianity is a history arranged by the will of God, then the history in the sense of Hegel will be a history arranged by reason and spirit. In fact, Hegel directly regards the whole process of history as the manifestation of spirit. In his Philosophy of History, Hegel said:

> To begin with, we must note that world history proceeds within the realm of Spirit. The term "world" includes both physical and psychical nature. Physical nature does play a part in world history, and from the very beginning we shall draw attention to the fundamental natural relations thus involved. But Spirit, and the course of its development, is the substance of history. We must not contemplate nature as a rational system in itself, in its own particular domain, but only in its relation to Spirit. Spirit, on the stage on which we observe it, that of world history, is in its most concrete reality.[2]

Freedom is the essence of spirit, the only truth of spirit. "The question of the means whereby Freedom develops itself into a world leads us directly to the phenomenon of history. Although Freedom as such, is primarily an internal idea, the means it uses are the external phenomena which in history present themselves directly before our eyes."[3] As early as ancient Greece, the world has been conceived as a rational world, but the reason in ancient Greece was still. Hegel tried to integrate reason with history, i.e.: he tried to integrate the spirit of ancient Greece with Christian spirit. The consequence of this integration essentially can also be considered as incorporating reason and spirit into the structure of the Christian concept on history and handing God's function over to rational

---

1 [German] Karl Lowith: World History and Salvation History, p.120.
2 [German] Hegel: Philosophy of History, p.16.
3 The same book as above, p.20.

spirit. Hegel looks at the world with "rational eyes" other than God's eyes. It is not difficult for us to see that the history in the sense of Hegel also points at an ultimate goal, which is infinitely rich and concrete spirit.

The full realization of spirit should be the whole of history, and also the termination of history. In this way, Hegel successfully projects Christian sacred history on secular world, thus secular reason possesses the nature of holiness. Hegel said: "That the History of the World, with all the changing scenes which its annals present, is this process of development and the realization of Spirit – this is the true Theodicaea, the justification of God in History. Only this insight can reconcile Spirit with the History of the World – viz., that what has happened, and is happening every day, is not only not "without God," but is essentially His Work."[1]

No matter how the realm of ideality is conceived, history as a process to this realm has become a basic Western concept. But we know, before Marx the so-called history was always an abstract history other than a concrete and real history. It is not to say that the history always points to an ultimate goal, rather it is to say that the previous history was a history conceived by proceeding from an ideal goal, other than a history conceived by proceeding from the real and finite existence of man. In fact, the history conceived by Marx also points to a specific ideal goal. In terms of its form, it also shares the same structure with Christian concept of history. If not so, we could only conceive Marxist doctrine as a still view of world or a cyclical theory of history. But the key of the issue is not that what structure they share, but the key issue is that, what this structure means. In terms of the previous so-called history, that history points at God or reason does not start from true real life, but since from the starting point it was set by god or the starting point of the **Reason,** thus this history was impossibly a real history. It was just the process of realization of Divine Will or **Reason.** Marx thinks:

> We must begin by stating the first premise of all human existence and, there-fore, of all history, the premise, namely, that men must be in a position to live in order to be able to "make history." But life involves before everything

---

1 [German] Hegel: Philosophy of History, p.451.

else eating and drinking, a habitation, clothing and many other things. The first historical act is thus the production of the means to satisfy these needs, the production of material life itself. And, indeed this is an historical act, a fundamental condition of all history, which today, as it was thousands of years ago, must daily and hourly be fulfilled merely in order to sustain human life.[1]

In essence, Marx explores for a secular premise and a secular start for history. This premise and start are enough to distinguish Marxist theory of history from any of the past theories on history because only in this way people can truly discover real history. If we proceed from such a real basis and start, the realm of ideality pointed at by history can be conceived only through this basis. Above we have illustrated it to some extent, but we still need to further explain what the difference between the realm of ideality pointed at by real history and the previous telos of history is, and what this difference means to history and our real life. Here we have to more concretely and profoundly involve Marx's realm of freedom – communist theory, for we know the history conceived by Marx exactly points at communism as the realm of freedom.

Marx's visual sphere on history

Early-modern philosophy failed in all of its efforts in solving the basic contradiction of human existence. The fundamental reason for the failure was that they did not concretely cognize human life-world or the contradiction between the finity and ideality in the human existence, and could not reach the concept of real history. The philosophy before Marx was conscious of this contraction only in an abstract form and expressed the solution to this contradiction as a process in which the opposition between thought and being was decomposed in history. Due to this abstract grasp of history, they were doomed to failure and could not reasonably solve the basic contradiction of human existence. Therefore, we must go on and grasp this basic contradiction of human existence and grasp the real human history in a concrete form. It requires us to start

---

1 Marx & Engels Selected Works, Edition 2, Vol.1, p.78~79.

from concrete human life, from the real finite subject and from "real individuals. By starting from "real individuals", the fundamental contradiction of human existence will be really grasped. Thus, it is possible for
us to proceed from reality and obtain a real solution to this contradiction.
Because, the difference of Marx's modern practical philosophy from the
other modern practical philosophies is that, it regards productive practice
as the most fundamental human activity, the primary human activity,
then proceeding from productive practice and its historical development
will be the only way to solve this issue.

Marx's modern practical philosophy and productive practice

Production on the one hand is the relation between man and nature and
on the other hand, it is also the relation between man and man. From
the perspective of the relation between man and nature alone, the freedom as self-realization as conceived by Marx, is decided by the amount
of the free time left after his activity time, --left after the necessary time
needed for the subsistence of the labourer(man). i.e.: which offers the
possibility for comprehensive and free development of man's potential,
Generally speaking, the activity time for a man is a determined constant,
so the premise for the increase of free time should be the reduction of
necessary labour time; and the premise for the reduction of that necessary
labour time must be the advanced development of productive forces,
particularly science and technology. That is to say, from the perspective
of the relation between man and nature alone, the possibility of man's
free development is in a simple direct proportion to the development of
productive force. Each step of progress in productive forces means the
reduction of the necessary time of labour for subsistence and the increase
of the free time available for free development. However, in real historical
process, the relation between the development of productive forces and
the development of man is not such a simple linear relation, but it is a
more complex and tortuous process. When men's productive forces
reaches a level high enough to provide surplus products and expresses a
sign for the ability to freely develop themselves, this advanced productive

forces do not only lead to the free development of human abilities. But on the contrary they lead to enslavement and oppression, as well as majority people's loss of the possibility of free development. How does this antinomy between social development and individual development occur in the process of history?

It is sure that people's productive force will develop to some extent following the accumulation of labour skills and experiences, and by the increase of population. The development of productive forces certainly will result in the change of interpersonal communication forms – which is the content of historical necessity, i.e.: the development in the division of labour. In terms of its immediate effect, the division of labour makes man's activity professional and can greatly raise labour productivity, thus elevating the level of productive forces; in terms of its far-reaching effect, the division of mental labour and physical labour resulting from the development of division of labour ultimately will inevitably lead to the emergence of science as an independent mental production department, thus providing the most powerful means for the development of productive force. Therefore, in view of its immediate effect and far-reaching effect, division of labour is a necessary condition for the development of productive force. However, the results produced from the division of labour are absolutely not only these. While promoting the development of productive force, the division of labour also generates another serious consequence – the tortuous development of human history.

The alienation

Firstly, division of labour makes the development of human ability specialized. In terms of the potential requirements for the development of human ability, everybody points at the comprehensiveness of freedom, but division of labour restricts this comprehensiveness and makes freedom develop in a specific aspect. In this way, the development of division of labour makes labour lose the finite sense of art, which used to be an exhibition of its own power in a sense, and turns labour into dull, boring and tedious pure output of physical and mental power; division of labour turns man into an abstracted and one-sided man.

Secondly, more importantly, it has to do with man's abstraction and one-sidedness. "The division of labour implies the possibility, not only the fact that intellectual and material activity – enjoyment and labour, production and consumption – devolve on different individuals, but makes possible that the only possibility of their not coming into contradiction lies in the negation in its turn of the division of labour."[1] Thus, the development of division of labour is closely related to the development of productive forces. On the one hand, the development of productive force pushes the development of division of labour; on the other hand, the development of division of labour in return promotes the development of productive force. When productive forces are developed to certain extent, surplus products will appear. Surplus products make private appropriation possible, i.e.: and make the snatch of surplus products through private appropriation possible, while individuals' different positions in the division of labour in social activities turns the unfair private appropriation into reality and results in private property. Hence, division of labour will inevitably result in the destruction of the previous unified social communities which equally communicate with each other. They are polarized into the opposition between the haves and the have-nots, and between ruling class and the ruled class. "Division of labour and private property are, moreover, identical expressions: in the one the same thing is affirmed with reference to activity as is affirmed in the other with reference to the product of the activity."[2] The generation of private property makes the wealth increase due to the elevated level of productive forces, and the wealth is completely seized by minority private owners, while the free time thus obtained and available for development of self ability is completely monopolized by a minority of private owners, too. In this case, division of labour is a forceful means to accelerate development, while for a majority of individuals, they not only do not obtain any possibility of free development but also lose the "primitive richness" in their previous activities.

---

1 Marx & Engels Selected Works, Edition 2, Vol.1, p.83.
2 The same book as above, p.84.

Thirdly, the interpersonal communication as a necessary result of the development of division of labour will be extended all over the world in the end. In addition, there will also be such a circumstance: "The social power, i.e., the multiplied productive forces, which arises through the co-operation of different individuals as it is determined by the division of labour, appears to these individuals, --since their co-operation is not voluntary, but has come about naturally,-- not as their own united powers, but as an alien forces existing outside them. And, -as alien forces-the origin and goal of which they are ignorant, which they thus cannot control, which on the contrary passes through a peculiar series of phases and stages independent of their will and the action of man, nay even being the prime governor of these".[1] Moreover, "separate individuals have, with the broadening of their activity into a world-historical activity, become more and more enslaved under a power alien to them (a pressure which they have conceived of as a dirty trick on the part of the so-called universal spirit, etc.), a power which has become more and more enormous and, in the last instance, turns out to be the world market".[2] This social power spontaneously generated by the division of labour and intercourse, owing to its spontaneity and owing to the mutual dispersivity and contrariety resulting from division of labour, is manifested as an alien force completely independent of each and every individual separated from them and completely free, and out of their control.

In a word, the development of division of labour results in such a circumstance: on the one hand, due to division of labour, the subject of activity makes its own development abstracted and one-sided, and due to private property, is deprived of the increasing free time brought by the development of productive force, thus deprived of the possibility of free development, and becomes a pure labour force; on the other hand, these multiplied productive forces, due to division of labour, becomes an alien force independent of individuals, i.e.: one is the development of the social forces opposite to individuals and the other is the abstraction and

---

1 Marx & Engels Selected Works, Edition 2, Vol.1, p.85~86.
2 The same book as above, p.89.

poverty of individuals. "It is one of the chief factors in historical development up till now."[1]

In this case, the antinomy between social development and individual development exactly results from the mutual mediation between the material exchange activity between man and nature, and the communicative activity between man and man, i.e.: the mutual mediation between the natural necessity that controls the relation between man and nature, and the historical necessity that controls the relation between man and man. The simple linear relation of man and nature, due to the intervention of the relation of man and man, becomes such a complex and tortuous relation. Due to the mutual mediation between two necessities, the opposition between man and thing restricted by the blindness of natural necessity is not sublated by improved productive force. On the contrary, this improvement adds to it a new opposition – between individuals and the productive forces they create, between living labour and materialized labour. This latter opposition caused by blind historical necessity, in a sense, is an opposition more puzzling and insufferable than the former opposition caused by blind natural necessity. For this reason, philosophers have paid more attention to this second opposition.

It goes without saying, that the people long before Marx have known this antinomic phenomenon of history, but generally speaking, none of the previous thinkers could really conceive this phenomenon. They have only explained this phenomenon in various mysterious forms. The earliest explanation should be the religious myth in Holy Bible: man ate fruit of wisdom, thus could identify good and evil and had degraded, so they must be saved by God to return to the arms of God. Vico and Rousseau in early modern times both clearly knew this contradiction. Vico introduced the theory of unintended consequences of social activity to indicate the deviation between the end and consequence of this social activity. Rousseau had pointed out, the advance of science and art had not only played a role in corrupting customs but also is the very root cause for enslavement and inequality as it aroused man's many desires.

---

1 The same book as above, p.85.

When men was in a primitive state, "they lived free, healthy, honest and happy lives, so long as their nature allowed, and as they continued to enjoy the pleasures of mutual and independent intercourse", whereas "all subsequent advances have been apparently so many steps towards the perfection of the individual, but in reality towards the decrepitude of the species."[1] Kant, Fichte, Schelling and other people tried to explain this deviation with the mysterious theory of "Plan of Nature" or "Plan of Universe". Hegel's "cunning of reason" is even the culmination of such a theory. As far as this antinomic fact in human development is concerned, nature is more profound than ancient people's direct attitude and early-modern didacticists' innocent optimism, but in terms of their concrete interpretations, all of them ran into mystery, even materialist Feuerbach's "species-essence alienation theory" was mysterious.

If we start from real individuals and regard human history as human activity process which is limited and restricted by natural necessity and historical necessity, then the solution to the issue of the relation between freedom and necessity must proceed from both the transcendence and relation of the two necessities. That is to say, the freedom of "everybody's comprehensive and free development" as man's ultimate goal is limited and restricted both by natural necessity and historical necessity. Historical necessity on the one hand is limited by natural necessity and on the other hand it also limits the activities of human individuals. In this sense, historical necessity becomes a medium between individual free development and natural necessity. In other words, historical necessity is the actions that men have to take in order to control external nature and turn external nature into a being meeting men's need. Therefore, we may also say that historical necessity is an extrinsic means, which men consciously or unconsciously use to sublate natural necessity. This means is what men have to resort to, but it itself is a means only but anything ultimate, so it inevitably changes with the change in the relation between man and nature. In this case, the transcendence of historical necessity is closely related to and restricted by the transcendence of the natural necessity.

---

1 [French] Rousseau: Discourse on the Origin of Inequality Among Men, p.120, Beijing, Commercial Press, 1962.

Above we have indicated that, in human history, the concrete manifestations of historical necessity's restriction on man's comprehensive and free development are division of labour and private property. Therefore, the transcendence of the historical necessity is also the elimination of division of labour and private property which restricts man's development and which turns man into abstract being. But since division of labour is the certain result of the improvement of productive force, the so-called elimination of division of labour can only have two possible ways: one possible way is to force productive forces back to below that level which is high enough to cause the generation of division of labour, just like the old man described by Chuang Tzu. He drew water with an urn and refused to use any mechanism that could raise efficiency, for it might destroy primitive "perfection". This passive way to eliminate division of labour was proposed time and time again in the history and is still heard from time to time, nowadays. But as a truth, this solution is unrealizable in real history. Hegel ever pointed out: "For the state of innocence, the paradisaical condition, is that of the brute. Paradise is a park, where only brutes, not men, can remain. ... The Fall is therefore the eternal Mythus of Man – in fact, the very transition by which he becomes man."[1] Therefore, for man, it is impossible to eliminate division of labour by returning to pre-historical state through abandoning sacrament and wisdom. However, there is another way to eliminate division of labour. That is the great development of productive force. It is the positive way.

People's division of labour in productive activity is the need for the development of productive forces. Productive activity is a basic condition for all history. Men have to finish it every day for survival; on the other hand, under normal conditions of health, physical strength, spirit, craftsmanship and skill, an individual also has the demand for engaging in normal labour and stopping ease, in other words, productive activity meanwhile is also a way of individual's self-realization.[2] That is to say, productive activity per se is also a form of development of human po-

---

1 [German] Hegel: Philosophy of History, p.318.
2 Collected Works of Karl Marx and Frederick Engels, Chinese version 1, Vol.46 (II), p.112~113.

tential, but in a sense, the abilities which man possesses is infinite, so the free development of these abilities requires extremely rich diversity of human activities. In a primitive state – a state without real division of labour, though individual's activity has a kind of "primitive richness", it is extremely finite integrity. Therefore, whether for meeting man's material demand to a larger degree or for further developing man's potential, it is necessary to break through this primitive integrity. The only way to break it and achieve free development is to limit individual's activity to some specific aspects, specialize it, integrate this kind of activities which exist as special abilities in various individuals into an activity of the totality and achieve the integrity of man "species" or to the society which possesses the level of totality. That is to say, to integrate individuals' activities which used to be like mutually irrelevant atoms into overall activity so as to break through primitive finity and obtain finite overall richness which greatly outdoes the previous one. Whereas, to integrate previously homogeneous atoms or individuals –individuals engaging in similar activities into overall activity cannot rely on the simple addition of atomic individuals. The only way is to specialize individuals' activities– turn individual into a specialized "organ" of overall activity. This is the so-called division of labour. In fact, division of labour is not to separate people's activities but to specialize individuals' activities so as to integrate them into an overall activity and integrate previous atoms into an organic polymer and an object. That is to say, division of labour and socialization of activity are associated and are the two aspects of the same process. Division of labour on the one hand results in great development of the ability of men as "species" and as a society, and on the other hand greatly abstracts and monotonizes the development of men as individuals and makes production lose the sense of art from previous finite integrity and become a tedious activity that men have to do in order to survive.

However, the development of productive forces resulting by the development of division of labour enables the existence of a social group which is completely away from material productive activity and exclusively engages in spiritual productive activity, possible. Hence, under the premise of "separation of material labour and mental labour" which was called "real division of labour" by Marx, finally the scientific theoretical activity which is dedicated to the symbolic comprehension of nature is formed. The development of science and its role in material production create such a trend: the work which used to be performed by man's natural organs is substituted by artificial organs. The so-called application of science in production is, in essence, to substitute natural organs with artificial organs for production. The development trend of this substitution progresses from a local substitution to a general substitution, from the substitution of man's hands and feet, to man's physical strength and finally to human brain. As a result, machines completely substitute men to do material productive labour, even some mechanical mental labour. Hegel saw this development trend of material production in a very early time. He said,

> The universal and objective in work is to be found in the abstraction which, giving rise to the specialization of means and wants, causes the specialization also of the production. This is the division of labour. By it the labour of the individual becomes more simple, his skill in his abstract work greater, and the amount he produces larger. The result of the abstraction of skill and means is that men's interdependence or mutual relation is completed. It becomes a thorough necessity. Moreover, the abstraction of production causes work to be continually more mechanical, until it is at last possible for man to step out and let the machine take his place.[1]

However, Hegel did not get a correct conclusion from this development trend. Instead, he led it to his development theory of spirit. By starting from human activity theory, we may obtain a thoroughly different conclusion. That is to say, when the development of science and its application in production enable man to step out of direct production process, it is also the time when division of labour is really eliminated, because under such condition, division of labour not only no longer plays a role in promoting the development of productive force as before, but also becomes a shackle for productive forces. In this case, the elimination of division of labour is not only for the free development of human ability but also for the further development of productive force.

---

1 [German] Hegel: Philosophy of Right, p.210.

Human activity and communism

The elimination of division of labour will certainly result in the elimination of private property, at the same time, while the elimination of private property and division of labour meanwhile is also the ally for individuals, on the basis established by modern productive forces and world intercourse. Hence the re-control of the power of the things individuals create through their ally is the transcendence of the historical necessity which used to blindly control human activity and is the establishment of communism, while the system established by communism is exactly the basis of this reality and excludes all things existing independent of individuals.[1] It establishes the rule over contingency and relation and substitutes the rule of relation and contingency over individuals.[2] Therefore, communism on the one hand is the transcendence of previously alien historical necessity and is the freedom from historical necessity. From this historical height, firstly the conscious transcendence of necessity is not merely an issue of cognition and is not an issue of first cognition then action, either. Fundamentally speaking, it is an issue of historical practice; secondly, the historical necessity, which as an alien force, has controlled the man in history, was not as imagined by old philosophy. It is something like "Providence" and "Plan of Universe" which regards man as a tool, or rather, in view of man's ultimate transcendence of his externality and alienation, historical necessity is more like a tool or means by which man realizes his end, i.e.: in order to realize his goal of free development, man has to resort to the medium of historical necessity.

But the transcendence of the historical necessity in only the necessary condition for achieving "each individual's comprehensive and free development" other than the sufficient condition; the freedom of independent labour realized by the transcendence of historical necessity, i.e.: elimination of division of labour and private property is only a freedom in a finite sense and not the freedom in a sense of "each individual's comprehensive and free development". Marx had pointed out pro-

---

1 Collected Works of Karl Marx and Frederick Engels, Chinese version 1, Vol.3, p.79.
2 The same book as above,

foundly, "Freedom in this sphere (material production) can only consist in socialized man, the associated producers, rationally regulating their interchange with Nature, bringing it under their common control, instead of being ruled by it as by the blind forces of Nature; and achieving this with the least expenditure of energy and under conditions most favourable to them, and worthy of, their human nature. But it nonetheless still remains a realm of necessity." According to Marx, "realm of true freedom" is a sphere not stipulated by external end and is on the other shore of the realm of necessity. Therefore, not only the transcendence of historical necessity, i.e.: the elimination of division of labour and private property enables the consequence of human activity no longer be an alien force which rules over man, but also more fundamentally, only the transcendence of natural necessity, i.e.: the advanced development of productive force constitutes the sufficient conditions for "each individual's comprehensive and free development", because "the realm of true freedom, which, however, can blossom forth only with this realm of necessity as its basis. The shortening of the working-day is its basic prerequisite".[1] The shortening of the working-day means the lengthening of free time. Only in free time, "everybody's comprehensive and free development" is possible.

Here we see what Marx is different from all previous thinkers, with is his huge sense of historical reality. Not like previous thinkers who have imagined man's freedom or free development as a pure spiritual state and a non-historical subjective behavior, Marx realistically and historically reduces comprehensive and free development to free time and directly associates the realization of free development with the historical development of material productive forces. In this way, communism as a result of historical movement, is the transcendence of previous blind historical necessity and more fundamentally the transcendence of natural necessity. The transcendence of these two aspects jointly constitutes the premise of the realm of freedom.

---

1 Collected Works of Karl Marx and Frederick Engels, Chinese version 1, Vol.25, p.927.

Marx's view on freedom and his "production – art" paradigm

Now the question is: what is the content of this "realm of true freedom"? Marx said: "Beyond it begins that development of human energy which is an end in itself, the realm of true freedom."[1] Thus it can be seen that, in the sense of Marx, the connotation of this "realm of true freedom" is "development of human energy which is an end in itself". Then, our next question will be: what does "development of human energy which is an end in itself" mean, or under what condition may human energy be developed as "an end itself". That is to say, under what condition can "each individual's comprehensive and free development" be realized"? On this question, we see that, Marx's definition has experienced a development process. In Marx's thought, the realm of freedom as man' ultimate ideal is conceived as the comprehensive and free development of human energy. He did not change this conviction in his whole life, but the conditions or forms for the realization of the development of human energy, changed many times along with the development of his thought. What restricting this change was the change of Marx's understanding on the relation between production and art. In Chapter 2, we have indicated Marx's understanding on practice is a "production – art" paradigm, while art is a model for free activity, so whether production can be like art fundamentally decides the possibility of the realization of freedom. Largely, Economic and Philosophical Manuscripts of 1844, The German Ideology, 1857-1858 Economic Manuscript and Capital form the stages of the development of Marx's view on freedom.

The first systematic enunciation of Marx's view on freedom is found in his Economic and Philosophical Manuscripts of 1844. In this early works, Marx defines the species-essence of man as a free and conscious activity. On this basis, through comparison with animal's unconscious activity, Marx points out that, human activity essentially is a free activity, comprehensive activity, and in this activity, man as subject will achieve comprehensive development and realizes his species-essence; moreover,

---

1 Collected Works of Karl Marx and Frederick Engels, Chinese version 1, Vol.25, p.927.

this activity itself is performed "in accordance with the laws of beauty", so essentially it is also an aesthetic artistic activity. Marx further states that, man, when designing the objective, he really proves himself to be a species-being. Such production is his active species-life. Through it, nature appears as his work and his reality. The object of labour is, therefore, the objectification of the species-life of man: because man produces himself not only intellectually, in his consciousness, but actively and actually, and he can therefore contemplate himself in a world he himself has created. To objectify his species-essence as free and conscious activity in external real world and facilitate it with a sensuous form – the sensuous manifestation of the essence of man's free activity, is undoubtedly a kind of artistic creation, realization of freedom.

But "in tearing away the object of his production from man, estranged labour therefore tears away from him his species-life, his true species-objectivity, and transforms his advantage over animals into the disadvantage that his inorganic body, nature, is taken from him."[1] "In the same way as estranged labour reduces spontaneous and free activity to a means, it makes man's species-life a means of his physical existence".[2] Therefore, the realization of man's free development is to transcend alienated labour and restore the essence of man's species-life. But as "private property is therefore the product, result, and necessary consequence of alienated labour, of the external relation of the worker to nature and to himself",[3] the transcendence of alienated labour is also the transcendence of private property. This is communism. Marx, writes:"Communism as the positive transcendence of private property as human self-estrangement, and therefore as the real appropriation of the human essence by and for man; communism therefore as the complete return of man to himself as a social (i.e., human) being – a return which is accomplished consciously and embracing the entire wealth of previous development. This communism, as fully developed naturalism, equals humanism, and as fully developed humanism equals naturalism; it is the genuine resolution of the conflict

1 Collected Works of Karl Marx and Frederick Engels, Chinese version 1, Vol.25, p.927.
2 Collected Works of Karl Marx and Frederick Engels, Chinese version 1, Vol.42, p.97.
3 Collected Works of Karl Marx and Frederick Engels, Chinese version 1, Vol.42, p.97.

between man and nature and between man and man – the true resolution of the strife between existence and essence, between objectification and self-confirmation, between freedom and necessity, between the individual and the species."[1] Therefore, in Economic and Philosophical Manuscripts of 1844, Marx conceives the realization of man's free development and man's free activity as the realization of true human essence which transcends estrangement and private property, that is to say, "man appropriates his comprehensive essence in a comprehensive manner, that is to say, as a whole man".[2] This appropriation of man's own essence achieves a kind of fully independent labour. In other words, in this stage, Marx thinks man's free development, man as a whole man, is directly realized in the independent labour that transcends estrangement.

However, there were two defects in Economic and Philosophical Manuscripts of 1844. One is that it only regards labour as the realization of man's species-essence, but does not clearly disclose that labour meets man's material needs, this most fundamental aim, so it was impossible to reasonably explain the origin of division of labour and private property; the other is that it starts directly from man's species-essence and deems it's a ready thing, and not starts from real individuals, so it is impossible to reasonably explain the role of interpersonal relations which mediates the relation between man and nature, thus it is difficult to reasonably explain the origin of division of labour and private property. In this book, the circular reasoning of the occurrence of estranged labour and the generation of private property is the necessary result of these two defects. Therefore, improvement should be be made.

But, The German Ideology starts from real individuals and regards labour, firstly as a means of subsistence, so the above two defects are sublated. In addition, it also defines new stipulations on the conditions of man's free development. Now the concept of alienation is established on the basis of the theory of division of labour, so the transcendence of alienation, the realization of independent labour firstly is established on the

---

1 Collected Works of Karl Marx and Frederick Engels, Chinese version 1, Vol.42, p.120.

2 The same book as above, p.123.

basis of the development of productive labour, the content of the transcendence of alienation is defined as the elimination of division of labour.
But here, the sphere of material production, i.e.: productive activity, is
still deemed as a major sphere for the realization of man's free development. In it, free activity and independent labour still have same meaning, "whole individuals", "personalized individuals" also have the same
meaning with the individuals associated under the conditions of eliminated division of labour and private property, i.e.: "The appropriation
of the totality of instruments of production is, for this very reason, the
development of the totality of capacities in the individuals themselves".[1] Here, obviously Marx particularly stresses the pre-conditional
significance of the transcendence of historical necessity for man's free
development on the basis of advanced development of productive
forces, while is yet to make any in-depth study on the deeper concrete
conditions and on the sphere of free development. Therefore, sometimes, he had even borrowed some ideas of Utopian socialists. For example, he thinks, "in communist society, where nobody has one
exclusive sphere of activity but each can become accomplished in any
branch he wishes, society regulates the general production and thus
makes it possible for me to do one thing today and another tomorrow,
to hunt in the morning, fish in the afternoon, rear cattle in the evening,
criticize after dinner, just as I have a mind, without ever becoming
hunter, fisherman, herdsman or critic".[2]

In the 1857-1858 Economic Manuscripts, on the basis of in-depth research on economics, Marx started further defining the conditions for
man's free development. In these new works, Marx points out to a differentiation, in social forms in human history: "personal dependence as the
"first social form" and personal independence founded on objective dependence as "the second great social form", and the society in the future
as the "third stage" is as "free individuality, based on the universal development of individuals and based on their subordination to their com-

---

1 Marx & Engels Selected Works, Edition 2, Vol.1, p.129.
2 The same book as above, p.85.

munal, social productivity as their social wealth".[1] To make this individuality possible, the development of ability must reach certain degree and universality.[2] These basic stipulations are largely the same as those stated in The German Ideology. The difference is that here Marx further stipulates the conditions and activity sphere for man's free development. Particular attention should be paid to two aspects.

Realm of freedom and beauty

On the one hand, Marx, this time gives more concrete stipulations on under what conditions labour of material production can become individual's self-realization. He points out that, the work in material production can become attractive work, the individual's self-relation only "(1) when its social character is posited, (2) when it gains a scientific and at the same time general character, not merely human exertion as a specifically harnessed natural force, but exertion as subject, which appears in the production process not in a merely natural, spontaneous form, but as an activity regulating all the forces of nature."[3] In this passage, the labour is social, refers that under the premise of eliminating private property, individual labour is directly social labour, without having to rely on exchanges. The so-called scientificalness refers to that on the basis of advanced development of science, man as a subject of the labour, possesses a great ability to control nature due to the application of science. Under such condition, the subject of labour achieves "rich individuality", "which is at the same time all-sided in its production as in its consumption, and whose labour also therefore appears no longer as labour, but as the full development of activity itself, in which natural necessity in its direct form has disappeared".[4] That is to say, in the labour process under this condition, natural necessity is transcended, and man's free development can also be realized. Here, Marx opposes the understanding ; "as Fourier,

---

1 Collected Works of Karl Marx and Frederick Engels, Chinese version 1, Vol.46(I), p.104.
2 The same book as above, 108.
3 Collected Works of Karl Marx and Frederick Engels, Chinese version 1, Vol.46(II), p.113.
4 Collected Works of Karl Marx and Frederick Engels, Chinese version 1, Vol.46(I), p.287

with grisette-like naivete, conceives it", and considers that the labour under that condition as nothing but a kind of entertainment and recreation. He points out: true free labour, such as: music composition, is also a very serious and extremely stressed thing.[1]   Here interestingly, Marx regards artist's creative activity or man's artistic activity as a model for "true free labour". This shows certain continuity with the idea of "man also produces in accordance with the laws of beauty" as stated in *Economic and Philosophical Manuscripts of 1844*.

Another noteworthy aspect is that in this works, Marx for the first time stipulates the condition for man's free development in another aspect or from another angle. It is to stipulate the condition of man's free development from the perspective of disposable time or free time. He points out, "the free development of individualities, and hence not the reduction of necessary labour time so as to posit surplus labour, but rather the general reduction of the necessary labour of society to a minimum, which then corresponds to the artistic, scientific etc. development of the individuals in the time set free, and with the means created, for all of them."[2] "The measure of wealth is then not any longer, in any way, labour time, but rather disposable time".[3] In free time, man truly obtains the condition for free development, i.e.: "all free time is for free development",[4] or "time for the full development of the individual".[5]

The reason, why Marx drew the above conclusion is that during his intensive research on capitalist production process, he discovered that; following the progress of science and its application in production, "labour no longer appears so much to be included within the production process; rather, the human being comes to relate more as watchman and regulator to the production process itself. He writes: "(What holds for machinery holds likewise for the combination of human activities and the development of human intercourse.) No longer does the worker insert a modi-

---

1 Collected Works of Karl Marx and Frederick Engels, Chinese version 1, Vol.46(II), p.113.

2 The same book as above, p.218~219.

3 The same book as above, p.222.

4 The same book as above, p.139.

5 Collected Works of Karl Marx and Frederick Engels, Chinese version 1, Vol.46(II), p.225.

fied natural thing [ger. Naturgegenstand] as middle link between the object [ger.Objekt] and himself; rather, he inserts the process of nature, transformed into an industrial process, as a means between himself and inorganic nature, mastering it. He steps to the side of the production process instead of being its chief actor".[1] This indicates "to what degree general social knowledge has become a direct force of production, and to what degree, hence, the conditions of the process of social life itself have come under the control of the general intellect and been transformed in accordance with it",[2] while this transformation "reduces labour time for the whole society to a diminishing minimum, and thus frees everyone's time for their own development".[3] Just because Marx saw this trend in production process, Marx abandoned the previous utopian stipulation on the condition of man's free development, and sought more concrete stipulation on the real basis of the development of productive forces. In this stage, the stipulation that man's free development can be realized in the sphere of material production is co-exists together with the stipulation of "free time for the full development of the individual". Marx had not yet explained the relation between these two stipulations. This indicates Marx was still seeking a sounder stipulation on this issue.

But in the last manuscripts of Capital, Marx develops the concrete stipulation on man's free development. It is to seek the concrete conditions for man's free development, within the changes in the relations by different forms of human activity. Here, Marx thinks that, in the sphere of material production, it is impossible for man to avoid the control caused by natural necessity,and cannot transcend historical necessity through eliminating division of labour and private property, cannot make it no longer be a blind force to rule itself and cannot carry out production in the most reasonable condition, because this sphere is always a realm of necessity. Therefore, what man can finally realize in the sphere of material production is only the finite development of human energy, finite freedom, i.e.: freedom from historical necessity, while the sphere of the com-

---

1 The same book as above, p.218.
2 The same book as above, p.219~220.
3 The same book as above, p.221.

prehensive and free development of human energy is "realm of true free-dom". This indicates Marx ultimately thinks the sphere where man's free development is fully realized is not the sphere of material production, but outside it, i.e.: the other shore of the sphere of true material produc-tion. Then, where is this sphere? It is reasonable for us to say this sphere which enables the realization of man's comprehensive, free and sufficient development is nothing, but the sphere of man's artistic activity. We still remember that regardless of his early or late periods, when Marx had stip-ulated the condition of man's free development, he had always associated man's free development with aesthetic activity, and always regarded artistic activity as a model for truly free labour. Therefore, when Marx ultimately thinks the sphere of material production is always a realm of necessity other than the sphere of free development of human energy, the realm of true freedom in his sense is no one but the sphere of artistic activity, the realm of aesthetics. The realm of freedom is also the realm of beauty.

In Marx's philosophy, productive activity is primary activity, while labour tool is the primary medium for the realization of man's aim. In order to realize his aim, man must go in for productive activity according to the law of tool operation. But, going in for productive activity according to the law of tool operation, means man is controlled by the law of tools, while man uses tools to carry out activity in order to realize aim. This con-trolling state obviously is not what man's aim itself desires for, therefore it is unfreedom, regular unfreedom – the necessity. In this way, the subject of activity faces such a choice: either to be controlled by tool when using tool in order to realize the aim, and lose another freedom while realizing the aim; or to refuse the use of tool. However, people usually choose the former without any hesitation. Of course, in human history, some nostalgic people refused to use tools, like the abovementioned old man who would rather draw water with an urn than raise efficiency with lever mechanism. Nonetheless, nostalgists, only refuse new tools other than all tools, so they do not belong to the latter case. Thus, the realization of a kind of freedom is inevitably associated with the use of tool.

The use of tool makes the opposition between man and nature concrete and puts him into an opposition with the medium. On the one hand, internal aim walks out of the interior of subject and permeates towards object; on the other hand, the concrete stipulations of the object are delivered to subject through tools, the necessity of the object becomes something with stipulation and content. However, the stipulation and concrete content in the necessity of object are manifested through tools, in other words, subject is grasped through tool, so the necessity of the object is directly manifested as the necessity of the tool in the sense of the subject. Consequently, in terms of direct form, the contradiction between the inner freedom of the subject and the necessity of the object is manifested as the opposition between the inner freedom of the subject and the necessity of the tool.

Theoretical activity pursuing for absolute necessity

The use of the tool presupposes another modality in human activity. In productive activity, initially there was only, the abstract opposition between the aim and the object. The use of tool transcends that abstractness of the opposition and also makes the realization of the aim indirect. In order to realize the direct aim, it is necessary to establish a mediated relation at first and regard this medium as a direct aim; while in order to realize this aim, it is necessary to establish another mediated relation, too, and so on and so forth, and this sequence can be extended to infinity. In this extension, the initial direct aim becomes vague and unclear and retreats to a remote place, while only medium is presented before subject. The retirement of the initial aim makes medium itself an aim pursued by activity. Medium by nature is necessity, the necessity man must submit to, during realization of his aim. Hence, in the process of the establishment of a medium, subject shifts itself from the direct pursuit of initial aim to the pursuit of necessity. Thus, it turns out to be a theoretical attitude. This theoretical attitude and the medium of theoretical activity – lansign, constitute man's theoretical activity. Theoretical activity, therefore in terms of its aim, is the activity pursuing necessity other than the activity pursuing freedom. Theoretical activity not only pursues necessity as a general rule but also pursues absolute necessity. The highest aim of theoretical activity is to reduce or arrange all things into an absolutely necessary system and conceive the whole world as a gigantic machine.

Although productive activity delays its initial aim under the action of medium, man as a subject cannot abandon his initial aim after all. If productive activity is to impose the will of the subject on nature and make nature accord with his aim, its standpoint should be subjectivity; while if theoretical activity is to completely accept object and make subject completely submerge in the necessity of object, its standpoint should be objectivity. In this way, the opposition between practical attitude and theoretical attitude will be manifested. Theoretical activity is converted from the activity of establishing tool medium, thus essentially it can return to tool medium. Under this circumstance, theoretical activity mediates productive activity in fact. This mediation or this permeation of theoretical activity towards productive activity was manifested as a continuously expanded trend in history. Therefore, the opposition between practical attitude and theoretical attitude enters the interior of productive activity, or in other words returns to the opposition between the inner aim and means of productive activity. Nowadays, theoretical activity represented by natural science is so advanced, productive activity is so deeply mediated by theoretical activity that we can hardly imagine how those many spheres of productive activity will go on, if without theoretical activity. Thus, man should enter necessity at first, if he wants to pursue freedom. Necessity ubiquitously stands before subject and pushes the realization of freedom farther. The development of productive activity is getting more attached to theoretical activity, but the consequences of theoretical activity is necessity other than freedom. People engage in productive activity in order to obtain freedom, but they first receive necessity; what is more, the greater the freedom desired is, the greater the necessity will be there. When man uses a tool to realize his aim, it seems that "cunning of reason" defeats natural necessity, but when we look back, we will find this acquisition is at the cost of an advance payment.

Therefore, we see in the sphere of theoretical activity, people hang up on subjective aim and only pursue objective necessity and regard the grasp of this objective necessity as their aim. Theory itself in fact is evolved from the tool or means system of human activity, so the aim of theoretical activity should be subordinate to the aim of practice. However, due to the independence of theoretical activity, in theoretical activity aim is completely dissolved into means, whereas means becomes aim. That is to say, in the sphere of theoretical activity, necessity is an absolute dominant force, while freedom is to conceive this necessity and consciously obeys it. Here, for human activity, aim and means only possess a kind of abstract identity. In other words, in the sphere of theoretical activity, it is impossible for man to realize comprehensive and free development; whereas in the sphere of productive activity, practice always needs to use tools, resort to the means for different aims and take theoretical activity as medium, and only when it complies with the natural necessity grasped by tool or theoretical activity, subjective aim can be realized, so in productive activity, inevitably human capacity can only obtain a limited development. During production, aim and means are identical only in a limited sense – and means is identical to the aim only in a limited aspect in which it can realize aim, while in other aspects, it is intrinsic. Therefore, means always limits the aim and makes the aim be realized only to a limited extent. In the three spheres of human activity, man's free development can be realized, only in artistic activity or aesthetic sphere.

Above we have indicated that the aesthetic activity or artistic activity is considered the highest form to sublate the opposition of man and nature and the opposition between freedom and necessity. This idea was first systematically put forth by Kant and then developed by Schiller, Schelling and Hegel. But judgment activity as an activity which associates freedom and necessity only has pure subjective sense, i.e.: it "seems like" that, where and what it is like in fact is unknown. In any case, it is a matter of significance that Kant regards artistic activity as a medium linking freedom and necessity. After Kant, Schelling regards artistic contemplation or aesthetic activity as a way to grasp the Absolute, in the primitive identity between spirit and nature. Hence, Schelling leads the understanding on artistic activity completely to complete objective idealism and regards artwork as the highest presentation of the Absolute. Hegel's attitude towards artistic activity is the same as Schelling's in essence. Only he thinks the forms to achieve the Absolute also include religion and philosophy, in addition to art, and art is a lower form among them. Nevertheless, the two do not have essential difference in the idea that "beauty is the perceptual manifestation of ideas". That is to say, Schelling and Hegel in fact regard the subject of art as absolute idea other than infinite man.

The one who really developed Kantian theory from the aspect of reality is the poet and philosopher Schiller. He concludes from the opposition between man's perceptual impulse and formal impulse that in order to realize the harmonious development of the two impulses in experience, the third impulse – play impulse should exist, its object "may bear the name of living form; a term that serves to describe all aesthetic qualities of phenomena, and what people style, in the widest sense, beauty".[1] As the aesthetic state is a middle state between natural state and logical and moral state, and is a kind of substantial infinity, "this medium situation in which the soul is neither physically nor morally constrained, and yet is in both ways active, merits essentially the name of a free situation" -- "on the part of nature, it is made profitable for him to make of himself what he will; that the freedom to be what he ought to be is restored perfectly to him", while "freedom is taken from man by the one-sided compulsion of nature in feeling, and by the exclusive legislation of the reason in thinking".[2] Schiller on the one hand tries to demonstrate the objectivity of beauty according to Kant's definition of beauty, similar to all subjective breakthroughs achieved before and on the other hand, as a poet, he expresses more sense of reality than Schelling and Hegel.

Obviously, Kant, Schiller, Schelling and Hegel's thought that aesthetic activity dissolves the opposition between freedom and nature is rather profound and can give us a great enlightenment. It is also obvious that fundamentally speaking, as their philosophy does not grasp human's productive activity, this most fundamental sphere of human existence, their

1 [German] Friedrich Von Schiller: Letters Upon the Aesthetic Education of Man, p.86, Beijing, China Federation of Literary and Art Circles Publishing Corporation, 1984.
2 The same book as above, p.107~110.

definitions on the essence of beauty also have certain illusoriness. As a result, they ran into difficulty in the attempt to use aesthetic activity as a transition from nature to freedom. This is prominently manifested by the theory of organic nature conforming to aim, i.e.: they have both proposed the concept of nature conforming to aim, so that the transition from nature to spirit is tenable. Kant starts from dualism, so this principle of nature conforming to aim was only the subjective principle of judgment. Schelling and Hegel had started from their objective idealism and considered that; nature conforming to aim is caused by the estrangement of spirit. Schiller had swayed between these two notions. However, starting from the principle of nature's conformity to aim, people are unable to reasonably explain why the aesthetic value of mountains and seas as inorganic beings is higher than the aesthetic value of caterpillars as organic beings. This conflict with daily aesthetic experience indicates nature's conformity to aim as advocated by Kant and other people is ridiculous. What they did not see is exactly man's productive activity, this real and purposive activity. Truly speaking, it is man's productive activity that constitutes the transition from nature to freedom, while natural being's conformity to aim does not possess the effect of transition. For human being, the conformity of any natural being to aim can be judged only from man's aim other than natural being itself. In terms of natural being alone, the existence of organic matter no doubt shows higher inherent conformity to aim than the existence of inorganic matter does, but in terms of human being, the conformity of every natural being to aim must be re-arranged according to man's aim and must be re-contemplated under the universal light of human activity.

Therefore, from the perspective of modern practical philosophy, aesthetic activity or artistic activity is based on productive activity. Productive activity as a real activity mode to solve the basic contradiction of human existence is unable to sublate the externality of aim and means due to its reality, thus unable to realize the supreme ideal of man's free development. That is to say, in the mode of productive activity, the finity of productive activity is contradictory with the infinity of human's ideal for free development. Aesthetic artistic activity, due to the help of symbolic

medium, breaks through the finity of productive activity and can symbolically realize the ideal of free development of human energy. Therefore, starting from Marxist standpoint, we may reach such a conclusion:
beauty is the symbol of freely developing man or whole man. This definition on the essence of beauty indicates that although beauty stems from
man's productive activity, productive activity itself is not beauty. Beauty
is to transcend the finity of practice and reach an infinite sphere, i.e.:
transcend the restriction of the finity of productive activity on man's free
development and point at a sphere where human capacity can be developed without limit. However, this sphere does not have the reality of the
sphere of productive practice and is only symbolic existence. Therefore,
aesthetic or artistic activity is the symbolic compensation on man's real
existence, i.e.: the disclosure of man's truest end. Or, in other words, just
through this disclosure, the compensation on man's real finite existence
is achieved and the existence of man intrudes in a symbolic way into the
realm where finity is transcended. For this reason, all great artworks are
immortal. All activities in other spheres, due to their finity, can hardly
surpass the then historical value. Only the great artworks can transcend
history and leave people a feeling of beauty forever. Therefore, the dimension of aesthetics is the dimension of the infinity in man's existence,
and man becomes true man, due to the existence of the dimension of
aesthetics. If art has not ever existed or had been abolished, the existence
of man will lose its finity and purely become the existence of the present.
Of course, aesthetic activity is only an activity of symbolic compensation
on human existence, so once the symbolized object becomes the object
of real activity, symbol will lose the sense of compensation and retreat
from this sphere.

Besides, all human activities are activities in time dimension, so under
the premise that the total time of human activities is not changed, the
free time needed by artistic activity has a reciprocal relationship with the
necessary labour time needed by productive practice, thus the increase
of free time is directly determined by the quantity of necessary labour
time determined by the level of productive activity, whereas the level of
productive activity is determined by the level of theoretical activity rep-

resented by science, as well as by its application in productive practice. In view of the distribution of human activity time in different activity spheres, aesthetic activity as the realm of true freedom cannot exist independently and must be established on the basis of productive practice – which is a realm of necessity. Only in the free time provided by the development of productive activity and theoretical activity, men can enter the palace of art and the kingdom of aesthetics. That means the development level of productive activity and theoretical activity is in proportion to the increase of free time. The development of modern science seems to presuppose such a prospect: following the development of the latest technological revolution symbolized by devices with artificial intelligence, mechanical devices can not only substitute human limbs but also will substitute human brain in production. In this way, it is possible that in the end the process of material production is completely performed by machines and man is completely liberated from this process. By then, artistic activity will become man's most principal activity mode, or as Maxim Gorky put it, aesthetics will become the ethics of future society.[1] In this case, when we look back, we will discover man's submission to necessity in productive activity and theoretical activity not only plays a role in realizing finite aim but also is closely related to the possibility of the realization of the realm of true freedom – the infinite realm of aesthetic activity. Only when people can grasp a broader range of necessity and use it to mediate productive activity, can they obtain more free time, thus having greater possibility of free development.

We see, Marx regards artistic activity as man's free existence condition, in other words regards artistic activity as the true state of human existence. Although Marx had regarded independent labour as the realization of freedom in his early ages and regarded productive labour as a realm of necessity and placed the realm of freedom on the other shore of production sphere in his old ages, no matter how different the concept of freedom is in his early ages and old ages, we can easily see from the above analysis that throughout Marxist thought, artistic activity has always been

---

1 Translation of Aesthetics, Book 1, p.2, Beijing, China Social Sciences Press, 1980.

deemed as a typical sphere of man's free development. In his early ages, Marx thought the realm of freedom can be reached as long as alienated labour is transcended because then Marx had thought that true productive labour was a creative activity similar to art, while in his old ages, Marx thought the sphere of material production was always a realm of necessity, because Marx then realized that; the modern production had lost its finite sense of art, which used to be embodied in the production of traditional handicraft industry. Just based on this cognition, Marx had resolutely excluded production from the realm of freedom. Obviously, the difference between Marx's view of freedom and the freedom as described in traditional textbooks in socialist countries have possessed a remarkably different cognition on necessity. This is mainly bygone in China for some time. In the sense of Marx, people's cognition and submission to necessity in productive activity and theoretical activity not only plays a role in realizing finite aim but also is closely related to the possibility of realizing the realm of true freedom, but this cognition and submission are not freedom, and the satisfaction for obtaining a need is not true freedom, either. The true freedom rests with the increase of free time brought about by this cognition and submission, and rests with man's comprehensive and free play of his capacity in the free time, i.e.: infinite creation of art.

PART III

DIALECTIC AS
PRACTICAL WISDOM

CHAPTER THREE

Looking into Marx's Realm of Ideal from the Angle of Real History

Karl Mannheim, thinks socialism and communism are same as the Christian Millenarianism, liberalism and conservatism. They are all Utopia.[1] Without doubt, the communism is considered as an ideal here. In addition, he thinks the existence of these ideals has its root in finite real life. We cannot deny that Mannheim saw the formal "isomorphism" among the communist ideal, the Christian ideal, the liberal ideal as well as the ideals of other doctrines, but obviously we cannot thus say he has revealed the essence of communism or covered all content of communism. Based on this isomorphism, Karl Lowith also attempted to illustrate Marx's doctrine of history from the Christian history of salvation. In his sense, historical materialism, is a salvation history, speaking through the language of "political-economics" by A.Smith or Ricardo. He said ; "The real driving force behind this conception is a transparent messianism which has its unconscious root in Marx's own being, even in his race. He, was a Jew of Old Testament, satirist, though an emancipated Jew of

---

1 [German] Karl Mannheim: Ideology and Utopia, p.244~253.

the nineteenth century, who felt strongly anti-religious and even anti-Semitic. It is the old Jewish messianism and prophetisms – unaltered by two thousand years of economic history from handicraft to large-scale industry – and Jewish insistence on absolute righteousness which explains the idealistic basis of Marx's materialism. Though perverted into secular prognosis, the Communist Manifesto still retains the basic features of a messianic faith: 'the assurance of things to be hoped for'".[1] Same as Mannheim, Lowith had only grasped the formal similarity between Marx's communist ideal and the Christian ideal, but they did not understand the difference of Marx's communist ideal from previous ideals. It is consciously constructed based both on real and finite existence, thus possesses the reality in another sense. This is the difference of the communist ideal from previous ideals, Utopian socialism in particular.

Here, we can easily comprehend the significance of communism in two aspects: its identity and difference from previous ideals. The two aspects can be conceived as the two aspects in which communism bears realistic significance. The first aspect is the realistic significance of the existence of the ideal. This aspect we have previously investigated above. That is, ideal is the appeal that people are based on and transcend finite existence. This ideal is also a value standard for the critique of real life. The second aspect is on the feasibility of the ideal. That is to say, communism is an ideal, but Marx thinks there is a valid channel between it and the reality, which is the real history. In order to distinguish communism from previous ideals, utopian socialism in particular, Marx and Engels has paid more attention to the significance of communism in the second aspect, while have talked little of the first aspect; on the contrary, many non-Marxist thinkers often saw the sameness aspect between communism and the ideals of man in different periods and tried to negate the difference aspect. We should say, neglecting the significance of communism in the first aspect is the incomplete understanding on communism, while only seeing the significance in the first aspect will often lead to misunderstanding on communism. Therefore, we should combine the significance of the two aspects.

---

1 [German] Karl Lowith: World History and Salvation History, p.52~53.

In fact, in terms of the realistic significance of the existence of ideal, it is not that there is no difference between communism and the other human ideals. The construction of the communist ideal is a conscious process starting from the real and the finite existence, but for other types of human ideals, real life is not really perceived; communism is perfect as an ideal because real life is finite and imperfect, This finity and imperfection are considered the most authentic, while the perfection of other human ideals is often believed natural, whereas the finite real world is often thought to be unreal. Of course, from today's point of view, the relation between the latter ideal and real life is a distorted relation, and this relation can be appropriately conceived only when it is incorporated into the relation between communism and real life. Because if we do not set foothold at real finite existence, no ideal can be appropriately conceived.

In any case, the realm of ideality can be conceived as another "true" world constructed by people in order to transcend the finity of the real life. This truth not only rests with the fact that ideal stems from real life but also rests with its critical and guiding role in real life. That is to say, it is impossible that ideal is only hanged high above real life. Instead, it should be able to interact with real life in all kinds of ways. On the one hand, since ideal originates from real life, then following the change of real life, the realm of ideality should be changed, too. Thus, different historical periods have generated different ideals. Even if in the same historical period, different social classes may have different ideals. As Mannheim thinks, the utopian elements in human consciousness are invariable in content and form. This essential and formal changes in numerous Utopia does not take place in the spheres irrelevant with social life. On the contrary, it can be seen that particularly in the development of modern history, a series of forms of Utopia were closely related to certain stages of historical development and every form of them was closely related to a special social class.[1] For the moment, we do not discuss whether Mannhein's Utopia is identical to the concept of ideal, we discuss here. The fact that the realm of ideality changes with real life is certain. This

---

1 [German] Karl Mannheim: Ideology and Utopia, p.210.

also helps us to understand why communism had only emerged in the era of Marx other than any era before.

On the other hand, since ideal is a world constructed in an attempt to transcend the real finity, it certainly keeps certain distance from real life and is manifested as people's pursuit to value, thus generating a critical effect on reality in the aspect of value. We can understand without diffi-culty that to raise and follow any ideal essentially means a kind of critique on reality. In the sense of Christianity, the state before the Fall of Mankind and the state after the last judgment undoubtedly are the ideal state, but this ideal state is relative to the "vicious" human nature in the secular world. The tension between this ideal and reality is the power which drives the history forward. Of course, all these ultimately originate from God. The ideal of enlightenment thinkers is reason. The expansion of subjective reason in early-modern philosophy corresponds to the un-reasonable social life. Engels said:

> The great men, who in France prepared men's minds for the coming revolu-tion, were themselves extreme revolutionists. They recognized no external authority of any kind whatever. Religion, natural science, society, political institutions — everything was subjected to the most unsparing criticism; everything must justify its existence before the judgment-seat of reason or give up existence. Reason became the sole measure of everything.[1]

Utopian socialists including Charles Fourier think, "for the bourgeois world, based upon the principles of these philosophers, is quite as irra-tional and unjust, and, therefore, finds its way to the dust-hole quite as readily as feudalism and all the earlier stages of society. If pure reason and justice have not, hitherto, ruled the world, this has been the case only because men have not rightly understood them."[2] In fact, commu-nism has possessed the dimension of value critique of real world from the very beginning. In Economic and Philosophical Manuscripts of 1844, Marx's introduction in communism starts from the analysis and criticism on man's self-alienation in reality, "while communism is the ac-tive transcendence of the private property – man's self-alienation, so it is

---

1 Marx & Engels Selected Works, Edition 2, Vol.3, p.719.
2 The same book as above, p.721~722.

the real possession of human essence through man and for man; therefore, it is man's return to himself and social man. This return is complete and conscious and maintains all wealth developed before. This communism as completed naturalism is equal to humanism, while as completed humanism is equal to naturalism. It is the real solution to the contradiction between man and nature, and between man and man, and is the real solution to the conflict between, being and essence, objectification and self-verification, freedom and necessity, and individual and species."

In Communist Manifesto, Marx and Engels have expressed that; bourgeoisie and capitalism had won over feudalism through substituting the exploitation, veiled by religious and political illusions with naked, shameless, direct, brutal exploitation; what the bourgeoisie therefore "produces, above all, are its own grave-diggers". "its fall and the victory of the proletariat are equally inevitable". "In place of the old bourgeois society, with its classes and class antagonisms, we shall have an association in which the free development of each will be the condition for the free development of all."[1]

It goes without saying, in terms of critique of the reality, communists' "each individual's free development is the condition of all human's free development" has the same function with the enlightenment thinkers' "reason" and "justice" and the utopian socialists' "all human beings should labour" (Saint-Simon). In this sense, it is valid for people including Mannheim who put communism on a par with other human ideals. Rorty, has also noticed this similarity. He compared the Communist Manifesto with the Christian Holy Bible and thought "the authors of these two works both want to make a prediction on the forthcoming events, based on the super-excellent cognition on the force that decides human history".[2] Both of theses literatures criticize the suffering and unfairness in current life and provide a hope for people, i.e.: at a future moment, "we are willing to and also can treat the needs of all human beings in a way needed by the man who is closest to us and loved most by us"[3].

---

1 Marx & Engels Selected Works, Edition 2, Vol.1, p.294.
2 [American] Richard Rorty: Post-metaphysical Hope, p.345, Shanghai, Shanghai Translation Publishing House, 2003.
3 The same book as above, p.347.

Therefore, in the sense of Rorty, although many of Marx's predictions have been proved untrue, it does not indicate communism is unrealistic, just as many of the predictions in the Holy Bible have been proved false, this cannot stop people from reading it and obtaining inspiring force of life from it.

Anyway, communism is understood in a one-sided manner here. Its significance is much more than this. It also has another kind of important reality. The previous human ideals can only be used as ideals and all have a sense of fantasticality, but communism is not merely an ideal high above real life. In the sense of Marx, there exists a real historical channel accessible to communism. Although each ideal contains a kind of reachable promise, the channel of communism is different from others, because communism is not a world constructed on an abstract principle. It is not merely the projection of wishes generated from the discontentment with current status. It is an ideal constructed by consciously starting from finite human real life.

Saint-Simon said: "all should labour." This idea was raised in a form of moral requirement. The socialism envisaged by him does not exceed the scope of this moral requirement. It expresses people's wish, which first of all is, based on the discontentment with reality. His socialism was formed by many similar wishes. In essence, any human ideal may more or less have this character, i.e.: the character of criticism at current life. However, the communist ideal raised by Marx and Engels is not only the criticism at reality and not only expresses a kind of "should". It is the revelation of historical necessity. This necessity is not based on a pure belief but on "science".

In fact, the theoretical activity in the whole life of Marx can be considered as the effort to pursue such a historical science and seek a real road to communism. In Economic and Philosophical Manuscripts of 1844, Marx thinks communism is the active transcendence of private property – human's self alienation, and is the return of man to himself and social man. The driving force of this return is the internal contradiction in alienated life, because "the entire revolutionary movement necessarily finds both its empirical and its theoretical basis in the movement of private property – more precisely, in that of the economy."[1] Marx's dissertation here is obviously Hegelian. Nevertheless, the contradictions he observes are the contradictions in productive labour and economic life. The development of these contradictions is a channel to communism. Obviously, Marx's proving here is rather derived from contemplation other than real contradictions because in fact Marx starts from the species essence of man other than from real individuals. In The German Ideology, Marx starts from real individuals, thus communism is given a new meaning. Here the finity of human life is conceived under the theory of division of labour, so the sublation of this finity is firstly established on the basis of the development of productive forces. Consequently, the sublation of this finity is stipulated as the elimination of division of labour. In the last draft of Capital, Marx explores a more realistic route to communism. That is to seek the concrete conditions for the realization of communism through the changes in the relations of modes based on real human activities. Here, in Capital, Marx thinks the sphere of material production is always a "realm of necessity", while the realm of true freedom obviously exists outside the sphere of material production.[2] Marx thinks communism as a sphere of artistic activity which exists in the free time created by productive activity, so its conditions also exist in real life. Following the development of productive forces, the necessary labour time expended in human life will be shortened infinitely, while free time will increase infinitely. In this way, communism will be realized in real life.

Two contemporary challenges facing Marxism

Marx's this theory has numerous supporters, but some people has doubted its reality since the very beginning, too. I think no sufficient reason can justify that it is a truth which needs no modification, and meanwhile no reason can convince people to completely give up, this

---

1 Collected Works of Karl Marx and Frederick Engels, Chinese version 1, Vol.42, p.120~121.
2 Collected Works of Karl Marx and Frederick Engels, Chinese version 1, Vol.25, p.926.

ideal. At least, when we look from the perspective of theory, into Marx's communism theory and investigate on the challenge it faces; in our sense, Marx's communism theory faces two challenges and the challenges are exactly targeted on the two assumptions of the theory.

First, is the possibility of infinite increase in productive forces. A key link of Marx's reasoning is that the increase of free time relies on the continuous development of the level of productive forces caused by the development of science, while the precondition for the continuous development in the level of productive forces is that resources can infinitely support the development of productive forces. The infinity of natural resources was not a problem in the 19th century, but it is no longer, a non-problem in the 21st century. If productive forces are unable to develop infinitely, then how should we handle the question on the realization of the realm of freedom? This is a question unavoidable for a strict Marxist. Neither simply thinking on Marx's reasoning is thoroughly out of date nor equally simply affirming this reasoning is tenable. The conscience of theory requires our review on this fundamental question.

The second, is whether the growth of productive forces, inevitably brings about the freedom of man. We should say Marx has been aware of the paradoxical nature of human development since he dissertated on the theory of division of labour, but this paradox was not fully considered in his communist theory. Over the past century, huge development in human productive forces has been achieved. It has significantly enriched people's material life, but human also has an increasingly stronger uneasiness, feeling dominated by these productive forces. The rise of the theory of technical critique after Weber also includes a critique on Marx's communism theory to some extent – although technology is not equal to Marxist productive activity. This is the second fact that Marx's communism theory must face. Therefore, I think the perfection and development of communist theory must include the rediscovery of Marx's thought of technical critique and the construction of technical critique theory.

Even if the complete realization of the realm of freedom is hanged up due to the restriction of the development of productive force, does Marx's view of freedom thus lose its realistic significance? Not at all. The exploration of the way to realize freedom runs through Marx's theoretical activity. This fully indicates the free development of man is the end-result of Marx's all theoretical activities. This is exactly what Marx tried to disclose when he criticized capitalism – a special existence form of market economy. In capitalism, or an ordinary society of market economy, the characteristic of production is to produce for production, while generally the fundamental meaning of human existence is forgotten. Therefore, warning critique on this mode of social production is absolutely necessary for the healthy development of this society. This critique is a kind of correction. Then, what standard do we use to correct this society which has completely fallen into the worship of wealth? No like Hegel who entrusts everything to the course of world history and regards everything in reality is reasonable, the only way for us is to compare the reality with an unreal and ideal mode of existence and the perfection of artistic activity and make people aware of the dimension of human divinity and the finity of reality, thus improving the quality of human existence.

About the Authors

Wang Nanshi, a native of Fengxiang, Shaanxi, China, born in July 1953, professor in the Department of Philosophy of Nankai University. Main research fields include contemporary Marxist philosophy and social and political philosophy. Main works: Introduction to Human Activity Theory (as co-author, 1993), Introduction to Modern Materialism (as co-author, 1996), From Domain Integration to Domain Separation (1998), Social Philosophy (2001) and Coming of the Era of Polytonal Culture (2002; written more than 100 published academic articles.

Xie Yongkang, a native of Liupanshui, Guizhou, China, born in October 1978, doctor in the Department of Philosophy of Nankai University. Research direction is contemporary Marxist philosophy. A number of his academic articles were published in the Journal of Tianjin Social Sciences, Journal of Seeking Truth and other publications.

Printed in P.R.C

www.ingramcontent.com/pod-product-compliance
Lightning Source LLC
Chambersburg PA
CBHW071700120626
46550CB00001B/49